ED

CHILDREN OF THE NEW AGE

'a much-needed and necessary history of New Age phenomena . . . impressive, sensible and insightful. . . . This book will stand out.'
Professor Daniel Wojcik, *University of Oregon*

Elements of New Age culture have emerged from the underground to become a central part of everyday life for many in the West. The demand for organic foods and natural remedies; the growing general interest in spirituality and healing; the peace and anti-road lobbies; and the burgeoning global rave scene are all influenced by the variegated counterculture that New Age represents. But what exactly *is* New Age? How should we define its impact upon contemporary Western culture?

Children of the New Age, a pioneering history of the New Age phenomenon, combines original ethnographic research with rare archival material to give a definitive overview of New Age belief and practice from the 1930s to the present day. It chronicles the development of alternative spirituality from embryonic beginnings to a universal trend: from its inception within enclaves of Rosicrucians, occultists and Alice Bailey's neo-theosophists to its modern-day incursions into mainstream political, musical and artistic cultures. But this is also a distinctly *critical* history. New Age culture, says Steven J. Sutcliffe, is notoriously variegated and hotly contested, exposed to competing strands of revelation and apocalypse. Caught between the hippy explosion and the doomsday scenarios of millennial Christianity and UFO groups, it has been the preserve both of extreme religious ascetics and of humanistic countercultures lauding the Edenic perfection of this-worldly existence. At stake in its history are controversial questions of value, and of its perceived status as a discrete and unified movement. What 'counts' as New Age? To whom does New Age culture belong? Is it now genuinely mainstream, or does its egalitarian, grass-roots, small-group ethos resist easy appropriation and succinct politicisation?

Supported by first-hand accounts of the author's adventures in alternative culture, including firewalking and spiritual healing workshops and life at the Findhorn community, and by archival correspondence and publications recovering the 'lost' history of alternative spirituality during the 1950s and 1960s, this is an incisive and colourful survey of New Age trends and controversies. It calls for a fresh understanding of New Age as an emergent and fragmented folk idiom, complete with its own revealing loyalties and fractures; not a unified 'movement' or 'new religion', but a diffuse cultural force reflecting ever-shifting currents of popular sentiment.

Steven J. Sutcliffe is a Research Fellow in Religious Studies at the University of Stirling. He is co-editor of *Beyond New Age: Exploring Alternative Spirituality* (2000) and author of numerous papers on counterculture and popular religion.

CHILDREN OF THE NEW AGE

A history of spiritual practices

Steven J. Sutcliffe

Routledge
Taylor & Francis Group

LONDON AND NEW YORK

First published 2003
by Routledge
11 New Fetter Lane, London EC4P 4EE

Simultaneously published in the USA and Canada
by Routledge
29 West 35th Street, New York, NY 10001

Routledge is an imprint of the Taylor & Francis Group

Typeset in Bembo by Steven Gardiner Ltd, Cambridge
Printed and bound in Great Britain by MPG Books Ltd, Bodmin

British Library Cataloguing in Publication Data
A catalogue record for this book is available from the British Library

Library of Congress Cataloging in Publication Data
Sutcliffe, Steven, 1961–
Children of the New Age: a history of alternative spirituality
/ Steven J. Sutcliffe
p. cm.
Includes bibliographical references and index.
1. New Age movement – History – 20th century. I. Title.
BP605.N48 S867 2002
299'.93 – dc21
2002031680

ISBN 0-415-24298-3 (hbk)
ISBN 0-415-24299-1 (pbk)

FOR OWEN (b. 1994) AND NEIL (b. 1999)

CONTENTS

ACKNOWLEDGMENTS

At various stages of researching and writing this book I enjoyed illuminating exchanges with a range of scholars. Here I would like to acknowledge in particular Terence Thomas, who first saw potential in my work and passed on his passion for methodology, and Gwilym Beckerlegge who offered shrewd early insights. I would also like to thank in particular John Drane, Paul Heelas, Daren Kemp, Russell McCutcheon, Graham Monteith, Chrissie Steyn, Kevin Tingay, and Matthew Wood. None of them is responsible for the argument in this book, of course. My students on the Open University course 'World Religions', which I taught for three years between 1998 and 2000, helped sharpen my thoughts on the relationship between methodology and pedagogy, as did students at Sunderland University who took my module 'New Age and Paganism: the Return of Popular Religion' in Autumn 2000. Being appointed to a Research Fellowship in Religious Studies in Autumn 2001 at the University of Stirling finally gave me time and space to complete the book. I am also very grateful for the personal encouragement of Malory Nye at Stirling and James Cox at Edinburgh. Staff at Routledge were courteous and helpful, and my thanks are due in particular to Adrian Driscoll who took the proposal on, to Roger Thorp who patiently saw it through and to Clare Johnson for her attention to detail.

I was given excellent service by library staff at The Open University, Stirling University, Southampton University (special collections), Sunderland University, the Mitchell Library in Glasgow, the National Library of Scotland, and the British Library. The *Scottish Daily Record* and *Sunday Mail* press library in Glasgow, Psychic Press in Essex, the Shropshire Records and Research Centre in Shrewsbury, and the Dumfries Register of Deaths were also very helpful.

I am grateful to the Findhorn Foundation for permission to quote from their archives held in the National Library of Scotland; to Michael Forster for help in distributing an early questionnaire at Findhorn and for feedback on a very early draft of Chapter 7; and to all those at Findhorn who took the time and effort to respond to my questionnaire. In particular I thank my fellow participants in 'Experience Week' and hope they recognise something of themselves and the Findhorn experience in this chapter.

My thanks also to Eileen Caddy, Dorothy Maclean and Anthony Brooke for answering letters; to Ruth Nesfield-Cookson for information on Attingham Park and the networks of the 1960s; and to Daphne Davis, David Govan and Rosemary Main for sharing recollections of their aunt, Sheena Govan. I would like to thank the Unit of Service, in particular Alison, Patrick and Deirdre (pseudonyms), for their generous time and patience, and further thanks to Alison and Patrick for interviews, correspondence and critical feedback on drafts of Chapter 6. I am also grateful to Steve Nation of the Lucis Trust in London for hospitality during my visit. Thanks also to several dozen people who completed questionnaires with me at alternative health fairs in Edinburgh; to Hazel Price, firewalker (pseudonym); to residents at the Salisbury Centre, Edinburgh, for informal conversations; and to members of the Theosophical Society in Edinburgh who welcomed my early visits.

Despite her own demanding teaching schedule and other family duties, my wife Jo Miller always encouraged this book as did my parents-in-law, John and Kathleen Miller. Godfrey Smith and Sheila Mackay gave me shelter (and much else) in Galloway. Manda Miller, Nicky Ferrie and Donna Rodgers were at different periods loving childminders to our sons Owen and Neil: without them I could have done very little of this work. Last but not least, I thank my parents, Marjorie and Trevor Sutcliffe, who first set me on the scholarly road.

Finally, the 'Children of the New Age' invoked in my title is the name Sheena Govan (1912–1967) gave to her small group of spiritual seekers in the mid-1950s (according to Glasgow's *Sunday Mail*). This trace of an oral tradition in popular culture serves as an appropriate title for the 'New Age' genealogy proposed here; it also acknowledges the unique contribution of a forgotten architect of 'New Age'.

Steven J. Sutcliffe
Stirling, February 2002

INTRODUCTION

On the genealogy of 'New Age': a field note

> Genealogy does not resemble the evolution of a species and does
> not map the destiny of a people. On the contrary, to follow the
> complex course of descent is to maintain passing events in their
> proper dispersion; it is to identify the accidents, the minute
> deviations – or conversely, the complete reversals – the errors, the
> false appraisals, and the faulty calculations that gave birth to those
> things that continue to exist and have value for us; it is to discover
> that truth or being do not lie at the root of what we know and
> what we are, but the exteriority of accidents.
>
> (Foucault 1977: 146)

This book is an historical ethnography of 'New Age' spirituality in
Anglo–American culture between the 1930s and the 1990s. My first contact
with this polyvalent expression 'New Age' was in the mid-1970s when I bought
a second-hand copy of a book by Alice Bailey, grandly entitled *A Treatise on
Cosmic Fire*. I remember the sombre, plain, midnight-blue jacket – the house
style of the Bailey books – and the sheer bulk of the book. Although its
1,283 pages of text defeated me, I was intrigued to find in the endpapers the
following invitation:

> Training for new age discipleship is provided by the *Arcane School*.
> The principles of the Ageless Wisdom are presented through esoteric
> meditation, study and service as a *way of life*. [Emphasis in original]

Then in 1982, I was hitch-hiking to Southampton one evening to visit a
friend when I met an older traveller, heading north. He told me his destination
was Findhorn. I was surprised, for I knew Findhorn was at the other end
of the British mainland and it seemed late in the day to be starting out so
far. But the hitchhiker made light of this, confessing a long-standing attraction
to Findhorn. 'We're all searching for something, aren't we?', he said, as we
parted.

1

My own spell 'on the road' was then only just beginning. My friend in Southampton was working with young people in and out of psychiatric institutions, and I naively associated their careers with a psychic rebellion against the *status quo*. I was also immersed in punk rock, which meant I scorned the 'hippy-ish' sentiments – that 'searching for something' – of my fellow-hitchhiker. I thought all *I* was seeking was the quickest lift into Southampton – certainly not the meaning of life. But punk itself can be seen as an expression of a wider 'secular apocalyptic' folk culture, as Wojcik (1997: 121ff.) has convincingly argued, and from this perspective there was more in common between the punk music apocalypse of the late 1970s and certain 'New Age' prophecies of the 1950s and 1960s than either of us could have guessed that afternoon beside the dusty dual carriageway.[1]

In the event I was to spend much of the 1980s seeking out spiritual alternatives to the conservative Anglicanism I'd grown up with on the one hand, and 'the system' in general on the other. I remember savouring the books of the popular writer Colin Wilson (b. 1930), including his new romantic manifesto *The Outsider* (1956) and his digest of 'alternative' religion, *The Occult* (1978 [1971]), my paperback copy of which carries the spectacular blurb 'the ultimate book for those who would walk with the Gods'. I also read *Peace News* and the anarchist bulletin *Freedom*. In 1982 I came to Scotland to work as a volunteer for the Edinburgh Cyrenians, first in their city hostel for homeless and 'at risk' young people, later at a rural small-holding. I became a vegetarian and lived in a co-operative household where a lively 'alternative' culture unfolded, incorporating sexual politics (feminist and anti-sexist men's groups), a wholefoods co-op – and a healthy crop of cannabis plants in the sunny lounge. Between 1983 and 1986, in no particular order, I read popular accounts of Buddhism and Taoism, consulted the *I Ching*, learnt to read Tarot cards at the Salisbury Centre, and had my astrological birthchart prepared and interpreted (Sun in Aries, Moon in Libra, Leo rising, as it happens). I practised Zen meditation and struggled with T'ai Chi Chuan. I visited the Samye Ling Tibetan Buddhist Centre in Dumfriesshire and hovered on the brink of formally converting to Buddhism. I also found time to spend periods on the dole and to work as a busker and community musician. One regular musician friend was a TM practitioner and Gurdjieff reader, another belonged to the School of Economic Science. In 1986 I became informally apprenticed to a craft shoemaker who followed Rudolf Steiner's Anthroposophy and spent a couple of years making shoes in the south-west of Scotland. Later still, back in Edinburgh, I joined groups in Gestalt therapy and assertiveness training, and helped to organise several men's gatherings. In short, throughout the 1980s I rode the carousel of emergent spiritualities. I sought with a vengeance.

And yet 'New Age' – as slogan, emblem, formal ideology – was scarcely an item in this eclectic mix. I encountered the expression, if at all, largely in connection with the Findhorn community, and this despite the fact that many of my pursuits at this time – communal and co-operative living, reading 'mystical' texts, practising meditation, using occult divination and personal growth techniques – are widely said to be signs of belonging to a 'New Age movement'. But I met no one in Edinburgh in the 1980s who prophesied a New Age, who described themselves as a 'New Ager', or who identified with a 'New Age movement'. Certainly a diffuse collectivity of individuals, networks, societies and small groups existed that amounted to a loose culture of 'alternative' spirituality. But when in the mid-1990s I found myself researching 'New Age' in an academic role, I was puzzled to find the experts directing me back to what were, to me, familiar haunts and practices – except that now they had been definitively repackaged. Confusion increased when I began to reconstruct a genealogy of the field and discovered a lost history of 'New Age' as an apocalyptic emblem in the 1950s and 1960s. In fact 'New Age' had been employed in this way from at least the late 1930s/early 1940s in a tradition of functional spirituality irrigated equally by 'alternative' and 'popular' discourses. Practitioners drew on occult, Eastern and neo-Christian practices and motifs, developed in a lay and amateurist culture, in order to prepare themselves for an imminent 'New Age'. This would be a new world order that would be inherited by the chosen few who had survived the predicted social and economic collapse or – after 1945 – possible nuclear holocaust (versions varied).

This particular history of alternative spiritual practice has nowadays been almost entirely obscured by a preference on the part of commentators to conflate 'New Age' with the post-1970s idiom of 'mind, body and spirit'. The latter, although certainly connected with earlier manifestations, is – as I will show – substantively a very different kettle of fish from the apocalyptic millennialism of the mid-century Anglo–American subcultures. So how could such radically different versions of 'New Age' arise? The first 'New Age' currents – pre-1970s – tended to be ascetic, puritanical and other-worldly; the second – post-1970s – were emotionally expressive, hedonistic and firmly this-worldly. What kind of a 'movement' could so radically change its stripes? The genealogy of 'New Age' made it clear that some elementary empirical questions remained unanswered.

Apart from giving a taste of some of the basic problems tackled in this book, the point of this reflexive 'field note' is neither to celebrate my affiliations to 'New Age' – whatever this turns out to be – nor to deny them. Rather it is simply to indicate my own historical engagement with the field so that the reader knows that my approach is informed by 'emic' as well as 'etic' knowlege – a crucial distinction I elaborate in Chapter 1. Ross (1992: 554) is surely correct when he remarks:

> I don't believe that anyone undertakes any kind of cultural study – chooses an object for such a study – that one is not personally invested in. All such research is deeply autobiographical – how could it not be?

Yet having acknowledged this, care is required. Reflexivity arising from one's embodied presence – one's personal 'stake' – in a field can be overplayed. The subjectivity of the participant–author in a book which, like this one, incorporates fieldwork observation and participation as well as primary source analysis, should not be allowed to overshadow the total picture.[2] By acknowledging my earlier career as a 'seeker' in and on the fringes of 'New Age', then, I recognise the methodological requirement for scholars to position themselves within their narratives – without, however, taking them over.

Related to this point is my interest in working with a reflexive model of Religious Studies as critical research done 'at home', on 'ourselves', in line with critiques in anthropology of the traditional disciplinary preoccupation with studying 'exotic others elsewhere' (Davies 1999: 32–8). By researching familiar territory – my own 'backyard' biographically, culturally and geographically – this book contributes modestly, I hope, to the wider project of placing important aspects of Anglo–American culture in proper historical and anthropological context. The historical evidence assembled in this book is vital, for it both severely undermines the unity and homogeneity of what has been passed off as the 'New Age movement' at the same time as it recovers a real social milieu – or, better, an overlapping series of milieus – connected (here explicitly, there obliquely) with the emblem. But to claim that 'New Age' is a term operationalised and interpreted within a series of social collectivities is a far cry from identifying a *movement* or even a coherent complex of ideas or *Weltanschauung*. What we find – to cite Foucault again – is more like an 'exteriority of accidents': a bricolage of more or less interchangeable practices and values given focus by an ambiguous eschatological emblem. Nevertheless I do not propose a relativist account of 'New Age'. I want to argue against Drane's (1991: 18–19) claim that 'the amazing diversity of the ingredients that go into the New Age mixture will always ensure that any definition we come up with can, with perfectly good reason, be challenged by someone else whose experience of it has been quite different', on the grounds that some definitions, reconstructions and genealogies are simply more plausible than others. This book attempts to supply them. So I offer a critical realist analysis of 'New Age', by which I mean merely that I assume the existence of a social world and our ability, through reflexive methodology and critical self-consciousness, to gain useful, replicable knowledge of it (cf. Davies 1999: 17–25).

Before I sketch the book's argument, let me clarify its methodological base. This is eclectic and interdisciplinary, as befits its hybrid subject, and generally conforms to Martin's (1990: 116) call for histories of religion to be 'conceived in an ethnographic grain'. The book aims to reconstruct the lost history of 'New Age', incorporating Foucauldian genealogy, reflexive ethnography and an anthropological approach to popular reading practices. It aims to reconfigure 'New Age' studies from the ground up, thereby closing down some stale avenues for good and opening up a new set of problematics for future work. To accomplish this I move regularly between a broad lens and close, detailed study.

I attempt a number of specific operations: I deconstruct the received wisdom of a 'New Age Movement'; I reconstruct a viable genealogy of 'New Age'; I recover lost histories and ethnographies of popular practice and spiritual biography; and I reconfigure 'New Age' as a modern domain of popular religious discourse and practice. This strategy effectively removes 'New Age' from the field of 'movement' studies (new social movements, new religious movements) altogether and reconceives it as a harbinger of the shift in contemporary religion to small group practice and a discourse of 'spirituality'.

A few words are required on this discourse. There is now a wide range of spiritualities on offer in Anglo–American culture, and it can be argued that their often sympathetic interaction with emergent cultural values problematises 'alternative' as their most accurate descriptor. Some spiritual styles remain dissident or countercultural; many are evidently *an* alternative in the sense that they are distinctive, even quirky, options but nevertheless are now generally regarded as 'variant' rather than 'deviant'; others have fully entered popular culture and are diffused in advertising, television, the world-wide web, paperbacks and magazines. Nevertheless I do use 'alternative spirituality' as a convenient tag for the extensive historical field from which 'New Age' emerged. This should also make clear that the book in no way *conflates* 'alternative spirituality' and 'New Age'. Quite the opposite: I argue that 'New Age' is merely a particular genealogy within a far broader field.

Case studies, largely though not entirely from the British mainland, carry the narrative and substantiate an argument that might equally well have been sourced primarily in North America, North/Western Europe or Australasia. However, certain key networks and groups are, as we shall see, unique to the UK. In Chapter 1 I set the scene, set out my methodology, establish the book's arguments, and review the existing field of 'New Age' studies. Chapter 2 gives a broad historical survey of currents of alternative spirituality in the 1920s and 1930s before focusing on Alice Bailey's post-Theosophical ideology of a 'New Age' as a primary discursive source for post-war activists, often mentioned by commentators but never properly unpacked. Chapters 3 and 4 provide a detailed, contextualised narrative history of the acts and communications of key agents in British 'New Age' networks in the 1950s and 1960s. I focus in particular on the pre-history and germination of the Findhorn community, probably the best-known 'New Age' centre in the world, but I also trace and substantiate international connections to the US and New Zealand. Chapter 5 is in effect the lynchpin of the book, arguing that a popular hermeneutical shift in the meaning of 'New Age' took place at the turn of the 1970s, in which 'New Age' as apocalyptic *emblem* of the near future gave way to 'New Age' as humanistic *idiom* of self-realisation in the here-and-now. Chapters 6 to 8 then document this more recent, idiomatic 'New Age' in the form of ethnographies of my own involvement as a participant–observer in the mid-to-late 1990s in certain prominent Scottish sites and activities implicated in the earlier genealogy of 'New Age'. These include an Alice Bailey meditation group, the

Findhorn colony, and various workshops and fairs in holistic health networks. Chapter 9 reviews the evidence of previous chapters and argues for a shift in focus away from fantasies of a 'New Age Movement' and towards contextualised accounts and analyses of 'seeking', the emergent discourse on a reflexive lay 'spirituality', and the nature and function of the small, flexible cultural institutions that emerge once the 'New Age' dust has settled. Throughout I use inverted commas around the expression:[3] this is not a fad but a necessary device to keep my problematisation of this category constantly in the reader's gaze and hence to defer that mystification which is the inevitable result of slippage from taxon to essence.

Part 1

EMBLEM

1

THE LIFE AND
TIMES OF 'NEW AGE'

It is . . . not the religion of the professionals, religion in its doctrinal purity, that I have sought to recover, but rather concrete religious phenomena with all the impurities of a specific social context.

(Obelkevich 1976: vii).

Different kinds of practice and discourse are intrinsic to the field in which religious representations (like any representation) acquire their identity and their truthfulness. From this it does not follow that the meanings of religious practices and utterances are to be sought in social phenomena, but only that their possibility and their authoritative status are to be explained as products of historically distinctive disciplines and forces. The anthropological student of *particular* religions should therefore begin from this point, in a sense unpacking the comprehensive concept which he or she translates as 'religion' into heterogenous elements according to its historical character.

(Asad 1993: 53–4)

This book proposes a thorough deconstruction and reconfiguration of 'New Age' in which both the label itself and the phenomena associated with it are subjected to critical scrutiny or a 'hermeneutic of suspicion' in the sense identified (if not endorsed by) Ricoeur (1970: 32–3). My general argument runs as follows. First, I unpack the concepts 'New Age Movement' and 'The New Age'. That is, I take issue with the hegemonic view that 'New Age' is a 'movement' of some kind or even a homogeneous entity at all. Such formulations essentialise a set of mixed, meandering, even divergent social processes more akin in presentation to Deleuze and Guattari's (1988: 3ff.) proliferating 'rhizome' than to a unified organic entity. I also question the covert metaphysics informing the reifying expression 'The New Age', which effectively periodises manifestations by assigning them to a homogeneous cultural epoch or astrological era. Both terms are unsatisfactory: 'New Age' as a 'movement' is, as I will show, a false etic category and a formulation such as 'The New Age' simply reproduces an emic agenda.[1] In fact, 'New Age' represents at its narrowest a specific millennialistic emblem, and at its most diffuse – at its most symbolically overdetermined – a loose idiom of humanistic potential and psychotherapeutic change that could be, and has been, called anything from 'human potential' to 'mind body spirit', from 'holistic' to 'spiritual growth'. Asad's call to recover the 'heterogenous elements' of particular religious formations is apt here, for little else in the history of modern religion turns out on close inspection to be as variegated and diffuse in character as 'New Age'.

To deconstruct 'New Age' in this way is also to engage with the long-standing debate in Religious Studies on the analytical purchase of broad categories such as 'world religion', 'religion' and 'religions', even particular constructs such as 'Hinduism' (Baird 1971, Fitzgerald 2000). Such debates have called the universalism of this vocabulary of religions into question, underscoring the specific historical circumstances of its genesis and development. 'New Age' is no exception here; indeed, it exemplifies an enduring mystification in category formation in Religious Studies.

Approaching the subject through a hermeneutic of suspicion also raises the question of whose interests are served in classifying as 'New Age' the Fortean diversity of phenomena typically associated with the term.[2] Through taxonomic sleight-of-hand the phenomena have been accorded a homogeneity and concrete presence that the historical record simply does not permit. But this does allow 'New Age' to be set up like a stooge to be knocked down by a variety of vested interests. For example, it has been demonised by conservative evangelical Christians, particularly in the US, as is evident in the very titles of Constance Cumbey's *The Hidden Dangers of the Rainbow: The New Age Movement and Our Coming Age of Barbarism* (1983) and Texe Marrs' *Dark Secrets of the New Age* (1987).[3] In other constituencies, 'New Age' is sniggered at as 'touchy–feely' spiritual consumerism. Parties with axes to grind here include rationalist sceptics (Basil 1988) and paternalist social scientists (Bruce 1998), for whom 'New Age' is a codeword for a shallow, self-indulgent, even – one senses – *plebeian* and *vulgar* spirituality that should not be given scholarly oxygen. This unlikely confluence of critics shows that 'New Age' has triggered curiously exaggerated and intemperate reactions in very different social power bases. This only reinforces an important but largely occluded function of 'New Age' studies: to connect data about alternative spirituality and religious innovation to comparative studies in the sociology of knowledge and anthropology of culture, rather than remaining a pocket of colourful anecdotalism tagged on to the end of Religious Studies.

Deconstructing 'New Age' has a second major revisionist function: it contributes to the wider process of recovering and reassessing 'lost' expressions of religion, for 'New Age' flourished as a major current within a much broader field of popular religious practice. When William Bloom, an influential activist in 1980s and 1990s Britain, describes 'New Age' as the visible tip of the iceberg of a mass movement in which humanity is reasserting its right to explore spirituality in total freedom.

(Bloom [ed.] 1991: xvi)

we can identify some typical concerns of religion in a popular mode: grassroots activism, strategies for everyday living, ideals of spiritual autonomy and egalitarianism, and – not least – an ideology of direct, unmediated access to 'experiences'. Nevertheless, I shall be arguing throughout this book that the cultural arena within which such voices are raised has no overarching purpose, no compelling agenda, beyond that of expressing whatever 'spiritual' values are deemed appropriate for the moment and – through a radical tolerance – upholding the rights of others to do the same. That is, what debate there has been among practitioners on the meaning of 'New Age' has most often amounted simply to a nexus of conversations, occasionally arguments, within a decentred and theoretically unbounded matrix of viewpoints and pressure groups, here locally-focused, there widely-dispersed, but almost always mutually tolerant and hence diffusive rather than regulative. Rather than constituting a social movement or a new religious movement, then, 'New Age' was originally an apocalyptic emblem whose encoded semantics were sufficiently rich and multiform for a later generation to take it over as a codeword for currents in post-1960s popular religion.

And this is the third point in my argument: 'New Age' is not a distinctive empirical formation but a (now rather stale) codeword for the heterogeneity of alternative spirituality, best classified as a sub-type of 'popular religion'. Here are two simple definitions of 'popular religion'. The first is from Thomas (1995: 387):

If 'official' religion [is] defined as religion founded on authoritative documents and propagated by religious specialists, priests or hierarchy, then the term 'popular' can apply to any layperson, whether peasant or ruling-class, who adopts beliefs and practices which may be at odds with the religious specialists' views.

A clear illustration of this can be found in the rhetoric of David Icke, a former footballer, broadcaster and Green Party spokesman, now a prominent contemporary advocate of 'New Age'. In his early memoir-*cum*-manifesto *The Truth Vibrations* he writes:

The new spirituality involves a one-to-one relationship with the Godhead and the higher intelligences. We will no longer believe that all our sins can be forgiven by a priest appointed by the church hierarchy. Why do we need a human to arbitrate between ourselves and God when we have our own link?

(Icke 1991: 127)

Icke's is an unusually combative declaration of anti-clericalism and anti-institutionalism. But of course the problem with this definition of popular religion is that it reproduces a crude dichotomy between 'official' and 'popular', which – although clearly attractive to Icke, for example – may not always, or even typically, obtain in the field. This is particularly the case in 'New Age', where to the extent that Thomas's 'specialists, priests, or hierarchy' can be found at all, they exist in secondary institutions with relatively high-turnover user groups. Although a strong strain of neo-Christian piety and mysticism has flavoured the arena, the stance is less one of being 'at odds' with Christianity than with the hegemony of 'institutional religion'. At the same time such disdain for 'tradition' does not prevent practitioners from co-opting historical formations deemed fit and useful for everyday spirituality, including popularising mystics of the Christian churches as spiritual rebels. Hence a second working definition of popular religion teases out some important social psychological dimensions underpinning 'New Age's disdain for institutional religion:

> Popular religion is the quest for (a) *more simple*, (b) *more direct*, and (c) *more profitable relationships with the divine*.
> (Maldonado 1986: 6; emphasis in original)

The field is replete with evidence of appeals to less complex, less mediated and more rewarding ideas and practices. The aforementioned William Bloom urges readers to 'do something, anything, to deepen your relationship with the sacred' (Bloom 1993b: 18, 19). Gill Edwards, one of a plethora of independent workshop leaders in 1990s Britain, writes in *Stepping Into The Magic*: 'It is time for *everyone* to become a shaman, a metaphysician, a dream-weaver, a walker-between-worlds – each in our unique way' (Edwards 1993: 192).

This brings me to my fourth and final point, one that is in fact applicable to all academic study of religion. Obelkevich's conceptualisation of his subject as 'concrete religious phenomena with all the impurities of a specific social context' precisely describes my own view of religion as a cultural institution among others. The special interest of 'New Age' manifestations is that, by dint of their fluidity, ephemerality and heteroglossia, they compel us to reassess the implicit boundary maintained by most scholars between 'culture' and 'religion'. I would argue that this differentiation functions to safeguard the agential purity of the latter from the contaminating contingency of the former. 'New Age', however, is contaminated – that is, hybrid and syncretic – culture *par excellence*, and proper comprehension and extension of this insight dissolves the scholastic illusion of 'world religions' and their sub-types. In the dizzying field of cultural hybridity that opens out before us once the 'New Age' umbrella is collapsed, we can glimpse the truth of Deleuze and Gauttari's (1988: 7) application of the rhizome to linguistics 'there is no language in itself . . . only a throng of dialects, patois, slangs, and specialised languages'. In Religious Studies this amounts to

Martin's (2000: 282) reconceptualisation of religion as 'the ubiquity of locally contingent and syncretistic formations', which is to say that 'local variation *is all there is!*'

Fieldwork, history, text: methodology in the study of 'New Age'

Any theory of religion must be able to deal adequately not only with structure but with change and must include within its stipulations historical as well as contemporary data.

(Martin 1990: 112)

The qualitative researcher is not unlike the detective in the classic murder mystery. Starting with a few clues, the detective questions persons connected with the case, develops hunches, questions further on the basis of those hunches, begins to see a picture of 'what happened' start to emerge, looks for evidence pro and con, elaborating or modifying that picture – until finally the unknown is known. The murderer is caught; what was once a mystery is now understandable.

(Wiseman 1979: 113)

Since I am concerned in part with the methodological shortcomings of the field, a brief review of my own methods follows in the interests of transparency and reflexivity. To begin with I employed ethnographic fieldwork and textual analysis, with Denzin's (1970: 307–10) well-known principle of 'methodological triangulation' in mind – meaning the generation of multiple measures or profiles of one and the same phenomenon. This is particularly germane to the study of religion, which – *pace* the efforts of anthropologists and ethnographers – still tends to be dominated by analyses based largely on texts. That this is still largely the case in 'New Age' studies is suggested by Heelas's admission (1996: 7) that 'academics . . . simply do not know much, if anything, of the thousands of different things that are going on'. One aim of the present study is to map historically and ethnographically the sheer variety of people's popular practices and interpretations, which scholars can find when they start to look for religion in its proper habitat.

I conducted the bulk of my fieldwork in Scotland. Given my rationale for a multidisciplinary approach to the subject it seemed realistic to tackle an accessible arena. In the end, most of the fieldwork was done within a few hours of where I live in central Scotland, some of it in 'old haunts' mentioned in the introduction. Doing ethnography 'at home' in a compact European country (population *c.* 5 million) that is also a keenly theorised cultural–political community (Paterson 1998, Sutcliffe 2002) certainly encouraged serendipitous connections between people and places that kept warm my autobiographical stake in the field. For example, while browsing for primary sources in an

Edinburgh second-hand bookshop I discovered that the proprietor was a nephew of Peter Caddy, co-founder of the Findhorn community and one-time husband of Sheena Govan, the charismatic teacher of the proto-Findhorn group in 1950s London. Later I found that, at the time of her death, Govan herself had been lodging in the same village in south-west Scotland where I myself, a generation later, had lived during my shoemaking career. Not only this, but a certain Alice Bailey had in 1895 first encountered her spiritual 'Master' at an aunt's country estate in the same locality (Bailey 1973: 35). I interpreted these developments as pleasing coincidences, although they were later reinterpreted by one or two informants as Jungian 'synchronicities' which demonstrated that, esoterically, I was 'meant' to write this book. That aside, some details were clearly chance incursions into the area: Sheena Govan had no previous connections with the south-west of Scotland, and Alice Bailey came from a very wealthy Manchester family and could presumably just as easily have met her 'Master' at another country seat. Similarly, the colony that became the Findhorn Foundation community might have sprung up in the Trossachs if the staff group of Peter and Eileen Caddy and Dorothy Maclean had been laid off there, instead of in the north-east of Scotland. Indeed, but for Sheena Govan's family connections in Scotland, the proto-Findhorn group would have had no reason to move to Scotland at all. And yet, as I will show, Sheena Govan is a key figure in the genealogy of 'New Age', Bailey its chief theorist and the Findhorn colony an international site of 'New Age' practice. The contingent turns out to be essential.

There is an additional reason for restricting the ethnographies to Scotland. The distinctiveness of Scotland within the UK, demonstrated on educational, legal and ecclesiastical grounds since 1707, presents an opportunity to remark in passing upon the differing acculturative potential of 'New Age' in a society that still retains a Presbyterian cultural resistance to Anglo–American popular culture (Highet 1972, Brown 1997). The demographic profile of Scotland's prime 'New Age' site, the Findhorn colony, demonstrates this by default: founded by English and Canadian nationals, Findhorn has been dominated by American, German and English people, with Scots scarcely represented at all. But notwithstanding the residual cultural resistance of Presbyterianism, the contemporary profile of 'New Age' in Scotland appears to be coming into line with other countries in the grip of globalising and postmodernising forces: the rest of mainland Britain, Western Europe, North America and Australasia. Hence at the same moment that Highet (1972) was arguing for the distinctiveness of Presbyterian culture, the directory *Alternative Scotland* (Wright and Worsley 1975: 114) reported 'a great upsurge of non-Christian religion' and 'an increasing number of groups simply interested in borrowing from any religion or none for the purpose of developing the potential of the individual'. By the 1990s the Church of Scotland (1993: 44) was reporting 'active promotion of New Age ideas and practices in Scotland' with Drane (1993: 57) now claiming that 'most unchurched people in Scotland today are more likely to construct their worldview from aspects of the New Age outlook than from elements of mainstream Christianity'. And a founder-proprietor of the successful 'Body and Soul' bookshop in Edinburgh told me in January 2000 that the 'New Age' idiom was now diffused through the general culture and was actually 'more widely accepted' in Scotland than in England, where he thought it had become a middle-class preserve.

Overall the Scottish experience serves to emphasise the ability of 'New Age' to override certain indices of social and cultural difference through trafficking in a common currency, a point reinforced by Hanegraaff's (1996: 13) observation on 'New Age' discourse in The Netherlands and Germany as 'an English–American affair by any standards'. The Scottish ethnographies presented in Chapters 6 to 8 can thus be read as a particular – a Scottish – case study in the dissemination of an Anglo–Americanised praxis. That is, their Scottish markings represent a vernacularisation of a common stock predominantly moulded by Anglo–American popular cultural values. These in turn reproduce a model of 'spirituality' in which reflexive and interactive agents work within a web of egalitarian social relationships, drawing upon a cluster of populistic beliefs and practices.[4]

The emics and etics of New Age

All notions of replicability and testability fly up the chimney when the world as seen by the observed is capriciously muddled with the world as seen by the observer.

(Harris 1969: 33)

The final product, it seems to me, should reflect a kind of biculturalism in which the ethnographer understands cultural phenomena in both emic (native) and etic (outsider) ways.

(Wagner 1997: 90)

Earlier I referred to the 'emics and etics' of 'New Age'. This terminology refers to the epistemic frame of the interpretations we hear in any particular account of cultural events. The neologisms 'emic' and 'etic' were first used in print in the 1950s by a linguist, Kenneth Pike, who dropped the prefix from the conceptual pair 'phonemic/phonetic' to develop a more parsimonious, higher-order terminology derived from linguistics but applicable to culture in general (Headland 1990: 15). According to Pike 'an emic unit' is 'a physical or mental item or system treated by insiders as relevant to their system of behaviour and as the same emic unit in spite of etic variability' (Pike 1990: 28). An etic unit, on the other hand, is an 'outside disciplinary system' (ibid.) formulated for the purposes of scanning and then de-coding an unfamiliar emic system (ibid.: 34). In Pike's view, 'etics' – or cross–cultural 'science' – is the means to emic – indigenous – ends.

In the 1960s the anthropologist Marvin Harris began to theorise the emic/etic distinction in a way that challenged Pike's prioritisation of 'emics' (Harris 1990: 48–50). Harris accepted Pike's basic understanding of the emic unit but introduced a strong etic agenda: namely, 'the task of building a diachronic, synchronic, comparative, and global science of society and culture' (ibid.: 49). For Harris, etics are something more than emics writ large; indeed, if etics can be shown to be merely artificially extended 'local' categories, they fail the test and remain merely emic. In Harris's view etics provide the basic epistemology of academic knowledge: they are literally that which 'makes the social sciences possible' (ibid.). They are 'accounts, descriptions, and analyses expressed in terms of the conceptual schemes and categories regarded as meaningful and appropriate by the community of scientific observers' (Lett 1990: 131).

Clearly the emics and etics of culture go to the heart of contemporary debates on the flaws in the so-called 'Enlightenment project' of generating universal categories and explanations. For my purposes, it is the cognitive, and specifically epistemic, dimension of emics/etics that is particularly stimulating: as Lett (1990: 132) notes, 'it is our *understanding* of the phenomena, not the phenomena themselves, that is either emic or etic'. Emics and etics are not a fixed dichotomy of representation but dynamic and symbiotic frames of discourse: emics can transform into etics and back again. The important point is making the epistemic shift a conscious, predictive and transparent act, which underscores the active or operative nature of the distinction between emics and etics. That is, while etics cannot but be emics at their point of origin, etic viability lies precisely in the ability to function as cross-cultural explanatory units. In claiming to have achieved this, etics lay themselves open to testing as 'fakes', and indeed may be exposed as such. In this sense, an etic formulation is falsifiable whereas emics simply are not. Purported etic formulations such as 'The New Age' or 'New Age Movement' are a case in point: as we shall see, they are fakes.

Hence I would agree with Wagner's 'biculturalism', quoted at the head of this section: that is, an appropriate academic agenda for an intercultural, polycentric world is to obtain and 'broker' *both* kinds of knowledge – emic and etic, 'insider' and 'outsider'. This strategy is particularly applicable to the task of reconstructing the subjectivities of religious discourses on the one hand, and locating these in historical and cultural context on the other, such as I attempt to do here with 'New Age'. However we juggle the precise weighting of emics and etics in the final reckoning, what is crucial is to preserve the creative epistemic tension between them. This functions to preserve alterity or 'otherness' in social life because it builds in cognitive difference. This in turn exposes the 'moccasin-walking' model of 'empathetic' Religious Studies as a hollow, even mystified, metaphor: we can never 'get into someone else's shoes' in any useful academic sense. By explicitly and transparently differentiating between emic and etic 'voices', then, we can avoid this 'capricious muddle' of categories and explanations.

This brief excursus into emics and etics benefits 'New Age' studies twofold. First, it allows a real emic history of the 'New Age' emblem to be envisaged and recovered, something impossible before, because the (false etic) discourse on a 'New Age Movement' erased traces of difference. Second, the genealogical approach I use also throws light on the wider field of alternative spirituality in which 'New Age' has been deployed (Sutcliffe and Bowman 2000). Neither of these benefits is available in extant portrayals of the field, which overwhelmingly homogenise 'New Age' by collapsing emic and etic differentials, as we see in a brief review of the secondary literature to follow. In short, throughout the book I counterpoise emic and etic categories to generate a dynamic, reflexive and transparent account of 'New Age' and its location in a broader field of alternative spiritual practice.

Fieldwork: roles and ethics

Fieldwork practice invariably shades off into a grey zone in which the line between the 'informed' and 'uninformed' consent of practitioners becomes blurred (Richardson 1991: 64). As Fine (1993: 268) bluntly asserts, 'the world is secured on secrets'.[5] Taking into account these realistic constraints on a theoretically 'pure' fieldwork, I nevertheless almost always worked openly rather than covertly: that is, telling participants who I was, what I was doing, and – if I knew at the time – why. Usually I mentioned my own thoughts and feelings on the practice or issue at hand. But sometimes I was vague about my motives and opinions since – as Fine (1993:274) shrewdly puts it –'not only are we unsure of the effects of explaining our plans but often we do not know what we want until well into the research project'. An open or 'overt' approach allows for a degree of negotiation, accommodation and – if necessary – disillusion on all sides. Consequently the difference between emic and etic perspectives that a covert approach would collapse through concealment is stimulated in overt work:

> There can be no question of total commitment, 'surrender' or 'becoming'. There must always remain some part held back, some social and intellectual 'distance'. For it is in the 'space' created by this distance that the analytic work gets done,
>
> (Hammersley and Atkinson 1992: 102)

We can now grasp emics/etics as a cognitive correlate to the fieldworker's embodied marginality. Instead of the alterity of researcher and researched – and of emics and etics – being a problem, it becomes a boon, a positive tool for comparative knowledge and theory. Nevertheless, the indeterminate nature of the role of participant–observer, the dynamic relationship between emics and etics, and the fluid and deregulated arena of practice that constitutes the 'New Age' field created an ambiguous experience of fieldwork, since my presentation to other practitioners was hard to distinguish from the exploratory, 'taste it and see' tactics adopted by novices, the 'creative exploitation' of opportunities for spiritual growth practised by the dedicated 'seeker' (Straus 1976). Drawing on her own experience of research with a small spiritual group, Wagner (1997: 91) explains a delicate situation well:

> To me, I was a member of the group because I was studying it. To the group, I was a member who was also studying it. Although the group leaders and most of the members knew I was a student of the group, they insisted from time to time that I was undergoing spiritual growth, just as they were. If I did not protest, I would be uncomfortable. If I protested too much, it would make the group uncomfortable.

This, of course, replays the esoteric interpretation of a *hidden purpose* behind my research mentioned earlier. Such a 'cosmic' level of unfalsifiability defies all attempts at transparency and disclosure and suggests that Shaffir's (1991: 77) conclusion is realistic: 'Despite a commitment to conducting research overtly, deception is, nonetheless, inherent in participant observation'.

History and genealogy

> People who profess to ignore history are nevertheless compelled to make historical assumptions at every turn.
>
> (Tosh 1984: 1)

> The search for descent is not the erecting of foundations: on the contrary, it disturbs what was previously considered immobile; it fragments what was thought unified; it shows the heterogeneity of what was imagined consistent with itself.
>
> (Foucault 1977: 147)

Factoring emics and etics into the methodological equation convinced me that historical perspective, in particular a Foucauldian genealogical analysis, was also required to complete the reconstruction of 'New Age'. As I have said, my approach conforms to Martin's (1990: 116) call for histories of religion to be 'conceived in an ethnographic grain'. This is in one sense simply to follow Baird's (1971: 33) theory of history of religions as a 'temporal study [which] attempts to locate religion in its cultural setting, and to reveal sequential connections'.[6] But the special problem of the 'New Age' field lies in the fact that its boundaries are highly indeterminate, its empirical history is largely unknown and its celebration of subjectivities corrodes a steady morphology. I cannot therefore simply 'read off' the history of an agreed phenomenon. 'New Age' must be reconstructed from scattered and internally inconsistent sources. To do this properly we must in the first place acknowledge as serious empirical evidence spiritual practices and ideological motifs that until recently have been disparaged and marginalised. It also means taking seriously Foucault's call for genealogy to maintain 'passing events in their proper dispersion', which means identifying 'the accidents, the minute deviations – or conversely, the complete reversals – the errors, the false appraisals, and the faulty calculations that gave birth to those things' (Foucault 1977: 146). Following the lead of cultural studies in restoring subcultures, countercultures and popular culture to the scholarly agenda, not only is there intrinsic interest in recovering the history and ethnography of 'lost' spiritualities but considerable theoretical pay-off accrues in understanding the cultural dynamics of religious change and innovation. The sum is that this book is not a celebration of 'colourful' marginality or eccentricity but a genealogical reconstruction that leads us from an 'exteriority of accidents', through murky arenas and surprising contiguities, to the heart of contemporary religious expression.

Popular sources

Alongside my ethnographical and historical work, I trawled the field of 'New Age' writing and publishing. An important body of evidence lies in correspondence, newsletters and mailing lists, particularly in the 1950s and 1960s. Much of this is by nature ephemeral or held in private collections and is thus difficult to trace. From the outset I interpreted 'texts' very broadly from the conviction that a search for a 'canon' is particularly inappropriate to this field. For while most practitioners – Findhorn residents, UFO contactees, spiritual healers – continually test their experiences against written material of all kinds (including their own) they have little use for textual 'closure', preferring to study what comes to hand through personal recommendation and network culture. An idea of the voracious appetite for popular printed material can be had from the pages of the bulletin of the New Zealand-based *Heralds of the New Age*, begun in the mid-1950s. An editorial in 1964 reveals the domestic storage and dissemination of group texts:

> Completely unpaid, our librarian runs what amounts to a suburban library (housed in her home). She selects, wraps and despatches hundreds of books monthly.[7]

An article by the librarian herself lists her most borrowed stock, ranging from the Christian Bible and the Bhagavad-Gita to Shakespeare and Swedenborg, the Theosophical writings of C. W. Leadbeater and H. P. Blavatsky, the Oahspe and Urantia bibles, the spiritual healers Edgar Cayce and Harry Edwards and assorted popularisers of 'Eastern' spirituality such as Paul Brunton and

Paramahansa Yogananda.[8] That the library content remained 'open' to new spiritual trends is proved by material in later issues: a 1986 bulletin gives considerable space to the Indian *guru* Sai Baba whose teachings, we are now told, 'many of our readers have come to accept'.[9]

Searching for a fixed canon in this popular marketplace of ideas only perpetuates an implicit model of Christian biblical exegesis. What is required in 'New Age' studies as elsewhere in Religious Studies is the contextualisation of textual exegesis in an ethnography of readership. This will certainly include analysis of textual content but it must pay attention to popular rather than elite hermeneutics and it must address the material culture of texts. In short, what is of interest to me is less what the texts 'say', 'defer' or 'elide' than their conditions of production and distribution, and the ways in which their audience *uses* them. This point refers not just to the manufacture and circulation of ideas typical of this domain but to the physical properties of the material in which discourse is inscribed and transmitted. In 'New Age' groups of the early period, talks were taken down in shorthand, letters typed (with carbon copies kept and filed), newsletters and information sheets crudely duplicated, contact rotas maintained, mailing lists up-dated on card files, and – in larger groups – several hundred envelopes stuffed and posted by hand. The resulting 'endless typing' – in the words of the editor of the *Herald*s bulletin – indicates the 'home industry' conditions under which 'New Age' discourse gestated and circulated, suggesting a degree of physical time and effort which lessened markedly once fax and computer culture began to kick in in the 1970s. This also hints at the powerful, if masked, material base of discourse, since it suggests that the earlier career of 'New Age' as a specific social emblem reflects in part the pioneers' substantial investments of domestic space and elbow grease. Once the material gets into the hands of its audience, a new set of problematics arise, for as Avryl Lambert, the Heralds' librarian, herself put it: 'There are hundreds of books to help stretch your mental horizons, but we must all seek to digest and to PUT INTO PRACTICE the wisdom of authors'. Only an ethnography of readership can gauge how, if at all, this norm translates into practice. There are some indications of the fruitfulness of such an approach in the ethnographies of Chapter 6 and 7.

So I draw upon a spectrum of popular primary sources, including an extensive private archive of the foremost international 'New Age' organisation, the Findhorn Foundation. As a reflexive 'check' on these I also draw on my own occasional correspondence and conversations with practitioners over ten years or more. Since I am principally interested in the corroborative value of these sources in tracing the genealogy of 'New Age' and in their function as populist modes of expression, my discussions of textual content *per se* are restricted. But I do provide a broad discussion of Alice Bailey's texts of the 1930s in Chapter 2, and I discuss the popular hermeneutics of 'New Age', encoded in some seminal texts of the 1970s onwards, in Chapter 5.[10]

Hunting the snark: the
'New Age Movement' in secondary sources

If the genealogist refuses to extend his faith in metaphysics, if he listens
to history, he finds that there is 'something altogether different' behind
things: not a timeless and essential secret, but the secret that they have
no essence or that their essence was fabricated in a piecemeal fashion
from alien forms.

(Foucault 1977: 142)

There is now a vast literature on 'New Age', including Christian theological
assessments (Saliba 1999) and rationalist debunking (Basil 1988), neither of
which I will treat here. Nor will I consider anthropologies of distinctive
practices or sites classified as 'New Age' – for example, Danforth (1989) on
firewalking, Brown, M. (1997) on channelling, or Prince and Riches (2001)
on Glastonbury – although clearly these are the kinds of contextualised study
the field urgently requires. But here I am interested in the bigger picture, and
so I will focus upon a handful of major texts that, from the late 1980s to
the present, have manufactured the academic orthodoxy that there is an
identifiable religious movement known as the 'New Age' or the 'New Age
Movement'.

J. Gordon Melton has provided several wide-ranging accounts of 'New Age'
as a 'new popular religious movement'.[11] In his view 'New Age'

> is a genuine *movement* – it has no central headquarters, and its
> adherents hold widely varying opinions concerning its exact nature
> and goals. . . . The movement is, however loosely, held together by
> its very real transformative vision of a new world and of new people
> who will transcend the limitations of narrowly chauvinistic cultures,
> religions, and political systems, and will surpass the outmoded
> thought-forms of 'old age' theologies and beliefs.
>
> (Melton 1988: 35–6)

Actually Melton is describing no more than a collection of individuals with a
common utopian ideal. Ironically the absence of just those empirical variables
appropriate to a new social movement (NSM) or new religious movement
(NRM) – leader, headquarters, prescribed text, boundaries, public policy,
common goal – is seen as confirmation.[12] Certainly when it comes to questions
of doctrine and belief, Melton acknowledges some discrepancies:

> The ideas of the New Age Movement are difficult for many to grasp,
> as they grow more out of intuition and experience than doctrines
> or logical reasoning. Moreover, the movement tends to embrace
> mutually contradictory ideas, and among its spokespersons are people

who voice opinions completely unacceptable to the movement as a whole.

(1988: 45–6)

This representational indeterminacy also colours the collection of essays entitled *Perspectives on the New Age* (Lewis and Melton 1992) which contains a vast range of phenomena said to constitute 'New Age', as a brief tour of chapter contents makes plain. 'New Age' is variously linked to humanistic and transpersonal psychology, to Hinduism, to Spiritualism; it interacts closely with New Thought, Pagan witchcraft and alternative spirituality in general; it penetrates corporate business; and it permeates popular arenas of healing and channelling.[13] The editors' introduction identifies 'narrow' and 'broad' definitions of 'New Age' (Lewis and Melton 1992: x–xi) linked with a 'spiritual subculture' on the one hand and media stereotyping on the other. To confuse matters they say that the 'spiritual subculture' includes people who would 'explicitly *reject* this particular label [New Age]' due to perceptions of media stereotyping. They also say that 'one of the traits of the New Age is that major subjects of interest vary from time to time'; hence 'New Age will persist in some form (though perhaps under a different name) into the foreseeable future' (ibid.: xii, x). The sum of these generalisations is a remarkably chameleonic 'movement', one that can apparently change its corporate stripes, shift its principal interests and synthesise everything from witchcraft to corporate business while simultaneously cohering as an empirical collectivity. Lewis (1992: 2) even claims – without explanation – that researchers 'can no longer simply ask respondents in a straightforward manner whether they consider themselves part of the New Age'. But what kind of viable movement – save for one in enemy territory or with illegal or clandestine aims (clearly not the case here) – would be put in jeopardy by simple public affiliation? The data presented under Lewis and Melton's editorship in fact suggest a far more amorphous phenomenon of collective behaviour that is insufficiently institutionalised to be certain of goals, ideology, or even formal identity. Their attempt to make the expression 'New Age Movement' – or even 'New Age' – stick to this diffuse collectivity is pursued in the teeth of the evidence.

An assumption has been made and a trend set. Most accounts of the 1990s accept *a priori* the existence of some kind of movement connected to 'New Age': the main task is now assumed to be identifying the *kind* of movement it is. For example, in the introduction to his pioneering study *The Emerging Network*, Michael York explains that his aim is 'to arrive at some understanding of what the New Age Movement is; how it is formed; who is involved, who its leading spokespersons are' (York 1995: xiii). But elsewhere York's account is interestingly contradictory, for he also correctly says that 'New Age' is 'an umbrella term that includes a great variety of groups and identities', that adherents 'drift between a range of meetings, workshops, lectures or ceremonies', that it is 'not doctrinaire and consequently means many different things to many different people', that it is 'largely composed of short-lived groups' and hence is characterised by 'ephemerality' and, finally and crucially, it does not 'formulate any clearly expressed idea of religious or organisational boundaries to be maintained' (ibid.: 1, 26, 35, 148). But while York is prescient in stressing the field's network properties, his ultimate solution to the definitional problem is to subsume 'New Age' under an impossibly inclusive higher-order category, the 'holistic movement' (York 1995: 330), which includes

> New Age, Neo-paganism, the ecology movement, feminism, the Goddess movement, the human potential movement, Eastern mysticism groups, liberal/liberation politics, the Aquarian Conspiracy, etc.

That Fortean 'etc.' gives the game away: 'New Age' is still an open case.

York's hyper-inclusive 'holistic movement' bears some resemblance to Paul Heelas's *The New Age Movement* (Heelas 1996), in which the term 'New Age' is uncoupled from emic usage and read back into twentieth-century alternative religion as a whole. Encouragingly, Heelas (1996: 5) understands 'New Age' as a 'cultural and practical resource employed in everyday life' and presents 'a study of "popular" values, aspirations and endeavours'. Chief among these is 'interest in the self, its values, capacities and problems' (ibid.: 173). But Heelas compromises this important enquiry by extravagantly extending the boundaries of 'New Age': his 'key figures' are Blavatsky, Jung and Gurdjieff, while men as diverse as A. R. Orage, Carl Rogers, Prince Charles, Aldous Huxley, and Paul Tillich are yoked in; even NRMs like Transcendental Meditation, Soka Gakkai and the Church of Satan are incorporated. The problem is that there is no useful boundary to Heelas's 'New Age Movement'. He himself admits this when he writes that 'the word "movement" should not be taken to imply that the New Age is in any sense an organised entity', but his alternative definition – 'the assumption that humanity is progressing into a new era' (ibid.: 16) – is not convincing, an 'assumption' being far too weak a term to evince a sociocultural movement. By uncritically adopting 'New Age' as an etic term, the very real emic career of the emblem is lost. It is then only a short step to conflating 'New Age' with modern alternative religion as a whole. Consequently the analytic purchase of the taxon, and the empirical history of the field, are severely compromised.

In contrast, Chrissie Steyn's phenomenological investigation *Worldviews in Transition* (Steyn 1994) patiently reconstructs emic content and categories. The bulk of her text stems from thirty extensive interviews in South Africa in the early 1990s with activists and purveyors of 'New Age' services. This attention to 'insider' accounts yields a very different profile. Steyn finds that a diffuse Theosophy structures 'New Age' in South Africa (ibid.: 27). In particular, two-thirds of her interviewees 'had been markedly influenced by the [Alice] Bailey teachings' (ibid.: 101). Heelas (1996: 45), in contrast, claims that Theosophy is 'not especially significant today' and makes only passing reference to Alice Bailey. Consequently Steyn models a gently other-worldly, millennialistic approach against Heelas's (1996: 16) humanistic 'inner spirituality'. Like Lewis and Melton, Steyn acknowledges the controversy attending 'New Age' self-identification among practitioners, observing that many of her interviewees 'were reluctant to use the term' and some were 'appalled at the idea of being labelled "New Agers" ' (ibid.: xiii). She also problematises the 'movement' tag: 'it is not an organisation which people can join and it has no creed that everyone should confess' (ibid.: 6). Nevertheless, she uses the construct 'New Age movement' throughout the book and even concludes with a profile of an 'ideal-typical New Ager' (ibid.: 302).[14]

In *New Age Religion and Western Culture* (1996) Wouter Hanegraaff depicts 'New Age' as a commodification of Western esoteric thought for a secular culture. The text is thus in part given over to an historical discussion of 'esotericism'. Hanegraaff's argument for its impact on modern alternative spirituality is potentially instructive but his presentation of 'New Age' suffers from the by-now familiar definitional a priorism:

> Whatever the nature of the New Age movement will turn out to be, the absence of generally recognised leaders and organisations, norma-tive doctrines and common practices effectively distinguishes it as a whole from the many movements which do have these characteristics.
>
> (ibid.: 14)

'New Age' is rendered a priori unique. But how could a 'movement' exist without the kinds of feature repudiated by Hanegraaff? He finds a solution to the problem of fuzzy boundaries in Colin Campbell's (1972) notion of the 'cultic milieu', meaning the alternative spiritual subculture which has been a persistent feature of modern urban societies. Hanegraaff conflates 'New Age' with this 'cultic milieu' (op. cit.: 17, 522), suggesting that the latter became at some point self-consciously aligned as 'the New Age movement'. But he advances little evidence for how, why, when, where, and by whom this transform-ation came about. The bulk of *New Age Religion and Western Culture* consists of detailed expositions of ideas and themes culled from over one hundred texts selected by Hanegraaff from 'leading New Age bookstores' (ibid.: 17). This cer-tainly provides a rich digest of the popular religious imagination in post-1960s Anglo–American culture. But since he asserts rather than demonstrates his bold claim that 'a considerable part of the literature is little more than the written reflection of New Age practices' (ibid.: 18), and since the tag or emblem itself – 'New Age' – scarcely features in the titles of his representative publications, Hanegraaff's model of 'New Age religion' remains curiously decontextualised.

Finally, I come to Jon Bloch's interesting but restricted sociological study, *New Spirituality, Self and Belonging* (Bloch 1998). Despite the fact that this is the slimmest volume on offer and is based entirely on a small sample of interviews, it takes emic discourse seriously, a position sorely under-represented in other studies.[15] Bloch's method is qualitative ethnographic interviewing, from which he develops an argument that what he calls the 'new spirituality' is a style of popular discourse constructed by participants to minimise the social strain they experience between diverging needs of self-autonomy and collective belonging. The performative function of this discourse is well-observed by Bloch, but his argument that this amounts to 'a fluid, modern social movement' is constrained by the book's brevity and the lack of sustained examination of wider sociocultural factors moulding the discourse.

What can we make of these key secondary sources? They share a consensus that beneath the outward diversity of 'New Age' is a substantive core of ideas and values. Holding to this almost as an article of faith allows the authors to speak either of a 'New Age Movement', thereby aligning themselves with a major sociological sub-industry on NRMs, or of an entity or timespan, 'The New Age', in which case identifying with emic metaphysics. Melton and York represent this homogeneity largely in terms of a family of networks; Heelas via an ambiguous relationship with the values of modernity; Steyn through Theosophical lineage; Hanegraaff in terms of textual ideas; and Bloch through innovative communication codes. The sum is a complex overview that – as one might expect – is strong on texts, beliefs and ideas, but less sure, even contradictory, on ethnography, genealogy and empirical structure. In other words, the precise location in time and space of 'New Age' remains remarkably unclear despite the assumption that 'New Age' is now a secure etic term.[16] Is it 'a religion of revelation' (Hanegraaff 1996: 27), a 'genuine movement' (Melton 1988: 35) or an embodiment of 'self-spirituality' (Heelas 1996: 18)? Or is Steyn (1994: 6) correct to claim that 'it is not an organisation which people can join and it has no creed that everyone should confess'?

The fact is, no one is sure.

'New Age': tangled emics

The special potency of 'New Age' lies in its range of possible interpretations and associations. These include a modernist 'new world order', a resacralised cosmos and – not least – an era of human empowerment and fulfilment in a post-scarcity society. In short, the phrase 'New Age' evokes large-scale cultural change, reflecting exciting yet also risky developments in the modern world: technological revolution and the boom in travel and cultural tourism, certainly, but also the disruptions of the industrial revolution and, more darkly, the globalisation of war and the money economy. These multiple meanings ensure that ideological ambiguity inheres in any particular invocation of 'New Age'. The eschatological question of whether the 'New Age' is to be 'secular' or 'religious', (human) made or (divinely) revealed, is left unresolved.

There is scattered usage of 'New Age' from the mid-Victorian era onwards, but here I want to focus on a twentieth-century genealogy, when the emblem is used with increasingly stylised connotations and the social contexts of its use can be cross-referenced. In Wellesley Tudor Pole's *Private Dowding*, for example, a Spiritualist exegesis of the sufferings of the First World War, a Christ-like figure called 'The Messenger' tells the author that 'a spiritual remedy is becoming available [that] will veritably prove the elixir of the new age and will be within reach of all mankind' (Pole 1917: 95). The appeal to things 'spiritual' and egalitarian are perennial ingredients of dissident religiosity. But a Christian element also enters in: harbinger of this 'new age' is 'the Christ spirit' which 'will dwell among men with healing in its wings'. Pole later surfaces in 'New Age' circles in England in the 1960s, as we see in Chapter 4. Meanwhile, in South Africa, Johanna Brandt, wife of a minister in the Dutch Reformed Church, received a series of revelations from a 'Messenger'. First published in Dutch in 1918, *Die Millenium: ein voorspelling* [The Millennium: a Prophetic Forecast] announced that 'an altogether new epoch' was imminent and that 'the first great miracles of the new age of mystic revelation' were about to be revealed in South Africa (Steyn 2001).

The relationship of 'The Christ' to this imminent new era, which had preoccupied Wellesley Tudor Pole in England and Johanna Brandt in South Africa, was taken up in earnest in the US in the 1930s by Alice Bailey, a former Anglican and Theosophist who eventually published a vast corpus of books outlining her system of 'eschatological Theosophy' (Ellwood 1995: 321). Culminating in the two-volume *Discipleship in the New Age* (1944, 1955), *The Return of the Christ* (1948), and *Education in the New Age* (1954), Bailey's epic texts prophesied an esoteric 'New Age' to be inaugurated by Christ's return. But although Bailey's 'New Age' was persuasive, it was never entirely hegemonic: the deregulated, lay praxis of what would soon be termed 'postmodernity' put paid to that. Others who toyed with the emblem could put their own spin on it to suit the moment. For example, among groups providing spiritual alternatives in the aftermath of the Second World War was 'World Union', which offered study courses in 'New Age Citizenship' and 'New Age Health' from a London address.[17] An indefatigable English pamphleteer, Basil Stewart, added a twelve-page booklet entitled *The Aquarian Age: What it Connotes and the Phenomena that Will Usher it In* (Stewart 1942) and the more substantial *Spiritual Truth: the Pure and Universal Religion of the New Era of the Aquarian Age* (Stewart [n.d.]) to his roster of self-published tracts on a range of issues from Spiritualism to anti-Catholicism. And as we already know, in New Zealand in 1956 the Heralds of the New Age began to publish booklets of messages channelled from spirit guides, 'space brothers' and deceased religious leaders, while pockets of a 'New Age subculture' emerged (Spangler 1984: 26) in the US.

In 1967 two modest English publications championed the 'New Age' emblem. They merit a few comments, since the late 1960s is a key period for mapping the hermeneutic shift in New Age.[18] *Revelation for the New Age* (Brooke 1967) and *A Faith for the New Age* (Vaughan 1967) were both published by Regency Press, an outlet associated with Spiritualist and

Psychic publications. Indeed, the author of the former was a member of both the Society for Psychical Research and the Churches' Fellowship for Psychical and Spiritual Studies, while several well-known Spiritualist sources are included in the extracts of writing in *A Faith for the New Age*. This is essentially a plea for a more broadly 'supernaturalistic' (ibid.: 200) and millennialistic Christianity, based on what the author calls 'widespread expectation' of an 'immanent Manifestation or Second Coming' (ibid.: xliii) that will 'open up vast new continents of mind and soul for mankind to explore in a truly New Renaissance and a truly New Reformation in a truly New Age'. Similar influences shape the collage of views and experiences in *Revelation for the New Age*, a collection of talks given by the author in the early 1960s to small groups in the US and UK. Brooke's material adds some exotic seasonings to Vaughan's neo-Christian manifesto, including Indian mysticism, psychic surgery, UFOs, and the *lingua franca* of Esperanto. These and other elements are considered to be 'signs' foreshadowing 'a dramatic breakthrough of spiritual values which will sweep us all into a worldwide co-operative community', which Brooke calls 'the world administration of the new age' (ibid.: 7).

But ambiguity haunts the form this revelation will take. Will Christ return as the bearded Palestinian famous from European church statuary, as the cover picture of *Revelation for the New Age* suggests? Or in the guise of a contemporary charismatic figure – perhaps the emerging Korean guru, Sun Myung Moon (Brooke was among the first to publicise Moon's Unificationist theology in the West), or Sri Aurobindo? Or perhaps the revelation will be more diffuse – a matter of 'a new realisation dawning in the hearts of men'? (ibid.: 8).

It is clear that in these early statements on 'New Age', authored between the 1930s and late 1960s, there was real discussion and debate, and even a degree of consensus, on the timing and nature of this new order. The meaning of the emblem at this time was evidently in part negotiated within a community of users. In other words, 'New Age' carried literal status, in sharp contrast to the proliferation of referents, and their increasing metaphorisation, that characterises 'New Age' discourse from the 1970s onwards. I explore this point in detail in Chapter 5, but it is worth emphasising here that in the 1960s a variety of small projects explicitly identified themselves with a dawning 'New Age', presented as a public revelation of spiritual power on the point of engulfing the whole planet. In the US an information network called, simply, 'New Age Teachings', issued a monthly bulletin of 'channelled' messages to subscribers in some thirty countries around the globe (Melton *et al.* 1990: 326). In north-east Scotland, a small community beside the coastal village of Findhorn described itself as 'pioneering a new way for the New Age'.[19] An American activist, David Spangler, lived at Findhorn in the early 1970s and wrote a book there called *Revelation: The Birth of a New Age* (Spangler 1977 [1971]).

In contrast, there are also references in several directories of alternative spirituality documenting an emergent 'umbrella' function. A self-styled 'New Age Group' in Blackpool, England, for example, was holding regular meetings to discuss 'colour, numerology, practical mysticism, esoteric astrology, unity and yoga', while 'The New Age Research Fellowship' in Epsom concentrated on 'absent and contact healing, rescue work, meditation, [and] discussion on occult matters' (Strachan 1970: 120–1) and the Middle Piccadilly Farm at Sherbourne, Dorset, listed itself as a 'small New Age community' specialising in 'self-exploration workshops' (Khalsa 1981: 50). What exactly is 'New Age' about all these latter associations? Since they do not explain their grounds for adopting a 'New Age' identity we can only surmise that the term was 'in the air' and seemed a potent and accessible slogan to organise and perhaps market diverse wares and practices. The so-called 'New Age Travellers' who emerged in the 1980s were different again. A picaresque hybrid of punk and 'free festival' hippies in the English countryside (Lowe and Shaw 1993, Hetherington 2000), the 'travellers' were for a time entirely identified with 'New Age' in popular discourse in the UK and counted as the most common category mistake made by friends and colleagues when I first told them of my research in the mid-1990s. Confusions stemming from the co-existence of at least two broad currents of popular hermeneutic – one apocalyptic and eschatological, the other expressive and humanistic – reminds us of the point of embarking on a genealogical investigation in the first place, since the a prioristic assumption of a 'New Age Movement' obliterates nuanced emic differences by default.

Enough has been said here to indicate that some specific historical currents of alternative spirituality that fall short of a 'movement' in any useful sense have nurtured 'New Age' discourse. A recent revival of the term 'Aquarian' as a rival emblem must also be mentioned for the sake of completeness. It derives from astrological calculations on the earth's movement from Pisces into Aquarius, the new sphere of celestial influence (Kelly 1990). Astrology had been popularised in the 1920s – for example, *The Message of Aquaria* (Curtiss and Curtiss 1921) and *The Riddle of the Aquarian Age* (Bennet 1925) – and in the 1930s it entered British daily newspapers. In the contemporary period the 'Aquarian' motif can be traced to the late 1960s: the musical *Hair* had the chorus line 'this is the dawning of the Age of Aquarius', and the famous Woodstock music festival was billed as an 'Aquarian Exposition' (Makower 1989: 106). The trope also drives texts like *A Vision of the Aquarian Age* (Trevelyan 1977) and *The Aquarian Conspiracy* (Ferguson 1982). Sometimes the expressions 'New Age' and 'Age of Aquarius' are interchangeable: a recent book by David Spangler is called *Pilgrim in Aquarius* (Spangler 1996). But 'Aquarian' has also been an alternative tag for Pagan practitioners seeking to celebrate the dawn of a new cycle of spirituality while distancing themselves from the stark modernism, and perceived mercantilism,[20] of 'New Age'. Thus Marian Green, editor of *Quest* magazine in England, is said to be typical of some British Pagans in the early 1990s in that she 'entertains the New Age idiom as a compatible frame of reference' (York 1995: 151). And in the US, Adler (1981: 402) reproduces a 1973 'Aquarian Manifesto' celebrating 'Aquarians Together', denoting 'Witches, Warlocks, and Wizards, Psychics, Priests and Parapsychologists; Mystics, Mediums, and

Magicians; Astrologers, Diviners and Occultists'. In the light of this and other evidence of blurred boundaries, recent Pagan claims of sharp differentiation from 'New Age' must be treated as strategy rather than history.[21]

Deconstructing 'New Age'

The term 'New Age', like the earlier terms 'hippie' and 'yuppie', is partly an accurate designation and partly a mass media stereotype, a symbolic canopy beneath which a very wide variety of phenomena are thrown. There is *something* going on, everyone agrees, but what?

(Simmons 1990: 203–4)

The search for descent . . . shows the heterogeneity of what was imagined consistent with itself.

(Foucault 1977: 147)

In short, I argue in this book that 'New Age' was originally an apocalyptic emblem and is now a tag or codeword for a 'spiritual' idiom. In both cases 'New Age' lacks predictable content and fixed referents: it is always interpreted vernacularly, although the literalist tendencies of the earlier period allow far less hermeneutical latitude than do the polysemic fragmentations of post-1970s spirituality. In order fully to deconstruct 'New Age' and refocus academic attention, I need to show how 'New Age' is intimately linked to wider spiritual experimentation. To this end I exhume in the first part of the book, entitled 'Emblem', some key early episodes in 'New Age' discourse. The ideology of an imminent 'New' or 'Aquarian' age that became available in the 1930s has as a primary source the post-Theosophical writings of Alice Bailey, but it also reflects complex popular cultural dynamics in the period and a growing constituency of seekers hungry for new spiritual syncretisms. After the Second World War the nuclear age and the 'space race' added urgency to this discourse; one sketch of the régime at the Findhorn community in 1968, before the incursions of the counterculture, characterises this 'early' New Age discourse as

a spiritual cargo cult, waiting for something to happen. From the skies, through world events, or from within, they were waiting for that signal, that sign, the ineffable essence of a new 'reality' that would tell them that the old was passing away and the New Age was beginning.

(Hawken 1990: 180–1)

In the second part of the book, entitled 'Idiom', I build a contrastive profile of 'late' New Age. Following a hermeneutical shift in the early 1970s, and under pressure from new developments in alternative religion – including the vigorous evangelising of NRMs (Clarke 1987), the 'do your own thing' ethos of the counterculture (Neville 1970) and the diffusion of 'personal growth' and human potential pursuits in popular culture (Heelas 2000, Puttick 2000) – 'New Age' became an increasingly multivalent signifier. By the 1980s and 1990s 'New Age' had metamorphosed into a label for a sensual and somatic idiom of contemporary popular religion containing a little bit of just about everything. This shift from sharply-focused, apocalyptic emblem to diffuse humanistic idiom is the axis around which the book turns.

2

'OLIGARCHY OF ELECT SOULS'

Alice Bailey's New Age in context

A new world war was not only predictable, but routinely predicted. Those who became adults in the 1930s expected it. The image of fleets of airplanes dropping bombs on cities and of nightmare figures in gasmasks tapping their way like blind people through the fog of poison gas, haunted my generation.

(Hobsbawm 1995: 35)

After the war of 1914–18, wherever I went, no matter whether in England, on the Continent, in America or the Far East, conversation was likely to turn to supernatural subjects. It looked as though many people were feeling that their daily lives were only an illusion, and that somehow there must somewhere be a greater reality.

(Landau 1935: 4)

Without any exoteric organisation, ceremonials, or outer form, there is integrating – silently, steadily and powerfully – a group of men and women who will supersede eventually the previous hierarchical effort. They will supersede all churches, all groups, and all organisations and will eventually constitute that oligarchy of elect souls who will govern and guide the world.

(Bailey 1991a [1934], *A Treatise on White Magic*, 399–400)[1]

In the 1930s Europeans had barely recovered from the 'Great War' of 1914–18, which cost Britain eight hundred thousand lives (more than half of them under the age of thirty), France more than a million and a half, and Germany nearly two million, before international conflict was again rearing its head (Hobsbawm 1995: 26). The human casualties, material damage, political instability, and psychological impact of this 'world' war had been on a scale and intensity hitherto unknown, while the range of territories that experienced military action graphically announced the age of globalisation. Almost all of Europe fought. Other continents were embroiled: New Zealanders and Australians came to the Aegean, Canadians and Americans fought in France. The naval war spread from the Falkland islands to the North Atlantic. Similar globalising trends were to shape the Spanish civil war of 1936–9 and the 'second' world war of 1939–45, which as William Thompson points out, ironically engendered an 'amazing planetary system of coordination – one that organised the movements of armies, peoples, and industries across the Atlantic and the Pacific' (Spangler and Thompson 1993: 170).

Peacetime crises followed. The economic slump of 1929–34 generated unemployment on an unprecedented scale in the US, Germany and the UK. Revolution in Tzarist Russia in 1917 vanquished the *ancien regime* in favour of the Union of Soviet Socialist Republics (USSR), a vast new experiment in Marxist–Leninist economics. A wave of political–economic grand plans and projects ensued, from Lenin's New Economic Policy (1921) and Stalin's Five-Year Plans (1928 onwards) to Roosevelt's New Deal in the US (1933), and from Fascism in Italy, Spain and Germany to proposals for Social Credit in Canada and the UK.

The impact of this 'world crisis' – as it was commonly called – was vividly captured by the contemporary English popular philosopher and broadcaster C. E. M. Joad:

> The nineteenth century believed in progress, yet, believing also that it knew the main lines upon which progress would proceed, it was little interested in what was to come. . . . Our interest [is] in what is to come, which expresses itself in a constant stream of books and pamphlets on every possible aspect of the future, ranging from the 'Future of Clothes' to the 'Future of Physics'. . . . This looking forward is, I suggest, an outcome of the felt uncertainties of the present. We have come, we feel, to a definite break in the tradition of our civilisation. The nineteenth century was the end of an epoch; we, it is increasingly evident, are at the beginning of another.
>
> (Joad 1933: 23–4)

This sense of an epochal turn – making a 'clean break' with the past – manifests in popular, middle-brow and elite cultures alike in the interwar period. In 1920s London, jazz and night-clubs were 'characteristic iconoclasms' (Seaman 1970: 23) and the power of popular music ensured that the first radio broadcast from the BBC's new headquarters in London in 1932 featured a modern dance orchestra. By 1936 the first television broadcasts were vying with the cinema for popular attention. In art, Dada and Surrealism propagated play and rupture: Duchamp displayed a signed urinal; Magritte undercut the relationship between signifier and sign and with his picture of a pipe infuriatingly entitled 'ceci n'est pas une pipe'.

Literary journalism, architecture and music all grappled with new aesthetic orders. A restless new editor, A. R. Orage, took over *The New Age*; T. S. Eliot published *The Waste Land*. The architecture of Walter Gropius and the Bauhaus was welcomed as a celebration of

> the creative energy of this world in which we live and work and which we want to master, a world of science and technology, of speed and danger, of hard struggles and no personal security.
>
> (Pevsner 1975 [orig. 1936]: 217)

In orchestral music, the atonalism of Schoenberg and his pupils Berg and Webern caused a sensation, decentring musical expectations in the cause of

> a chromatic freedom in which notes are organised in a way that avoids most of the characteristic features of tonal music [in which] there is a distinct hierarchy of sounds. . . . With atonal music all notes are equal, and consequently there is no tonal centre.
>
> (Karolyi 1995: 3)

In the political realm, revulsion at the carnage of the Western Front and internationalist and pacifist aspirations were all brought together under the sign of the League of Nations, set up in 1919 to broker a fragile peace. However, its political successes were limited. More significant was the idealistic capital invested in it, for utopian speculation was closely associated with the League. For example, H. G. Wells was both a supporter of the League and a writer who expounded visions of 'progress' in books like *Men Like Gods* (1922), *The Work, Wealth and Happiness of Mankind* (1931) and *The Shape of Things to Come* (1933). Wells' fictions ruminated on science, social planning and utopias. Like their dystopian shadow of the same period, Aldous Huxley's *Brave New World* (1932), they infused the newly-emergent 'science fiction' genre with learned prognostications on the cultural impact of technological change and the shape of new world orders. *The Shape of Things to Come* (Wells 1933), for example, paints an epic vision of the future from 1929 to 2106 in which a new world war triggers a lengthy period of global chaos before a group of intellectuals decides that a world state is the only solution. After trials and tribulations – including a thirty-year plan and a world council – the utopian state is achieved. *The Shape of Things to Come* epitomises the 1930s *zeitgeist*. The dizzying order envisaged by Wells's elite had clear affinities with the aspirations of the League of Nations and reflected key obsessions of the 1930s: social planning, the role of 'strong' individuals and cadres, and the 'long arm' of international politics.

There were also substantial political changes in the period: the achievement of full suffrage for women in 1920 in the US and in 1928 in the UK, for example, or the election of the first Labour government in Britain in 1924. And for consumers, new wealth was quietly germinating. Stevenson and Cook (1994: 11, 13) argue that alongside the pictures of dole queues and hunger marches must be placed those of another Britain, of new industries, prosperous suburbs and a rising standard of living. . . . For many salaried people affluence began not in the 1950s but in the Thirties, when it became possible for an average salaried person to buy his own house, usually on a mortgage, run a car, and begin to afford a range of consumer durables and household goods hitherto considered quite out of reach.

House building and home ownership increased sharply between the wars, new roads and motor traffic proliferated, and the UK rail network expanded to the full (Clarke 1996: 145–6, 151). By 1933 the electricity grid in the UK – a potent symbol of new technology – was among the most advanced in the world: in 1920, only one house in seventeen had electricity; by the end of the 1930s, it was two out of three (Stevenson and Cook 1994: 17). Massive circulation of mail – around four items posted weekly by each British adult (Clarke 1996: 113) – indicates a revolution in communications in which publishing of all kinds expanded, including intense newspaper circulation battles, the first paperbacks (the 'Penguin' imprint of 1935), and various book clubs and part-exchange library schemes. Weekly cinema audiences in mid-decade averaged nearly twenty million (Thorpe 1992: 107), and most homes had a wireless, factors which contributed to the increasing influence of popular media and a domestication of culture and leisure. The rise of a popular consumer culture vied with the totalistic solutions of the utopian planners and the new Modernist aesthetic alike, generating rich but volatile subjectivities in everyday life. In this religion was no exception.

The alternative turn: doing religion differently

'The British soldier has certainly got religion; I am not so sure, however, that he has got Christianity'.

(Army chaplain, 1917, quoted in Winter 1992: 190)

As hardly any of the exoteric cults in the world to-day are really able to show men *how* to overcome the world (though enjoining them earnestly to do so): and as not one of them is able to offer any really convincing *proof* of the truth of its creeds, it is not surprising that vast numbers of thoughtful and even spiritual people are turning away from 'organised religion' and looking in other directions for a sure foundation upon which to build their lives.

(Baker-Beall 1932: 300)

The type of literature which deals with the spiritual quest, especially from the psychological point of view, is becoming increasingly popular.

(Editorial in *Occult Review* 62/4, 1935, p. 219)

The 1920s and 1930s are a key period for the development of religion in twentieth-century Anglo–American culture, mixing elements of innovation, consolidation and revival. I have space here only to sketch the emergence of a loosely institutionalised constituency of 'seekers' practising a hybridised lay 'spirituality' which, together with the sociocultural developments outlined above, provide an audience and a context for Alice Bailey's seminal 'New Age' discourse. But I cannot treat here the acculturation of migrant traditions in Anglo–American culture such as Buddhism, Hinduism, and Sufism – which richly deserve extended analyses – nor can I consider the equally important impact upon alternative spirituality of the interfaith movement, whose public success was exemplified in the World Congress of Faiths held in London in 1936. Instead I focus on what was then often termed 'the occult': a broad field whose detraditionalised practice combined with a yearning for a re-enchanted cosmos to create an ideal seedbed for a 'New Age' prophetic discourse.

Theosophy and Spiritualism are prime indices of the cultural diffusion of such a field. These class-aligned, competing ideologies were at their peak of social influence in the 1920s and 1930s. The aestheticised spirituality of the Theosophical movement was bound up with a series of progressive political causes from women's suffrage to Indian independence: 'to be a Theosophist', recalls one woman, 'you had to take part in all the big problems and questions that were going on around you in society' (Akhtar and Humphries 1999: 19). In its spiritual teachings Theosophy celebrated a mysterious cosmos and the occult potential of humankind, and the original Theosophical Society, now under the leadership of Annie Besant and C. W. Leadbeater and trading heavily on the charismatic figurehead of Jiddu Krishnamurti, the anticipated 'world teacher', reached a membership peak in 1929 of some 45,000 worldwide (Campbell 1980: 128). Theosophy also supplied a *lingua franca* for other occultists in bourgeois culture, colourfully dramatised in the aristocratic spiritual milieu portrayed in Cyril Scott's didactic *Initiate* trilogy (1920–32). It also generated several enduring schismatic movements including Alice Bailey's Arcane School in 1923, of which more anon. And a separate genealogy of populist groups indebted to a broad occult–Theosophical discourse arose from the 1930s onwards which migrated and recruited across class lines, such as Guy and Edna Ballard's 'Mighty I AM' movement in 1930s America and George King's Aetherius Society in 1950s England.[2]

Theosophy partly defined itself over and against the 'vulgar' search for empirical proofs of survival after death such as defined the more plebeian Spiritualist community, an equally prominent star in the alternative spiritual constellation. Winter (1992: 191) points out that, across the trenches during the 1914–18 war, 'spiritualist images, stories, and legends proliferated. . . . Some were about the dead, others about magical forces affecting the living'. Spiritualism was rejuvenated in the culture of bereavement (Winter 1995) that succeeded the war when over 40,000 war cemeteries and memorials sprang up across the UK alone (Davies 1993: 26) and mass pilgrimages were organised to war cemeteries at Ypres, Gallipoli and Flanders (Walter 1993: 65). In the late 1920s and early 1930s there were around one quarter of a million practising Spiritualists and some two thousand Spiritualist societies in the UK in addition to flourishing microcultures of platform mediumship and 'home circles' (Nelson 1969: 161; Hazelgrove 2000). Like Theosophy, Spiritualism in the 1920s and 1930s is best understood as a recrudescence of Edwardian and Victorian spiritual concerns – a revival rather than an innovation – but, unlike Theosophy, with a particular purchase in working class and lower-middle-class cultures. Ironically, the Spiritualist cause was fostered in the media by the public conversions of prominent figures whose social status and cultural capital were, in fact, atypical of the movement as a whole: in the UK these included the physicist Sir Oliver Lodge, the writer Sir Arthur Conan Doyle, and the newspaper editor Hannen Swaffer.

Theosophy and Spiritualism benefited from the consolidation of a more diffuse occult culture which celebrated the recondite, magical powers of the person in a resacralised cosmic order.[3] Astrology was the populist face of this revival: its stellar blueprints of influence and constraint seriously challenged traditional Christian theodicies in the uncertain moral order of the 1920s and 1930s. R. H. Naylor cast the first newspaper horoscope in the UK in the *Sunday Express*, for the newly-born Princess Margaret; a column followed in the *Daily Express* in 1931. By the late 1940s one Christian apologist complained that horoscopes were 'an essential component of a successful Sunday newspaper' and that astrology was 'galloping through the homes of the people of Britain' (Davies 1954: 106).

There were inevitably many levels of engagement with these practices. Uncomplicated recreation was one. In 1935 the *Daily Express* published a popular compendium called *The Book of Fortune-Telling: How to Tell Character and the Future by Palmistry, Cards, Numbers, Phrenology, Handwriting, Dreams, Astrology, Etc* (*Daily Express* 1935). The volume was described as being 'for amusement only' (ibid.: 5), promising that 'you are quite sure of being in demand at all parties and gatherings if you can put on a mysterious air and read the future!' (ibid.). Serious spiritual diagnosis was another angle, vigorously defended by the Theosophical practitioners 'Sepharial' and 'Leo'; Alice Bailey also delved here (her *Esoteric Astrology* was published posthumously in 1951). And if required, intellectual legitimation for these enthusiasms was available in the work of C. G. Jung, who studied astrology and *I Ching* in the 1920s and 1930s (Main 1997: 11–14).

Clearly astrology could travel socially and speak both to everyday concerns of love and happiness and grand theories of meaningful coincidence. One member of an astrological society in London in the 1930s recalls that

> people were feeling the need for additional information to help them plan their lives. It gave clues that you got nowhere else, it told you things that you knew next to nothing about.
>
> (Akhtar and Humphries 1999: 112)

In the re-enchanted cosmos fed by Theosophy, Spiritualism and popular occultism alike, the charisma of the individual – and of small illuminated groups and circles – waxed. Exotic cultures were scanned for useful spiritual technologies. Sensational gurus from far corners of the Empire and beyond held court in metropolitan centres, such as Gurdjieff, Krishnamurti and Meher Baba. The indigenous peoples of North America became spirit guides for mediums, such as the messages from 'Silver Birch' published in the new weekly magazine *Psychic News*. Amateur healers flourished: for example, a New Zealander, J. J. Thomas – a self-styled 'psychic surgeon' – gave spiritual healing under the direction of his Zulu spirit guide 'Good Fellow' in a room above his motorcycle garage business in East London (Thomas 1957). More radically still, Archie Belaney from Hastings, England, moved to Canada, renamed himself 'Grey Owl', and had a meteoric career as an indigenous backwoodsman lecturing on an early form of eco-spirituality (Dickson 1976).

And we are still only scratching the surface of a vast arena of hybrid spiritualities. For example, towards the end of the 1930s Wicca was germinating in the imagination of colonial administrator Gerald Gardner, and Peter Caddy – future Findhorn founder and 'New Age' prophet of the 1960s – had embarked upon a Rosicrucian apprenticeship (which we follow more closely below). The young Alan Watts – later a guru of the Beats and Hippies – was mixing Buddhism, Theosophy and occultism (Snelling *et al.* 1987). Mary Swainson, a pioneer 'New Age' counsellor and psychic, was 'testing out everything from spiritualism to psychic science' (Swainson 1977: 204). A former army intelligence officer, J. G. Bennett, had embarked upon his lifelong 'spiritual quest' (Bennett 1962: 221) through Sufism, Ouspensky and Gurdjieff. And so on: this kind of list exemplifies the rhizomic outcomes – the Fortean *et cetera* – characteristic of alternative spirituality. What is clear enough is that these and other undercurrents of alternative spirituality popularised an ideology of radical personal transformation that crystallised in the model of the self as a 'seeker', navigating strange but exciting cultural waters (Sutcliffe 2000a). The contemporary religionist was adopting – implicitly or explicitly – the normative identity of a 'special agent' who could 'spiritualise' society with potent practices and infuse the religious vocabulary of the day with new terms and concepts.

'Armchair' spiritualities and 'cottage' religion: readers and seekers at large

Who provided the curricula and resources for these new seekers? In 1935 the journalist Rom Landau identified one source. His seminal survey, *God is My Adventure: A Book on Modern Mystics, Masters and Teachers*, investigated a number of heterodox spiritual teachers active in England and Europe at the time. Such was the book's popularity that it was reprinted seven times between 1935 and 1939 alone and made Landau's reputation as a knowledgeable commentator on alternative religion (Alan Watts [1973: 119] describes him as the delegated 'authority on modern cult-religions' at the World Congress of Faiths in 1936). Landau's book is interesting on several counts: it maps a range of alternative teachers now proselytising in the heart of Enlightenment Europe; it hints at the impact on contemporary religion of the forces of globalisation and population displacement set loose by the 1914–18 war; and it documents the privileged social background – the 'drawing-room culture' – of one particular sector of alternative spirituality.

The title, *God is My Adventure*, is immediately revealing. 'God' is presented as the object of a personalised human quest, while 'adventure' suggests excitement, diversion, even dalliance. The subtitle indicates further detraditionalisation of religion: the pursuit is not to be among priests, theologians and churches – the standard authorities – but in the company of an arresting collection of 'mystics, masters and teachers'. Landau's heroes (there are no heroines) are independent teachers offering a functional spirituality for lay practitioners. The nominal Christians in Landau's pantheon are the American–Swiss Frank Buchman, founder of the Oxford Group movement (later Moral Re-Armament), and the Welshman George Jeffreys, evangelical principal of the Elim Pentecostal Church. The rest are firmly non-Christian or else can only be construed as 'Christian' in the most attenuated sense. The Greek–Armenian G. I. Gurdjieff and the Hungarian Rudolf Steiner are perhaps 'esoteric' Christians, although each was teaching his own system. So was Jiddu Krishnamurti, a Brahmin's son from the Theosophical headquarters in India, who had recently renounced his leadership of the Order of the Star in the East to proclaim, famously, that 'truth is a pathless land'. Meher Baba was from a Zoroastrian family in Poona, India, and claimed to be an *avatar* for the Modern Age. Others – the Russian mathematician and occultist P. D. Ouspensky, the Estonian aristocrat Hermann Keyserling and the German poet Stefan George – practised mystically-nuanced Stoic philosophies.

Not only the teachings but the ethnic origins of these gurus – Greek–Armenian, Hungarian, Indian, Russian, Estonian – are at some variance with those of typical clergy and congregation of the period (Mews 1994). Gurdjieff and Meher Baba are particularly strong representatives of the biographical hybridity swirling beneath the surface of these new spiritualities. Born to an Armenian mother and a Greek father in the Caucasus, Gurdjieff's family moved to Kars in Turkey where he absorbed his father's oral tradition while also receiving instruction from an Orthodox priest. Meher Baba's Zoroastrian parents had emigrated to India from Persia; he himself claimed initiation first from a female Sufi (itself an arresting status) and later by a Hindu guru, and his ashram at Bombay in the early 1920s attracted followers of all these religious systems. He synthesised these perspectives in spectacular fashion when, in 1932, in an interview on the front page of the *Sunday Express* in London, he claimed 'I am one with God. I live in Him like Buddha, like Christ, like Krishna' (cited in Landau 1935: 131).

God is My Adventure not only documented new discourses in spirituality; it catered for a developing public interest in 'alternative' religion in general. Literary modernism was already exploring heterodox symbologies: T. S. Eliot's poem *The Waste Land* (1922), for example, includes a Tarot card reading by 'Madame Sosostris, famous clairvoyante' and references to the Buddha's 'fire sermon' and the Upanishads, and the piece as a whole is framed by an Arthurian 'holy grail' mythology. Nor was Eliot's interest in comparative religion eccentric: other modernists were drawn by these vistas, including Eliot's colleague Ezra Pound – *The Waste Land*'s dedicatee – who sought inspiration in Chinese nature poetry, and Aldous Huxley, whose practical tastes ranged in mid-century from palmistry to vedanta to mescalin.

As publishing of all kinds expanded, so different audiences emerged for 'genre' and 'niche' interests, in religion as in everything else. By the close of the 1930s dedicated Spiritualist, Psychic and Occult book clubs (Nelson 1969: 162) were mining the popular readership opened up in 1935 by Penguin paperbacks. A steady flow of periodicals came off the presses in Britain. Some were literary, quasi-academic publications like G. R. S. Mead's *The Quest* (1909–30) and *The Search* (1931–4), which spawned their own dedicated societies. Others were respected middlebrow journals like Ralph Shirley's *Occult Review* (1905–51). Others still were eclectic and often short-lived, such as *Proteus*, concerned with 'Natural therapeutics, Scientific physiognomy and phrenology, Dream analysis, Psychic phenomena, scientific astrology and herbalism'.[4]

The Shrine of Wisdom is an interesting example of a publication connected with a group of practitioners. Published in Cheshire, England, by the 'Hermetic Truth Society' (affiliated to the equally portentious 'Order of Ancient Wisdom'), it described itself as 'a quarterly devoted to synthetic philosophy, Religion and Mysticism'. The autumn 1920 issue featured an article on 'Spiritual Exercises for Mystics' and a 'hermetic biography' of Pythagoras. Members' notices register a successful summer retreat for the Order in North Wales and a call for help at headquarters 'typing copies of Lections and Rites, duplicating documents, copying music, transcribing MSS., addressing envelopes, making vestments, insignia, badges, etc'.[5] Clearly there was a ceremonial practice of some kind, but the journal's contents – largely popular discussions of Hellenistic mysticism – give scant clues to this.[6]

But the most tenacious twentieth-century occult periodical was undoubtedly the *Occult Review*, published by Rider for nearly fifty years from 1905 and distributed in the UK, US and Australasia. A typical interwar issue might include articles on astral travel, alternative healing, Eastern religious texts, interpretations of karma and reincarnation, and profiles of contemporary teachers and gurus. Several pages of advertisements featured groups and societies, and products and services such as talismen, astrology, and clairvoyance. Spiritualism and Theosophy were the enduring influences, the former usually as critical foil to the latter's benchmark spiritual acumen (or snobbery). Editorials critiqued fraudulent mediums, mused on teachings of 'the Masters', and delineated the nature and scope of occultism in general, particularly its claimed consonance with scientific methodology and its potential as a functional spirituality for modernity. Hence a 1932 editorial, entitled 'Linking Up', describes 'true occultism' as 'the science of spirituality' that has 'no concern with creeds, either religious or theosophical'. It proposes setting up a 'Spiritual League' to co-ordinate those 'scattered spiritual units' exploring 'inner life and its manifold problems'.[7] These 'scattered spiritual units', of course, could be construed as not only the various small groups and societies of the day but also the *Occult Review*'s atomised readership. In this way the private hermeneutics of solitary readers – their 'armchair spiritualites' – could be reconfigured as a vital contribution to occult praxis, since in the materialist metaphysics of occult spirituality, the 'life of the mind' was no metaphor but a real location in which to perform work to change the world.

Certainly if one could or would not practise alternative spirituality collectively, print culture was available as a material resource for inspiration and reflection. Disencumbered of the constraints of collective ritual, readers' subjectivities could flourish, even run riot. Compelling evidence that texts functioned as a very practical resource for solitary hermeneutics can be found in the preface to the 1945 revised edition of *God is My Adventure*. Here Rom Landau puts his book's success down to the existence of a buoyant market among 'seekers' (his term) for 'the spiritual experiences of a fellow seeker'. He also acknowledged a more diffuse spiritual curiosity in the population at large based on evidence that

> many others, disillusioned by the Churches, were only too willing to delve into the ways and methods of unorthodox schools of thought, yet without at the same time feeling compelled to accept this or that method as the only valid one.
>
> (Landau 1945: 7)

In other words, dedicated 'seekers' – and I return to this term later – took to the book immediately; still others browsed and dabbled, but held back. Significantly, both readerships resisted 'being pontifically forced by the author into accepting a certain point of view' (ibid.). Overall this new preface evokes a 'bookish' constituency of reader – practitioners who consider themselves 'seekers', relish eclecticism, and equivocate on the existential 'closure' implied by unreserved commitment.[8]

The popularisation and dissemination of previously elite discourses on spiritual development at all cultural levels – from Eliot's *Waste Land* to the *Occult Review* to newspaper astrology – evinces a pervasive print culture. Landau's book was reprinted eleven times in as many years; another example of the genre, Paul Brunton's *A Search in Secret India* (1934), was reprinted six times between 1934 and 1938 alone. Books, of course, require manufacture, distribution and promotion. In London the latest titles could be found in specialist bookshops like Atlantis and Watkins. The proprietor of the latter, John Watkins senior, was himself a student of H. P. Blavatsky's Theosophy, and the young Alan Watts (1973: 107) remembered that Watkins' son acted as his 'trusted adviser on the various gurus, pandits, and psychotherapists' active in late 1930s London. Others preferred Atlantis, where the shop's owner, Michael Houghton, apparently led his own 'Order of the Hidden Masters' from the basement (Wise 1995). Such establishments not only supplied books, then, but functioned as contact points – even ritual venues – for spiritual seekers.[9]

Domestic premises and hired rooms also played a part in the generation and practice of what we might call 'cottage' spirituality. A rash of grandly-named small groups were active during the interwar period with varying numbers, lifespans, and cultural impact, from the aforementioned 'Quest' and 'Search' societies, and the Order of Ancient Wisdom, to 'Woodcraft' groups with a mystical and 'animist' view of nature such as the Order of Woodcraft Chivalry (Hutton 2001: 165–70). Pitched somewhere in values and praxis between magical orders, Freemasonry and 'Friendly' societies, these were essentially middle-class and lower middle-class social groups with an amateurist intellec-tual ethos and a corresponding taste for innovative ceremonial. Typically they met on private premises or in discreetly hired rooms and communicated through their own networks and publications.

A Rosicrucian group in England

One of these small groups in particular, the Rosicrucian Order Crotona Fellowship, is of historical significance out of all proportion to its sociological profile due to its role in the genesis of two major currents of twentieth-century alternative religion. Its function as portal into a surviving witchcraft coven, according to the claim of Gerald Gardner, founder of Wicca, is one point of departure.[10] But the Order was also a formative resource in the long spiritual career of Peter Caddy, a central protagonist in international 'New Age' circles between the 1950s and 1970s, including the early years of the Findhorn colony.

The Rosicrucian Order Crotona Fellowship (hereafter ROCF) was a quasi-initiatory body whose oath – 'Silence, Secrecy, Sincerity and Service' (Slocombe 1995: 1) – does not, on the face of it, augur great disclosure. It was most prominent in the late 1930s – thirty-six members apparently attended its 'annual conclave' in 1937 – although it endured into the early 1950s (Heselton 2000: 76, 89). Although the Order published an extensive series of small booklets and pamphlets through the 1920s and 1930s and at its peak received regular coverage in the local press (perhaps surprisingly, given the first two injunctions of its oath), it has had a very restricted influence on occult culture in general. Nevertheless, a colleague of Caddy's has plausibly argued that the latter's approach to Findhorn practice in the 1960s 'was *directly* and *deliberately* drawn from his Rosicrucian training' (Slocombe 1995: 2). This is borne out by correspondence between Caddy and the secretary of the ROCF as late as 1971, which discusses the transfer of surviving ROCF regalia from its old centre to Findhorn to be used in a 'consecrated area . . . where the power can be focused'.[11] In fact the ROCF's small group structure represents a seminal lay response to the perceived stagnation of 'organised religion' between the world wars, and its lay esotericism played a formative role in Peter Caddy's auto-biographical development. So my sketch here of its history and structure not only allows me to recover another 'lost' spiritual culture in 'New Age' genealogy but also enables me to isolate an emergent 'New Age' biography among the welter of competing identities of spiritual seekership in the 1920s and 1930s.

Peter Caddy (1917–94) was brought up in a middle-class Methodist household in Ruislip in Middlesex. He describes himself as a 'loner' who learned 'obedience, discipline and to ignore physical pain' at an early age. He received a socially conservative and privileged English education, attending public school and becoming a King's Scout (Caddy 1996: 19–25). In the late 1920s his father – whom he describes as 'a model of conventional high-Christian morality' (ibid.: 77) – began an eclectic search for relief from chronic back pain, trying alternative cures such as chiropractic and homeopathy. He also received spiritual healing from a medium called Grace Cooke and her 'guide' White Eagle. Peter Caddy describes this encounter as 'my first experience of a spiritual nature' (ibid.: 21) and although his father returned to orthodox Methodism, Caddy notes that a trend had been set: 'there was no turning back for me' (ibid.: 23). At the age of sixteen, he recalls, 'I began to question many of the things that had been taught by conventional religions, and started my own search for the truth through many "ologies" and "isms"' (ibid.: 25).

Caddy's 'search for the truth' began in earnest in the ROCF, a group which revolved around the charismatic leadership of a certain George A. Sullivan (1890–1942), who also used the pen-names of 'Alex Matthews', 'Aureolis' and 'Muser'. Sullivan set up the ROCF in the Liverpool area in the early 1920s, scripting its texts and developing a correspondence course. He was also active in the intersecting occult networks of the day, including Theosophical and Co-Masonic circles and a 'College of Psychotherapy and Natural Therapeutics' in Liverpool, and Heselton (2000: 58) also points out that an address at which he produced ROCF pamphlets in the 1920s belonged to a local Spiritualist church. In addition to his Rosicrucian activities, Sullivan was also an amateur actor, poet and playwright, and after moving to suburban Christchurch on the English south coast around 1935, he directed plays in the ROCF's 'ashrama', a wooden hall erected in the garden of Sullivan's new benefactor. Ambition grew, and in 1938 the ROCF built an elaborate private theatre in the same grounds.[12] Assessments of Sullivan's character differed widely in the English occult community. Some, it seems, accepted him as a 'Master' in the Theosophical tradition; others were less impressed.[13] In the ROCF, at any rate, he was considered a 'being of vast knowledge' (Caddy 1996: 32) and held the title 'Supreme Magus'. In 1936, aged nineteen and then serving a catering apprenticeship in London, Caddy was introduced to Sullivan by his brother-in-law. After answering Sullivan's 'probing questions' and 'meeting his inner scrutiny', Caddy was 'initiated' into the London-based branch of the Order (Caddy 1996: 32) and subsequently travelled regularly from London to Christchurch to attend ROCF gatherings.[14]

The ROCF's history – particularly its formation and development in the 1920s – remains under-researched.[15] In a small 1926 rulebook, Sullivan states that he founded the group in 1911 as 'The Order of Twelve'. This apparently disbanded in 1914 on the outbreak of war but was reconstituted by Sullivan around 1920 under its present name, rejuvenated by Rosicrucian lore Sullivan claimed to have learnt in Germany during a period in captivity. An alternative genealogy is given in another pamphlet, where the ROCF is said to have existed in its present form for 'at least one hundred years' and even to be descended from the 'Antient [sic] Rosicrucian Adepts of 1347'.[16] In the late 1930s Caddy (1996: 31) says it had chapters 'all over Britain' but despite these extravagant claims the Order was probably never very extensive and was largely associated with Sullivan's partner, friends and colleagues.[17] Its 'Grand Chapter' first operated in north-west England – in Birkenhead (c. 1924) and Liverpool (c. 1927) – before moving to Christchurch in late 1935 (Heselton 2000: 66) and – some time after Sullivan's death in 1942 – to Southampon (ibid.: 89). Since the only other branch that I have found a reference to is in London, it seems likely that there were only ever two branches of the ROCF – the mobile 'grand chapter' and a metropolitan recruitment outlet – plus an unknown (probably small) number of affiliates who maintained contact through a correspondence course. A pamphlet on the structure of 'The Chapter' throws light on the organisation of the ROCF. It outlines two types of ritual forum: a 'Plural Chapter' for group practice and a 'Singular Chapter' for individual use. The latter is a 'special place sanctified by a Rosicrucian Disciple in which he may individually practise the Rites and Ceremonies at the stated times in accordance with the Plural Chapters'.[18] The emphasis in this document on an implicitly solitary practice (no group ritual is mentioned) supports the surmise that 'plural' chapters were rare and that membership was largely a solo affair regulated by correspondence with Sullivan.

But there is no reason to doubt Peter Caddy's belief in the sincerity of both Sullivan and the Order. For example, he believed that Sullivan possessed an esoteric cipher manual of Francis Bacon's from the sixteenth century, handed down to him from previous 'Masters' in a Rosicrucian genealogy (Caddy 1996: 32), and certainly what survives of the ROCF's small library contains a range of occult and esoteric texts, including several antiquarian works.[19] He also held Sullivan's contemporary teachings in high regard. Shortly before his death Slocombe (1995: 1) says Caddy passed on to him

> a file of yellowed, dog-eared pamphlets and mimeographed papers
> [which] he had, he said, been carrying with him around the world

since the outbreak of World War Two. They were the original teachings and instructions given to him by his beloved mentor Dr. Sullivan, 'Aureolis', the Supreme Magus.

Notwithstanding the appeal to antiquity and lineage, these 'pamphlets' and 'mimeographed papers' strongly suggest a contemporary production base that was restricted, even domestic; certainly Heselton (2000: 66) states that parts of the correspondence course only exist in carbon copies.

Members seem to have practised Sullivan's Rosicrucianism largely through private reading, with ritual work (in the 'Singular Chapter') being performed in a home-made temple area. The working requirements of this space included a small altar, a cloth with the Rosicrucian emblem, incense, candles, appropriate ROCF literature, and a 'Collar or Robes' of the degree attained by the member.[20] A 'Plural Chapter', on the other hand, apparently required more elaborate regalia, including a charter from the Grand Chapter, swords, gauntlets, aprons, and gongs.[21] Weekend activities at the 'Grand Chapter' in Christchurch included 'church services and lectures' and there was an annual gathering at the 'ashrama' or meeting-hall. Group practice at Christchurch seems to have been a mixture of practical tasks, talks, drama, and games; some members acquired newly-built bungalows in the area in the late 1930s in order to live closer to the hub of activities.

What did the Crotona Fellowship teach? A 1925 pamphlet lists 132 lectures organised according to a hierarchical grade system, incorporating a wide range of occult and popular metaphysical material. A taste of this is provided by the 'Soul Science' postal lectures received by Caddy, which included instructions for practical exercises in 'positive thinking, healing techniques, empowering others, and growing into self-possession and self-control' (Caddy 1996: 33–4). Also taught was the power of the 'affirmation', a short statement designed to be spoken out loud or silently affirmed as a declaration of intent and focus of the will. Examples include:

> I am power. That power manifests in me, is directed by my thought to nothing but good.
> I create every mental condition, and that condition reflects in my environment. Therefore I create my life. I create it as I think it.
> (Cited in Slocombe 1995: 3)

Caddy himself succinctly summarises the thrust and appeal of Sullivan's Rosicrucianism thus:

> By thinking, you make your life whatever it is, and are thus either consciously or unconsciously your own creator, designing your own fate.
> (Caddy 1996: 33).

The sum is a radical populist idealism based on a belief in thought as an invisible – and hence 'secret' – causal agent possessing magical power.[22]

As I have said, the Order was probably never more than a small group and there is little evidence of the hiving off of 'Plural Chapters' beyond the Liverpool–London/Christchurch–London axes. The evidence suggests a quasi-endogamous network of couples, friends and mentors that, at the peak of its material resources in the late 1930s, numbered not more than a few dozen middle-class individuals: barristers, solicitors, small business operators, teachers, and clerical workers (Heselton 2000: 72ff.). The Order began to unravel after Sullivan's death, although Caddy (1996: 77) mentions that Sullivan's successor, Walter Bullock, was still giving talks in 1947 and Heselton (2000: 89) traces the group to Southampton in the early 1950s. But correspondence in the 1960s between Caddy and Bullock, and in the early 1970s between Caddy and Keen (Sullivan's former partner), suggests terminal decline. There are no new names in these letters, and a solitary reference to 'two very old London brethren' suggests the group now existed in memory only.[23] Keen herself died in 1972 and her large house – the Order's base – was demolished in 1976 (Heselton 2000: 73).

Nevertheless, in addition to its small group structure and lay, hybrid practice – features that broadly define alternative spirituality in the period – the ROCF influenced Peter Caddy's spiritual biography and, through this, the course of 'New Age' spirituality.[24] And as we have seen, the wider field of alternative spirituality within which the ROCF emerged functions as a diffuse and dynamic cultural context in itself: a series of overlapping networks created by the criss-crossing trajectories of numerous seekers, with nodal points in the form of talks and 'lectures', small group rituals and the occasional dedicated building or ritual space. Norms and values of 'seeking' are disseminated through print media and face-to-face interaction. Although stemming from a bourgeois ethos of 'spiritual self-help' (derived in turn from the largely professional and self-employed social bases of exponents), the reflexive institution of 'seekership' increasingly incorporated more egalitarian ideals, appealing to both sexes, and a wide range of social classes, as differences were smoothed out in the inclusive ideology of the group. By participating in a fresh and exciting culture of 'seekership', individuals across the social spectrum could have their subjectivities validated and celebrated, thereby securing a sense of place and agency in a re-enchanted cosmos, redefined now in terms of *quality* of experience. This loose, variegated constituency of 'seekers' formed the immediate audience for Alice Bailey's vision of a 'New Age' in the 1930s and provided recruits for its transmission and customisation in subsequent decades.

Alice Bailey and the Lucis Trust

Man is emerging into an era of peace and good-will, but a great effort is needed to force wide open the Door leading into the New Age.

(Alice Bailey, letter to *Occult Review*, 1932)[25]

My background has been that of an active worker in the Christian field, and I have been for many years a member of the Theosophical Society, but I work under no labels.

(Alice Bailey, letter to *Occult Review*, 1935)[26]

The subjective realm is vitally more real than is the objective, once it is entered and known.

(Alice Bailey, 1950, cited in Sinclair 1984: 66)

In sharp contrast to the notoriety of her Theosophical mentor, H. P. Blavatsky, the character of Alice A. Bailey (1880–1949) remains private, intense and elusive. 'I work under no labels', she wrote in the *Occult Review* in 1935. By her own account she was born into a wealthy Manchester family and received a privileged Anglican upbringing, largely at her paternal grandfather's country estate in Surrey.[27] Her childhood and early adulthood were unsettled and emotionally troubled. Her parents died when she was young, and – remarkably – she mentions three suicide attempts before the age of fifteen, indicating an intense and sensitive disposition (Bailey 1973: 21). She also described herself as 'a fundamentalist believing in a transcendent, often cruel God' (Judah 1967: 120). At an aunt's country estate in Kirkcudbrightshire, Scotland, she encountered a being she identified in retrospect as a 'Master' in the Theosophical tradition but who at the time she took to be Jesus. Following this revelation, she became a Sunday-school teacher and then, at twenty-two, an evangelist in soldiers' homes, a career which took her from Ireland to India. After a psychological breakdown of some kind – extant accounts gloss over this – she returned to England, only to emigrate to North America early in the twentieth century with a husband whom she had met through her army evangelism, and who was now training to be an Episcopalian minister. However, after a period of sustained domestic violence at his hands, she and their three children left him. A period of single motherhood and poverty followed in California where, around the age of thirty-five, Bailey encountered the Theosophical Society. She describes this as 'the opening of a new spiritual era in my life' (Bailey 1973: 133). In 1917 she moved to Hollywood to be near its (then) national headquarters. Subsequently she became editor of the Theosophical Society magazine *The Messenger* and married its secretary, Foster Bailey. Around 1919 she controversially claimed a fresh contact with a Master called 'Djwal Khul', known thereafter in Bailey's work as 'the Tibetan'. This marked the beginning of her true vocation as the Tibetan's 'secretary': it had been him and not Jesus, she now understood, who had appeared to her in Kirkcudbrightshire twenty years previously. She began her characteristic practice of recording clairaudient scripts from the Tibetan; this, along with founding and developing the organisations to disseminate these messages, would occupy the rest of her life.[28]

The first chapters of material from the Tibetan, later to be published as

Initiation Human and Solar (1922), appeared in *The Theosophist*, but controversy arose in the Theosophical Society concerning the legitimacy of these new revelations. Alice and Foster Bailey in turn became critical of organisational aspects of the Society and acrimoniously parted from it in 1920. Bailey continued to produce scripts by the Tibetan and began to teach her own interpretations of Blavatsky's key text, *The Secret Doctrine* (1888). In 1922 she set up the Lucis Trust, an educational charity, in New York.[29] It soon developed three main branches, which endure into the twenty-first century: the 'Arcane School', 'World Goodwill', and 'Triangles'. I will profile each of these in turn.

The Arcane School was founded in April 1923 to cater for the increasing numbers who were now writing to Bailey for personal advice in interpreting her 'esoteric philosophy'.[30] The impetus behind the formation of the Arcane School fits my thesis of an expanding culture of 'seekership' in the period. According to an introductory booklet, those contacting Bailey

> wanted to know more about meditation and how to practise it. They asked for guidance in their search for truth without being subjected to the usual limitations of dogmatic creeds and without pledging allegiance to some new cult or ism, some personality or authoritarian teaching.[31]

As I said in the Preface, the Arcane School specialises in 'training for new age discipleship' and functions as a private correspondence school, systematising and teaching a large body of ideas and meditations from the composite writings of Alice Bailey/the Tibetan. It claims a substantial body of students, the more dedicated of whom may study for ten years or more.

'Men of Goodwill' was set up in 1932 and changed its name to 'World Goodwill' in the 1950s in line with a resurgence of globalising, universalist ideals after the Second World War (Nation 1989: 7–8). Complementing the Arcane School's enquiries into subjectivity and soul-life, World Goodwill was oriented to political, cultural and interfaith activity, including championing the cause of the United Nations when this body was founded in 1945 to replace the discredited League of Nations.[32] World Goodwill has also promoted the idea of a 'new group of world servers': that is, a group 'of all races, classes and creeds' who 'serve the Plan, humanity, the Hierarchy and the Christ'. From this project came the idea of 'Units of Service', small groups of meditators quietly promoting Bailey's vision (see Chapter 6). In a redolent phrase from Bailey's 1934 publication *A Treatise on White Magic*, these new groups were to be understood as an 'oligarchy of elect souls' (Bailey 1991a: 400). In 1945 the 'Great Invocation' was published[33] and in 1952 an astrological occasion – the annual full moon in Gemini – was designated 'World Invocation Day' (Nation 1989: 8), described as 'a world day of prayer when men and women of every spiritual path join in a universal appeal to divinity for the release of energies to create the new civilisation'. To advertise this occasion, the Great Invocation was published in newspapers and displayed in sympathetic public premises, a practice which continues to the present day.[34]

'Triangles', a meditation network, began in 1937. Working in groups of three, participants resolve to link up in meditation once a day: 'it need take no more than a few moments and with practice can be done almost anywhere, and at any time'. A group triangle represents the 'Trinity of the Godhead' and multiple triangles represent a 'network of strands of lighted mental substance' embodying 'clear lines of spiritual relationship between human beings the world over'. The materialist analogy continues: 'Much as a sculptor shapes ideas into clay, so do Triangles workers build into mental substance the network of light and goodwill'. Sinclair (1984: 75) points out that three persons constitute the smallest possible group. Hence from the emic perspective, Triangles is a dynamic model of global–local relationships – in fact the quintessence of a transnational, globalised group identity – since participants in a triangle may live anywhere in the world. Hence where the Bailey books and the Arcane School explore 'esoteric philosophy', and World Goodwill seeks a universalised ethic, Triangles embodies a religionless 'spirituality':

> Triangles is not a religious movement but it *is* a spiritual project. As such it is inclusive of all faiths. 'Spirit' is the very essence of the Divine Life of God. 'Religion' is a human-made form for its containment and expression.

Such were the three linked projects which took shape under the Lucis Trust in the 1920s and 1930s. What of the content and style of Bailey's texts? Despite incorporating elements of debates in psychology, social planning and inter-national relations, these are indebted to Theosophical cosmology and indeed Bailey can only be described as a 'post-Theosophical' theorist. For example, by her own account she received instruction from former personal pupils of Blavatsky at the start of the 'new spiritual era' in her life, and she later admitted that 'none of my books would have been possible had I not made a very close study of *The Secret Doctrine*' (Bailey 1973: 138ff., 215). Her third book, *A Treatise on Cosmic Fire* (1925), is not only dedicated to Blavatsky but even reproduces the apocryphal 'Stanzas of Dzyan' upon which Blavatsky's own text had supposedly been based, while as late as 1936 the frontispiece of *Esoteric Psychology* carried a Blavatsky epigraph. Not only this, but the chief external authority in the Bailey oeuvre, the Master 'Djwhal Khul', known as 'the Tibetan', clearly invokes the authority of Blavatsky's early proclamation of Tibet as the spiritual home of the Masters.[35] Finally, Bailey sought to legitimate her own esoteric authority by two strategies: first by claiming more-or-less direct lineage to Blavatsky,[36] second by claiming to *transcend* even Blavatsky's authority in the final analysis by rooting the Arcane School in 'the Ancient Wisdom teaching'.[37] That the Theosophical Society also traced itself to such a source only entrenches the 'Theosophicality' of Bailey's work. Interestingly, Sinclair (1984: 50) implies that Bailey later rejoined the Theosophical Society, suggesting Bailey's persistent identification with a movement which, by her own admission, had given purpose to her life in strained circumstances.[38]

But Bailey also innovated upon Blavatsky's heritage by incorporating a millennialistic Christology, surely influenced by her early evangelicalism. Where Blavatsky was regularly and explicitly anti-Christian, Bailey was merely dismissive of her youthful convictions, describing her immature self as a 'rabid, orthodox [and] exceedingly narrow-minded Christian' (Bailey 1973: 1). So Bailey's stance was anti-*ecclesial* rather than anti-*Christian*: an important distinction that allowed her to retain and subsequently infuse into her writings a latent Evangelical piety. Thus in 1936 she wrote: 'The Christ is being born today in many a human being' (Bailey 1991b: 45) and in 1947: 'No man has ever been saved by theology, but only by the living Christ' (ibid.). Indeed, the Great Invocation fervently prays 'May Christ return to Earth'. This millennialistic thrust – Bailey's 'eschatological Theosophy' (Ellwood 1995: 321) – is central to the *telos* of her writings, making her much more than merely an interesting figure in Theosophical history. Her distinctive 'New Age' discourse, to which I now turn, is intimately tied up with expounding an esoteric, post-Christian *parousia*.[39]

Alice Bailey's New Age

According to Bloom (1991: 2), Bailey's total work contains some 285 passages referring to a 'New Age'. Three of her titles are explicit: the two volumes of *Discipleship in the New Age* (1944, 1955) and *Education in the New Age* (1954). But her first public reference to a 'New Age' comes in a 1932 volume, *From Intellect to Intuition*. The passage is worth citing at length, since it shows an early awareness of global flows and cultural syncretism and exemplifies her verbose Edwardian prose:

> We are now one people. The heritage of any race lies open to another; the best thought of the centuries is available for all; and ancient techniques and modern methods must meet and interchange. Each will have to modify its mode of presentation and each will have to make an effort to understand the underlying spirit which has produced a peculiar phraseology and imagery, but when these concessions are made, a structure of truth will be found to emerge which will embody the spirit of the New Age.
>
> (Bailey 1987: 4)

This leisurely, declamatory prose combines idealism and perennialism under the sign of the new, the modern and the epochal: in short, a 'New Age'. A 1936 volume, *Esoteric Psychology*, supplies the missing millennialistic dimension: 'There will be a pouring in of light upon mankind, which will alter his conditions of living [and] change his outlook upon world affairs' (Bailey 1991b: 276). This 'advent of Christ' may take the form of 'an actual physical coming' or a 'tremendous inflow of the Christ principle, the Christ life and love, working out through the human family' (ibid.: 46). In 1948, the year before her death, she devoted an entire volume to this topic, called *The Reappearance of the Christ*.

In addition to an eschatological Christology, the spiritual refinement of the individual is envisaged as a crucial factor in this new dispensation. In 1932 she writes:

> The individual must be given his full heritage, and special culture provided which will foster and strengthen the finest and the best amongst us, for in their achievement lies the promise of the New Age.
>
> (Bailey 1987: 27–8)

Such 'strengthened' individuals, she says, will function as a 'bridging body of men' to synthesise East and West. These 'pioneers of the New Age' will be

> practical men of affairs with their feet firmly planted on earth and yet, at the same time, be mystics and seers, living also in the world of spirit and carrying inspiration and illumination with them into the life of every day.
>
> (ibid.: 45)

In *A Treatise on White Magic* these Nietzschean seekers are said to exemplify a 'new group type', a 'true Aquarian', demonstrating

> a universal touch, an intense sensitivity, a highly organised mental apparatus, an astral equipment . . . responsive to the higher spiritual vibrations, a powerful and controlled energy body, and a sound physical body.
>
> (Bailey 1991a: 416)

To coordinate these virtuosic 'Aquarians', Bailey predicted the growth of loose networks of 'little groups'. Inclusive and organic, these groups will 'spring up here and there . . . as a man in this place and another in that place awakens to the new vision':

> They are not interested in dogmas or doctrines and have no shibboleths. Their outstanding characteristic will be an individual and group freedom from a critical spirit.
>
> (Bailey 1991a: 426).

According to Bailey, the concerns of these 'New Age groups' will be nothing less than 'world needs, world opportunities, and the rapid development of the consciousness of mankind' (ibid.: 427, 632). In *Discipleship in the New Age* Bailey (1981: 786) dates the beginning of this group programme to 1931 and in a 1937 address she celebrates the role of 'seed groups in the New Age' which

> tiny as they may be, will come to flower, and – through an eventual 'scattering of the seed', succeed finally in 'covering the earth with verdure'.
>
> (Bailey 1957: 26)

The sum of these experiments in spiritual education and group culture will be no less than an 'oligarchy of elect souls' to 'govern and guide the world' (Bailey 1991a: 400).

The significance of Alice Bailey's 'New Age'

> The New Age is upon us and we are witnessing the birth pangs of the new culture and the new civilisation.
>
> (Alice Bailey, *Discipleship in the New Age I*: 74])

The preceding material demonstrates the development in the 1930s of a potent discourse on 'New Age' that mixed contemporary economic and political ideas with a cultivation of interior, subjective and 'spiritual' states of awareness. These interests are in turn given direction by the *telos* of an imminent 'New Age'. The style is unmistakably bourgeois, even patrician, and the language of 'men', 'oligarchy' and 'race' will raise eyebrows in the early twenty-first century. But as I have tried to show in this chapter, Bailey's discourse took shape in an interwar context of radicalised economic theories and social policies and amid a globalising flow of cultural representations of alterity. Not least among these was the popularisation of 'alternative' spiritualities and 'other' religions with which Bailey was familiar and to which her message was in part directed. Hence her career is intimately bound up with the events and atmosphere of the 1920s and 1930s. Indeed, she first claimed contact with 'the Tibetan' in 1919; she became an independent teacher soon afterwards; and in the 1930s she contributed to wider debates on alternative spirituality, speaking at the Summer School for Spiritual Research at Ascona, Switzerland, between 1931 and 1933[40] and supplying introductions to popular 'quest' best-sellers like Paul Brunton's *The Secret Path* (1935) and Vera Stanley Alder's *The Third Eye* (1938). She contributed lengthy letters to the *Occult Review* on the impact of fear in global politics and defending 'Red Indian' spirit guides in Spiritualism.[41] In these and related contexts, Alice Bailey was a well-known contemporary ideologue: Scott (1935: 146), for example, thought her 'of considerable importance in the domain of modern Occultism'. Finally, of course, it was in this period that she outlined her 'New Age' vision and set up the institutions – a correspondence school, an educational project, a meditation network – to propagate it: the four introductory texts for Arcane School students were all composed in the politically, economically and militarily eventful decade between 1932 and 1942.[42]

Bailey's writings also anticipate the kind of intercultural, global flows of people, goods and values now taken for granted in debates on globalisation and postmodernity. Significantly, her expositions of group development and spirituality are consistently related to patterns of social organisation and bureaucracy in lay culture rather than to ecclesiastical settings or 'religion'. Thus her titles make plain that the texts are 'letters' and 'treatises' dealing in 'problems' and addressing roles ('discipleship') and institutions ('education'); they employ the language and organisational infrastructure of business and commerce – the Masters are likened to 'a worldwide group of executives' and 'the bringing in of the kingdom of God' requires 'sensible business procedures and carefully considered programmes';[43] and they are broken down into volumes and manifold internal divisions and sub-headings.

Her occult hermeneutics likewise reflect scientific and political innovation: for example, in 1947 she would write that 'the release of the energy of the atom' (following the bombing of Hiroshima and Nagasaki in 1945) had signalled the dawn of the 'New Age' (Bailey 1991b: 279), and in 1950 postumously claimed that even the League of Nations had been a project engineered by the 'Masters' (cited in Sinclair 1984: 42). Esoteric and exoteric – or 'inner' and 'outer' – realms were for Bailey, as for other occultists, inextricably interlinked; but their relationship needed to be revised. The former was actually the inner, spiritual cause of the latter. If social and economic reconstruction was to be realised, then, it would be as a direct result of inner, psychic growth. In other words, social reconstruction had to be reformulated as the organic outcome of co-ordinated subjectivities rather than a function of the tacked-on schemes and Five-Year Plans envisaged by the technocrats. This vision was encapsulated by Bailey in a magisterial passage reminiscent of, yet subjectivising, H. G. Wells's seminal utopian prophecy, *The Shape of Things to Come*:

All the postwar planning . . . and the seething turmoil reaching throughout all levels of the human consciousness, plus the inspiration of disaster and suffering, are blasting open hitherto sealed areas in the minds of men, letting in illumination, sweeping away the bad old conditions. This is symbolised for us in the destruction of ancient cities, and by the intermixture of races through the processes of war; this also signifies progress, and is preparatory to great expansions of consciousness [which] will, in the next one hundred and fifty years, completely alter the manner of man's thinking; they will change the techniques of religion; they will bring about compre- hension and fusion. When this work has been accomplished, we shall record an era of world peace which will be symbolic of the state of the human spirit.

(Bailey 1991b: 278)

Bailey's vision of a looming 'New Age', then, did not emerge in a vacuum but within a considerable turn in Anglo–American spirituality towards populistic and syncretic beliefs and practices articulated through seekers, groups and a new, non-aligned discourse on 'spirituality'. The range of interests and pursuits in the culture at large – 'secret' lore, esoteric groups, 'psychic' talent, 'oriental' wisdom, occult powers, a Nietzschean aesthetic – anticipate a shift in the function of religion from cementing traditional communities to legitimating new identities. These religious dynamics in turn must be set in the context of a period of significant economic and psychological uncertainty, overshadowed by the memory of one world war and anticipation of another. In such a period the notion of an esoteric quest – not just for oneself, but in the service of 'humanity' and a 'New Age' – offered an expanding population of 'seekers' an empowering role in their everyday lives to counter the emergent totali-tarianisms of Mussolini, Hitler and Stalin on the one hand, and the perceived dullness and doctrinal conformity of traditional churches on the other.

In Chapter 1 I claimed that Alice Bailey's discourse became the dominant model for 'New Age' activists in the second half of the twentieth century. As I have shown here, Bailey's 'New Age' could gather and affirm the many disparate, potentially fissiparous spiritual paths pursued by her readers. At the same time, a caveat: implicit in my argument is a good measure of historical serendipity or the 'exteriority of accidents' (Foucault 1977: 146). In the deregulated fields of alternative spirituality, causality is as likely to be a function of the tug and pull of popular discourse as it is to stem from the originality and calculation of irreplaceable activists. Bailey was neither the first nor the last prophet of a 'New Age', and if her formulation had not achieved a happy *lingua franca*, others who also dallied with the emblem – or similar – might have prospered in her place. In any case, as we have already glimpsed from my sketch of the influence of popular Rosicrucianism upon Peter Caddy, an entire series of 'alternative' genealogies have fed the practices of key 'New Age' activists. Nor was Bailey's vast occult cosmology unique: Aleister Crowley, Carl Jung, P. D. Ouspensky, Rudolf Steiner, and G. I. Gurdjieff, to mention just a few prominent contemporaries, were compiling similarly arcane, totalistic systems. Neverthe-less, Bailey's books were written in a recognisable Anglo–American idiom. Strikingly presented in austere midnight-blue cloth, they constituted a brand of alternative spirituality whose volumes could be built into a handsome library – and this at a time when Bailey's rivals had yet written nothing of coherence (Gurdjieff), were only publishable privately (Crowley), had not yet been widely translated (Steiner) or were simply too specialised (Ouspensky) or academic (Jung) for the ubiquitous 'man in the street'. In sum, Bailey offered an esotericism that was both satisfyingly *modern* (demonstrating a sophisticated secular awareness) and yet existentially *comprehensive*: subjectively rich, and simultaneously vast, bureaucratic and 'planned' down to the last detail. In theory meritocratic, it was directed by ascending cadres of spiritual masters from the relatively humble 'unit of service' to the pantheon of Masters, each in their place functioning as an 'oligarchy of elect souls' to inspire and guide those coming after.

But the Lucis Trust is no embryonic 'New Age Movement' and ultimately Bailey's 'New Age' discourse must be understood as merely one of several grand narratives then available under the sign of alternative spirituality, alongside Crowley's 'magick', Gurdjieff's 'Work', Jung's 'analytical psychology' and Steiner's 'Anthroposophy'. You could take it, leave it, or dilute it as you pleased, the principle being that 'in spiritual research the utmost personal freedom is a *sine qua non*' (Landau 1945: 7). Bailey's modernist 'New Age' was an eschatological emblem that seekers could use to navigate their own pathways through alternative spirituality. That the Arcane School had no monopoly over the emblem only accelerated its diffusion into the wider spiritual culture. The allure of Bailey's 'New Age' is attested by the strength of popular reference to her discourse among key post-war activists. For example, Findhorn founder Dorothy Maclean recalled using Bailey's language as 'basic spiritual teaching' in the 1950s and 1960s,[44] while Steyn (1994: 27, 101) found that, as late as the 1980s, two-thirds of her sample in South Africa were 'markedly influenced' by Bailey.

Some commentators have ignored or misread Bailey's place in the genealogy of 'New Age'. Heelas (1996) is an example of the latter, presumably because her quiet millennialism sits awkwardly with the exuberant 'self-spirituality' he singles out. But Heelas's eschewal of Bailey only reinforces my argument that there are no essentials in 'New Age' historiography, only contingencies and connections. My genealogy of 'New Age' certainly uncovers a tension between an 'early' asceticism and a 'late' hedonism as the emblem trickles down into the 1970s and 1980s. But rather than seek to collapse the difference between early and late 'New Age' periods and attitudes in a search for what Foucault calls an 'inviolable identity' underpinning the diversity of historical manifestations, I suggest that this difference or tension is a sign rather of the 'dimension of other things', that 'disparity' finally uncovered when one subjects such a variegated discourse as 'New Age' to genealogical scrutiny.

3

THE 'NAMELESS ONES'

Small groups in the nuclear age

Voices claim to come to us from Masters in the flesh – from Masters beyond the veil – from other planets – from spiritual realms – whence great groups of advanced Spirits are communicating to mankind what we need to know.

(Pugh 1957: 7)

You've got to remember that, in those days, the Cold War tension had gripped the world like an iron vice and the nuclear question was extremely worrying for people.

(Ray Nielsen, Aetherius Society member, cited in Akhtar and Humphries 1999: 163)

We were choosing to live our lives from a spiritual background, outside organised religions and their limitations.

(Dorothy Maclean on alternative spirituality in the 1950s)[1]

'Tuning in': making inner contact

She was not a spiritual teacher in the traditional sense. She had no programme, no classes nor meditation techniques, but would help people to see God in their lives.

(Sheena Govan, described by Peter Caddy, 1996: 74)

Between the 1940s and 1960s a series of slender networks of individuals and groups became preoccupied with the millennialistic associations of the 'New Age' emblem. One small group in particular explored methods of meditation, guidance and group attunement before settling in a caravan park near the small coastal village of Findhorn in northeast Scotland. By the 1970s this colony of alternative spirituality, known as the Findhorn community or simply Findhorn, was recognised as 'the most important New Age centre on the planet' (Bloom 1991: 2). Since Findhorn has readily proven historical associations with 'New Age' and because other experimenters in the field sooner or later found themselves in contact with the Findhorn pioneers, this chapter presents the formative years of Findhorn's founders as a historical case study in the growth and development of early 'New Age' culture.[2]

In March 1947, in the austere aftermath of the Second World War in which rationing and displacement were the order of the day, Peter Caddy – now an RAF officer – met a woman called Sheena Govan (1912–67) on the train from London to Bournemouth. Caddy remembers he was reading *The Aquarian Gospel of Jesus the Christ* on the train and that this triggered a conversation with Govan: as he puts it, 'we started talking about the forthcoming Age of Aquarius, the so-called New Age in which spiritual truths would come to the fore' (Caddy 1996: 72).

Sheena Govan was the youngest of four children of John Govan (1861–1927), the founder in Scotland in 1886 of the Faith Mission, one of many evangelistic groups and home missionary societies of the late Victorian period. The Faith Mission was a lay Protestant movement, described as a 'rural counterpart to the Salvation Army' (Warburton 1969: 82). It specialised in holding evangelistic meetings, taken by 'pilgrims' (its itinerant evangelists), in country areas of Scotland, Northern Ireland and East Anglia. Begun and largely administered by middle-class families, its historical appeal was to working-class and lower middle-class converts, and it had its greatest successes in the 1920s and 1930s when some 4,000 belonged to its Prayer Union (Warburton 1969: 86). It upholds a literalist interpretation of the Christian Bible, a practical theology of saving grace, and encourages a 'holiness' approach to personal spirituality: that is, exponents seek to become 'fully saved, cleansed from sin, and receive the power of the Holy Spirit' (ibid.: 76).

Sheena Govan was born in Edinburgh where the Faith Mission established its headquarters in 1913. She appears as the solitary little girl – aged about ten, smiling happily – in a group photograph of senior 'pilgrims' in the early 1920s (Govan 1978: f.p. 158). She has been disowned by the Faith Mission and I have been unable to find out much about her life before her association with Peter Caddy, when she was thirty-five.[3] Tabloid newspaper articles in the late 1950s describe a 'difficult' childhood and say she gave birth to an illegitimate child who was later adopted.[4] Certainly she is remembered by a nephew as 'wild' and 'theatrical', a 'rebellious' child who wanted to become an actress in a family groomed for evangelical service.[5] Her nieces remember her as a 'charming' and 'charismatic' woman, 'very beautiful' and 'very strong', but also 'a bit queer'.[6] Govan studied music in London, becoming a 'good violinist'[7] and a 'clever dramatist', and she performed solo shows for ENSA during the Second World War.[8]

When Caddy met her, Govan was enjoying an 'elegant' lifestyle in a 'smart flat' in Lupus Street, Pimlico[9] where she functioned as a lay spiritual director:

> Her flat was like a magnet. Throughout the day, people came for
> spiritual help and guidance; Sheena believed that at this time many

people were going through an initiatory experience of self-realisation that she called 'the birth of the Christ within'.

(Caddy 1996: 74)

Dorothy Maclean, also a future Findhorn founder, described her role as that of a 'spiritual midwife'. Peter Caddy (1996: 73) describes her as a 'vivacious and extraordinarily beautiful woman' who 'put her whole being into everything she did'. He began to stay in Govan's flat during his working week in London, returning to his family in Christchurch at weekends where he was still involved with the Rosicrucian Order. According to Caddy, Sheena Govan believed that she and him 'had been drawn together by God' and were 'two halves of the same soul'. Caddy duly separated from his first family, jettisoned his 'mystical and ancient-wisdom books' in readiness for the 'birth of the Christ within' (ibid.), and in 1948 married Govan (ibid.: 77).

Under her tutelage, Caddy recalls 'learning to do everything "unto the Lord", as she put it, with love, and to do it perfectly' (ibid.). Govan taught that this 'raises the "vibrations" – the quality of the atmosphere of a place and its conduciveness for spiritual work' (ibid.: 78). Mental alertness and concentration, and the honing of the will, seem to be the chief goals, applicable as much to household chores ('everything had to be perfect, shining and spotless') as to spiritual work. These 'raised vibrations' evidently helped Govan to contact 'higher and higher streams of intelligence in her meditations' (ibid.). Indeed, in the newspaper stories in 1957 Govan claimed to have received 'many revelations and communications from God, from some of his angels, and from some great souls who had visited this earth in the past'.

Notwithstanding Govan's unorthodox metaphysics, her practices of 'raising vibrations', 'receiving' messages, and attending to the 'Christ within' bear the impression of the Faith Mission's evangelical soteriology: what Govan (1978: 160) calls 'holy living and self-denying service through the power of the indwelling Christ'. The third Findhorn founder, Eileen Caddy, recalls that Govan offered her pupils a 'training' designed 'to reinforce our faith in this inner God and to follow it in our lives' (Caddy 1988: 31). This advocacy of 'living by the Lord' repays comparison with the passionate entreaty of Sheena Govan's evangelist father, John Govan, to

get into this position of entire surrender to God . . . He will show you when to wait upon Him, and how long to wait . . . and He will visit you and bless you.

(Govan 1978: 29)

Likewise Sheena Govan's notion of the 'Christ within' is foreshadowed by John Govan's sense of conviction as a young man that '*this* is what I need – a "clean heart", not just consecration, not a mere giving of myself to God, but a work of God to be done in my soul' (ibid.: 24), an experience known among evangelicals as 'full salvation'. Even the psychological nonconformity of Sheena Govan's circle has affinities with the 'spiritual curiosity' of late Victorian evangelism, as can be heard in John Govan's musings on his formative spiritual experiences in Glasgow:

> Personally I have received deep spiritual blessing. . . . But I am not at all satisfied yet with what I know about this gift of the Holy Ghost. I want a far deeper experience, and to see more of the signs following.
>
> (ibid.: 30)

Sheena Govan's mysticism flourished in intimate rather than public contexts, and it is difficult to imagine her thriving at the rallies and marathon prayer meetings of the Faith Mission. But like Alice Bailey, this sensitive, expressive and restless woman, once beyond the strict evangelical boundaries of her upbringing, would inevitably test out alternative models of experiential religion.

One early contact of Govan's was Dorothy Maclean (b. 1920), a Canadian graduate in Business Studies; they met in New York during the Second World War. Maclean, the only daughter of a middle-class Presbyterian household, was then working as a secretary for British Intelligence (Maclean 1980: 10). Maclean came to London with her husband, who was involved in Hazrat Inayat Khan's Western Sufi Order, and she was also initiated, remarking that 'Sufism, like other teachings I embraced along the way, pointed me inwards, always inwards' (ibid.: 12). Over the next few years Maclean explored many other spiritual groups in early 1950s Britain, including Theosophy, Anthroposophy, Alice Bailey, the White Eagle Lodge, and the Order of the Cross, and she recalls that others in Govan's group sometimes attended the meetings of these groups in London.

The third Findhorn founder to gravitate to Govan's circle in Pimlico was Eileen Combe (later Caddy).[10] Following the comfortable upbringing of many 'New Age' activists, she was born in 1917 in Alexandria, Egypt, where her father was a bank director. The family lived in 'a large and spacious home surrounded by a beautiful garden with palm trees and a long rolling lawn where my parents gave outdoor parties' (Caddy 1988: 11). But her private schooling in Ireland and elsewhere was unsettled: she reports frequent changes of institution, and her resistance to 'academic learning'. She attended church regularly with an aunt, but refused to be confirmed along with her peers: 'I wouldn't do it just to be like everyone else' (ibid.: 13).

After her father's death, Eileen returned to Alexandria to look after her mother and her younger brother. Her mother became interested in the curative potential of Christian Science for her brother's epilepsy, and she and Eileen began to read and practise together – although Eileen has denied active interest: 'I simply went along with her faith and beliefs because she was so completely shattered after my father's death'.[11] In any case her mother's commitment was strong, and in the 1930s the family moved to England so that her brother could enter a Christian Science supported residence (ibid.: 14). In due course Eileen married an RAF officer and renewed her international lifestyle, moving in turn to London, America and finally Iraq. Her husband was involved in Moral Re-Armament (MRA), which in the late 1920s and early 1930s had been known as the 'Oxford Group' movement and whose founder, Frank Buchman, was one of the 'modern masters and teachers' featured in Rom Landau's *God is My Adventure*. Eileen participated diffidently in MRA's characteristic 'quiet times' and 'guidance' sessions, although she later acknowledged that Christian Science and MRA had been 'stepping stones' on her 'spiritual path'. In fact, it was through MRA that Eileen met Peter Caddy when he was on RAF duty in the region. Caddy had been courted by Eileen's husband for recruitment to MRA following the publication of a short essay he had written calling for 'spiritual as well as military rearmament of the nation' and invoking Jesus Christ as a 'model leader' (Caddy 1996: 93).[12] But Peter held views over and above the piety he shared with MRA. According to Eileen this concerned 'psychics, spiritualism and the occult':

> he told me about spiritual masters on 'higher levels' who worked through people to impart spiritual knowledge and healing. . . . I knew he didn't go to church, but I sensed a commitment to something spiritual.
>
> (Caddy 1988: 19)

She certainly found him an 'extraordinary, powerful man' (Caddy 1988: 27) and for his part Peter became convinced that Eileen was the 'other half' (Caddy 1996: 101) he had previously sought in Sheena Govan. Soon Eileen had left her family and joined Peter in Govan's London circle.

'Sheena's group':[13] small group spirituality in 1950s London

Govan gave regular talks to her group.[14] Despite her role as *de facto* leader of the group, these addresses emphasised an egalitarian message: namely, 'the true teacher was within each one of us, and that the time would come when outer teachers would not be necessary' (Maclean 1980: 26). But there were unresolved tensions within the group. Despite her call for spiritual self-responsibility, Caddy (1996: 90) remembers Govan's authoritarianism:

> Sheena taught me the need for obedience as well as discipline. For example, when there was a crisis in the world, she'd have the group go on a fast, watch and pray for twenty-four hours, each taking two to three hour shifts, day and night. . . . For her followers, Sheena's word was law, to be obeyed immediately.

And Govan could be a subtle, demanding task-master. When she asked Dorothy Maclean to clean her rooms, the latter recalls:

> The idea of coming into Sheena's to dust every day seemed like just a waste of time, but I would do it with what I thought was a smile. One day Sheena asked me not to come anymore because my attitude was all wrong.
>
> (Argyris and Ward 1991: 10)

Eileen Caddy began her own gruelling apprenticeship with Govan, whom she remembers as 'very demanding', 'serious', and 'aloof'. She followed Govan's spiritual direction and also nursed her during bouts of illness over the following years (Caddy 1988: 31ff.). She undertook daily periods of meditation, listening for and writing down messages from the 'god within' – a voice she heard, she said, 'inside my head'. Her first contact with this source was in 1953, in Glastonbury, Somerset: perhaps the premier esoteric destination in Britain, with a recognised authority to legitimate heterodox practice. Her immediate model was, once again, Sheena Govan. Peter Caddy (1996: 113) recalls that 'Sheena had always gone there to renew her inspiration', and Maclean remembers that Govan had a caravan at Glastonbury that the Pimlico group would occasionally use.[15]

Sheena's group was small: according to Maclean, about five regular members. Participants were temperamentally diverse. Of Peter and Eileen, Maclean (1980: 26) writes 'neither were people towards whom I would have naturally gravitated'. Eileen Caddy (1988: 33) says of Maclean that 'we were as different as chalk and cheese'. Only mutual association with the charismatic Scot kept them together, since changes of mood and direction flourished in the hothouse conditions of the group. Peter Caddy (1996: 113–14) describes what he calls 'an extraordinary tangle of relationships':

> Eileen was married to, but separated from [her first husband]. Although I was legally still married to Sheena, Eileen and I were now living together as man and wife – with Sheena's blessing. Sheena's relationship with Jack, the naval commander, had passed into history, although Jack remained friends with all of us. Dorothy had divorced John Wood [her Sufi husband].

Notwithstanding the preoccupation with spirituality and the 'Christ within', it is difficult to miss a highly visceral, sexually and emotionally charged dimension to the group.[16] What would certainly have been considered in the early 1950s an epidemic of challenging sexual morality and a transgression of women's ascribed gender roles in particular – Sheena's illegitimate child and multiple relationships, Peter's serial marriages, Eileen's abandonment of her first husband and children, Peter and Eileen's co-habitation, Dorothy's divorce and independence – only anticipated the cocktail of sex and spirituality just around the corner in the 'Swinging Sixties' (Masters 1985).

The 'children of the New Age'[17]

I had to cast aside thirty years and become as a child again, a child of the new age, now dawning upon this fear-ridden earth.

(Jimmy Flangon, ex-seaman and painter,
member of Govan's group)[18]

The significance of Sheena Govan's small group in the genealogy of British 'New Age' cannot be overstated. The three founders of the future Findhorn colony were now working together, encouraged and sometimes goaded by Govan in a series of spiritual experiments that had already sampled Rosicrucianism, occultism, meditation, Western Sufism, and evangelical piety. All were white, middle-class British Commonwealth citizens aged in their mid-thirties or early forties, from privileged professional backgrounds and with extensive experience of international travel and residence. This partly reflected standard expatriate lifestyles, but the restless movement between countries and partners also suggested a wider trend in the displacement of individuals in the wake of another world war. Most significantly, like the virtuoso seekers of the 1930s before them and the popular seekership to come in the 1960s and 1970s, they had recognised in Govan a suitable Western *guru* who could teach and transmit a practical, everyday methodology of inner, spiritual guidance: an ideal portable resource for an exciting but risky time of international social reconstruction.

'New Age' is merely a background motif so far. Maclean (1980: 22) acknowledges its currency but also recalls that they did not use the expression much in the early days of Govan's group. In contrast, Caddy (1996: 72) remembers that his very first meeting with Govan turned on a chance conversation about 'the forthcoming Age of Aquarius, the so-called New Age'. Thus in what are among the first uses of the emblem in public discourse in Britain after the Second World War, the term is heavily qualified. Another decade will pass before it shifts to centre stage. Nevertheless, Govan's group provides the loam for a cluster of ideas and practices to germinate that have been associated with 'New Age' since Alice Bailey's discourse, including the vocation of spiritual seeking, the formative power of thinking as a creative act with real outcomes in the world, inner guidance obtainable in meditation, the elective affinity of seekers, the social potency of small groups, and – last but not least – a restrained but burgeoning millennialism.[19]

But the group's cohesion was to be tested as the 1950s wore on since, despite her earlier insistence on self-responsibility and inner spiritual authority, it seems that Govan increasingly encouraged the group to see her as a new Messiah with supreme authority.[20] Caddy (1996: 125) notes Govan's conviction 'to spread word of the coming New Age throughout Europe and beyond' and Maclean (ibid.: 34) writes of her 'impossible mission of changing the world'. This shift of emphasis in Govan's role, together with her increasingly extreme directives, marks a turn in the fortunes of the group in 1955. Eileen Caddy (1988: 39) now writes of Govan's 'whim' and 'crazy ways'. For example, Peter Caddy had recently resigned his commission in the RAF in order to live with Eileen, but under Sheena's spiritual direction he now separated from her to take a job in Ireland as a hotel 'kitchen boy', despite the fact that Eileen had just had their baby (Caddy 1996: 119–20). Meanwhile Maclean (1980: 33–4) resigned her secretarial post for a series of maverick jobs around the UK, including kitchen maid, nanny and school matron. A picture of uncertainty and unhappiness emerges. Eileen Caddy writes of a 'confused, nightmarish' time and mentions a suicide attempt (Caddy 1988: 38, 39). 'I seemed to have lost everything', recalls Peter Caddy (1996: 120–1), 'my life with Eileen, home, money, career . . . my spiritual path and inner direction'. When Sheena Govan declared Eileen Caddy unfit to care for her new baby and took custody of the child herself, personal tensions in the trio came to a head. Peter and Eileen rebelliously reunited, but 'Sheena would have none of this and said that from now on we would have to go it alone' (Caddy 1996: 121). Not for the first time, the Caddys parted company with Govan. In turn Govan headed north, drawn by the heartlands of Faith Mission evangelism in the west of Scotland.

But Govan's charismatic personality remained compelling, even at a distance of five hundred miles. Soon Peter Caddy had made the long journey north to visit her at a remote country cottage near Glenfinnan, from whence he embarked on a 'pilgrimage' – at Govan's suggestion – to the island of Iona (Caddy 1996: 125ff.). Govan's spiritual authority seemed restored and the Caddys duly decided to move north also. So Peter hunted for jobs in Glasgow while Eileen travelled to new lodgings of Govan's on the island of Mull, near Iona. Dorothy Maclean also arrived, ostensibly to bid a final farewell to her friends' 'freakish' lifestyle; nevertheless, she lingered in the vicinity, as did one or two other group members (Maclean 1980: 35–8). By early 1957, however, following yet another quarrel with their *guru*, Maclean and the Caddys had regrouped in Glasgow. Peter Caddy secured a post as a hotel manager in Forres, in the north-east of Scotland, but on the heels of this success, tabloid journalism caught up with the group and a sensational story appeared in the Scottish press about the activities of Sheena Govan, the 'woman they call the Messiah', and her 'disciples'.[21]

The tag given the group in the newspapers[22] – the 'Nameless Ones' – is actually quite appropriate to the group's lay anonymity. As one journalist noted, this was 'a group that has no name, no headquarters, no book of doctrine'.[23] Even more interesting, however, is the expression *Sunday Mail* journalists claimed Govan herself used to refer to the group at this time: the 'Children of the New Age'. Whether she used this expression repeatedly, or as a unique, casual remark to the reporter, is unclear. But the expression vividly captures the dramatic, expansive discourse of the group and the transformative potential of their biographies to express a new spiritual dispensation.

At the same time there is tension, even bathos, between the magisterial tone of this expression and the actual position of Govan's group. The 'children of the New Age' in 1957 were technically jobless, displaced and now in open conflict with the *guru* who had enticed them north. In the circumstances, the hotel staff positions which Peter Caddy secured for them and into which they were set-tling as newspaper stories about 'the nameless ones' flared up must have offered welcome respite. But in May 1957 the *Sunday Mail* unexpectedly ran a series of high-profile spreads including editorial comment, photographs, biographies, and interviews. The series began with a front-cover wedding-day photograph of Sheena Govan and Peter Caddy in 1948 with the caption 'Sheena Govan Tells All' and the subtitle 'The astonishing story of a woman her disciples claim is a Messiah'. Inside were photographs of the seven 'Children of the New Age', an article by Sheena Govan on her childhood, and a brief biography of Peter Caddy.[24] Subsequent weeks featured further statements by Govan and material on three more of the group, before interest petered out.[25] Caddy's new employers were understandably alarmed at this development and it was clear that the group's continuing connection with Govan would jeopardise their hard-won security. A final 'parting of the ways' became inevitable (Caddy 1988: 53). Peter Caddy (1996: 133) rationalises it in this way:

> The tremendous power [Sheena] channelled was taking its toll at last; she was beginning to become unhinged and to lose her discrimination; she developed a monomania about Love and its ability to save the world. It was distressing to see her subsequent deterioration but there was nothing we could do about it.

In the space of a few months Sheena had been transposed from *guru* of the Chelsea Embankment to Celtic witch. The transfer of charisma from teacher to pupil – specifically from Sheena Govan to Peter Caddy – is exemplified in a melodramatic set-piece in which Peter Caddy turns her away from the hotel during the staff group's first winter:

> [Sheena] had said to me that in the end, I would be so close to God that I would turn against her. . . . Now it was happening, just as she'd prophesied, and I watched with great sorrow the lonely figure of the woman I had loved and served, walking away down the frozen drive.

> (Caddy 1996: 146)

We have seen how the brilliant, rebellious daughter of an evangelical Christian sect precipitated the formation of a small group of seekers in 1950s Britain. This small group, or 'cell', in turn represents a broader culture of collective spiritual practice in structure (its intimate yet open form) and ideology (its discourse of 'spirituality' set over and against 'religion').[26] Sheena Govan's notion of a 'New Age' was latent and indicative rather than systematic and prescriptive, like Alice Bailey's, but powerful clues to the new spiritual culture she envisaged can be found in her techniques of inner listening, her eclectic and domestic approach to practice, and the subsumation of everyday work to the inspiration and spontaneity of the moment. The sum is a robust and practical appropriation of spirituality that anticipates popular culture of the 1960s and 1970s. Her secular methods have survived and prospered in the oral teachings and loose lineages transmitted by the three core Findhorn founders (Maclean and the Caddys) and have become institutionalised to a greater-or-lesser degree in the Findhorn community itself.

Yet contact with Sheena virtually ceased after 1957, even when in the early 1960s she was living in a small village close to the new colony at Findhorn.[27] When Sheena visited the colony Eileen Caddy portrays her as 'grey in feature, hair and clothes, hardly recognisable' (Caddy 1988: 82). The group's attitude towards Govan was now curt. Eileen Caddy's received unequivocal guidance: 'My beloved child, the past is past and finished' (Caddy 1988: 82). In 1965 Peter wrote to his old Rosicrucian mentor, Walter Bullock: 'Sheena had failed in her mission; the odds against her were too great. We now have no contact with her.'[28] In 1967 Govan was living in a rented house in the village of Dalry, Kirkcudbrightshire, and in October she died from a cerebral haemorrhage, 'poor and largely forgotten' (Hawken 1990: 217).

At 'God's hotel'[29]

> Eileen and I knew we were cornerstones of God's plan for the New Age. . . . We were to be one of the foundations upon which the New Age was to be built.
>
> (Peter Caddy, cited in Hawken 1990: 73–4)

In March 1957 Peter and Eileen Caddy – now married – and Dorothy Maclean took over management of the Cluny Hill Hotel in Forres, a small, prosperous market town east of Inverness. The hotel, an imposing Victorian building set in landscaped gardens, was originally built as a spa resort but was now struggling commercially. With the exception of Lena and Hugh Lamont, the new 'disciples' from Glasgow, the staff group was the same core of seekers who had crystallised around Sheena Govan in Pimlico a decade earlier.

The story of the group's restoration of the hotel's flagging fortunes can be pursued in the literature. Freed from Govan's eccentric regime, the group now thought of themselves as a special spiritual unit. 'The real work had begun', writes Eileen Caddy (1988: 52), and this centred upon the infusion of occult guidance and group consciousness into the everyday management of the hotel. External guidance gained by telepathy joined inner listening in the roster of daily practice. In the Philippines in 1953 Peter Caddy had met an older woman called Anne Edwards, usually known by her 'spiritual name', Naomi.[30] She was a relative of an American airforce officer and apparently a versatile 'sensitive': 'if Naomi were given a name to tune in to, she would be in immediate contact with that being, whether a space brother, a prophet of old, a member of the Hierarchy, or a person' (Caddy 1996: 107, 226). Naomi had been part of a small group developing a global 'Network of Light' via telepathic contact with several hundred similar groups. The overall aim was to channel and disseminate cosmic energies:

> Naomi gave as an example a high overlighting group covering the whole of Africa, which radiated to three overlighting stations or groups. These people then radiated to key stations or groups, and from these key stations to three other stations. That's the way the energy was stepped down by the system, or relay of transformers, so that it could be used in the everyday world – just like electricity when it finally reaches the home, and appliances can be plugged in.
>
> (Caddy 1996: 107)

As with Alice Bailey's cosmology, the structural image is once again hierarchical: the 'energy' – or power – is 'stepped down' from above, with elect groups controlling the process at each level. The egalitarian thrust of spiritual seekership and group dynamics is tempered by an implicitly differentiated, even authoritarian, structure to regulate and distribute the primary 'energy'. In other words, there could be a post-war 'energy crisis' in spirituality as much as in materialist economics.

An abstract but technical language of 'energy', 'power', 'love', and 'light' dominates the group's discourse at this time. In a 1960 diary entry Eileen Caddy (1988: 66) wrote of projecting 'love radiances' into the network: 'I felt rather like a radio station sending out hundreds of waves all over the world . . . I had this feeling of power leaving my being to be sent to those in need'. Her guidance reassured her that she was 'part of a tremendous network and each member is closely interlinked' (ibid.). As an image of a global web of consciousness, the 'Network of Light' can also be found in Alice Bailey's *Discipleship in the New Age*, published in 1944, where she describes an international 'network of spiritual energies' or 'golden network of light' generated by spiritual practitioners (Bailey 1981: 23, 75). Since Naomi was also in contact with 'the Tibetan' (Caddy 1996: 106), it seems plausible to suggest that she adapted the image from Bailey. In any case, files in the Findhorn archive document Naomi's version of the scheme, comprising international lists of groups and various telepathic messages.[31] Both are partially presented in a terse cipher carrying echoes of the American airbase where Naomi lived and worked. For example, Naomi's own group is called the 'Central Telepathic Station' or 'CTS' and a new contact is known as 'Y–4'. Other beings and powers also contribute to the network, including the 'Christ Forces', the 'Masters of Ra' and 'the Master Jesus'. Among many lengthy messages recorded by 'CTS' is this:

> The work you are doing is to become text books [*sic*] for New Age functioning. WE MUST WORK CONSISTENTLY AND CONSCIOUSLY PREPARING THE WAY FOR THE CHRIST.[32]

Popular metaphysics and military code create an intense mix here. An additional ingredient is UFO (Unidentified Flying Object) lore. Naomi was working at the height of UFO enthusiasm in popular culture, which had begun in North America in 1947 with a claimed sighting of 'nine silvery crescent-shaped objects' flying at high speed (Clark 1990: 476), and Caddy himself had written an article on the subject in 1954 (Caddy 1996: 116ff.). It is little surprise, then, that Naomi's telepathic contacts also brought messages from the 'space brothers', and UFO communications duly became woven into the guidance received at Cluny Hill Hotel. The resultant mixture of political hopes and fears and prognostications of general cultural change was intensified by nuclear competition and the space race between the US and the former USSR in the late 1950s. Belief grew in the group that extraterrestrials might intervene in the perilous climate. As Peter Caddy (1996: 161) explains:

> There was a real danger of total nuclear holocaust if the wrong finger was on the wrong button at the wrong time. Planetary crisis on such a scale would affect the balance of the whole solar system, so certain contingency plans had been made by extraterrestrial beings, and among the more desperate of these plans was one in which groups of people were to be evacuated from chosen places around the world.

As part of their now daily contact, the group made regular visits to the local beach in case spacecraft might land there. They did this at the full moon, a period also promoted by Alice Bailey as an auspicious time for spiritual work (see Chapter 6). Two unsuccessful landing attempts by UFO craft beside the hotel are reported by Caddy (ibid.: 161, 166), and messages received by Dorothy Maclean during this period reinforce apocalyptic expectations. Her notebook entry of 3 February 1962 announces sombrely: 'My child, the world is much nearer destruction than it thinks, and many people do think the end is near'.[33]

At first sight such other-worldly prophecy sits oddly with the managerial and domestic rhythms of hotel life. The cosmic and the quotidian jostle uneasily for attention: the group seems poised between an 'inner' doomsday scenario and the 'outer' minutiae of everyday life. When the former intruded on the latter, Eileen would 'drop whatever she was doing, such as cooking a meal or changing the baby's nappies, and immediately turn to God for an answer' (Caddy 1996: 142). In fact this dizzying zoom from God's-eye view to close-up and back again mirrors a wider global–local flow of politics and culture, and reflects the psychological strain of working for an international 'network of light' while managing the daily round in small-town Scotland.

The perfectionism that dominated the group's ethos at this time was perhaps a by-product of this dynamic tension between extraterrestrial contact and family rhythms. Expressed in the quality of attention paid both to inner guidance and domestic chores, the general attitude had been learnt in embryo from Sheena Govan who, Peter recalls, 'put her whole being into everything she did, with tremendous love, whether it was playing the violin . . . or scrubbing the floor' (ibid.: 73). In the group's eyes, their perfect labour was transforming the hotel into a 'centre of light' in the global network. Elbow-grease both material and spiritual was creating a 'powerhouse of Love and Light', a place of magical potency: 'If anyone tried to do harm to Cluny Hill and those who lived there, it rebounded in similar fashion' (ibid.: 153, 156). The hotel had a pioneering role to play, for places like it would increasingly 'replace the monastic sanctuaries where people sought solace from the chaotic world' (ibid.: 153).

The group understood themselves to be tapping god-like wisdom in an uncertain world. The Conservatives' slogan 'You've never had it so good', which helped their return to office for a third consecutive win in the 1959 General Election in the UK, played on common acknowledgment that this was now an era of 'affluence, appliances, and work' (Marwick 1982: 114ff.). But nuclear warheads were proliferating and the paranoia of Cold War sharpening: as Hobsbawm (1995: 226) puts it, 'entire generations grew up under the shadow of global nuclear battles which, it was widely believed, could break out at any moment'. The prevailing psychological culture encouraged privacy, discretion, even wariness, attitudes that turned individuals and groups in on themselves, endorsing exploration of 'inner' realms. A strain of apocalyptic fantasy in 'New Age' discourse in the 1950s can be explained in part as the diffuse psychological fruits of international political tensions.

Small group practice and 'New Age' discourse: some patterns in the 1950s

Sheena Govan's 'children of the new age' provide a British case study in alternative spirituality in the 1950s that is broadly representative of a wider Anglo–American culture of small group spirituality. Not only this, the group provides a genealogical link between the 1930s 'spiritual' milieu and Alice Bailey's 'New Age' discourse, and the mid-to-late 1960s when, as we shall see, a limited public forum emerged where the 'New Age' emblem was explicitly debated. But before we move into the 1960s there are several characteristics of Govan's group that should be noted.

First, the actors were socially and geographically mobile and marginal. Careers were typically in the Services, although often incomplete or truncated. Maclean had worked for British Intelligence; Peter and Eileen Caddy met through the RAF (from which Peter resigned his commission); Jimmy Flangon was a former merchant seaman; Sheena Govan's lover 'Jack' was a naval commander. Expatriation also plays a significant function. Govan, Maclean and the Caddys travelled and settled widely, particularly in the British Commonwealth and the Americas. Closer to home, Govan was that familiar figure in modern British cultural history, a Scot in London who returned to her roots under pressure. In turn Maclean, the Caddys, Jimmy Flangon and Fred Astell were English 'outsiders' when they followed Govan to rural Scotland. The proto-Findhorn group came from socially and economically privileged backgrounds, which they exchanged for 'odd' jobs and periods of unemployment (in an unusually buoyant economy). Women in particular occupied liminal roles, somewhere between the ascribed domesticity of tradition and the social independence to be sought by second-wave feminists within a generation. A similar mobility and marginality characterise the group's spiritual careers, which placed them well beyond the denominational mainstream of the day. Peter Caddy and Dorothy Maclean previously belonged to 'esoteric' spiritual groups (the ROCF and the Western Sufi Order) and Sheena Govan and Eileen Caddy had been involved in sectarian or heterodox Christian movements (Faith Mission, Christian Science, Moral Rearmament). Most also explored other groups and systems at the same time as they belonged to Govan's circle.

Second, the broad goal in group culture is to supersede rational decision-making in everyday life, including spirituality: to turn 'from intellect to intuition', as Alice Bailey's 1932 title had it. The precise mechanism might be intuition, guidance or listening to the heart: in each case, individuals strive to sidestep or bypass the curse of instrumental rationality – Weber's famous 'iron cage' of modernity, ratiocination as a systematic cognitive strategy for making plans and calculating outcomes in life. Instead, participants want to tap unsullied sources of information and wisdom that promise a more direct and immediate spiritual life. Eileen Caddy (1988: 31–3) explains that Sheena Govan taught her a painstaking schedule of daily meditation and writing in order to pick out 'God's voice' among the many different conversations she heard in her head. Peter Caddy's approach was to heed his intuition, emphasising quick discernment and spontaneous response. As he puts it:

> What I was developing was a powerful intuition, without allowing mental or emotional considerations to interfere with it, and *that* was 'the source of wisdom' I learned to act upon: a deep inner knowing, beyond words and pictures, that prompted immediate action.
>
> (Caddy 1996: 78)

However, the precise criteria for distinguishing authentic from ersatz spiritual promptings remain obscure: oral transmission may hold the key to developing a 'knack'. Assessing such practice is fraught with dangers, since calculating the level of competence achieved in following inner guidance depends upon an instrumental logic that by emic definition is eschewed in the act. 'Never question what you are asked to do', Govan apparently instructed, 'just act immediately and you will see later why it was so important' (Caddy 1988: 34). And a maxim of Peter Caddy's Rosicrucian mentor 'Aureolis' directly correlates personal charisma with the cultivation of feelings: 'the larger and deeper your emotional nature, the more your power is manifested' (Caddy 1996: 105). Nevertheless, retrospective rationalisation is built into this rhetoric; indeed, it is a recurrent epistemic strategy. This has the effect of protecting a supra-rational approach from falsification since whatever happens in the lifeworld can be – and frequently is – retrospectively interpreted as spiritual providence. In this light we might say that, contrary to emic claims, the operative condition – the net effect – is one of 'inner' intuition and guidance *complementing* rather than *super-seding* rational calculation in everyday life. Since biographies routinely include changing sexual partners, separating from one's children, and chopping and changing careers, in addition to specific spiritual work, there is also an issue of whether exalting intuition and emotion beyond rational scrutiny may become a gloss for whimsy or libidinous free-play. Enough has been said in this chapter to suggest that, in Pimlico at least, Govan's discourse on 'raising vibrations' and contacting the 'I AM within' (Caddy 1996: 78) could serve to justify capriciousness.[34]

Third, interpersonal relationships were beginning to mutate in anticipation of the 1960s' 'cultural revolution' (Marwick 1998) which included both sexual liberation and feminist critique. The key players were all divorced – in Peter Caddy's case, for the second time – when they finally parted company with Govan. Lovers, separations, split families, single people, intimate circles, emotional expressivity: in the bourgeois culture of the 1950s these were suspicious – in some cases even scandalous – phenomena in their own right, let alone in the service of religion or spirituality. As Peter Caddy (1996: 113) himself admits: 'Ours was an extraordinary tangle of relationships'. The restless sexual relationships and friendships reflected similar patterns in work, residence and spiritual seeking: change – sharp, swift, spirited – was the order of the day.

Fourth, gender asymmetry is inscribed in the group. The women in particular were exploring new openings to hold power and exercise authority. The obvious example is Sheena Govan, a fiercely independent musician, spiritual director and proclaimed Messiah of the 'New Age' – a 'Redeemer in the form of a woman', in Peter Caddy's words. But the picture is muddied by the fact that the core practice of the group, inner listening, depends upon the women – particularly Eileen Caddy and Dorothy Maclean – gaining access to 'other' levels of wisdom involving considerable self-sacrifice. In this they effectively repeat the passive role of 'secretary' assumed by Alice Bailey, a deeply ambiguous role connoting low social status – yet often wielding real power. There may be no 'Master' to attend in Govan's group, but the identity (and gender) of the source contacted by Eileen and Dorothy is not entirely clear. At the same time the group ideology gives them special status, and the transmission of technique from Sheena Govan to Dorothy Maclean and Eileen

Caddy (and thence to Findhorn) is effectively matrilineal. Peter Caddy, on the other hand, advocates greater spontaneity of action in relation to inner voices, as when he secured the hotel position for the group, handled the final split with Sheena Govan, and (as we will see) represented Findhorn at 'New Age' gatherings in the 1960s.

The empowerment inherent in Sheena Govan's role as a female Christ must also be tempered by the group's ultimate rejection of her, and her subsequent decline and early death. In sum, the status of 'New Age' women in the 1950s was ambiguous and unresolved. On the other hand we know that some women at least were practising and teaching spiritual techniques throughout the decade at a time when only one Christian denomination in the UK (Congregationalists), and no 'national' church, was prepared to ordain women priests. Furthermore, ascribed female domains move from background to foreground. Emotional and intuitional strategies for acquiring spiritual guidance have for a long time in Western cultures been feminised. Here they break loose from sharply gendered connotations either way. Jimmy Flangon confesses his need to 'become as a child again'; Peter Caddy not only exercises his own intuition but consults each of the women in the group at various points for guidance. And the group's ideology is dominated by metaphors and practices derived from housework and childrearing, domains of work traditionally ascribed to women: Maclean dusting Govan's flat as part of her apprenticeship, Govan herself described as a 'spiritual midwife', Eileen Caddy's guidance regularly couched in the maternal language of 'My Child'.

The final characteristic to note is the form of association adopted by these 'Children of the New Age'. 'Sheena's group' was not a recognisable sect, nor even a social movement with a clearly defined goal, but a small reflexive group. This format was ideally suited to the qualitative needs of the actors who could experience a high ratio of relationships, an intensity of emotional response, and considerable flexibility in what they did and when they met. The comradeship engendered by the group co-existed with a loose structure: there was no membership criterion to restrain a curious (or disaffected) participant from fishing in other waters, or drifting away altogether. Hence the spiritual career of the individual seeker remains paramount. The group coheres for as long as it is able to satisfy the needs of discrete careers at a particular moment in time, since the group itself is little more than a convenient assemblage of individuals. As Peter Caddy would later write to a correspondent expressing anxieties about flagging commitment in her own group: 'The human spirit must be free to move from one group to another. . . . Many of these groups are but stepping stones along the path'.[35]

The small group can be defined as 'a group all of whose members are known, at least by sight, to everyone of them' (Phillips 1965: 14). Groups percolated through Anglo–American culture in the years following the Second World War, influenced by American egalitarian values and functioning as a new social forum for mutual aid (Phillips 1965). But small groups have consistently played a definitive structural role in the development of alternative spirituality, from Spiritualism's home circles to the lodges of the Theosophical movement, the chapters of the ROCF and the covens of Gerald Gardner's Wicca. They served a similar function in evangelical Christian projects such as Frank Buchman's 'Oxford Groups' (Randall 1999: 238–68), which attained a high profile in interwar religion (Mews 1994) and attracted passing interest from Eileen and Peter Caddy, as we know. The intimate and expressive potential of small-group relationships also informs the house church movement in the 1970s and the Alpha Course in the 1990s. These and other post-war applications of spirituality bear the traces of humanistic theories on the therapeutic function of small groups, developed from the late 1940s onwards in the Training-group (T-group), Gestalt and Encounter movements in the US in particular (Alexander 1992). And these currents fed a diffuse post-Sixties movement for maximising 'human potential' which, as we see in Chapters 5 and 7, underpinned the hermeneutical shift in 'New Age' from apocalyptic emblem to humanistic idiom.

The sociologist Bryan Wilson (1965: 294) noted that small groups arise 'in societies marked by high rates of social mobility' where social stratification is 'unclearly articulated' and criteria of social differences are 'fluid and volatile'. This was increasingly the case in post-war Britain, where the stolid Conservatism of the 1950s temporarily masked complex processes of social and cultural reconfiguration and pluralisation. Groups were in part a response to the attenuation of traditional kinship support and to the erosion of ascribed statuses of class, gender and religion. Under such conditions the group provided some reassurance of status and also supplied norms and values to fill the hiatus caused by the reshuffling of the social order, encouraging emotional expressivity and interpersonal bonding across gender and class. The small group became increasingly recognised in the period as an appropriate social-psychological setting for social work, psychotherapy and management training, thereby functioning, in Wilson's tart summary, as a 'localized set of universal Joneses'.

The reflexive methodology of group practice represented in Sheena Govan's circle is reminiscent of Alice Bailey's prognosis in *A Treatise on White Magic* of 'little groups' which 'will spring up here and there', bent on 'group sentiency', 'freedom from a critical spirit' and 'development of consciousness' (Bailey 1991a: 321, 426–7). Bailey calls them 'seed groups in the New Age' (Bailey 1957: 26). We know that group members were familiar with Alice Bailey's writings and may have had individual contact with the Lucis Trust in London: they would certainly recognise the bones of Bailey's discourse. With their practice consolidated at Cluny Hill Hotel at the end of the 1950s, this group of seekers would go on in the 1960s to lay the foundations of the Findhorn colony and to send Peter Caddy as their representative to a seminal gathering of 'New Age group leaders' (Caddy 1996: 240). And as we shall see, the small group is the structural norm in the exponentially unfolding fields of post-Sixties spirituality tagged 'New Age'. The ethnographies in Chapters 6 to 8, for example, are grounded almost entirely in group experiences, yet still represent only a fraction of popular spiritual practice at the turn of the twenty-first century.[36]

Small–group spirituality in international context: mapping a 'New Age subculture'

The New Age will only be peopled by those who are ready . . . it's tantamount to the sorting of the wheat from the chaff.

(Ray Nielsen of the Aetherius Society, cited in Akhtar and Humphries 1999: 165)

We know that there were other spiritual groups of modest size active at this time. Some of them were known to Govan's group: Dorothy Maclean mentions Alice Bailey, the Order of the Cross and the White Eagle Lodge, among others. Examples of 'alternative' groups catering to other tastes could be multiplied extensively, from 'Work' groups in the Gurdjieff–Ouspensky tradition to the Wiccan covens described in Gerald Gardner's *Witchcraft Today* (1954).[37] But not all groups were open and inclusive: The 'Work' groups in particular could be notoriously selective, and until the rescinding of the 1736 Witchcraft Act in 1951, Wiccan practice technically risked prosecution and hence required vetting of neophytes' motives.

The closest comparisons to Govan's group in terms of method and demographic profile were groups making esoteric interpretations of UFOs. Interest in UFOs in the 1940s and early 1950s spread quickly through an international network largely defined by Anglo–American popular culture (Wojcik 1997). Typically UFOs were seen as the vanguard of cataclysmic change that would usher in a 'New Age' on Earth. Various ancient texts were scanned and decoded in this light (the apocalyptic and visionary literature of the Christian Bible in particular) and a surge of popular publishing ensued. A variety of spiritual study groups started up, both temporary and enduring. Among the latter is the Aetherius Society, formed in London in 1955 by a yoga practitioner, George King. He claimed to have made contact with Aetherius, a 'Cosmic Master' living on Venus, who subsequently relayed an extensive body of messages through King detailing the necessary practices and ideas to adopt for the Aquarian Age. As summarised by a later follower, George King

received a very definite message that there would be another coming, another Master would come to this earth to lead people into the New Age. This Master will not be born through the womb again but will actually land. This means he will use a spacecraft of some description.

We believe it will be a definite event when everybody will know and there'll be no doubt about it.

(Akhtar and Humphries 1999: 165)

There was some early interest in King's trance performances in London and people participated in the 'charging' of sites of spiritual power, including Exmoor and the Cairngorms. But the Aetherius Society struggled to expand in the UK and in the late 1950s King moved to America. Here he found a more receptive audience, which reflected the predominantly American construction of UFO practice in both its 'contactee' and 'channelled' expressions.[38] These included the founding myth of the movement – the sighting of an unidentified object over Mount Rainer, Washington, in 1947, called a 'flying saucer' by a journalist (Clark 1990: 476) – as well as the early proselytising by popular authorities such as George Adamski (author in 1953 of *Flying Saucers Have Landed*) and Daniel Fry.

The kind of small group spiritual culture in which this new source of revelation developed is encapsulated in the case of 'the Seekers'. In 1953–4 extraterrestrial prophecies were received by a suburban housewife, Mrs Keech, and interpreted by a church-based discussion group called 'the Seekers' (Festinger *et al.* 1964).[39] The intimate group dynamics merit comparison with Sheena Govan's group in the same period. Mrs Keech is of a similar age to Govan and her spiritual career – including Theosophy, Dianetics, and the 'I AM' movement (ibid.: 33–5) – follows a familiar pattern of seeking. Like the group at Cluny Hill, Mrs Keech establishes personal contact with a god-like source (this time not 'the Christ', but a 'space brother') who relays a series of messages advising her to develop her own spirituality and to assemble a group of sympathetic co-workers. Through mutual contacts she meets Dr Armstrong, organiser of a local church-based discussion group, the Seekers. Armstrong is described as 'a tall man in his early forties [with] an air of ease and self-assurance', which makes him close in age and demeanour to Peter Caddy. Also like Peter and Eileen Caddy, Armstrong and his wife have an expatriate, liberal Protestant background, and a wide and eclectic interest in 'mysticism and the occult' (ibid.: 39–40).

Like Govan's group across the Atlantic, the Seekers' weekly practice revolves around a 'lesson' received by Mrs Keech and studied in a small group (about fifteen individuals). This begins with meditation – to get 'in tune with each other' – and a 'nonsectarian Christian prayer' (ibid.: 71). After Mrs Keech's message has been relayed, Dr Armstrong provides a lengthy exposition, sampling a range of esoteric teachings – interplanetary travel, biblical passages, reincarnation, diet – as well as prophecies on the 'coming catastrophe' (ibid.: 73–4). Although the communications increasingly hint at catastrophe (first nuclear war, later a flood), the Seekers are promised that the 'end of the age of darkness' is at hand and that those upholding the 'new cycle' or 'age of light' will be 'evacuated' from the planet (ibid.: 36, 45, 57). Like Govan's group in

London, then, the Seekers in mid-America exemplify the functional ideology of spiritual electivity – the 'oligarchy of elect souls' – laid out in Alice Bailey's vision of a 'New Age' and confirmed in Ray Nielsen's understanding of 'the sorting of the wheat from the chaff'.

This kind of small group spirituality has been particularly strong in the northern hemisphere. But southern hemisphere manifestations can be found, particularly in colonial/Commonwealth outposts like South Africa (Oosthuizen 1992, Steyn 1994) and New Zealand, where a small group calling themselves the 'Heralds of the New Age' began in 1956 under the leadership of May Harvey. The Heralds brought together familiar elements of mediumship, healing, piety, UFO lore and a syncretic cosmology of 'Masters' and planes of existence. Their fortnightly meetings in Auckland began with a 'universal prayer for world peace'; May Harvey would then give a lecture and initiate discussion. Periods of silent meditation and absent healing followed. Finally, the group practised 'spiritual broadcasting': this meant visualising healing streams of light flowing from 'the Source of Holy Light' to sites of cataclysm and disaster around the world.[40]

The Heralds' favoured 'sensitives' would also record messages from various discarnate sources and publish these in regular bulletins.[41] Content from a late 1950s issue included 'A Message from Ashtar of Venus to All Who Are Endeavouring to Spread New Age Teachings'.[42] On the back cover of another was this arresting announcement:

> Do you realise the possibilities if we individuals and nations were to live in peace, love and harmony? Other planet civilizations do. Why can't we? . . . Know you that our Master Jesus is working ceaselessly and untiringly organising other planets and our spirit world to help us in the days to come. **Read the enclosed messages of great importance**.[43]

A 'Special Message to New Age Young People' in 1962 elaborated:

> You are now coming forth into a new age, into a new arc of light that shall raise the vibration of the planet and restore order out of chaos. . . . The Aquarian Age is at hand and a great exodus is taking place. Consciousness is being accelerated and a transformation will come into effect. You are part of the great nucleus of Earth which will usher in a new age.[44]

The Heralds also circulated messages received by groups in the US and England, and their contacts pages featured news from Australasia, Britain, the US and Canada, their prime mission territory.[45]

Like the other groups in this chapter, the Heralds of the New Age sprang from a syncretic, lay culture. The group was run by a core of dedicated and hardworking women, including the leader, the chief sensitives and the librarian who kept their substantial collection of books (likened in size to a suburban library). And like the other small 'seed groups' discussed, this female oligarchy invoked a discourse of selfless domestic labour to promote the coming 'New Age':

> Our work is voluntary in the fullest sense of the word. . . . No one makes a living within the Heralds. . . . We have no official residence. Our 'offices' are to be found in the private homes of our students whose diligence makes it possible to keep up card systems, write envelopes and execute the endless typing necessary for the compiling of our Folders. . . . Every penny received from your love offerings goes directly into the printing, stationery and mailing fund.[46]

In the US there was a 'circuit of groups' of this kind, particularly along the Atlantic and Pacific coasts and in the South-West. David Spangler (1984: 26) calls this a 'new age subculture'. Included here are study groups linked to post-Theosophical organisations as well as groups for psychic study and mediumship. 'Still others', Spangler claims, 'were formed around no particular teacher or with no discernible philosophy but simply to "study" or promote the "New Age" '(ibid.). In fact 'belief in the imminent dawning of a new age' (ibid.: 17) was the common denominator among disparate and fissiparous temperaments. Spangler's summary of the worldview of this loose 'new age subculture' is worth citing at length, since it puts the values and beliefs of one small group in north-east Scotland into international context:

> The earth was entering a new cycle of evolution, which would be marked by the appearance of a new consciousness within humanity that would give birth to a new civilization. Unfortunately, the present cultures of the world were so corrupt and locked into materialism that they would resist this change. Consequently, the transition from one age to another would be accomplished by the destruction of the old civilization, either by natural causes such as earthquakes or floods, or by a great world war, or by social collapse of an economic or political nature, or by combinations of these. However, those individuals whose consciousness could become attuned to and one with the qualities of the new culture would be protected in various ways and would survive the time of cataclysm and disasters. They would then enter a new age of abundance and spiritual enlightenment – the Age of Aquarius, as astrologers call it – in which, guided by advanced beings, perhaps angels or spiritual masters or perhaps emissaries from an extraterrestrial civilization whose spacecraft were the UFOs, they would help to create a new civilization.
>
> (Spangler 1984: 17–18)

Hence there was a wider syncretic culture of alternative spirituality to which the superficially *ad hoc* careers of Sheena Govan's 'Children of the New Age' were meaningfully related. Not only this, but popular media coverage of politics and science, together with a burgeoning science-fiction culture, ensured that a rich mix of information and speculation was available to seekers to factor into their spiritual work. As Festinger *et al.* (1964: 54) comment in respect of the substance of Mrs Keech's messages:

> Almost all her conceptions of the universe, the spiritual world, interplanetary communication and travel, and the dread possibilities of total atomic warfare can be found, in analogue or identity, in popular magazines, sensational books and even columns of daily papers.

The sum is that by the end of the 1950s certain key actors, ideas and practices encapsulating an international 'New Age' culture had become anchored in rural Scotland in the unlikely setting of a grandiose Victorian hotel. But the group's career was once more about to change course.

4

'THE END IS NIGH'
Doomsday premonitions

The great cleansing has begun, but I doubt if I shall be on Earth to see its finish.

> (Marjorie Lee, Isle of Man: communication to
> Heralds of the New Age, New Zealand, Christmas 1963)[1]

These are truly amazing prophecies. . . . It is strange how uplifting these words are: they speak of great disasters, they speak of an entire world being destroyed . . . and yet they uplift and bring security.

> (Group at Lake Titicaca: communication to
> Network of Light, November 1964)[2]

Have you anything coming through related to what one would call 'The Second Coming' and how we should prepare ourselves?

> (Monica Parish, London: letter to Peter Caddy,
> Findhorn, October 1965)

I am required at Findhorn due to the imminence of the landing of our space brothers.

> (Peter Caddy, letter to Monica Parish, April 1966)[3]

A domestic cell: caravan life at Findhorn, 1962–5

It is certainly true to say that without the teachings of my former wife, the late Miss Sheena Govan, who led a group which people called the 'Nameless Ones', this community would never have come about.

> (Peter Caddy)[4]

In November 1962, following their unexplained dismissal from the Cluny Hill Hotel (Caddy 1996: 173ff.), Peter and Eileen Caddy and their three children moved their large touring caravan onto a residential site outside the nearby village of Findhorn. From Victorian hotel to house on wheels was an abrupt transition. Peter Caddy (ibid.: 186) remembers their new habitat as a bleak, treeless and dreary place, with row after row of mobile homes lined up like shabby privates on parade along the concrete lanes that had served as dispersal bays for aircraft from the adjacent RAF base during the War.

In fact this new settlement – at first sight so inauspicious – would consolidate the group experiment begun in a Pimlico apartment and developed at 'God's hotel'. Certainly, the new base – a caravan – could not be more different, but then such extremity of lifestyle had always been a hallmark of 'Sheena's group'. A later resident recalled that Peter Caddy 'explained that we lived in mobile homes to remind us that we should be ready to move at a moment's notice' (Akhurst 1992: 113).[5]

Initially the group led a cramped existence in the caravan, as Eileen Caddy recalls:

> The three boys shared a small room at one end. . . . At the other end
> . . . was the living room, dining room and bedroom all in one. Our
> double bed folded up into the wall during the day. . . . The narrow
> passage between the boys' bedroom and the main room was my
> kitchen.
>
> (Caddy 1988: 76)

To increase pressure on space, Dorothy Maclean soon moved into an annexe to the caravan. But there was at least one advantage to living on top of each other: their caravan was 'well away from most of the other caravans' and hence 'secluded and private' (ibid.: 75). An early photograph illustrates this well (ibid.: f.p. 75): the three adults sit beside the caravan on a small patio enclosed by a head-high fence; one or two caravans are visible in the near distance on the dunes. The scene strongly evokes privacy and withdrawal: the caravan as secular monastic cell.

For three years, unemployed and 'virtually cut off from contact with the outside world', the group lived 'like hermits':

> Very few people came to visit us and apart from Peter and Dorothy's
> weekly trip to the labour exchange to collect their National Assistance
> money, we rarely went into town. My intense work in meditation
> made me increasingly sensitive and vulnerable. After a brief trip into
> Forres . . . I returned home weak and shaken. I felt like a snail without
> a shell and was reluctant to leave our quiet haven again.
>
> (Caddy 1988: 98, 90)

Life revolved around organic gardening, vegetarian food, physical exercise, the children's local schooling and, most importantly, 'inner work' (ibid.: 84). Eileen Caddy zealously meditated, using the public toilets for peace and quiet (ibid.:

78).[6] There was also group meditation for several hours each day, largely in the evenings when the children had gone to bed. According to Dorothy Maclean (1980: 45–6) the group worked with the Network of Light – 'sometimes receiving, sometimes broadcasting' – and also communicated telepathically with 'highly developed humans'. Peter Caddy worked on a garden of fruit and vegetables, making particular use of Maclean's guidance from 'nature spirits'.

'New Age' signs and wonders

It was the myth of the 'Findhorn Garden' that first attracted public interest in the community. In 1968 Sir George Trevelyan (see below) visited the community and described 'one of the most vigorous and productive gardens I have ever seen' in his report to the organic lobbying group, the Soil Association. Trevelyan crowned his enthusiastic assessment with an image that came to haunt the community: the garden had produced a '42 lb cabbage' (Caddy 1996: 282). This vision of a restored 'garden of Eden' became an important counter-balance to doomsday prophesying. In fact, the first commercial publication about the community – *The Magic of Findhorn* (Hawken 1990 [1975]) – promotes a miraculous image reminiscent of the 'signs and wonders' theology of conservative evangelical Christians. The back cover of the popular paperback edition superimposes the following text over a fantastically verdant woodland garden scene (with prominent cabbage):

> Findhorn: the extraordinary Scottish community where people talk to plants with amazing results; where vegetable and flower gardens are animated by angelic forms; where forty-pound cabbages and eight-foot delphiniums grow, where roses bloom in the snow; a land where nothing is impossible and legends are reborn.

The blurb summarises the 'full story of Findhorn: how a caravan was transformed into an oasis of spiritual communion, and a rubbish dump blossomed into a Garden of Eden'.

The richly multivalent images of 'garden' and 'nature' were to provide a bridging metaphor between the privations of caravan culture in the early 1960s and the flourishing colony which Findhorn was to become. As Clark (1992: 104) argues, by the 1970s the garden had become 'the organizing mythology of Findhorn, a metaphor for the growth, or the flowering, of human consciousness'. However, in the early days planting vegetables was clearly part of a subsistence lifestyle for an 'almost destitute' (Metcalf 1993: 2) group of incomers in an unfamiliar rural economy. It was also a chance for the energetic Peter Caddy to be busy. Around this time, he began to re-emphasise the benefits of 'positive thinking'. According to his wife, the point of learning to 'think positively' and to 'control our thoughts' was 'to learn how to create form by our thinking' (Caddy 1988: 95). Peter Caddy (1996: 214) described this technique as 'based on my Rosicrucian teachings'. Now termed 'manifestation', it soon became central to Findhorn ideology. Essentially, 'manifestation' involved becoming aware, through meditation, of a particular need, and then visualising its materialisation into form. The success of the process was gauged retrospectively: if something failed to come about, then *de facto* the requirement had been mistaken in the first place. Examples abound in the literature of manifestation in action: attracting money to pay bills, stimulating the donation or discovery of useful objects, even acquiring caravans and bungalows. Like the strategy of acting on intuition discussed in the previous chapter, manifestation was an unusually empowering principle since it could never be falsified: 'failure' to manifest could always be ascribed to faulty procedure (not getting properly focussed or attuned) rather than to the method itself.

Like 'God's hotel' previously, the caravan settlement soon became conceptualised in terms of power: 'we worked in the garden not just to feed ourselves; we were putting radiations into the ground' (Caddy 1988: 87). Meanwhile, apocalyptic messages intensified:

> The situation will become worse. Darkness will gather speed and envelop many of the countries of the world because people have turned their faces away from Me. . . . Think of the story of Noah. Your circumstances are very similar.
>
> (ibid.: 98)

Eileen Caddy identifies the personal pronoun here as 'your own inner God' (ibid.: 10). For those at Findhorn and (as we shall see) elsewhere, only this kind of immanent power could offset the psychological turbulence created by an economically 'hot' culture in an intensely 'cold' war: the Findhorn pioneers, after all, had moved into their caravan the month after the Cuban missile crisis of October 1962. By 1965 Peter Caddy was explaining to another group in the north that they were 'building an Ark, a place of refuge which will sustain us in the days of destruction ahead'.[7]

Around the same time comes first mention in the literature of a wider network of sympathetic activity in Britain: of 'people in spiritual circles' and a 'new spiritual movement' (Caddy 1988: 103, 115). According to Peter Caddy (1996: 233), the group's previous focus on 'inner connections' was shifting to 'making outer contact with like-minded people'. Caddy himself now began a series of lengthy journeys across the British mainland, meeting 'spiritual people' (ibid.: 233) in Edinburgh, Lancashire, Shropshire, Glastonbury, London, Hampshire, and Dorset. Through this process Caddy met George Trevelyan.

Sir George Trevelyan (1906–96) and Attingham Park

Peter Caddy has called Trevelyan 'the father of the new age in Britain' (in Trevelyan 1986: 8) and Perry (1992: 33) describes him as 'more influential than any other single person in the UK'. Trevelyan came from an aristocratic land-owning family in Northumbria, and was the son of a distinguished politician and nephew of the eminent historian.[8] He studied history at Cambridge University before becoming apprenticed as a furniture maker in the Arts and Crafts tradition in the Cotswolds, Gloucestershire. In the 1930s he began a long career in alternative education that included studying the 'Alexander technique' of posture training, and teaching at a progressive boarding-school, Gordonstoun, in Moray (where, by coincidence, Sheena Govan also briefly taught in the 1960s after the break with her group). Here Trevelyan taught, among others, the present Duke of Edinburgh, Prince Philip (b. 1921), whose son Charles (b.1948), present Prince of Wales, was also partly educated there. In 1947 Trevelyan was appointed Principal of a newly established Adult Education College at Attingham Park, a former country estate near the Welsh border. The new college was partly sponsored by Birmingham University in a general post-war reconstruction of higher and further education.[9] The prospectus was populist in appeal: 'No qualification is needed other than the enthusiasm to take part. The atmosphere is informal and no one need feel discouraged through lack of scholarship' (Lowe 1970: 91). Attingham itself is an extravagant and imposing eighteenth-century mansion house now in the care of the National Trust. Trevelyan worked there throughout the 1950s and 1960s, organising and frequently teaching innumerable short courses in arts subjects, including (discreetly) alternative spirituality. When he retired in 1971 he founded the Wrekin Trust to develop the latter interests further, and some of its functions were in turn taken over by the Scientific and Medical Network in 1973.

Since the early 1940s Trevelyan had studied Anthroposophy, the vast post-Theosophical cosmology of the Hungarian writer and lecturer Rudolf Steiner. Steiner's influence is evident in *A Vision of the Aquarian Age* (Trevelyan 1977), as is Alice Bailey: there are chapters called 'The Ageless Wisdom Re-emerges' and 'New Age Now', and the book concludes with her 'Great Invocation'. But Trevelyan also liked to quote visionary poets such as Wordsworth and Blake; he knew Spiritualist sources such as Grace Cooke's White Eagle teachings; and he was involved with the Soil Association, as we have seen, which met regularly at Attingham Park in the 1960s.[10] In short, like most of the person-alities in the early genealogy of 'New Age', Trevelyan's spirituality was eclectic, syncretic and proactive and cannot easily be aligned with any one current or tradition.

Throughout the 1950s and 1960s he quietly promoted a strain of alternative spirituality in Attingham's curriculum. His employers were reputedly uncomfortable with this aspect of the college but were otherwise pleased with Trevelyan's charismatic leadership. In fact, esoteric subjects were few and far between in Attingham's extensive curriculum of study weeks and week-ends, although Trevelyan kept what he called 'the significant mailing list' – one thousand or so names – in addition to the standard Attingham mailing list, to whom the courses in alternative spirituality were advertised. But in the 1950s there were on average only two a year: in 1951, 'The Festivals of the Year and the Changing Seasons' and 'The Universe and Man'; in 1957, 'Modern Man in Search of Himself' and 'Innocence and Experience' (on William Blake). A turning point came when around one hundred and seventy individuals – between twice and thrice the College's standard enrolment – attended a 1964 course, 'Death and Becoming'. From then until the end of the decade the yearly average of esoteric courses in the curriculum more than trebled. But even then the figure is dwarfed by Attingham's mainstream adult education events: 'Pointers to the New Age', for example, a week-end gathering in the summer of 1965, was just one out of a dozen events on offer.[11] Nevertheless, as Ruth Nesfield-Cookson recalls, the college offered a 'fantastic platform' since 'there was so little else going on'. One might add the rider: in *public*. In domestic, so-called 'private' settings, there was plenty afoot, as we are only just discovering.

Like so many others, Trevelyan had an equivocal relationship with the term 'New Age'. His secretary recalls that he 'didn't like the term' and 'rather used it in inverted commas'. It appears in the study programme on only a handful of occasions. 'Pointers to the New Age' in June 1965 sought 'to discuss the rising hope, now being held by an increasing number of people, that mankind is indeed moving into a New Age' and 'Living into the New Age' in June 1971 featured David Spangler, a key theorist of 'New Age' in the early 1970s (and whose 'New Age subculture' portrayal I cited in the last chapter). But the one of most interest to us here is a 'study weekend' in the autumn of 1965 for a 'small and mainly invited group'.[12]

'New Age group leaders' at Attingham Park, 1965

This is an age of conferences, discussion groups, study of 'group dynamics' and the like. The reason is that intense change and pressure in all parts of the social organism demands our learning to absorb new ideas which may have a transforming power. Here the group is a necessary instrument. It is an entity far greater in strength than the sum of its individual members. The right ordering of the New Society can be seen as a pattern of group relationships, from the small cell of a few closely-linked individuals to the world society of nations.

('The Significance of the Group in the New Age', 1–3 October 1965, Attingham Park Prospectus)

Through one of the 'people in spiritual circles' mentioned earlier (in fact the secretary of the Scottish UFO Society, discussed below) Peter Caddy heard of, and duly gate-crashed, a 'New Age group leaders' gathering at Attingham Park in October 1965 (Caddy 1996: 240). The attendees were 'leaders of the various spiritual groups and movements in Britain' (Caddy 1996: 241), presumably selected from Trevelyan's 'significant' list. American journalist Paul Hawken (1990: 159–60) – writing from a perspective partisan to Findhorn – describes the attendees as the '*crème de la crème*' of the 'clubby and convoluted world of British spiritual groups', a 'tight-knit and predominantly upper-middle-class coterie' dressed in 'tweeds and chiffon'. In contrast Hawken presents Caddy as a 'brash and tanned gardener from the North'. Caddy himself takes up the tale:

> The conference's first speaker . . . invited us all to pool ideas so we could formulate a charter for the founding of a New Age Community. The ensuing suggestions and discussion puzzled me and then began to try my patience, so I got up and said that we were already doing at Findhorn what they were all talking about. We had been guided in the moment by God, step by step, I explained. . . . It was nonsense to draw up 'charters' or 'blueprints'!
>
> (Caddy 1996: 242)

The clash of method is interesting in itself: the rational discussion, focused on 'charters' and 'blueprints', clearly goes against the grain of Findhorn guidance and spontaneity. But in other respects this small gathering of some thirty individuals (Hawken 1990: 159) provides a significant index of 'New Age' affiliation in Britain in the 1960s. Small as it is, it is a public 'New Age' event, although it offers only restricted access, being for a 'mainly invited group'. Caddy's memoirs provide a handful of names of participants. Let us probe their connections with other groups, as well as one or two other links that Trevelyan developed at Attingham Park, in order to gauge the wider constituency of interest in 'spiritual' matters potentially available for mobilisation under the banner of 'New Age' in mid-1960s Britain. We already know a little about Findhorn, represented here by Peter Caddy. But since the ideology of 'the group' in 'New Age' could override traditional allegiances of class and gender, at the other end of the social spectrum to the unemployed gardener stood a retired Air Marshal.

'Chalk and cheese' revisited: professionals and amateurs of the skies

Sir Victor Goddard (1897–1987) was a high-ranking RAF officer who on retirement in the 1950s became involved in psychic and esoteric circles, including Spiritualism. In addition to regular visits to Attingham he attended several London groups including the College of Psychic Studies – described in the same period by Mary Swainson (1977: 206) as 'a gold-mine for all seekers' – and the Centre for Spiritual and Religious Studies. Of the latter, Goddard (1975: 15) writes: 'Nothing could be more quietly untrammelled by authority and freely enquiring in its interests than was that loose-knit, fluid group of seekers'. Certainly this assessment is borne out by the Centre's own publicity in which it announces that 'in order to preserve the necessary fluidity, there is no membership or any form of organisation beyond that needed for the operation of its various activities'.[13]

The libertarian implications evident here as elsewhere in alternative spirituality circuits before the agitations of the counterculture in the late 1960s is the converse of Left–Marxian anarchism. On the evidence of his published writings (as well as his service rank in the RAF), Goddard was a conservative idealist. *Flight Towards Reality* (Goddard 1975), published a few years after the Attingham gathering, is a discursive memoir-cum-essay that touches upon some familiar themes – clairvoyance, mediumship, spiritual and transcendental realms, UFOs – with no interest in social context. Its central tenet is the art of 'imagining', evidently similar to the 'manifestation' practised at Findhorn: as Goddard defines it, 'imagining creates that which may be embodied and then dynamised' (ibid.: 99–100). Goddard was in fact a mature Establishment figure who relished institution and procedure. Hawken (1990: 160) indicates as much in his sketch of Goddard's response to Caddy's testimony at the Attingham gathering:

> Air Marshal Sir Victor Goddard, the second-highest ranking officer in the Royal Air Force, slowly rose. He stared at Peter and then addressed him: 'Would you like to say a few words and illuminate us all as to how you expect to finance your new age community?'

A very different figure again was Sheila Walker, secretary of the Scottish UFO Society. Walker was a middle-aged woman with a home in Edinburgh where Caddy would often break long north–south journeys. Walker's mother later bought one of the first mobile homes at the Findhorn colony, and Sheila Walker herself had informed Caddy of the 'New Age group leaders' event. Thus Walker functioned as a local contact in a wider web of interpersonal relationships comprising relatives, friends, and colleagues in the spiritual quest. If she lacked the social leverage of Trevelyan or Goddard, she could put individuals in touch with each other at a local, grass-roots level, and in a straightforward and practical manner. Nor was she afraid to voice her opinions, for as we shall see, she later clashed with Peter Caddy over the authority of Eileen's guidance at Findhorn.

Sheila Walker's involvement with UFOs is an index of the persistence of the extraterrestrial associations of 'New Age' throughout this period. In the US, several small concerns published pamphlets and booklets in the 1950s directly linking spacecraft to an imminent 'New Age'. A Los Angeles imprint calling itself, simply, 'New Age' published *The Beginning of the New Age* and *The Coming Golden Age: The Great Cosmic Changes Now in Progress and What the Future Holds for Us*. From the 'New Age Church and School of Truth' in Miami came *Flying Saucers: Vanguard of the New Age*, while the 'Coptic Fellowship of

America' in Los Angeles issued the *The Meaning of Flying Saucers in Reference to the New Age* (Melton and Eberhart 1995). In New Zealand the Heralds of the New Age continued to publish their thick booklets throughout the 1960s: in the year following the Attingham gathering, for example, a lengthy communication from Ashtar was published claiming that 'thousands now accept the truth of flying saucers'.[14] And in Britain, it is significant that Findhorn's first residential guest, shortly before the Attingham gathering, was Daniel Fry, an American UFO contactee who claimed to have travelled in a spaceship (Caddy 1996: 236). To cement the circle, Ellwood (1973: 143) reports that the main ritual in Fry's UFO group 'Understanding Unlimited' was to recite a 'New Age prayer derived from the Alice Bailey writings' (presumably the 'Great Invocation').

Clearly Goddard and Walker had different social backgrounds and gender ascriptions: Goddard public and professional, Walker domestic and amateur. Their joint attendance at the Attingham weekend recalls Eileen Caddy's (1988: 33) description of the personalities in Sheena Govan's group being 'as different as chalk and cheese'. But whether professionals in the armed services or amateur observers on the domestic 'front', all those attracted to the 'New Age' emblem were located in social networks of one kind or another which disseminated the news of a 'New Age' and its extraterrestrial harbingers. But the very process of 'spreading the word' through a polycentric network could unravel and dilute the prophecies' detailed references and hence undermine the specifics of the discourse. The simultaneous dissemination and declension of 'New Age' discourse under these conditions of popular exegesis is precisely the situation that obtains in the 1970s as 'New Age' gradually shifts from its function as an agreed emblem of an imminent new world order to become a contested idiom of spiritual practice in the here and now.

Spiritualist connections

Alongside the UFO connection we find Spiritualism, which provided a significant pool of interest in 'New Age' prophecies in the 1960s. Another named participant at the gathering was Kathleen Fleming, a 'widely loved sensitive' (Brooke 1967: 68): that is, a psychically-sensitive person receptive to a range of subtle communications, from intuitive 'hunches' to specific messages. Fleming accompanied Peter Caddy on several networking journeys in the 1960s, and alongside UFO enthusiasts, mediums travelling the circuit of Spiritualist churches to give 'platform' demonstrations represented the first spiritual subculture to show interest in the new Findhorn colony.

Correspondence in 1967 between Peter Caddy and Albert Best, a medium from Irvine in Ayrshire, Scotland, reveals the busy traffic of mediums and spiritual healers (often one and the same person) at the early colony. Albert Best first contacted Findhorn in early 1967, saying that he would be 'taking a public meeting in the British Legion hall, Inverness' and would like to visit

Findhorn while in the area.[15] This was clearly a success: Best gave a sitting for a small group to whom he delivered messages through his spirit guides 'Hans' and 'Ali'. Best's performance was sufficiently impressive for Caddy to visit his own sanctuary at Irvine later the same month. In May Caddy again contacted Best, asking him to 'let me know if you get anything your end regarding Ben Macdhui' – Ben Macdhui being a Cairngorm mountain boasting a considerable supernatural folklore. Caddy commends several other mediums in letters to Best, including Connie Reay, 'a remarkable medium' whose skills the Findhorn colonists employed to 'anchor' a 'blue healing ray' at the 'Power Point' on which the first Findhorn Sanctuary was built (see Chapter 7). There is also extensive correspondence between Peter Caddy and a couple called Harry and Lil Billington from south London, whose guide was 'Ee-ko' of 'Planet Moon', but this contact ended in a quarrel.[16] Other spirit guides who appeared at Findhorn in 1967 included 'Grey Cloud' and 'Chang', and such was the traffic that in July Caddy excitedly told another correspondent 'last week we had no less than six mediums and it was fascinating all the material that poured through'.[17]

The roles of sensitive, medium and spiritual healer in Spiritualist culture were clearly attractive to the Findhorn colonists and were in any case broadly analogous to their practices of meditation, guidance and intuition. A more philosophical, aristocratic perspective on spiritual realities was represented at Attingham Park in George Trevelyan, although his broad romantic idealism could as easily make room for Kathleen Fleming's 'sensitivity' and Albert Best's spirit guides as it could for Blakean speculation on the heavenly host. One admirer records that during his interview with Trevelyan some years later, the latter 'casually informed' him that the room was 'full of angels' (cited in Trevelyan 1986: 14).

But there were tensions in culture and aesthetic between working class and lower-middle class Spiritualists such as Albert Best and Harry and Lil Billington, and the more obviously professional, military and managerial classes, which were overrepresented at the Attingham gathering and to which key individuals – Trevelyan, Goddard, Caddy and others – belonged. Gender asymmetry was marked, too, among these 'New Age group leaders': despite the leading role played by women as teachers, mediums, sensitives, and even new messiahs in 'New Age' culture, men continued to dominate the public agenda and police the boundaries of appropriate discourse. These and other disruptive variables mean that delicate common ground could easily fracture. For example, the busy flow of Spiritualists to Findhorn declined in inverse proportion to the interest generated in the colony among young middle-class counterculturalists in the late 1960s. To put it bluntly, the higher mean age, poorer health and weaker economic resources of plebeian Spiritualists made for a far less attractive partnership in the eyes of the Findhorn pioneers compared to the young, able-bodied, college-educated seekers who were now flocking to their door.

Liebie Pugh (1888[18]–1966) and the 'Universal Link'

Kathleen Fleming was not only a link between Attingham Park and Spiritualism. Caddy had first met her in the prosperous seaside town of Lytham St
Anne's, near Blackpool, north-west England, where Fleming was an associate of
Liebie Pugh, an artist and Spiritualist. Pugh was the centre of a network called
the 'Universal Link' and Caddy described her as a 'key figure in this link-up
of the forces of Light'.[19] Her appearance was striking: Caddy (1996: 234)
remembers 'slightly yellow [skin] with the most wrinkles I have ever seen',
which Dorothy Maclean thought made her 'look Tibetan'.[20] Pugh mentions
her 'long study of occult and inner teachings' (Pugh 1957: 13) and Brooke
(1976: 51) found her 'equally at ease in discussions on Religion, Theosophy,
Christian Science, Spiritualism, various forms of Yoga, Subud, etc'. That closing
et cetera is interesting in itself, implying that Brooke had either lost track of
Pugh's multiple conversions or considered none of greater import than
others, a position which in either case markedly relativises practice. Pugh had
previously been well-known in Spiritualist circles but had fallen out of favour
– an ascerbic obituary in *Psychic News* described her as 'kindly, benevolent and
sincere' but 'credulous'.[21] In the mid-1950s she had owned a rural hotel in
southern England, where a small group of six met to explore mediumship,
radionic healing and the 'unique powers in ourselves' (Pugh 1957: 14). The
hotel was said to occupy 'a very ancient and highly magnetic centre', and a
meditation room was duly created in a cottage in the grounds where various
'Masters' could materialise and reside (Pugh 1957: 22). The comparisons to
Govan's group at 'God's Hotel' in Scotland are striking.

By the early 1960s Pugh was involved with the Universal Link, a loose
network that had 'no formal membership' and was 'never an organisation'.[22] It
existed largely through face-to-face contact at Pugh's base in Lytham St Anne's
and through newsletters disseminating the prophecies and guidance of several
linked mediums and sensitives (Brooke 1976: 52). The original focus of the
Universal Link were visions shared by Pugh in the north-west of England and
a businessman named Richard Graves in the south. Graves claimed to have had,
from 1961 onwards, a series of supernatural experiences connected with a
popular devotional painting of angels announcing the birth of Jesus. On one
occasion, Graves received a burn from 'a brilliant blaze of orange light' that
emanated from the picture; on other occasions drops of salt water 'of the
consistency of tears' (Brooke 1967: 61) appeared on the picture's surface. A
'bearded, Christ-like figure' also materialised whom Graves called 'the Master'
and Pugh called 'Limitless Love' (Brooke 1976: 50ff.). Pugh made a relief sculpture of this figure in modelling clay, a photograph of which appears on the front
covers of two seminal publications of the day: *Revelation for the New Age* (Brooke
1967) and *A Faith for the New Age* (Vaughan 1967), discussed in Chapter 1.

Graves's claims attracted a little media interest in the early 1960s, and another
'New Age' psychic team, White and Swainson (1971: 34), describe his visions as

a 'current phenomenon' in 1963. An intricate grass-roots debate developed among followers of Graves and Pugh that continued throughout the 1960s. The messages from 'the Master' or 'Limitless Love' were interpreted as prophecies of a new spiritual dispensation in which faculties of illumination and discernment would develop in the population at large, creating a 'universal link' in spiritual consciousness. An apocalyptic timetable was discerned in which the return of this Master would trigger a moment of 'Universal Revelation' following a 'major world conflict' in late 1967, and the 'New Age' would begin (Brooke 1976: 65ff.).

Thus far the interests of the Universal Link group represent little that is unfamiliar in post-war alternative spirituality. Grass-roots networks of individuals; apocalyptic prophecy; seekers and teachers; psychic and spiritual experiences; occultism and piety; technological imagery: these are established elements in the subcultures associated with 'New Age'. But now I wish to tease out a less-remarked ingredient: charisma. The sociologist Max Weber famously defines charisma as 'a certain quality of an individual personality by virtue of which he [sic] is set apart from ordinary men [sic] and treated as endowed with supernatural, superhuman, or at least specifically exceptional qualities' (Eisenstadt 1968: xviii). I highlight the gender exclusivity here precisely because in these circles women compete strongly for charismatic status. Liebie Pugh resembles so many of the teachers and gurus we have met in that she 'had an extraordinary effect' on devotees (Caddy 1996: 234). Her secretary is said to be 'obviously devoted' to her while Pugh induces a 'trance' in Naomi on their first meeting (ibid.). Eileen Caddy (1988: 118) professes 'indescribable love for her' and Ruth Nesfield-Cookson describes herself and George Trevelyan literally 'on the floor at Liebie's feet' during a visit to Pugh in 1966.[23]

The most dramatic parallel concerns Liebie Pugh and Sheena Govan. In both cases the women are attributed divine or Christ-like status and their suffering becomes redemptive for the community. The women acquire – however briefly – the messianic status traditionally reserved for male prophets and saviours. Here is Eileen Caddy's (1988: 115–16) vision of Pugh shortly before meeting her for the first time in person:

> I became aware of Liebie's presence there with us. Then I saw before me a being of great stature and light and I recognised the face of the master Jesus, the Christ. I heard a voice say distinctly, 'Master', and Liebie and the Master were one and the same.

Later, narrating this vision to a colleague at Findhorn, she feels 'utterly at one with Liebie and the Christ and I heard the words "I am the Way, the Truth and the Life"'. Alluding to Pugh's cancer (which killed her in 1966), another seeker in the 1960s networks, Monica Parish, explained in a letter to Peter Caddy that 'Liebie's body is registering the dis-ease [sic] of the world'.[24] As Peter Caddy recalled of Sheena Govan's recurring illnesses: 'she seemed to take on not only the cares of others, but also, at times, their physical ailments' (Caddy 1996: 86).

Like Govan, Pugh's charisma was considerable. Recognising this, Peter Caddy (1996: 245–6) wrote to her soon after the Attingham gathering to suggest that she and her associates come to live at Findhorn. There were sound political reasons for cementing association: before her death, Pugh apparently passed on to Caddy the name of a 'wealthy benefactor' as well as an active mailing list (ibid.: 268, 273). As a result, the Universal Link was effectively absorbed into Findhorn. Symbolic of this transfer of authority was the move to Findhorn of Pugh's secretary Joanie Hartnell-Beavis, who in the words of Hartnell-Beavis's own obituarist brought with her 'the lineage of Liebie'.[25]

But as with Sheena Govan, such an egregiously charismatic personality created tension in the otherwise egalitarian group ethos of the Universal Link and indeed in wider 'New Age' networks. There are certainly some contradictions between the transcendent norm of 'group sentiency' advocated by Alice Bailey, and the operative conditions of groups like Govan's and Pugh's. The promise of experiencing at least a degree of charisma and virtuosic self-expression was part of the allure of the spiritual quest and in part drove seekers into group fellowship in the first place. But too much of a good thing could undermine group harmony and trigger a cult of leadership of the kind that Bailey had warned against. David Spangler seems to allude to this when, several years later, he mentions 'a tendency to develop a cult' around Pugh (Spangler 1977: 37). But that he himself nevertheless sought to incorporate this source of revelation into his own discourse by becoming in turn a channel of 'Limitless Love' only provides further evidence of a very real genealogy of 'New Age' in this period and of sometimes blunt political struggles to shape and control it.

'New Age' globetrotting: Anthony Brooke (1912–) and the 'Universal Foundation'

During my travels in the early Sixties I came across small groups of people in different countries who were channelling information concerning earth changes and a 'New Age', 'the end of an epoch', 'the Second Coming of Christ'.[26]

Melton *et al.* (1990: 482) list the 'Universal Foundation' as a major disseminator of 'New Age' discourse in the late 1960s. It was the creation of a partnership between Anthony Brooke and Monica Parish, whom Peter Caddy met for the first time at Attingham Park. Anthony Brooke had been the last independent governor of Sarawak before its post-war annexation by the British. He was a traveller, lecturer and pamphleteer, and an enthusiastic spokesman for several idealistic groups and causes. The potted biography appended to one of his pamphlets, entitled *An Open Letter to Citizens of All Lands*, makes this plain:

Anthony Brooke has been linking with different groups throughout the world having a special concern for unity and peace and education for world citizenship. He is a member of the Supreme Council of the Commonwealth of World Citizens and a Vice-President of World Union, a life member of the Royal Institute of International Affairs, International Fellowship of Reconciliation, Churches' Fellowship for Psychical and Spiritual Study, Spiritual Frontiers Fellowship, Society for Psychical Research; a member of Fellowship of Friends of Truth and of the Wider Quaker Fellowship.[27]

From the mid-1960s – in a simple rendering of the executive–secretary relationship – Brooke headed the Universal Foundation while Parish acted as amanuensis. Nevertheless, the duo's aims were no less operatic than its name: 'to promote universal understanding by linking together in concord individual people everywhere, thus fostering for the betterment of the whole world the spiritual evolution of mankind'.[28] It was essentially a communication network, or web, 'spun' by Brooke during his extensive personal travels:

During the years 1966–1967 we acquired largely through personal contact the names of many individuals all over the world who expressed a desire to be kept in touch with modern revelatory messages and other information relating to what is generally called the New Age or the New Dispensation.[29]

Brooke's populism was flexible and spontaneous. He appeared to be as comfortable moving in the upper echelons of international politics – Caddy (1996: 241–2) says he knew U Thant, then Secretary-General of the United Nations, 'very well' – as he was participating at grass-roots level. In the latter realm he became a close associate of the early Findhorn community whence the Universal Foundation moved in 1968. He also lectured at Attingham, promoted the Universal Link, and proselytised extensively in North America, where he met the young David Spangler in 1967. This kind of face-to-face contact was typical of the interpersonal reticulation of 'New Age' discourse: it was also a particularly significant connection since, as we will see in Chapter 5, Spangler was already a busy speaker in the 'new age subculture' in the US and had recently published a booklet called *The Christ Experience and the New Age* (cited in Caddy 1996: 307). Brooke acquired a copy, colleagues at Findhorn read it and soon Spangler had moved to Findhorn, where he was to produce a series of texts that dramatically reinterpreted the 'New Age' message in the early 1970s.

Brooke has remained internationally mobile and at the time of writing he continues to campaign for utopian solutions to global problems. In Sweden in the mid-1970s he promoted 'The Foundation for Peace through Unity' (Brooke 1976: 132–3) and by the 1990s he had moved to New Zealand with a programme entitled 'Operation Peace through Unity' and the motto, 'A Strategy of Hope for a World in Crisis'.[30]

Esoteric Revival: Wellesley Tudor Pole, the Lamplighters and the 'Silent Minute'

In 1964 Trevelyan set up the 'Lamplighter' movement at Attingham to capitalise on the success of the 'Death and Becoming' course. Lamplighters maintained permanently burning lights in their homes, usually low-wattage electric bulbs. Trevelyan (1981: 154–5) explains the underlying metaphysics:

> [The lights] were to be amber, to represent the Spiritual Sun, the source of life and the Christ Impulse working down into the obscurity of matter.... What happens is that the little light, combined with the dedicated intent, prayer and meditation, draws down a response from the next level of life and being.... A chain of inter-lacing events is set going, and focal centres of light then begin to multiply.

A neo-platonic hierarchy, similar to Alice Bailey's occult cosmos, is evident in this scheme of descending levels of existence from (high) 'Spiritual Sun' to (low) 'little lights' in the material world. Trevelyan is anxious to stress that becoming a Lamplighter entails no 'obligations of membership' or 'dogma'. The rationale here is that the lack of such gross outward signs helps Lamplighters to blend seamlessly into the 'great network of Light Centres spreading across Britain and the world' (ibid.: 156).

Wellesley Tudor Pole (1884–1968) had inspired Trevelyan to start the Lamplighters network. Pole was a former Army Major in the 1914–18 war who later followed a hybrid career as dealer in art and tea, amateur archaeologist, and aristocratic writer on spiritual and esoteric matters (I mentioned his book *Private Dowding* [1917] in Chapter 1).[31] On his visits to Attingham Nesfield-Cookson remembers him as a 'very quiet' man 'communing with spiritual worlds'. Although Pole probably didn't attend the 'New Age group leaders' week-end, his trigger role in the Lamplighters network is significant since it cemented yet another interpersonal chain of contact and linked the network with a practice from 1940s Britain: the 'Silent Minute'.

With the support of King George VI and Prime Minister Winston Churchill, Pole had proposed that a one-minute period of silence be observed among the population at large each night at nine o'clock during the critical early days of the Second World War. During this 'silent minute' people were to pray for peace. According to Pole, by 1943 over ten million individuals were keeping the silent minute (Gaythorpe 1979: 189). The end of war in 1945 curtailed its scope although the practice persisted in some circles until as late as 1961.[32] Then Pole is said to have received instructions 'from a high spiritual source' that 'Light should replace Sound' as the symbolic focus of the practice in order to remodel it for new times.[33]

Both the 'Silent Minute' and the 'eternal flame' of the amber lamps anticipate the instrumentalist logic of the 'New Age' idiom. Trevelyan (1981: 156) considered that a lamplighter's relationship with 'the great network of Light centres' resembled 'the flow of electricity from generators and through transformers which reduce the voltage so that it may shine in little bulbs' – an image which exactly reproduces the 'circuitry' of Naomi's 'Network of Light' in the mid-1950s, and the general hierarchy of relationship between groups and Masters in Alice Bailey's occult pantheon. In structural terms the significance of the Lamplighters in the 1960s lay in their providing an established network of practitioners sympathetic to contiguous practices and values, and it is significant that, after the Attingham gathering, Peter Caddy wrote to thank George Trevelyan for providing a 'list of Lamplighters [which] will be invaluable to me when dashing around the countryside linking up the various points of light'.[34]

'Power spots' and the romance of landscape: Iona and Glastonbury

So far in this chapter I have discussed a number of individuals present at a small week-end gathering called 'The Significance of the Group in the New Age' at an adult education college near the English–Welsh border in 1965. Brief sketches of various individuals present, the College itself, and related projects – the Universal Link, the Universal Foundation, the Lamplighters' network and its predecessor, the 'silent minute' – have given us a broader context in which to place the development of the Findhorn group and the discourse on 'New Age' in the 1960s. Before we assess the evidence of the chapter as a whole, a final ingredient must be added: a cult of place, more particularly of certain land-scapes functioning as pilgrimage sites. In England, Canterbury and Walsingham have played this role for Christians, Avebury and Stonehenge for new generations of Pagans. Pre-eminent in British 'New Age' networks are Iona in Scotland and Glastonbury in England.

In the modern period a popular reverence has grown up around the island of Iona and the market town of Glastonbury. Interest in these sites has not been confined to practitioners of alternative spirituality but is manifest among writers, painters and folklorists as well as liberal pockets of Christian denominations: for example, the ecumenical 'Iona Community' founded within the Church of Scotland in 1938 (Monteith 2000) or the more recent 'Quest Community' in Glastonbury, modelled on the former, set up in 1993 (Bowman 2000: 96). Kathleen Fleming, for example, had visited both Iona and Glastonbury around the time of the Attingham gathering. So had Peter Caddy, who describes Iona as 'one of the major centres of spiritual power in Britain' (Caddy 1996: 126). He even briefly considered moving there after meeting the new owner of one of the island's hotels who, like Cluny Hill under Govan's group or Liebie Pugh's establishment in Surrey, was developing the hotel as a 'spiritual' centre (ibid.: 238–40). Caddy also recalls visiting a number of individuals on the island including a 'remarkable healing mystic', several 'ancient spiritual sites', and a private house containing a 'powerful sanctuary' that 'attracted people from all over the world' (Caddy 1996: 239). Caddy was no stranger to the island and had visited it as early as 1956 on Sheena Govan's prompting; indeed, it was he who found the cottage on Mull, just across the water from Iona, where Sheena, Eileen and Dorothy all spent time later that same year.

These and other trajectories of spiritual interest in the island suggest a diffuse pool of support for a 'New Age' spirituality, although other interests such as the revival of a 'Celtic' Christian spirituality are strongly represented on Iona and not easily disentangled (Meek 2000). This is also the case with Glastonbury, although the numbers involved are greater due to the town's proximity to major conurbations. A 'quiet sanctuary' in Glastonbury – a town 'dotted with holy wells and sacred sites', a place of 'special power' (Caddy 1988: 27) – had been the setting, in 1953, for Eileen Caddy's first contact with the 'God within' and effectively the beginning of her career as seer and sensitive. In turn, Maclean remembers that Sheena Govan's caravan was sited in the vicinity for a time and used on occasion by members of the Pimlico group.[35]

It was also in Glastonbury that Peter Caddy had met Wellesley Tudor Pole shortly before the Attingham gathering. Pole was then spokesman for the Chalice Well Trust, a body formed in 1959 to preserve a natural spring at the centre of Glastonbury lore. Pole had become a prominent figure in the Glastonbury cult, having made a pilgrimage there as a young man as early as 1904. A few years later he also visited Iona during a tour of 'important spiritual centres' in the UK, taking with him a blue bowl that had been unearthed near the Chalice Well spring following a vision. This bowl, it was claimed, was the Holy Grail, brought to Glastonbury according to legend by Joseph of Arimathea.

In the lay culture of 'New Age' seeking, the rich heritage of popular religion associated with sites like Iona and Glastonbury helped to legitimise new endeavours. When Eileen Caddy visited Iona with Peter shortly after the Attingham gathering, she was told in guidance: 'This has been a very important and valuable pilgrimage. The linking together of these three centres of light – Iona, Glastonbury and Findhorn – is very important' (Caddy 1988: 105). Such was its allure that Peter Caddy made eight dedicated journeys around Britain in connection with Glastonbury alone in the mid-1960s and, as with Iona, was tempted to move there to become the new 'guardian' of Chalice Well (Caddy 1996: 249, 252).

These offers to Peter Caddy to join new projects on Iona and at Glastonbury confirm his status as a powerful individual in the networks. These and other 'centres of light' were considered by Caddy, Pole and others to be spiritual resources for troubled times, and since other constituencies were interested in them, they required political representation. In 1966 Tudor Pole described his part in 'rekindling' various spiritual sites or 'beacons':

> In 1904 Glastonbury was dead, or anyway in coma, spiritually speaking. In 1905 I found Iona in similar condition, benumbed. In 1906 Devenish [Northern Ireland] was riddled with unattractive elementals. The first two have now been brought back to life, beacons re-kindled ...I have ...taken part in re-kindling some twenty-five centres, in our islands and right across Europe, the Middle East and Africa.
>
> (Gaythorpe 1979: 189)

Fresh 'spiritual centres' were also discerned and incorporated into the network to map out an emergent geography of alternative spirituality. A letter of Caddy's to Pole makes this plain:

> We at Findhorn wish to do all we can to bring unity to the many such centres in the British Isles as Glastonbury, Iona, Attingham, Strathmiglo, and Findhorn. We are now co-operating with centres of Light all over the world.[36]

Continuing a latent discourse on power in connection with certain practices and individuals, sites like Iona or Glastonbury are sometimes called 'power spots' or 'power centres': that is, places 'believed to possess an excess of available spiritual energy' and where 'spiritual disciplines such as meditation and yoga are facilitated by the very environment' (Melton *et al.* 1991: 124). A power spot might be a place of impressive natural beauty (say, Iona); a site of traditional, or 'ancient', worship (Glastonbury); or a functional redescription of an otherwise unremarkable site (Attingham, Strathmiglo and Findhorn). The term was known to previous generations of occultists. For example, Dion Fortune, who played a key role in the cult of Glastonbury in the interwar period, published an article on the 'Power Centres of Britain' in the *Occult Review* in 1931. This summarised what Fortune called 'our native esoteric tradition', incorporating standing stones, wells, springs, trees and groves (Fortune 1931: 106–8). Glastonbury and Iona are both mentioned, along with Lindisfarne on the Northumbrian coast and Snowden in Wales. In language recalling the 'ley line' theory of Alfred Watkins' *The Old Straight Track* (1925), Fortune concludes that 'not only are the centres themselves of importance, but there are lines of magnetic force stretching between them' (Fortune 1931: 110). In a variation upon the same theme of esoteric landscape, another practising sensitive and occultist, Katherine Maltwood, claimed in 1929 to be able to trace on Ordnance Survey maps of the Glastonbury area the figurative outlines of the twelve signs of the zodiac, marked out by earthworks, streams and other antiquarian features. Hence it was only in accord with esoteric tradition that the 'Harmonic Convergence' of 1987 – an informal 'New Age' gathering called to celebrate the impact of an unusually powerful cosmic force – was celebrated on Glastonbury Tor and the town itself affirmed as 'the new Heart Chakra of the world in this emerging Age of Aquarius'.[37]

'New Age' eddies and undercurrents in the 1960s

It is time to take stock. From the material presented in this chapter we can see that the 'New Age group leaders' weekend at Attingham Park in October 1965 drew both directly and indirectly upon a diffuse 'New Age' constituency in Britain in the mid-1960s. Several traits require brief mention.

First, a generational observation: the actors in these circles were almost without exception born in the inter-war period or earlier, in some cases in the Edwardian or even late Victorian period. The dominant bourgeois culture valued interpersonal discretion and formalised patterns of behaviour, a pattern that informs (if not entirely determines) representative groups of the 1950s and early 1960s such as Govan's circle, the Heralds of the New Age and the Attingham Park gathering, because key figures, even the bulk of participants, belonged to these earlier generations. I develop this generational analysis in Chapter 5, for it is directly linked to the seminal hermeneutical shift in 'New Age' that occurs around the turn of the 1970s. The point to grasp here is simply that the vigour of a new generation of seekers was required if a 'New Age' discourse was to be successfully and enduringly transmitted into the public arena. A youthful counterculture was already poised in the wings at the time of the Attingham gathering, fed by a post Second World War 'baby boom'. By the end of the 1960s these new seekers would begin to take up the baton of the pioneers: some in communes (Rigby 1974), others in a more diffuse 'occult revival' in popular culture (Truzzi 1972), still others in the burgeoning 'spiritual groups and growth centres' (the subtitle of *The Many Ways of Being*, Annett's seminal 1976 compendium) that were – and remain – the legacy of alternative practice.

Second, if there is little by way of incontrovertibly 'public' doctrine or deportment to distinguish a 'New Age' group leader at Attingham Park from the general public, certain marked instincts and practices had developed in 'private' – that is, among colleagues, in group work, or simply alone. For example, actors are more likely to meditate than to pray, and if prayer is practised, it is likely to be silent or contemplative. Participants will receive some kind of 'inner' guidance and may well claim skills like clairvoyance, prophecy and mediumship. Nurturing intense subjectivities and refining intuition and 'sensitivity' are everyday concerns. 'Consciousness' is a common thread: getting 'attuned', or sensitised, to its subtle dimensions and to the consciousness of others (making the 'universal link'); 'going within' and doing 'inner work'; expanding and endlessly fine-tuning one's receptivity and telepathic connectivity. Special diets are utilised to enhance the subtle capabilities of the organism, particularly organic foods and vegetarianism. At Findhorn, Eileen Caddy (1988: 91) recalls we learned to live on vegetables from the garden, honey and fruit. . . . We found our sensitivity grew and we became more in touch with the spiritual realms and nature forces in the gardens. . . . I ate only one meal a day of raw foods and drank pints and pints of pure, clear water, with no tea or coffee or stimulants of any kind.

The last item of common culture to note is that participants read and discuss a wide variety of esoteric literature. Home-made, labour-intensive publications of all kinds disseminate an author's message and communicate between groups, and a special agency is imparted to solitary reading through a special 'spiritual interface', as Liebie Pugh (1957: 13) explains with regard to her own text:

The invisible is to become visible. That is the sum and substance of this message, and my writing it and your reading it is, by some spiritual alchemy beyond our present understanding but wholly scientific, to be part of the means of the invisible becoming visible.

As discussed briefly in Chapter 2, the act of reading itself, when correctly undertaken, is an interactive spiritual work contributing to the realisation of a common aim, since the reader's consciousness is an empirical, if recondite, 'place', and her thoughts are *things* with an inescapable impact on the world.

So much for the subjectivities delineating 'New Age'. What about quantitative evidence of participation? It is extremely difficult to estimate numbers of participants, because of multiple mailing lists, overlapping circles of interest and the impossibility of drawing firm boundaries around the field. Furthermore, fissiparous structural tendencies combined with an affinity for discreet, private practice means that we simply don't know how many other small groups were scattered around the UK or middle America at this time. From the evidence assembled here, several hundred individuals in various informal interest groups and networks of a 'spiritual' nature in the UK must have been more-or-less directly implicated. If we take into account other indices of 'New Age' interest throughout the decade, we find greater numbers indicated – perhaps a few thousand – although they remain small overall, certainly in comparison with the numbers who became involved in new religious movements from the late 1960s onwards.

Diverse indices of 'New Age' in the UK range from a tiny group in Sutherland, northern Scotland, which published a pamphlet of messages from 'the archangel Michael' in the early 1960s, to the fifty or so individuals Peter Caddy mentions meeting in the course of his first journey as Findhorn 'ambassador' (Caddy 1996: 228, 237).[38] In 1964 a group of a dozen or so individuals in the Bournemouth area of England were passing round material from the Heralds of the New Age and from 'Mark-Age' in the US in a postal exchange network.[39] Later the same year around fifty individuals were present at a meeting Peter Caddy attended in Glastonbury (Caddy 1996: 249). An alternative health centre such as Westbank in rural Fife could act as a focus for various small group activities: in 1969 Caddy notes that a group of twenty-four were meeting there weekly.[40]

Even estimating the numbers involved in a group with a clear name, central figure and regular communications is tricky. Consider Liebie Pugh's Universal Link. Spangler (1977: 36) mentions a 'large mailing list': Caddy (1996: 273) claims it amounted to between six and seven thousand individuals. This seems an overly large figure, but put into an international context, and allowing for a considerable degree of isolated participation – that is, receiving, reading and 'contemplating' the newsletters – it may not be so wide of the mark. Certainly there is disagreement concerning the extent of Pugh's support. On the one hand, Caddy (1996: 234–5) claims that 'people came from all over the world to see her' and 'she knew more spiritually inclined groups and individuals than anybody I had met'. But Dorothy Maclean describes her as 'not a well-known person except in a small circle'.[41] Of course, 'small' is a relative term. In any case, emic assessment of value, derived as we have seen from intensely-felt subjectivities, is qualitative rather than quantitative. Bearing in mind the difference between generous, even extravagant, mailing shots and proactive participants, we might guess that no more than a few hundred people were regularly and actively involved with Universal Link in Britain; perhaps several hundred globally. The empirical influence of the Universal Foundation is even harder to gauge. Although Brooke mentions 'personal contact' with 'many individuals all over the world' the logistics of this again suggest a constituency in the hundreds rather than thousands. Brooke (1976: 8) also mentions other small groups promoting various ecumenical spiritual programmes such as Universal World Harmony and World Union, but we cannot assume that the grand rhetoric of these groups' names translates into substantial or enduring bodies of supporters.

We are on surer ground with regard to Attingham Park, where we know that Trevelyan's 'significant' mailing list numbered around a thousand[42] but we return to murky waters when we consider Sheila Walker's UFO constituency. Buckner (1968) suggests fifty or so affiliates to a typical American UFO group around the same time, and this seems a reasonable estimate, although many of these seekers would simultaneously be pursuing other interests and hence may turn up on other lists and in different groups. For example, Spiritualism threw up many independently-minded mediums who migrated to – or dipped in and out of – related fields of practice, as in the case of Spiritualists at Findhorn, or the 'readers' group' in England connected with the spirit guide 'Gildas' and his medium, Ruth White, which numbered twenty-five in 1962 and around three hundred by the end of the decade (Swainson 1977: 214).

When we collate all these figures and allow for significant duplication, as well as the possibility that many small groups simply remain unknown and uncounted, we can estimate that the total figure of those in Britain in the early-to-mid 1960s engaged with 'New Age' in the apocalyptic sense outlined here was not more than a few thousand.[43] But however numerically marginal, those involved were articulating real concerns and issues of the day. Anthony Brooke (1976: 57) touches on this when he remarks on

> the multiplicity of often quite small meditational and prayer groups, perhaps consisting of no more than three or four people regularly meeting together, which have been mushrooming up on a worldwide scale in a kind of spiritual explosion, almost *in counteraction to the atomic counterpart* [emphasis added].

The metaphor employed by Brooke is the release of 'internal' (spiritual) energies through the disintegration of monobloc (religious) structures. Clearly there is some bathos between the rhetoric of magnitude – the 'mushrooming up on a worldwide scale' – and the numerical reality of groups of 'three or four people'. Nevertheless, the argument from subjectivity makes sense: numbers may be small, but exponents' cultural capital (in Bourdieu's sense) is often considerable, and the extension and refinement of subjectivity is a pursuit complete in itself. Consider the pioneering independence of the many female teachers and sensitives, or the social competence and self-belief of prominent male activists who can operate resourcefully even when displaced from the social and political establishment.

But some severe difficulties confronted activists like Peter Caddy and Anthony Brooke who attempted to convert a diffuse domestic spirituality into a public discourse capable of mobilising recruits. To begin with, the underlying class base is indeterminate. Although it is broadly middle class in ideology and aesthetic and is sprinkled liberally with privileged or aristocratic men (Caddy, Brooke, Trevelyan), it does not correlate markedly with either social orthodoxy or deviancy: that is, it embraces establishment and other socially privileged figures, including some intellectuals, as well as ex-servicemen, hoteliers, the unemployed, and – significantly – mothers, housewives and independent single women. The bewildering profile of occupational roles in the Gildas group reveals this heterogeneity particularly well, incorporating 'academics engaged in psychic research, educationists, psychologists of various schools, hippies, occultists, housewives, [and] spiritualists' (White and Swainson 1971: 33). Such internal role differentiation is not conducive to political campaigning and may well exacerbate interpersonal animosities under pressure, leading to splintering and cleavage. And despite the rhetoric of universal comradeship and talk of co-ordinating a 'new spiritual movement', compelling evidence suggests that this was offset by spiritual rivalry, the politicking of charismatic personalities and simple lack of interest in a wider theoretical agenda on the part of some small groups who simply wanted to be left alone to 'do their own thing' (to use the countercultural slang soon to be sprung upon society).[44] Furthermore, the structures of assembly and recruitment – small groups, networks of family and friends, inexpensive print media of pamphlets and newsletters – are ephemeral and micro-scale phenomena not easy to translate into more substantial institutions without developing the strength of roles and bureaucracy that participants repudiate in the first place. As is abundantly clear, loose and shifting patterns of association and congregation around a number of more-or-less charismatic individuals is the norm here.

Further problems for activists like Caddy and Brooke concern the absence of a distinctive material culture and behavioural code. Participants' clothes, language and etiquette are largely indistinguishable from prevailing middle-class mores and fashions in the 1950s and early 1960s, certainly in Macmillan's Britain. They meet in secular buildings such as hotels, private houses, adult education establishments, and public meeting rooms, where the sole concession to a dedicated ritual space is likely to be a 'sanctuary' for meditation and guidance. Finally, the hermeneutics of 'alternative' and 'esoteric' spirituality favour the 'veiling' of meaning and the exercise of discretion and discernment in transmitting teachings to others. All these factors contribute to a significant empirical camouflaging of the phenomenon, a point underscored in an American journalist's interview with Eileen and Peter Caddy in 1977 which begins: 'For mystics, they looked so, well, normal'.[45]

Clearly in a cultural milieu as tolerant as alternative spirituality, a critical mass of belief and behaviour must be distilled if a viable collectivity is to develop over time. This chapter and the last have shown that 'New Age' was at least a recurring motif in the milieu, one that *could* function as a common standard under which otherwise fissiparous groups and factions *might* unite. For the most basic trait sabotaging the public impact of these rich prophecies of social collapse and spiritual renewal is the institutional impact of the motor of spiritual seekership. By definition, seekers do not join institutions; they *leave* them. Seekers are seceders and their participation in institutions of any kind is likely to be enthusiastic but temporary.

Nevertheless, that the early 'New Age' emblem could generate real if limited public discourse on a shared project can be demonstrated by the lively debate in letters and pamphlets from the mid-1960s and early 1970s. Shortly before the Attingham Park gathering, for example, Peter Caddy informed his old Rosicrucian associate Walter Bullock that 'there is a truly wonderful plan now in preparation for the saving of the remnants and for the bringing about of the new Heaven and the new Earth'.[46] And shortly after it, Monica Parish asked Peter Caddy if Findhorn had 'anything coming through' related to 'The Second Coming'.[47] This time in his reply Caddy alluded to the soteriological role of 'our space brothers', although a plethora of alternative soteriological messengers and attendant doomsday scenarios can be unearthed in the literature. Nuclear holocaust, earthquake, flood and fire; spacecraft, the Masters, the Christ: which of these will trigger the *real* 'New Age'? Although the variety of these and other speculations anticipates the hermeneutic proliferation to come, there is an important difference: at this high-water mark of early 'New

Age', currents of debate and dissent are present, if sometimes only weakly, that are later almost completely silent or missing. Simultaneously there is an important basic agreement that the 'New Age' is a real historical event that has not yet come to pass. The points at issue are rather what kind of event it will be, when it will come, whose guidance is most authoritative, and what should be done by way of spiritual preparation. Consider the fiery letter from Peter Caddy to Sheila Walker on the occasion of her questioning the source of Eileen Caddy's guidance:

> These messages are God's Word sent out under His direct guidance. The whole of Findhorn and everything we are doing here is guided in this manner. Do I take it then that you do not accept that Elixir's [Eileen's] messages are from God?[48]

The implication is that while universal guidance is the norm, some channels of information and their centres are more sacrosanct than others. In short, it is the kind of emotionally charged response one might expect to receive in a debate where real historical outcomes are at stake and will be contested by participants. The stark political proof of this lies in Findhorn's subsequent ascendancy to the international 'New Age' crown and the historical elision of Sheila Walker and the Scottish UFO Society.

Hence debate over the 'New Age' emblem, including questions of stewardship and interpretation, is manifestly a sign that something *public* – status, leadership, authority – is at stake. Consider traces of other political rivalries in the literature. The Attingham Park gathering gave rise to personality clashes among 'New Age group leaders', as we saw in the case of Peter Caddy and Sir Victor Goddard. In the tea break Peter Caddy recalls that

> a woman came up to me and said that in olden times I would have been burned at the stake for saying some of the things I'd said. 'Then aren't we lucky to be alive today?', I said sweetly, thinking that she would have been one of the first to reach for the matches.
>
> (Caddy 1996: 242–3)

At Glastonbury too, it seems, 'all was not well'. A long-standing 'spiritual rivalry' had apparently come to a head between Tudor Pole at Chalice Well and another faction in the town (Caddy 1996: 253). Despite his light narrative tone, Caddy's commentary shows that very real political differences could develop:

> Eileen had several visions relating to the battle between these spiritual giants, and guidance that I was to bring them together, but the result of my efforts to do so was that both of them turned on me, each thinking that I was in the other's camp!
>
> (ibid.: 253)

Less dramatically, discussion and debate at the personal level could find minds changing, plans altering, allegiances shifting. This might mean simply a change in direction to one's spiritual seeking. But this in turn might influence public discourse if the individual concerned carried sufficient status and therefore had views meriting wider consideration. For example, there was a sharp change in the significance given to UFOs at Findhorn in the mid-1960s when, abruptly, Peter Caddy (1996: 262) announced that

> all that had been prophesied in the early years was no longer true. There was no need for an extraterrestrial 'rescue mission'. . . . The spacecraft that had come, as we thought, to arrange one such evacuation had in fact 'popped in' to tell us that everything was all right.

This breezy shift from the old certainties that the 'New Age' would only dawn after a catastrophic 'cleansing' of the planet was troubling for those who continued to receive stark prophecies of disaster. Correspondence between Peter Caddy and Lanakila Brandt, the leader of a Hawaiian group, illuminates the hermeneutic space that could open up between conservatives and liberals. In July 1970 Caddy explained to Brandt that the earlier messages of 'disaster and destruction' previously received at Findhorn – and, as we know, elsewhere – were being replaced by a new vision:

> Sufficient light has been anchored in the various centres of light around the world to prevent disaster. There will, of course, be much chaos, turmoil and confusion in the world as we move into the New Age. It is therefore vital that each centre concentrate on the Light, on the glorious Golden Age which is ahead, and rises above the chaos, confusion and disaster in the world.

In this revised scenario, 'New Age' is uncoupled from its traditional role as an emblem of post-apocalyptic utopia – the shape of things to come *after* the 'cleansing' forces of catastrophe – and envisioned as the process of averting or at least minimising such disasters before they even strike. What is noticeable about this is the move away from the might of implacable transcendental forces to the agency of human beings on the 'earth plane', a crucial shift that I discuss in some detail in the next chapter. Caddy continues his explanation in a psychological vein:

> Many mediums throughout the world have continually prophesied disasters in different areas, and these have not come about. It would seem that they have tuned in to planes of illusion created by man's fears and thoughts and in some cases, subconscious desires.[49]

Here Caddy tactfully suggests that the dramatic prophecies reported by Lanakila Brandt's group are coloured by psychological fantasies. She, however, is undaunted. 'The Prophets of Doom are still postulating world destruction', she replies, 'and the pictures that I have personally received indicate tremendous upheaval, appalling destruction'. Caddy then puts his cards on the table:

> Briefly, we have been told that the earth will not now be destroyed –
> although of course there will be much destruction and devastation as
> we move into the New Age, but this will not affect those of the Light.
> I am sure too that there will be much suffering in the world for those
> who have chosen the way of the self.

This paragraph opens the door to a psychological hermeneutic of 'New Age' in which the apocalypse is no longer the destruction of the planet at a fixed point in time, but the death of the insensitive, rationalistic ego in an ongoing process of human growth.

But if minds were changing at Findhorn, Lanakila Brandt – like many – remained wedded to traditional prophecies. Three years later she again told Caddy that 'we are extremely troubled':

> We have been receiving constant warnings of impending cataclysm,
> a global holocaust; constant urgings that we must *now* establish our
> bastion, our emergency resources.

This international conversation continued over a period of several years and reveals an informed exchange of opinion and interpretation. This becomes increasingly rare in the later 1970s and beyond as the pendulum of popular opinion swings towards human choice and agency as providing the proper motor of the 'New Age', the supernatural cosmos of Masters and space brothers fading accordingly. In fact, Peter Caddy's public assertion of commitment at the Attingham Park gathering in 1965 – 'one gives up everything to put God and His Will first, then all one's needs are met perfectly from His abundant supply' (Caddy 1996: 242) – sounds disturbingly dogmatic to the spiritual heirs of 'New Age' in the 1990s, as will become evident from the ethnographies in Chapters 6 to 8.

And yet the empirical boundaries that could cement individuals and groups into a distinctive collectivity under the auspices of the 'New Age' emblem are largely absent. As we have seen, participation and belonging – even to local groups – proceeds on an attenuated and self-selected basis. Certainly a collective Anglo–American culture of sorts exists: Peter Caddy maintains a flourishing correspondence from the north-east of Scotland; the Heralds of the New Age in New Zealand and George Trevelyan and the Universal Link in England all have impressive mailing lists; and scores if not hundreds of small groups and micro-networks exist for discussion, speculation and meditation.

Within this unstable milieu, a cluster of ideas, techniques and terminology associated with a 'New Age' led a chequered career in the 1950s and 1960s. As I indicated in Chapter 2 and argue in Chapter 9, this alternative spiritual domain is best understood as the creation of seekers, gathered in groups within wider networks of interest and association. But what kind of collectivity do these networks of lay spirituality amount to? Can these diverse articulations of a 'New Dispensation' or 'New Age' be said to be a 'movement' in any viable sense? Or do they simply amount to an aggregate of small groups, societies and individuals 'mushrooming up on a worldwide scale in a kind of spiritual explosion' (Brooke 1976: 57)?

I return to these and related questions in Chapter 9 after we have assessed the ethnographic evidence of Chapters 6 to 8. In the meantime, I close this chapter, as I began the previous one, on a decisive moment in the spiritual biography of Peter Caddy. The Attingham gathering of 1965 gave Caddy a new lease of life, for it gave him access to a fresh network of spiritual seekers just at the moment that the fledgling Findhorn colony was emerging from isolation. Through the list of contacts he collected at Attingham, Caddy proudly claims that by the end of the year he had 'visited most of the key people and centres in Britain that were seeking or already expressing a spiritual vision for the New Age, and played my part in making them aware of each other' (Caddy 1996: 253). He also boasts – probably correctly – that 'within a few years nearly everyone at that conference would come to visit us at Findhorn' (ibid.: 243).

Part 2

IDIOM

5

HEAVEN ON EARTH

From apocalypse to self-realisation

All that had been prophesied in the early years was no longer true.
(Caddy 1996: 262)

A guy just wants to practise his religion, just wants to do his thing, man.
(Otis Cook, American hippie: cited in Neville 1971: 203)

Introduction

The function of this chapter is to link the previous historical narratives with the ethnographies of 'New Age' activities in Chapters 6 to 8. First, this chapter profiles the impact of the counterculture and a new generation of seekers on 'New Age' enclaves of the late 1960s. Second, it shows how a shift in the hermeneutics of 'New Age' – from 'public' event to 'private' gnosis or from apocalypse to self-realisation – came about in the 1970s. Third, the chapter portrays the subsequent referential heterogeneity of the expression: in effect, its gradual fragmentation as a unifying ideological emblem or metanarrative device. I do not, however, pursue a strict chronology of developments beyond this point, since once the basic hermeneutical shift from 'emblem' to 'idiom' has been made, the hermeneutical floodgates are flung wide, and historical sequence becomes redundant. A general pattern of disintegration and diffusion can be plotted in which the seekers, groups and networks characteristic of the 1950s and 1960s simply diversify and proliferate radically, indeed almost beyond measure. As a result, in this 'late' period of use, 'New Age' can mean just about anything, as we will see.

'Paradise now':[1] spirituality and the counterculture

The counter culture is a revolt of the unoppressed. It is a response not to constraint, but to openness. It is a search for new interactional norms in the widening, more diffuse margins of postindustrial societies.
(Musgrove 1974: 19)

> Society was subverted ... by a new culture which is alive, exciting, fun, ephemeral, disposable, unified, unpredictable, uncontrollable, lateral, organic and popular.
>
> (Neville 1971: 52)

The extant texts largely conflate 'New Age' with the counterculture of the late 1960s and 1970s,[2] which was itself an untidy aggregate of 'hippie',[3] 'underground'[4] and 'alternative'[5] cultures. A more accurate description is that the counterculture serendipitously incorporated the expression 'New Age' into an already variegated agenda. Using the UK as a case study, it is partly the purpose of this chapter to argue that the counterculture acquired the emblem 'New Age' or its cognate form 'Age of Aquarius' from two principal sources: the subcultural pioneers at Findhorn, Attingham Park, Glastonbury, and elsewhere; and the broader 'occult revival' in popular culture'.[6]

The counterculture had been nourished by a variety of post-war developments. On the one hand anti-nuclear bomb and peace protesters – exemplified by CND (Campaign for Nuclear Disarmament), set up in 1958 and, briefly, the Committee of 100, set up on the back of CND's early successes to practise direct action – represented an unstable coalition of pacifist, anarchist, and Marxist attacks on authority and tradition that peaked in the early 1960s. In this sense the alliance indicated a political response to the Cold War climate of unease and suspicion analogous to the spiritual reactions of the 'New Age' groups discussed earlier. As Marwick (1998: 66) suggests, it also provided a link between the New Left revival of the 1950s and radical student movements in Europe and America in the mid-to-late 1960s. Serious, sustained politics was the exception rather than the norm, however, and Musgrove (1974: 19) is surely correct to see the counterculture as 'an exploratory curriculum, a range of experiences and exposures' rather than a politically revolutionary ideology. This point is amplified in Green's (1998) exhaustive account of the place of drugs, sex and psychotherapeutic experiment in various 'anti-institutions' of the period. The counterculture emerged in part out of a boom in education, employment and consumer confidence, which also fed the popular culture of the 'Swinging Sixties' (Masters 1985). A diffuse anti-authoritarianism, the student experience, widespread affluence: these and other social variables impacted powerfully on Anglo–American culture.

Chief among these was youth, reflecting a 'baby boom' in the populations of the USA and the UK following the Second World War. The titles of some seminal texts make this plain: *The Making of a Counter Culture: Reflections on the Technocratic Society and Its Youthful Opposition* (Roszak 1971), *Playpower* (Neville 1971), *Young Outsiders* (Mills 1973), *Youthquake* (Leech 1976). In the US the Youth International Party briefly emerged: its protagonists, known as Yippies (on the model of 'hippies'), 'extracted their world view from an intense, electrifying generational communion' (Neville 1971: 32–3). In sum, according to Clarke's (1996: 291) testy but succinct summary: 'A conspicuous and noisy youth culture, which had been hotting up for years, came to the boil in the 1960s'. A crucial feature of this youth culture was its tendency to mask traditional social stratification so that now 'styles marked off generations rather than classes' (Clarke 1996: 292). A self-conscious 'youth' constituency effectively became 'an independent social agent', spearheaded by a burgeoning trans-national community of students 'moving and communicating ideas and experiences across frontiers with ease and speed' (Hobsbawm 1995: 324). Demotic and antinomian values marked certain tendencies within this 'global youth culture'; others embraced entrepreneurship and 'the kind of high-spending consumer society long familiar from American films' (Marwick 1982: 114).

So much for the wider cultural background. We are now in a basic position to examine the spirituality of the counterculture and to note the place of the 'New Age' emblem within it. Let us begin with the simplest part of this proposal. How prominent is the expression 'New Age'?

Briefly, not very. Usage is comparatively rare. Certainly Muz Murray, in his seminal alternative magazine *Gandalf's Garden*, based in London, had proclaimed in 1968 that a 'long awaited Dawn of Consciousness' was finally 'glimmering in the minds of New Age Man-to-Come'.[7] And the cognate form 'Aquarian' turns up in the chorus of *Hair* – 'This is the dawning of the Age of Aquarius!' – and in advertisements for the 1969 Woodstock music festival in New York state. But evidence elsewhere is pretty thin. *The Aquarian Guide to Occult, Mystical, Religious, Magical London and around* lists just two explicitly 'New Age' bodies (Strachan 1970: 120–1). A representative countercultural 'mystic' interviewed by Musgrove (1974: 140ff.) acknowledges Egyptian, Buddhist and 'witch' teachers, meditates and uses the *I Ching*, but makes no reference to 'New Age'. Roszak (1971: 140) finds the pages of American underground magazines 'swarming with Christ and the prophets, Zen, Sufism, Hinduism, primitive shamanism, Theosophy, the Left-Handed Tantra' but not, apparently, 'New Age'. The odd 'Aquarian' reference in, for example, Mills (1973) and Leech (1976) cannot make up for this deficiency. The lack of reference in Leech (1976) in particular – an attentive account of 'the spiritual quest among the young' which draws extensively on emic sources – only presses home the point that 'New Age' was a marginal presence in the counterculture, quite insignificant in the heterodox spirituality of the day in comparison with well-documented discourse on, say, consciousness-expansion, drug-induced experiences and various kinds of magic.[8]

Even allowing for a time-lag in the migration of the 'New Age' emblem from the subcultures of Findhorn, Attingham and the Universal Link into the liberal/libertarian counterculture, the evidence of usage is weak. *Self-Exploration* (Saunders 1975), a digest of alternative spiritualities and therapies currently available in England and Wales, has just one explicitly 'New Age', and two 'Aquarian', entries among some two hundred. Furthermore, these three entries are survivals from previous decades, since the 'Meditation Group for the New

Age' is an offshoot of the Alice Bailey work, the 'Aquarian Centre' has as its primary interests the exploration of the Glastonbury Zodiac and ley lines (ibid.: 50) and 'Viewpoint Aquarius' is described as 'a society involved with the esoteric side of UFOs and Theosophy' (ibid.: 59). Another British directory of similar scope, *The Many Ways of Being* adds only two further items to these entries: a 'New Age Education Group', a lending source for audio-tapes, and the 'Bath New Age Centre' (Annett 1976: 268, 270). But since its remit also includes Scotland, *The Many Ways of Being* includes an entry on Findhorn, described as a 'spiritual community trying to demonstrate a "new age" life-style' (ibid.: 131). Note, however, the self-conscious use of inverted commas around the term, a typographical device that appears from the 1970s onwards.

Enough has been said by now to demonstrate that 'New Age' was a marginal emblem in Anglo–American countercultural spirituality in the early 1970s. On the basis of the British evidence it is coinage largely in circles established by an earlier generation of seekers. At the same time our discussion has pointed to a rich mix of spiritual styles available to a large constituency of economically and educationally advantaged, inquisitive and restless young people. For example, *Gandalf's Garden's* base in Chelsea, London, is described as an

> experimental, spiritually hip community evolving a lifestyle and producing a mystical scene magazine, shop and meeting place selling hand-made goods, occult books, exotic teas and health snacks; also free food and free notice board, yoga classes and weekly mantra meditations, talks, gurus, occultists, yogis, seekers for the miraculous, every Friday at 7.30 pm.
>
> (Strachan 1970: 20)

The *Garden's* bustling bazaar of activities, identities and products is reflected in the breathless syntax of this directory entry. But who used the centre? There are many testimonies by the new spiritual seekers. For example, Heelas (1996: 51) himself recalls that

> we did not have a very good idea of what we were looking for. But off we went: perhaps to a favoured farm, located in the Welsh borders, where we would talk of mysteries, take hallucinogens, watch sunsets, use the I Ching or Tarot, listen to The Incredible String Band, read Carlos Castaneda's *The Teachings of Don Juan* or Herman Hesse's *Siddhartha*.

Otis Cook, a veteran from the Korean war, takes this preoccupation with drugs and consciousness to a logical conclusion when he concludes his auto-biographical sketch, 'A Hippie Odyssey', with the affirmation cited at the head of this chapter: 'A guy just wants to practise his religion, just wants to do his thing, man' (Neville 1971: 203).

One contemporary activist informally told me that, among key 'New Age' proponents of the 1980s and 1990s, 'most' used LSD in the 1960s.[9] This makes them in part the heirs of the counterculture, since drug use – particularly cannabis and LSD – is widely agreed to have been a prominent signifier of affiliation (Leech 1976: 29ff., Green 1998: 173ff.). The expansive metabolic effects of cannabis and LSD found affinities with alternative ideologies of spirituality. In Mouledoux's (1972: 118) study of ritual drug use and communal living in the US, for example, daily ingestion of LSD and marijuana was one part of a lifestyle cocktail that also embraced popular discourse on 'astrology, the Tarot, I Ching, Zen, Sufism, Hinduism, rural communes [and] the inadequacies of the contemporary plastic-scientific world'. But a journalist in the American rock music magazine *Rolling Stone* later noted the ambivalence of discourse on spirituality in the counterculture: 'Turning on was a metaphor for becoming enlightened, but it also had a straightforward meaning: having sex and taking drugs'.[10] In other words, there were no sharp boundaries in the emic view between spiritual, sexual and 'psychedelic' practice.

As we see in the ethnographies of Chapters 6 to 8, the spiritual bricolage practised in the counterculture of the late 1960s and early 1970s has remained the staple strategy of spiritual seekers up to the present day. With certain obvious lifestyle exceptions – drug use (although see below), flamboyant dress, de-inhibited language and deportment – it is also characteristic of the more ascetic and disciplined behaviour of the 'New Age' pioneers in the 1950s and early 1960s. What has changed in each instance is the legitimacy of the cultural identity assumed by exponents. To map this crudely, we can say that in the early period, this identity was implicitly subcultural: Govan's group, Trevelyan's 'significant list' and Spangler's 'circuit' understood themselves to be a dissenting but righteous minority within a hegemonic but ignorant mainstream. In the middle period, the stance becomes countercultural: dissidence is still proclaimed, but the processes of wider cultural change that I touched on earlier have the effect of removing adherents from social quarantine and deploying them on a wider popular front of social and generational resistance to the *status quo*. In the final phase the grand narrative of 'alternative' culture as a distinct, even pure, contestatory force collapses as its rhetoric of difference and prescriptions for change are recuperated by popular culture for consumption in the self-service cafeteria of contemporary spirituality. We glimpse this process at work in print later in this chapter and follow its fortunes in the subsequent ethnographies.

Clearly this neat compartmentalisation of subculture, counterculture and popular culture should not be taken too rigidly: there are elements of a common discourse that can surprise hasty closure. For example, there is a functional relationship between drug use and meditation practice. The claim of an interviewee in Tomory (1996: 94) that 'early in the psychedelic era it had become a tradition to trip out under the full moon, when psychic energies were at their most intense' can be juxtaposed profitably with the structured meditation at the full moon devised by Alice Bailey's Lucis Trust (see Chapters 2 and 6). And in an early account of the Findhorn colony, just when it was being extensively settled by members of the counterculture, Rigby and Turner (1972: 76) note that 'the goals of drug-taking have been frequently phrased in terms of "expanding the consciousness", a phrase which is constantly used at Findhorn'. They go on to argue that 'the sense of deep personal relationship with fellow "trippers" is mirrored in the sense of community and group consciousness'.

In other words, there is sufficient cross-generational continuity in discourse and practice to allow us to think in terms of a lineage of spiritual seekers through different periods of time and cultural identities. In the present period, evidence for 'New Age' affiliation is as meagre as that for the wider field of alternative spirituality is plentiful. 'New Age' only begins to permeate the 'cultic milieu' of the 1970s (Campbell 1972) once sufficient numbers of the new generation of seekers have made contact with the earlier generation, in person or in text. This indeed happened, largely at the pioneers' favoured sites, resulting in a modest resurgence of 'New Age' discourse around the turn of the 1980s. By this time, however, 'New Age' had undergone a hermeneutical metamorphosis, as we shall see.

New seekers: the 'baby-boom' generation

Let me put my argument in a nutshell: between around 1967 and 1974 the 'New Age' emblem was passed – like a relay baton – from subcultural pioneers to countercultural baby boomers, undergoing in the process a fundamental transformation in meaning and reference as it passed out of the hands of a supernaturalistic apocalypticism into a this-worldly humanism. But before we consider in detail this hermeneutical shift, we must return to the role of the seeker, since it is the crucial bond between pioneer and youth. In Chapter 2 I picked out the function of this role in the creation and transmission of alternative spirituality in the interwar period, and Chapters 3 and 4 followed in some detail the quests and travels of key players in 'New Age' networks of the 1950s and 1960s. Now we must take into account a new generation of seekers: those who reached early adulthood in the late 1960s and early 1970s and hence were poised as young adults to take maximum advantage of the expansion of education, the generous economy and the gamut of new experiences informing Anglo–American culture at this time. It follows that these new seekers must have been born in the late 1940s and early 1950s – that is, in the immediate post-war period. Indeed, Roof (1993: 1, 2) has pointed out that those born between 1946 and 1964 now constitute about one third of the US's entire population. A strong element of religious questioning and exper-imentation has been characteristic of this 'baby boom' cohort whom Roof (1993) characterises as 'a generation of seekers'. This cohort has reconfigured American religiosity from the ground up in response to the unprecedentedly broad range of options, or 'pluralisation of life-worlds' (Berger *et al.* 1974: 62ff.), characteristic of the contemporary world. As Roof (1993: 8) puts it: 'Baby boomers have to discover for themselves what gives their lives meaning'.

One of the biographies which Roof adduces as evidence of this new generation's seeking proclivities is Mollie Stone's. In her view, 'life is a journey in which you learn from your experiences and grow as a person' (ibid.: 21). Significantly, her career begins in the counterculture, where she describes spending 'whole days in Central Park getting stoned'. She describes this as 'lots of fun as well as a spiritual experience' (ibid.: 22). Roof (ibid.) continues:

> Mollie has been on a spiritual quest ever since. She has explored many
> of the spiritual and human potential alternatives of the post-Sixties
> period: holistic health, macrobiotics, Zen Buddhism, Native American
> rituals, New Age in its many versions. . . . She's an explorer down many
> religious paths.

Notice here that 'New Age in its many versions' is, correctly, merely one of several 'religious paths' rather than a generic term. Apart from this small but significant detail, Mollie's explorations strongly recall the hybridity of *Gandalf's Garden* in London or Paul Heelas's account of drugs and mysticism in rural Wales cited earlier.

Her biography also has affinities with the career of a prominent British activist, William Bloom (b. 1948). Bloom grew up in a similarly secularised post-war household. In the 1960s, he tells us, 'I grew my hair long, wore an earring, and surrendered to flower power' (Bloom 1991: 1). He contributed to the English 'underground' publication *International Times* (or *IT*) and wrote a novel about 'swinging' London called *Softly, Children, I'm Coming* (Bloom 1971), revealingly described on the paperback cover as 'today's sizzling dish: sex, violence, drugs, the generation gap'. Bloom has described the counterculture's general resonance with alternative spirituality:

> Through its psychedelic experiences and its exploration of eastern
> and shamanic techniques for altering consciousness, counter-culture
> supported the notion of an invisible reality; and through its alignment
> with surrealism and situationism it also sought to create events which
> altered perspective and experience.
>
> (Bloom 1992: 3)

In a project which exemplified this cross-over, Bloom embarked upon a six-month retreat near the foremost beat-hippie destination of Marrakesh, Morocco, in 1972 (Bloom 1992). It is surely no accident that the fifteenth-century ritual he undertook here had previously been attempted by Aleister Crowley (1989: 184ff.) at the turn of the century: Crowley was a posthumous guru to the counterculture, and at least two versions of his memoirs discussing the ritual had been published by the early 1970s. However, Bloom nowhere mentions Crowley, preferring to emphasise his reading of a very different guru, Alice Bailey, from whom, he says, 'I absorbed the term "New Age" ' (Bloom 1991: 2).

Innumerable variations upon the spiritual quests undertaken by Mollie Stone and William Bloom were pursued by other young Europeans and Americans entranced by the potential of a radically *different* spirituality to expand the horizons of their everyday lives. Between 1965 and 1975 many thousands made the adventurous journey overland to India on what became known as the 'hippie trail' (Tomory 1996: xi). But for the veteran seeker, India was the tip of the iceberg: Muz Murray, founder of *Gandalf's Garden*, had previously spent 'seven years of vagabondage around the world . . . sifting the sands of many spiritual cultures for guidance on the inner way' (Murray 1989: 7, x).

As we shall see in the following chapters, this post-war 'generation of seekers' now makes up the bulk of new spiritual enthusiasts in the early twenty-first century. For example, in an important empirical survey of subscribers to the British magazine *Kindred Spirit*, Rose (1998: 8) found that more than half of his respondents – twice the equivalent proportion of the national population – belong to this broad cohort. The careers of these new seekers represent virtuosic variations upon a common generational experience that at its most intense mixed drug use, alternative spiritualities, communal and neo-tribal social forms, and extensive international travel. But 'New Age' remains a relatively rare rallying cry, and generally only where contact has been established with the pioneers, either in person (at Findhorn, say) or through their texts (Bailey is the obvious example). Given also the correlation I am establishing between generational cohort and the flavour or style of spiritual practice, there are significant implications here for the long-term strength and vitality of 'New Age' as a meaningful brand of spirituality, which leads me to press my argument against a 'New Age movement' ever more forcefully. And there is still another factor to take into account: the hermeneutical shift from emblem to idiom.

From apocalypse to self-realisation: the shift in 'New Age' hermeneutics

Thirty-seven years later, I see the New Age as an idea, not as an event.
(Spangler 1996: 55)

Your feeling of uplifted consciousness is the start of great changes that will be felt by each individual everywhere.
(Eileen Caddy's guidance, Christmas Eve, 1967:
in Caddy 1998: 122)

We have seen how, for much of the 1960s, 'New Age' was a viable emblem only within certain restricted networks of alternative spirituality. Its adherents were largely middle-aged, even elderly, and numerically fairly static, if not actually in decline. Furthermore, these networks shouldered the burden of their sensitives' catastrophic prophecies on top of the psychological stresses of 'cold' war and the post Second World War 'culture of austerity' (Marwick 1982: 78). The result was a restrained, formalised code of behaviour and aesthetic. Thus in 1967, a year in which a 'summer of love' was celebrated in San Francisco, London and other metropolitan centres, most of the 'New Age' pioneers were expecting nuclear fall-out and the evacuation of the planet. And in marked contrast to the popular hippie maxim 'never trust anyone over thirty',[11] an older age cohort dominated. The three Findhorn founders, Anthony Brooke and George Trevelyan were all aged between fifty and sixty; Alice Bailey, Sheena Govan and Liebie Pugh were dead. With very few exceptions, the pioneers of 'New Age' represented a generation born around the time of the 1914–18 war or even earlier, and in many cases belonged to the upper echelons of that same staid – 'square' – élite that the new generation of seekers was angrily spurning. In dramatic contrast, the English counterculture throughout 1967 was drawn by a different kind of UFO: London's briefly notorious 'U.F.O.' ('underground freak out') club, a large venue for live music, slide projections and psychedelic mayhem (Neville 1971: 24–6). 'Love-ins' were held at worthy English landmarks like the Alexandra Palace and Woburn Abbey (ibid.: 26) and the Woodstock festival in New York state – billed as an 'Aquarian' event – attracted some half a million young people in 1969 (Marwick 1998: 497).

Also in 1967, certain prophecies and their outcomes set in motion a process of hermeneutical reflection in 'New Age' circles that indicated a need both for new recruits and a more affirmatory, empowering message. The forecasts of imminent planetary 'changes' were reaching a crescendo. Eileen Caddy (1988: 121) noted 'a great many predictions from all sorts of sources that the world was going to end'. Gildas's group in England prepared for 'the imminent spring cleaning of the world' (White and Swainson 1971: 91). In Denmark, followers of the Universal Link built a nuclear shelter.[12] And Liebie Pugh, recently-deceased, warned the Heralds of the New Age in New Zealand, via spirit contact, that 'much sorrow will be seen at this time'.[13]

Some of these prophecies were couched in the figurative language of Christian adventism. For example, Monica Parish urgently passed on to Findhorn

> wonderful confirmations of the Glorious joy and *total* changes about to burst on the world. . . . Please share with *all* your group that we may all keep total vigil until His coming within 40 days now, and do exactly His will in this most vital period.[14]

Others used an abstract, quasi-Nietzschean language of 'energy' or 'power' that reformulated in vernacular speech elements of Prime Minister Harold Wilson's pervasive sloganeering on the 'white heat of technology'. At Findhorn, Eileen

Caddy received detailed instructions that she, her husband Peter, and her friend Joanie Hartnell-Beavis (Liebie Pugh's former secretary) were to go to a local hill at midnight on Christmas Eve, 1967. This they did, and stood there in a circle, holding hands. Eileen Caddy's guidance had foretold a tremendous but controlled 'force of power' that would flow through them all. She described her experience like this:

> I felt my body fill with light. I began to tremble violently and then collapsed, unconscious ... As I came to, I felt an absolute oneness with Peter, with Joanie and with the entire universe. I felt I was plugged into the cosmic power source and that we three had provided some sort of anchor or earthing point.
>
> (Caddy 1988: 121–2)

But there was no cataclysm, no apocalypse, no evacuation: the world was not swept away. 'Exhilarated' but very much with their feet on the ground, Eileen Caddy and her companions returned to their caravan. Her guidance subsequently told her 'nothing has gone wrong. It is simply that man has misinterpreted what has been prophesied'. In other words, the anticipated 'cosmic power' had indeed been 'released', but in a hidden, occult form rather than publicly and incontrovertibly. In the US in the same period – and with apparently no prior connection to Findhorn or other 'New Age' activists – an academic historian, William Thompson (1975: 158), reported a similar experience of inner certitude that encouraged him to leave his job: 'my meditation was quieter and deeper than it had ever been before. I had no words, voices or concepts to deal with what was going on in me ... but I could feel my life turning'. The American 'New Age' activist, David Spangler (see below), was convinced: 'By Christmas 1967', he wrote in *Revelation: the Birth of a New Age*, 'the New Age had been born' (Spangler 1977: 127). In Spangler's reading, the 'New Age' was no longer a future state. It was here, now, a state of mind triggered by experiences of ecstasy and illumination such as Eileen Caddy had experienced.

But not everyone was so sure. Early in 1968 a letter sent out by Anthony Brooke's Universal Foundation registered widespread uncertainty: 'Letters and reports are still being received from those who are making claims that the prophecy was, or was not, fulfilled, according to their consciousness and under-standing'.[15] That final clause pinpoints the crux of the matter, for it allows entirely subjective and localised exegeses to supplant the hitherto consensual forecast. Not only this, but the terminology in which the revelation is couched dramatically loses its emotional charge. As the letter continues: 'At Christmas, 1967, the Earth reached a significant turning point. We enter 1968 with a new consciousness'. The mild phrase 'turning point' and the psychologistic concept of 'new consciousness' replace the passionate rhetoric of a 'great cleansing' and a 'Second Coming', which we saw typified earlier discourse. An altogether more mundane and incremental series of changes in personal understanding and attitudes is implied in this modest language, which undermines the hitherto dominant hermeneutic of global drama and group salvation. The Universal Foundation was not alone in trying out this interpretation: we followed Peter Caddy's patient attempts to transmit the new understanding to Lanakila Brandt in Hawaii at the end of the last chapter. Similarly, in England the Gildas group understood that a 'final release' through war or atomic error was no longer likely (White and Swainson 1971: 101). As Peter Caddy (1996: 262) briskly remarked: 'All that had been prophesied in the early years was no longer true'.

A new consensus began to emerge in which 'New Age' was recast as a humanistic project of spiritual growth and self-realisation in the here-and-now. As Peter Caddy had presciently written from Findhorn in the spring of 1967 to Sheila Walker in Edinburgh:

> The sort of New Age group that we are pioneering is a group where each individual has come along a different path. . . . Each one must find out for themselves their own contribution . . . and not follow in the footsteps of another.[16]

And yet there is contradiction in Caddy's position, since a few months later – as we glimpsed in the last chapter – Caddy berates Walker for casting doubt on the authority of Eileen Caddy's guidance at Findhorn, a directive that undermines the *laissez-faire* approach to spirituality advocated above. But we should not expect to find in popular religious practice a sustained and systematic theology and attempts to do so inevitably distort the *ad hoc* reality of 'lay' spirituality in particular. Caddy's different strategies of legitimation may also reflect his own uncertainty regarding how to position himself – and Findhorn – now that the old prophecies were not, after all, being fulfilled, or at least not in the expected fashion.

In any case, a substantial degree of 'doom and gloom' (Caddy 1988: 121) and deferred expectations persisted. In late 1967, in classic 'New Age' prophetic mode, Gildas had announced: 'The day will soon dawn when all tears shall be wiped away, all sufferings appeased, all questions answered, and man shall live in peace with man in the age of gold' (White and Swainson 1971: 94). Yet in 1970 the day of reckoning apparently remained as elusive as ever and Gildas now advised: 'In many ways the changes are beginning, but as yet the time is not ready for the final acceleration to the moment of change' (ibid.: 106). A sense of insecurity – of wobbling on the cusp of change – haunts this transitional period in 'New Age' hermeneutics. David Spangler, who seemed quite sure that the New Age 'had been born' at the end of 1967, proclaims in the very next paragraph that 1970 is actually the date when the 'New Age energies' would 'begin to descend' (Spangler 1977: 127). And clearly the qualification in that last clause leaves the matter open to endless deferring, for when will this 'descent' be complete, and according to whose criteria?

Thus ran various intense attempts to fashion a popular hermeneutic to explain this risky but electric turn in 'New Age' prophecy. That this was attempted at all signalled awareness of a changing culture in the world at large and the fact that the very survival of an empirical collectivity to transmit the pioneers' experiences appeared now to be at stake. Consider the British profile of 'New Age' towards the close of the 1960s. The Findhorn colony at this point consisted of just twenty residents, many of whom were senior citizens (Rigby and Turner 1972: 82). Liebie Pugh's death had deflated the Universal Link, and her secretary had moved to Findhorn. George Trevelyan was poised to retire from Attingham Park. The Universal Foundation remained effectively a two-person agency. Yet at the same time, public interest in all things 'spiritual', 'esoteric' and 'magical' was growing sharply, particularly among the 'baby-boom' generation, as we have seen. The pioneers could not escape this fact.

In each of the years 1969 and 1970 Findhorn, for example, received some six hundred visitors, and by 1972 it had grown sixfold in numbers to accommodate around one hundred and twenty residents (Walker 1994: 59). It now palpably projected identity and purpose: a letter of Peter Caddy's in June 1972 to Alice Bailey's Lucis Trust in London claimed that the colony was now 'in touch' with 'at least' five hundred non-governmental organisations – an extraordinary change from the traffic in mediums just five years earlier.[17] The largest proportion of new residents at Findhorn were young people. Significantly, one resident's account notices a gap in residents' age cohorts 'between the early 30s and the late 50s',[18] which correlates with the distinctive generational profiles predicted by my argument on 'New Age' demography.

A qualitative distinction that supports this observation is made by Rigby (1974: 113), who contrasted residents from the 'spiritual/mystical wing of the international youth culture' with those from the 'relatively affluent middle class' previously involved in 'religious and esoteric groups such as the Theosophists'. In any case, in 1968 Peter Caddy (1996: 289) remembers with evident satisfaction 'a stream of hippies, hitchhiking to Findhorn from the South' and he considered Muz Murray's visit in 1969 from *Gandalf's Garden* 'a very significant contact'.[19] But he also alludes to potential rivalry, couched in terms of 'the generation gap': 'The hippies felt that they *were* the New Age, and that anybody else, over the age of twenty-five, who dressed normally or had short hair were of the old and couldn't move into the new' (ibid.: 286). There could be dramatic attitudinal and behavioural differences between the early 'sensitives' and the post-war 'freaks'. Caddy records that the latter 'had to learn that dirty, torn and slovenly clothes were not acceptable at Findhorn' – nor elsewhere, for when he introduced John Michell, a young writer on Glastonbury mysteries, to Major Bruce MacManaway, founder of the Westbank Centre in Fife (see Chapter 8), MacManaway 'looked John up and down and said, "Would you like a bath?"' (ibid.: 288). Eileen Caddy (1988: 131) notes firmly that visitors who treated Findhorn as a 'hippy commune complete with long hair, dirt and drugs' were 'sent on their way', although Craig Gibsone, who made a successful

118

transition from the drug culture to Findhorn leadership, remembers marijuana being grown and smoked clandestinely in the 1970s (Riddell 1991: 212). But when Eileen Caddy confessed difficulties 'dealing with physical sex because of the intensity of my inner life in meditation' (Caddy 1988: 137), her attitude could not have contrasted more sharply with the 'happy, hippie playful sex' (Neville 1971: 224–5) of the counterculture.[20]

The paths of sensitives and freaks also converged elsewhere. George Trevelyan held a special gathering for sixty-five of the latter at Attingham Park (Caddy 1996: 289), while in California, Ellwood (1973: 105) notes 'young people with long hair and beards' attending full moon meditation groups alongside those 'in conventional dress'. Back in Britain, Nicholas Saunders' hand-book *Self Exploration* warns readers that the School of Universal Philosophy and Healing in London is 'very sensitive to psychic forces being upset, and had to ask drug users to leave', but that the Aquarian Centre in Glastonbury is more laid-back, with meetings attended by 'a happy mixture of old ladies and young freaks' (Saunders 1975: 61, 50).

The latter entry invites inquiry into contemporary change in Glastonbury's spiritual culture. In 1969 a *Guardian* correspondent wrote:

> Hundreds of young people – hippies, poets, mystics, weirdies and sundry unclassifiables – have hitch-hiked and tramped into the town from all over Britain, Europe and even America . . . looking for 'vibrations'.
>
> (Cited in Leech [1976: 83])

A special issue of *Gandalf's Garden* was devoted to Glastonbury (White 1974: 133) and a music, arts and crafts festival, the Glastonbury Fayre (forerunner of the popular Glastonbury Festival), was staged in 1971, attracting an audience of some twenty thousand (Hexham 1983: 4). Hexham also notes 'an increasing number of young people' in Glastonbury 'on what they claimed was a "spiritual quest" '. These 'freaks' were taken under the wing of a segment of the resident community he calls the 'spirituals':

> The spirituals tended to be sympathetic to the freaks, seeing in them fellow pilgrims seeking religious truth . . . they hoped to exercise a steadying influence upon them. . . . They also told the freaks their own particular views on Glastonbury and its religious significance, as well as suggesting and lending more general books.
>
> (ibid.: 4)

Hexham's 'spirituals' and the 'sensitives' of the present book are clearly cognates, as are their respective relationships with the new seekers. If they, for their part, were drawn to the spiritual portfolios and experiences of the 'New Age' veterans, the latter increasingly needed the physical energy and enthusiasm of the younger generation if their legacy was to be consolidated and transmitted.

In short, this was a transmission in oral history and popular textual hermeneutics between Great War and post Second World War generations: between those who had expected the 'New Age' as an eschatological future, a 'world to come', and those who saw it as a realised present, a 'paradise now'. These two positions define a spectrum of interpretations of the emblem that would soon become available in popular culture.

At Findhorn the 'paradise now', or 'heaven on earth', option of the new seekers was boosted by the arrival in 1970 of David Spangler (b. 1945) and Myrtle Glines, who had previously been active in the North American 'new age subculture' (Spangler 1984: 25). Riddell (1991: 78) describes Spangler as 'the last of the Findhorn Community's founding figures' and his three years' residence in the colony correlates with the international shift in 'New Age' hermeneutics. Spangler formalised the colony's educational agenda: in addition to teaching and lecturing there and elsewhere on the 'New Age' circuit, he published several books and pamphlets while living at Findhorn that formed the basis of an expanding curriculum and generally propagated the message of Findhorn as a 'New Age' community. Meanwhile his partner Myrtle Glines offered practical skills for dealing with the inevitable stresses of colony life: Caddy (1996: 308) describes her as 'expert at dealing with and counselling people'. In sum, the partnership of Spangler and Glines supplied a down-to-earth frame of reference that emphasised the grounded interpersonal skills required by a growing community of mixed age cohorts and social etiquette.

In the process they opened a way into the colony for a diffuse discourse on 'human potential'. In the tradition of the American 'T-group' or training-group methodology mentioned in Chapter 3, this privileged the expression of feelings over emotional reticence, bodily awareness over ratiocination, and a general process-oriented approach to interpersonal relationships.[21] The result was increasingly a preoccupation with the inter-subjective experiences of individuals in everyday life, which suited the here-and-now focus of this new 'New Age'. I later heard long-term Findhorn resident Nick Rose compare Findhorn to a theatre without an audience where everyone is the cast: 'it is a hall of mirrors', he continued, 'a place to meet yourself round every corner, in every object and every person you meet'.[22] 'Experience Week', the standard induction into the Findhorn lifestyle from the 1980s to the present, which I describe in Chapter 7, is steeped in this approach.

Spangler and Glines were particularly keen to tackle the lingering notion of 'New Age' as some future cataclysmic revelation. Spangler (1984: 28) considered that such an interpretation

> shifted accountability away from individual persons and onto the back of vast impersonal forces, whether astrological, extraterrestrial or divine. It took away an individual's sense of being a cocreator with history, of being involved in a process of conscious and participatory evolution.

His solution was to drop the eschatology altogether. Peter Caddy (1996: 309) explains:

> His idea of what we were doing at Findhorn had nothing to do with maintaining 'a kind of survival centre, waiting for the coming of space brothers, waiting for apocalypse, and waiting for the New Age'. Instead we should be proclaiming that the New Age had already arrived.

As Spangler (1977: 181) later wrote: 'Revelation is not a great Being telling Man what to do. It is his own being seeking to release itself'.

But while challenging received wisdoms, Spangler also made sure to align himself with certain 'traditional' sources of authority. Soon after arriving at Findhorn, for example, he channelled 'Limitless Love and Truth', a source of guidance previously associated with the Universal Link, as we saw in Chapter 4. Just as Hartnell-Beavis's move to Findhorn symbolised the material transfer of allegiance from a fading 'centre of light' to an emergent leader, so did Spangler's connection with 'Limitless Love and Truth' subtly consolidate Findhorn's ascendancy. In general, however, channelling at Findhorn as elsewhere was gradually changing, becoming demythologised and democratised in line with the humanistic tendencies of human potential discourse. For example, as the 1970s progressed, Spangler's preferred channelling source was no longer 'the Christ', a 'Master', or even his 'Higher Self', the spiritual authorities that had previously guided him. He turned increasingly towards a source he carefully describes as 'not a guide' but a 'friend and coworker' who advocated 'mutual empowerment and freedom from dependency'. The simple first name by which this guide is known encapsulates the democratic turn: 'John' is a suitably plain, homely name for this domesticated arena of everyday spiritual work (Spangler 1984: 67).[23]

In line with the egalitarian flavour of 'John', the earlier *primus inter pares* model of illuminated leadership, wherein Govan, the Caddys, the Heralds and others rotated special status in a relentless traffic of mediums and messages, gave way to an ideology of diffuse, universalised charisma. Gnosis and spiritual power were for everyone: the ideal 'New Age' community or society would be an aggregate of individuals working together in enlightened self-interest. Although this had always been implicit in the talk of 'finding one's own path' and actively 'seeking truth', it was now directly and vigorously articulated. At Findhorn, the practice ceased whereby Eileen Caddy's guidance was read out to the community at morning meditation as a blueprint for the day ahead. Now her guidance wisely told her: 'Let go, stand back and allow all to live a life guided and directed by Me' (Caddy 1988: 166). It was now up to the individual to demonstrate her own direction. This was a radical hermeneutic shift that, while functionally aligning Findhorn with the individualism – the 'doing your own thing' – of youth and counterculture, amounted to a strong interiorisation of

'New Age' and thereby drove it 'underground' once more: in effect, for good. Bloom (1991: xvi) captures this modulation some years later when he alludes to 'a thousand different ways of exploring inner reality' and advises: 'Go where your intelligence and intuition lead you. Trust yourself'. Such radical egalitarianism was of course also in some tension with the oligarchic discourse of the pioneers that was (in theory at least) wary of individualism, considering this a manifestation of the unruly ego which should be subordinate to the spiritual discipline of the group.

The success of this humanisation of 'New Age' through a radical hermeneutic shift in its referent and a corresponding democratisation and domestication of its sources of authority can be gauged from Riddell's (1991: 78) remark that, when Spangler departed in 1974, Findhorn 'had oriented itself towards spiritual education, and had a much more youthful personnel'. If we take seriously Bloom's (1991: 2) assessment of Findhorn as 'the most important New Age centre on the planet', then by extrapolation this shift becomes a model for the international 'New Age' community. The gist of the shift is that a 'world-denying' eschatology gives way to a 'world-affirming' idiom of human potential: apocalypse gives way to self-realisation. The turn to subjectivity encoded in this new 'revelation' (now very much in the lower case) renders it a subtle, adaptable and genuinely popular cultural resource. But this comes at the price of relinquishing the last chance of finding a social basis for a 'New Age' movement. For when David Spangler (1977: 181) writes whimsically of one's 'own New Age seeking to blend with the New Age of others', it is clear that there can now be as many 'New Ages' as there are 'New Agers'.

'New Age' now: popular taxonomies

> The 'new age' label has in recent years been slapped on record sleeves, books, style magazines, sections of newspapers, fashion accessories, nightclub walls and advertising billboards.
>
> (Button and Bloom 1992: 16)

Since the 1970s, a populist and resilient 'spirituality' (whether or not it is labelled 'New Age') has attracted increasing numbers of seekers who are disengaging from traditional religious institutions while continuing to congregate on an *ad hoc* basis to sift and mix religious ideas and techniques. In this sense the spiritual cocktail at Findhorn – where 'followers of Bhagwan Shree Rajneesh worked next to followers of Madame Blavatsky' and 'British psychic healers sat in morning meditation with American PhDs in philosophy' – is rightly seen by Clark (1992: 100) as manifesting the 'plastic quality' of 'New Age' (ibid.: 104). At the same time, what 'New Age' now signifies varies considerably. Quite different representations have emerged ranging from 'religion for yuppies' (Tulloch 1991: 213) to 'New Age travellers' (Lowe and

Shaw 1993, Hetherington 2000). It would require a separate study altogether to chart recent 'spins' on the emblem, which in any case differ only in their degree of hermeneutic plasticity from the case investigated here. Nevertheless, I will now indicate a little of the heterogeneity of the 'New Age' subject in the 1980s and 1990s by way of introducing the ethnographies of Chapters 6 to 8.

I touched on the etic shortcomings of the taxon 'New Age Movement' in Chapter 1 and I return to the subject in Chapter 9, so I will say no more here. A slightly less reifying term is 'the New Age' (for example, employed socio-logically by Barker 1994) which appropriately conveys the idea of a 'pool' or 'milieu' of activity that has no particular end other than to manifest the creativity and resourcefulness of its actors. However, since it is unclear exactly when one is 'in' or 'out' of this pool, or indeed how it is constructed and where it is located in the first place, ontological and spatial confusions persist. Both 'the New Age Movement' and 'the New Age', then, are terms that subordinate passionate emic voices to a false etic category.

On the other hand, there is still some emic usage of the emblem. 'New Age' organisations and individuals certainly exist, although by no means as thick on the ground as popular opinion has it, and their exception only proves a general rule. As we will see in Chapter 6, the Alice Bailey projects are one such source, if now somewhat muted. The Aetherius Society, mentioned in Chapter 3 in connection with UFOs, is another. Since the 1950s, this body has incorporated 'New Age' into an eclectic programme of healing, self-development and ufology, describing itself in leaflets and flyers I obtained at holistic health fairs in Scotland as 'an International Spiritual Brotherhood which teaches and practises New Age Wisdom' and which is 'dedicated to creating a New Age on earth'. Among individuals, William Bloom has publicly (if inconsistently) affiliated himself with the term. During a talk I attended at Findhorn in 1995, Bloom declared himself 'a self-confessed New Ager'. 'I'm happy to associate myself with the phrase', he said, 'it feels great!'[24] However, when I asked him the following year at an 'Alternatives' evening in London about the appro-priateness of the term 'New Age' to delineate a broad range of contemporary spiritualities, Bloom now thought it only 'as good a term as any'.[25] For Bloom, as for others less prominent or prolific, 'New Age' would appear to be not so much a uniformly-understood emblem or code to nail one's spiritual colours to (as it certainly did function in the 1950s and 1960s) but merely one of a proliferating supply of contemporary spiritual tags and signs. In this sense 'New Age' may rise and fall in the spiritual stock market, and its recent decline does not necessarily obviate future revival. A case in point here is the career of the term on the holistic healing circuit. Vic Spence, organiser of a 'Mystic, Body, Mind and Soul' fair in Glasgow in 1995 told me that 'New Age' had 'hippy-ish' connotations but that the qualifier 'alternative' – as in alternative health or alternative spirituality – also 'gives the wrong idea'. He favoured 'new consciousness' or 'holistic' as an appropriate umbrella term. This distrust of

'New Age' was shared by the bookshop and accessories supplier, Body and Soul. Established in Edinburgh in 1988, the shop also organises health fairs in Scotland and north-east England. When I first visited their premises in October 1994, the proprietor was adamant that the shop would not call itself 'New Age' as this was 'more of an American term' and 'misleading'. Despite this earlier disavowal, a co-proprietor at a Body and Soul health fair in Stirling in January 2000 told me that the bookshop staff themselves now followed a 'New Age lifestyle' and that 'New Age' was being quietly but proudly reclaimed as a spiritual tag, much like 'queer' among homosexuals.

This indeterminate picture is replicated in publications that have repeatedly been invoked as founding texts of an eponymous movement. One or two of these in the 1970s did indeed promote the emblem, most notably David Spangler's *Revelation: the Birth of a New Age* (1977), from Scotland, and Mark Satin's *New Age Politics: Healing Self and Society* (1978), from Canada. Although Spangler's concerns are theosophical–metaphysical and Satin's secular–humanistic, Spangler would surely agree with Satin's (1978: 153) basic thesis, namely: 'If we want to change North America in a New Age direction, then we're going to have to begin with our selves [*sic*]'. If the limited circulation of Satin's self-published book belied his expansive rhetoric, this was not the case with *The Aquarian Conspiracy: Personal and Social Transformation in the 1980s* (Ferguson 1982), which was issued by a mainstream publisher and brought a hitherto subcultural term – 'Aquarian' – into the public arena. The author's explanation for her choice of this term is immediately instructive: 'I was drawn to the symbolic power of the pervasive dream in our popular culture: that after a dark, violent age, the Piscean, we are entering a millennium of love and light' (Ferguson 1982: 19). Technically, there is only one 'New Age' entry in the entire index. But Ferguson's characterisation of the networked structure of a very broad field of practice fits Alice Bailey's vision and post-1970s American practice alike. According to Ferguson, small groups 'networking and pamphlet-eering', 'little clusters and loose networks' and a 'turnabout in consciousness of a critical number of individuals' are now significant variables in popular and business cultures (Ferguson 1982: 24–6).

Hence *The Aquarian Conspiracy* traces the recent legitimation in Anglo–American popular culture of previously marginal social forms and identities. For example, the former American president Bill Clinton was dubbed a 'New Age president' for attending family therapy sessions and a purported 'search for the inner self'.[26] And Mikhail Gorbachev, former Soviet premier, has reportedly called for 'an integrated universal consciousness' to generate 'spiritual communion and rebirth for mankind'.[27] Similar processes have been at work in British culture, not least in the ranks of the aristocracy and celebrity culture: for example, Diana, Princess of Wales, was regularly involved with therapists and healers operating in a 'New Age' idiom (Heelas 1999, Woodhead 1999). And the success story of 1980s entrepreneurship was an international cosmetics franchise called The Body Shop, promoting holistic values to its franchisees and customers. In founder Anita Roddick's memoir of her business success, a handful of phrases – 'enlightened capitalism', 'green consumers' – hint at an emancipatory consumerism, while the word 'global' is said to have a 'multicultural and spiritual tone' (Roddick 1991: 253). Her closing chapter is entitled 'Towards the New Age?' (Roddick 1991: 239ff.) – although note the indeterminacy of that final question mark.

Related to these processes of cultural drift and dilution is the vague generic status acquired by 'New Age': it becomes a catch-all label. In popular use such inclusivity is relatively unproblematic and not particularly interesting in itself. But what if referential specificity and comparative analysis are required? Anthony Brooke's lay logic, like Peter Caddy's earlier hermeneutical equivocation, demonstrates the pitfalls in uncritically transferring emics into etics, for Brooke recalls that he used the term 'until the proliferation of its use in all manner of ways came to divest it of any specific meaning'.[28] As we have seen, the early networks produced apocalyptic forecasts that were quite specific in date, place and agency. This is the gist of the problem: 'New Age' slips in the blink of an eye from a historically specific *noun* to an indicative *attribute*. A similar dilution of impact obtains when an anodyne cognate replaces 'New Age', as in the titles of Adams's (1982) *New Times Network* or Peter Caddy's (1996) subtitle *Memoirs of a Man for the New Millennium*. The confusion of 'new times' and 'new millennium' with everyday figures of speech may be designed to help smuggle a message into popular discourse but, again, at the cost of losing referential specificity and hence political potency.

The emblem acquires fresh connotations in another directory, *The Whole Person Catalogue* (Considine 1992). This publication claims to be serving 'the Holistic health/New Age field' and includes a short section on what it calls 'the "New Age"', but again, notice the uncertainty and self-consciousness signalled by the forward slash and inverted commas of these respective typographical formulations. But *The Whole Person Catalogue* also carries a large advertisement for a London nightclub that dramatically repackages many practices associated with the 'New Age' idiom into a complete contemporary leisure experience:

SEED
IS FOR DREAMERS

London's leading **New Age** club '**SEED**' offers a total experience. No other club in Britain features **Live New Age Bands** from around the world every week, plus **brain machines**, **Shiatsu/massage** and introductions to fascinating **therapies**. **SEED** reaches all parts of the **Mind**, **Body** and **Spirit**.

As you step into the club **TASTE** the psychoactive guarana-based Brain Punch, **LIE BACK AND SAMPLE** the Brain Machines, **FEEL** the gentle healing touch of **Shiatsu**, **DELVE** into your future with **Tarot**, **crystal healing**, or even **Hopi ear candles**. **IMMERSE** in ambient sounds, **NETWORK** with guest mystics, musicians, artists, therapists, film-makers and other fascinating explorers of the new millenia [*sic*] and transformation.

(ibid.: n.p.)

Such an uncomplicated invitation to sensuous pleasure under the aegis of 'New Age' would have taken the pioneers aback but was not atypical of alternative spirituality in the 1990s. In England, a programme of talks by William Bloom is described as 'an enjoyable introduction to the inner world of energies and consciousness . . . informative and fun'.[29] And at the book launch of *The Christ Sparks* (Bloom 1995), which I attended at Findhorn in 1995, Bloom described the 'ease, fun, simplicity and playfulness' that accompanied his composition of the text, ending the launch by taking his audience through a guided meditation in which we were required to visualise a 'smile' opening out in our chests and spreading throughout our bodies.

Similarly, the well-established 'Alternatives' programme of events in central London promises a 'relaxed and friendly atmosphere' in which 'to taste the best'.[30] Back at Findhorn, a trade-marked product called the 'Transformation Game' has been marketed since 1978. Its inventor describes it as a 'fun and complex boardgame' which 'offers a playful yet substantial way of under-standing and gracefully transforming the way you play your life' (Inglis 1992: viii). Further afield, Skyros has offered holidays 'for the mind, the body and the spirit' at its Greek island centres since 1979, and more recently at its winter site on Tobago in the Caribbean. The company describes itself as 'world leader in alternative holidays' and provides holidays with holistic, spiritual and expressive content like 'Life Transformation and Self-Healing', 'Opening Your Heart' and 'Reiki Healing', in addition to more familiar holiday pursuits of swimming, socialising and sunbathing.[31]

Back in the UK one can browse for books and small ritual items in shops such as Watkins in London, Gothic Image in Glastonbury, Body and Soul in Edinburgh, or the Phoenix Shop at Findhorn. Storm (1991: 1) neatly captures their ambience:

The air will be lightly scented with incense and aromatherapy oils, the talk will be hushed, even reverent, and a taped cassette of waves lapping on a beach, or perhaps some Tibetan chanting, will be gently playing in the background. A noticeboard will be swamped with information on forthcoming events, from rebirthing courses to sacred dance classes, Tarot readings, meditation sessions and holidays to the pyramids. There may well be a couple of stands displaying crystal or Celtic jewellery, and another of New Age magazines. The books themselves will cover every imaginable esoteric, religious and occult tradition – as well as many freshly concocted spiritual paths.

The 'New Age' idiom can also crop up surprisingly in everyday encounters and conversations. In the course of researching this book I had many casual encounters with spiritual practitioners in very ordinary contexts. On the Stirling university campus one August lunchtime in 1995 I chatted with an Open University summer school tutor in his mid-thirties who had just returned from the Osho ashram in Poona. He produced a double-ended crystal from his shirt pocket and asked me to put it against my 'third eye' and see what happened, then explained in great detail his project to create an 'electronic buddhafield' in cyberspace to link up international spiritual colonies. On the train from Edinburgh to Lancaster in 1996 to give a paper on 'New Age' at an academic conference, I happened to sit beside a woman in her late forties. She told me she was involved in spiritual healing and showed me her pack of crystal healing cards – small aluminium rectangles in bright colours, impregnated with crushed crystals. She also practised astrology and was studying James Redfield's *The Celestine Prophecy* (1994), a popular text of the 1990s whose principal teaching – that there are 'no coincidences in life' – she used to explain the significance of our own meeting on the train that day. In 1997 I was surprised to find that an avowedly 'New Age' shop had opened in a small arcade in Stirling town centre, within a mile of my home. 'Healthworks' had been newly painted in pastel washes and displayed a stock broadly similar to the merchandise described by Storm. Upstairs was space for holistic healing classes. The proprietor told me that the premises had been 'feng shui-d' by a leading local practitioner (one of the Macmanaway family at the Westbank Centre, discussed in Chapter 8) who'd 'given it the thumbs up'. Our conversation was interrupted by two young men buying a Bach Flower remedy. Such is the risk inherent in alternative–holistic entrepreneurship, however, that two years later the shop was gone, a sign on the door thanking customers and blessing the next stage on their spiritual journeys.

That these recent examples of popular spirituality are far removed from the lifestyle of the early networks is evident if we juxtapose them with the drawing-room esoterics of Alice Bailey, the privations of the 'Nameless Ones' and the severe psychological culture of the early sensitives. The accent is now firmly on sensuality, self-expression and relaxation, rather than the demanding work schedules of the pioneers. Yet despite this significant shift from other worldly to naturalistic outlook, affinities remain in such areas as healing technologies and practices, popular epistemologies of experience, emotion and intuition, and pervasive structures of kinship and friendship. But the commonalities are between aspects of function and structure, not between stages in the life of a single movement.

The same point can be made by reference to various directories which appeared in the UK in the 1980s and early 1990s. Compare *The Seeker's Guide: a New Age Resource Book* (Button and Bloom 1992) with *New Green Pages: a Directory of Natural Products, Services, Resources and Ideas* (Button 1990). From a taxonomic perspective it is instructive to note that in its 'Therapy and

Spirituality' section (ibid.: 167ff.), *Green Pages* covers remarkably similar ground to *The Seeker's Guide* overall. Pursuing this point, we can find 'Green' as well as 'New Age' material in the chapters of an earlier directory-cum-survey, *Alternatives: New Approaches to Health, Education, Energy, the Family and the Aquarian Age* (Osmond and Graham 1984). Here, however, the controlling trope is 'Alternative'. These examples all hint at the haphazard distribution of the same or very closely related subjects among rival categories, which in turn puts them at the disposal of quite different political agendas. In other words, since the 1970s the same group or practice might be designated 'New Age', 'Green', 'Alternative', 'Holistic' or 'Spiritual' depending upon activist, context, agenda or even serendipity. This only emphasises once more the contingent foothold of the term 'New Age' in the fuzzy arena of contemporary popular spirituality and the need to move beyond theories of the field as exclusively countercultural and dissident practice in the early twenty-first century.[32]

David Spangler's engagement with the emblem functions in many ways as a barometer of its stock. As we now know, Spangler has written and spoken on the subject for over four decades from his early pamphlet *The Christ Experience and the New Age* (1967 – cited in Caddy 1996: 307) to *Pilgrim in Aquarius* (Spangler 1996). His earlier confidence in the emblem (Spangler 1977) has given way to a revisionist defence in the face of commercialisation and media criticism.[33] In any case by the early 1980s Spangler had acknowledged an increasing multifunctionality to the expression:

> It can be seen as a vision of technological process, as a spiritual renaissance, as a set of strategies for personal and social transformation, as a network of individuals and groups implementing those strategies, as a state of mind, and even as a divine revelation. . . . Which is the 'real' new age depends on the point of view.
>
> (Spangler 1984: 36)

The subjectivist 'turn' which I noted above is by now quite entrenched: the idea that 'New Age' might somehow be not 'real' would have made no sense to the pioneers in the 1950s and 1960s. The final index of Spangler's complicated feelings towards an emblem he had very much made his own is his reported reluctance (Riddell 1991: 79) to have reissued the extensive body of material he wrote and published at Findhorn in the 1970s. Perhaps one reason for this is his frank acknowledgment that 'to be called New Age today is the kiss of death intellectually, academically, and professionally' (Spangler and Thompson 1991: 31).

Findhorn's current self-description is 'spiritual community'. Indeed, on the occasion of my first enquiry I was told: 'The general feeling here is that the "New Age" is over'. But if 'New Age' is finished among informed spiritual activists, it remains very much alive in popular strategies of identification and demarcation where it is clear that it functions as a convenient tag meaning almost anything 'alternative' in religion or 'spiritual' in culture. Such usage is particularly pervasive in the media where the kinds of idiosyncrasy we have been discussing are exaggerated and widely disseminated. To close this chapter, a cursory glance at some examples from the British media in the mid-to-late 1990s will serve to demonstrate just how far and wide the expression has travelled since its inception; and how vacant it has become.

Television exposure, a profusion of internet sites, and regular bandying of the term in newspapers and magazines demonstrate a capricious popular career in the 1990s.[34] In a particularly interesting development, the discrete category of 'New Age travellers' emerged in England in the 1980s to denote mobile communities living in old ambulances and converted vans, or in teepees and benders, subsisting on casual labour and state benefits (Lowe and Shaw 1993). There are strong generational and attitudinal connections with the earlier 'freak' culture. As one traveller remarks: 'My bus has got hippie written all over it, or rather "new age traveller" as they call it now' (ibid.: 110). Indeed, in casual conversations with colleagues in social and community work my research was as often taken to be about this subculture as it was about an ameliorative middle class spirituality. 'New Age' has here acquired a strongly 'alternative' stance of anger and dispossession but it is unclear – as of course befits popular usage – exactly whence the distinctive coupling of 'New Age' with 'traveller' originates. Certainly the lifestyle of the 'New Age' travellers contrasts markedly both with the quiet demeanour of the early networks and the 'Mind Body Spirit' culture of personal growth, healing and well-being in the 1980s and 1990s. One journalist, alert to the incompatibilities, revealingly contrasts Findhorn, which he calls 'the respectable, clean-cut face of New Age', with marginalised travellers parked in a West Highlands lay-by.[35]

In contrast to this 'deviant', subcultural representation of 'New Age', other journalists have concentrated on intellectual culture and religious markers of identity. One commentator claims that 'New Age' represents the maturation of a 'culture of the irrational'.[36] Others have written about so-called 'New Age monks' living in London's Kentish Town or the 'New Age bazaar' of the Mind Body Spirit festival in Edinburgh.[37] The declining membership of the Church of England is said to be threatened by 'New Age-ism', described as a ' "pick-and-mix" religion' of 'paganism, astrology, the paranormal and cult television programmes'.[38] Various new religious movements have been yoked to the cause: for example, Marshall Applewhite and his fellow suicides in the 'Heaven's Gate' group were linked to 'America's New Age devotees', and Applewhite himself describes how he set up the group in the 1970s by 'searching religious scriptures, new age materials, anything'.[39]

The term also drifts into the realms of 'lifestyle' choices. Vague connotations accrue: a health resort on the island of Madeira is described as 'New Agey', indicating that it is 'an informal place where diaphanous hippy wear is acceptable' with an emphasis on 'relaxation, nutrition and nature'.[40] And a report in 1997 by the British policy organisation Demos, entitled *Tomorrow's*

Women, identified five group-types of 'modern womanhood', one of which were the 'New Age Angelas', said to be 'confident but reject materialism' and 'keen on personal discovery'.[41]

It is clear, then, that a single, unified conception of 'New Age' has manifestly failed to persist in the face of a battery of cultural pressures since the late 1960s. These have steadily fragmented the real but limited public vision of the pioneers. Their earlier prophecies of catastrophe have become purely optional, just one of a variety of possible scenarios. Among these, visions of self-healing and worldly abundance have come to predominate. The scales have tipped from disaster to abundance. Cosmic judgment has given way to human potential, an uncertain future to the utopian present, and the 'New Age' idiom has in the process diffused into popular culture. In other words, 'New Age' has become the joker in the pack of modern religion, a 'wild' card that can be made to mean exactly what its users want. It should also be clear that 'spirituality', rather than 'religion', is now firmly on the public agenda, and in retrospect making spirituality public – enabling an autonomous spirituality to 'come out', so to speak – can be seen to have been a major function of alternative spirituality in general and the networks associated with the incubation of 'New Age' in particular.

So, far from being a 'movement', let alone a separate 'religion', might we conclude that 'New Age' is now merely an occasional 'alternative' rhetorical flourish in contemporary spiritual discourse? Is 'New Age' now, as David Spangler suggested in the late 1980s, actually 'a mnemonic device far more than a prophecy' (York 1995: 49)? The following three chapters address these and related questions through an ethnographic cross-section of recent activity in Scotland. These chapters feature a 'Unit of Service' meditation group in Edinburgh, the Findhorn community in the rural north-east, and snapshots from holistic health practice in the central belt, including a firewalking workshop. All have very close, sometimes formative, historical connections with 'New Age'. I link each chapter to the basic socio-structural elements of, respectively, small group, centre/colony, and solo seekership, but just as I tracked the untidy careers of individuals and groups across boundaries in the 1950s and 1960s, so an adjunct aim of the ethnographical chapters is to indicate the continuing traffic of 'life' across neat boundaries right up to the present day. By extrapolation this material is also broadly representative of dominant patterns in popular spirituality throughout Anglo–American culture in the early twenty-first century. This Scottish cross-section reveals the range and diversity of activities in question, the strength of articulation of the 'New Age' emblem itself, the degree to which a normative lifestyle is present, and the often unrecognised and sometimes surprising lineages concealed under the tangle of what, ultimately, is a proliferating popular spirituality – under whatever name it goes.

6

A GROUP OF SEEKERS

The unit of service

Units of service are laying the necessary foundation for the emerging new age.

(Leaflet: *Units of Service*, Lucis Trust, n.d.)[1]

The aim of our group is spiritual and practical service in the world.

(Alison, Unit of Service)[2]

Making contact

A group of people, working in a united effort, guided by a common purpose, can have an effect on their environment far out of proportion to their numerical strength.

(Alison, Unit of Service)[3]

In October 1994 at a holistic health fair in Glasgow's City Halls I came across a small group – two women and a man – sitting behind a trestle table covered with pamphlets, information sheets, small cards, and a selection of thick paperback books with austere midnight-blue covers. The sober and restrained presentation of this stall stood out in the otherwise bustling and sensuous ambience of the fair as a whole (mapped in Chapter 8), and the books really caught my eye. I discovered that these were the 'Bailey books', of which around 8,000 are sold per annum in Europe and the British Commonwealth and as many as 24,000 in North America.[4]

I told the group of my attempt some twenty years previously to read Bailey's 1925 blockbuster, *A Treatise on Cosmic Fire*. The elder woman nodded sympathetically:'that's a *hard* one'. The group were linked to Alice Bailey's ideas. They called themselves a 'Unit of Service' and their principal activity was a short group meditation at the time of the full moon. 'It's not about witchcraft or anything', she said,'it's just that the energies are at their peak then – it's a kind of high tide – which means our meditation can be of most service'. She handed me a flyer which explained the metaphysics behind this:

> The moon itself has no influence on our work; but the fully lighted orb of the moon is indicative of the free and unimpeded alignment which exists between our planet and the *Sun* . . . the energy source for all life on earth of *physical consciousness,* of *soul awareness* and of *spiritual life.*

'We're giving a talk and meditation in December', said the man, handing me details. 'Help yourself', said the other woman, indicating the cards and pamphlets, 'it's free'. A small bowl for donations stood discreetly to the side. I selected a sample, deposited some small change, and moved on to the next stall.

That evening I read the material. It was detailed yet curiously abstract, and immensely wide-ranging. In one pamphlet, entitled *Preparation for the Reappearance of the Christ,* I read of 'a great and divine plan' in which 'a Spiritual Hierarchy guides humanity'. The head of this Hierarchy in the present period was 'the Christ', it seemed, and its 'Senior Members' were the 'Masters of the Wisdom'. A leaflet entitled *One World – One Humanity* listed some key words for our times: Goodwill, Interdependence, Co-Operation, Global Spirituality. Two other pamphlets were called *Education in the New Age* and *The New World Religion.*

On a wintry December weekend I travelled to a large warehouse building on an industrial site in Livingston, a new town in Scotland's central belt, to investigate further. Inside the air was sweet with incense as another holistic health fair got under way. This time it was a small, friendly event similar to the one in Glasgow but with a larger 'psychic' contingent (and hence a more plebeian social base) of scryers and Tarot readers. Once again, the Unit had its stall, but this time the elder woman – its founder, as I later discovered – was to give a talk. The typescript described her as a Quaker and 'for over twenty years a student of the Alice Bailey books and of the esoteric traditions of many world religions'.

I joined a very modest audience. The talk was entitled 'Meditation as a form of service'. It discussed the power of thought, the importance of the right kind of meditation, and the background to the Unit's activities. Addressing herself to 'students of the spiritual path, or seekers', the speaker quickly outlined a metaphysic in which 'action is a result of inner causes' and correct meditation a 'form of extended mental concentration'. Such 'sustained thinking' could, over time, open us to the powers of 'the Soul'. These powers generated love, described as 'a fine unimpeded inflow from the higher nature'. In short, through meditation and sustained concentration we were to 'go beyond the desires of the little self and begin to serve as the soul'. She mentioned various promotional techniques and activities connected with the Alice Bailey books, which in turn provided the requisite 'esoteric teaching' to 'precede and condition the "New Age"'.[5]

After the talk, a group meditation was proposed. A complicated six-stage procedure, typed out on an A4 sheet, was passed around. In Stage I, we were to imagine ourselves linked up 'in thought' with sympathetic individuals throughout the world. Then we spoke aloud this 'mantram':

The sons of men are one and I am one with them.
I seek to love, not hate.
I seek to serve and not exact due service.
I seek to heal, not hurt.

Next we were to turn our attention to 'the inner Spiritual Kingdom of the planet' and picture ourselves 'immersed in the consciousness of the Christ'. We were then to utter the following:

In the centre of all Love I stand;
From that centre I, the soul, will outward move;
From that centre I, the one who serves, will work.
May the love of the divine Self be shed abroad,
In my heart, through my group, and throughout the world.

Now we were to visualise 'the energy of love flowing into the hearts and minds of men' and to 'meditate on ways of spreading goodwill and wholeness'. To accomplish this, we were to act as a channel between 'the inner Spiritual Kingdom' and the everyday world. Finally, we finished with the grand prayer of the Bailey work, the Great Invocation (see below). The entire process lasted some fifteen minutes, during which we sat upright with eyes closed, and hands on laps or knees. The contrast between an active, engaged mind and bodily quiescence could not have been more marked: I found the combination of sustained concentration and alert posture surprisingly tiring.

Afterwards I bought an early Bailey title, *From Intellect to Intuition* (Bailey 1987), and joined the group for lunch in the vegetarian cafe. The speaker and *de facto* leader, Alison, who was also the founder of the Unit, was explaining the enthusiasm of 'spiritual seekers' today to be a direct result of increasing numbers of 'young souls reincarnating'. 'Never before has there been such an interest in spirituality and meditation', she assured us, 'and this fair is proof of it'. Gill, the other woman, nodded sympathetically. I discussed my research interests with Patrick and we compared backgrounds. He had pursued research in philosophy before becoming disillusioned with academic epistemology. He described himself as an 'ex-Catholic' who occasionally attended Mass ('for aesthetic reasons') but who rejected papal authority and church dogma. But in any case Patrick stressed that 'religion' was of little import or interest within the Unit. Its purpose was to practice 'spirituality' and 'world service'.

Group meditation at the full moon

We meet together at the time of the full moon to meditate, as a group, and as such to serve through the power of united thought and love. We are in this work acting as channels through which the energies of love and light can flow for healing and stimulation in the planet.[6]

Just before Christmas I attended a full moon meditation. It was held at eight o'clock in the evening at Alison's small flat, two storeys up in a tenement building in one of the larger Scottish cities. We met in Alison's living-room-cum-kitchen. The walls carry some of her work – she is an accomplished painter and wood engraver trained at London art schools – and the flat doubles as a workplace, exuding a cluttered domesticity.

On this occasion there were seven of us altogether: four women and three men, all apparently in their thirties or forties. We sat on cushions on the floor, or on upright chairs. The sole armchair was occupied by Alison. There were the three faces I already knew – Alison, Gill and Patrick – plus two other women – Deirdre and Pam – and Iain, a newcomer like myself. Iain knew Alison from Quaker meetings in the city, which she sometimes attended. I knew Iain from previous contact in Scottish alternative circles when he had been training as a Reichian therapist, and we had been partners in a massage workshop at the Salisbury Centre (see Chapter 8). But our paths had not crossed for several years: 'I've been here and there', he explained, 'I lived in Denmark for a while'.

In a short preamble Alison explained the timing of our gathering in terms of planetary 'alignment' and astrological rhythms. Then she gave a lengthy talk on this month's zodiacal sign, Sagittarius, drawing liberally on Alice Bailey's writings. Her exposition was detailed and sometimes abstruse, but I wasn't sure whether this was down to Alison or ambiguities in the Bailey books. Sinclair (1984: 111) freely admits, however, that Bailey's style

> militates against superficial reading: one has to read the passages back and forth and often go back to the beginning of a sentence before one has come to the end of it. There are qualifications, provisos, and endless subheadings.

Alison spoke from a small exercise book for nearly half-an-hour. We listened attentively, the soft hiss of the gas fire underscoring an impression of group readiness and commitment. Some sat cross-legged, others with closed eyes or lowered gaze. At the end there was a pause, and then Alison handed round a meditation schedule. The particular meditation performed at the full moon is called 'Letting in the Light'. In silence, and once more with closed eyes, we worked our way through seven titled sections, taking our lead from Alison who quietly announced each new section. We began with 'Group Fusion', in which we announced our intention to join 'the New Group of World Servers' in special work 'mediating between Hierarchy and humanity'. In 'Alignment' we were to 'project a line of lighted energy towards the Spiritual Hierarchy of the planet – the great Ashram of Sanat Kumara': at this point in the meditation our group was deemed receptive to 'extra-planetary energies'. We next contemplated 'the reappearance of the Christ' and meditated upon a 'seed thought' connected to the astrological sign of Sagittarius: this was 'I see the goal. I reach that goal and then I see another'. Then followed a stage called

'Precipitation', in which we visualised 'energies of Light, Love and the Will-to-Good pouring throughout the planet and becoming anchored on Earth'. In 'Lower Interlude' we had to 'refocus the consciousness' and recite another affirmation. Finally, the 'Great Invocation' brought matters to a close. We recited it slowly and sonorously together:

From the point of Light within the Mind of God
   Let light stream forth into the minds of men.
      Let Light descend on Earth.

From the point of Love within the Heart of God
   Let love stream forth into the hearts of men.
      May Christ return to Earth.

From the centre where the Will of God is known
   Let purpose guide the little wills of men –
The Purpose which the Masters know and serve.

From the centre which we call the race of men
   Let the Plan of Love and Light work out
   And may it seal the door where evil dwells.

Let Light and Love and Power restore the Plan on Earth.

We finished by humming an 'Om' syllable three times in unison.

The meditation lasted about twenty-five minutes. People opened their eyes slowly, smiled quietly or stretched. 'I'll put the kettle on', said Alison, rising from her chair. 'That was powerful!', said Deirdre, looking round the circle. 'Wasn't it?', agreed Gill. 'They always are, but they're different every month', said Alison. Iain said it reminded him of Liberal Catholic Church ceremonies he had attended in Denmark. I asked the group who the 'Masters' were. 'A good question', said Gill, with an enigmatic smile. There was reluctance to respond among the group: finally Patrick suggested: 'Enlightened beings?'. 'It's not about glamour', explained Alison hurriedly, 'it's not helpful to speculate on identities'. 'A Master *might* be a world leader, or a figure in the news' explained Deirdre. 'Or they *could* be you or me' said Patrick, adding hurriedly 'I'm not saying they *are*'. What, then, was 'the Plan'? This provided relaxed amusement. Alison said: 'It's easier to describe it by what it isn't', implying that 'everything' was part of its grand unfolding. Patrick alluded to a vast emergent cosmology in which only God ultimately knew the Plan for each particular planet or even solar system.

Were there other Units of Service in Scotland, I asked? No one seemed sure, or even particularly interested. Patrick said he thought there was 'similar stuff' going on at Findhorn. Alison said that there were a 'good many' individuals connected with the Unit who lived too far away to attend meetings. The Unit also had connections with groups in Dublin and Cork. A brief conversation arose among Alison, Deirdre and Gill concerning the 'peace processes' in Northern Ireland and Palestine: the gist of their discussion was that we all needed to remain optimistic and to continue thinking and working positively for peace. There was a final conversation on symbols. The group consensus was that the more dynamic form of the spiral was supplanting the circle as the appropriate emblem of our times: 'humanity', someone said, had had enough of 'going round in circles'; evolutionary energies were now urging things on and *up*. Gill emphasised the power of the upward spiral: one kept returning to the 'same' place, but always 'higher up'. 'Anyway, the darkness will give way to light in the end', she said simply. As the meeting broke up, Alison lent me her copy of Alice Bailey's *Unfinished Autobiography* (Bailey 1973). We descended into the cold street to go our respective ways: Gill to her flat nearby, Iain and Pam to local buses, Patrick and Deirdre by car across central Scotland, and myself on the train to Stirling.

The Unit of Service in context

ARE YOU A SEEKER?

Searching for answers to your innermost spiritual questions

* *the purpose of life*
* *the power of love*
* *the meaning of death*

Insights from the teachings of Alice Bailey give keys to spiritual growth and loving service[7]

This group was part of a wider network of Units of Service, of which there are just two or three in Scotland and some thirty in England and Wales, in addition to some two hundred others around the world including the US, South America, and Africa. These small clusters of seekers are described in a directory as 'groups and individuals working in co-operation with the service activities of the Lucis Trust'.[8] Most of the British groups appear to have started up since the 1960s; several have only been together a few years. However, the idea of such groups goes back to the 1930s, when they were called 'Goodwill Action Committees' (Nation 1989: 7), and the 1940s, when the present title seems to have emerged.[9] Our group had been formed in 1984 and its principal activities were holding full-moon meditations, distributing Bailey literature and (more recently) maintaining a low-key public profile at holistic health fairs.

Units of Service thus belong to the wider network of projects constituting the Lucis Trust, namely the Arcane School, World Goodwill, Triangles meditation and, not least, faithful study of the Bailey books. As I sketched out in Chapter 2, this cluster of initiatives stems from the post-Theosophical career of Alice Bailey in the 1920s and 1930s, and her claimed contact with a Tibetan Master, Djwhal Khul ('the Tibetan'), which produced a vast corpus of 'received' or 'channelled' texts. While there is no requirement for Unit members to participate in other Lucis Trust activities – indeed the opinion was forcefully expressed within our group on several occasions that the Unit was not exclusively a 'Bailey' group – the three most regular attendees in our group were all involved in 'triangles' meditation and in the Arcane School. Emic protestations notwithstanding, the weight of evidence is that the Units of Service are essentially an Alice Bailey project, derive almost all their ideology from this and sibling sources, and are largely sustained by committed students of the Bailey work.

As we saw in Chapter 2, Bailey set up the Arcane School to offer systematic study for individuals looking for 'guidance in their search for truth without being subjected to the usual limitations of dogmatic creeds'.[10] According to the Lucis Trust, it has around three thousand students worldwide at any one time, four hundred or so of whom live in the UK. In the seventy or so years between the early 1920s and the late 1990s this translates into 'tens of thousands' who have participated for various lengths of time, including a proportion who have 'passed right through' – that is, spent ten years or more in School study.[11] The majority of students have no religious affiliation other than to the Arcane School, although there are notable minorities, including Christians, Muslims and Rosicrucians. The organisation was summarised by one former student as a 'correspondence school keeping people of like mind in touch' through the teaching of a 'Christianised, interfaith Theosophy'.[12] Material for study consists largely in thematic excerpts from the Bailey books coupled with extracts from other post-Theosophical writers and assorted psychological and environmental sources. Written assignments are assessed by senior students known as 'secretaries', who typically work in different countries and are swapped around periodically to encourage impersonality in Arcane School relationships and foster the desired shift from 'ego' level to 'soul' work. Specified daily meditations and mantras (uttered aloud if appropriate, otherwise affirmed silently) complete the student's curriculum. Some breathing exercises, to be undertaken prior to meditation practice, are added at a later date.[13]

Patrick's weekly practice incorporated eight or nine specific meditations to be done on different days or at certain times of the day, in addition to the recommended half an hour of daily study. He summarised the work as 'pretty much reading, writing and meditating', understanding the latter in particular as a simple yet profound act of 'world service'. Details of the meditations are not available outside the School in order to 'safeguard' the work. Patrick explained that because meditation was working with energy, one had to be careful how to approach it: 'if you're not prepared, if you're not ready for a particular stage, it could create difficulties'. But it is unlikely that the meditations differ significantly from the two outlines discussed in this chapter, and others readily available elsewhere, in their serial procedures of aligning with higher energies, meditating on them, and then occultly distributing the 'grounded' energies. Like the Rosicrucian Order, Crotona Fellowship in the 1920s and 1930s, the governing ethos is 'private' rather than 'initiatic' or 'secret': for example, Alison said forcefully 'I *never ever* talk about AAB [Bailey] or the books in my daily life'.[14]

This impression of discretion and selection was reinforced when I attended the annual conference of the Arcane School in London in 1996. Certainly the morning sessions of the conference were for students only, but the afternoon sessions were open to the public and were structured around a formal schedule of meditation, the Great Invocation, addresses by speakers, and small discussion groups. The atmosphere was keen, animated and open, but the parameters of discussion were fairly circumscribed. This impression continued when I visited the Lucis Trust headquarters. These could scarcely be less evidently 'religious' in presentation and were more like a government department or a firm of stockbrokers. The Trust occupies a suite of sizeable rooms in an imposing neoclassical building behind Whitehall in central London. Here a few paid staff and a handful of volunteers co-ordinate the Trust's various projects, largely financed by donations and legacies.[15] I was courteously shown around the premises by an Arcane School co-ordinator who, like the seven or eight other people I met that afternoon, was in his late thirties or early forties. Nationalities were markedly mixed: my guide was English, but others came from Egypt, Greece, Ireland, and New Zealand. The atmosphere was calm, sober and somewhat bureaucratic: the general impression was of a small business or family firm. Sober oil portraits of Alice and Foster Bailey hung discreetly on one internal wall, and administration was centred on specific 'desks' – the 'Triangles desk', 'World Goodwill desk' and so on. The language of corporate business has also contributed to the Trust's stock of esoteric metaphors: hence the 'Masters' are described in an early (but still circulated) pamphlet as 'a worldwide group of executives . . . far more practical and realistic than the most efficient big business executives', and initiating 'the kingdom of God' requires 'sensible business procedures and carefully considered programmes'.[16] In the basement is a small printing press that maintains the pamphleteering side of the work, together with similar plant in New York and Geneva. The thick, midnight-blue Bailey books, on the other hand, are all printed in the US. The office suite also houses an eclectic lending library on popular esotericism, with an understandable bias towards its own material.

The 'New Age' remains a focus for the Lucis Trust. A new Bailey compilation was published in 1996 as *The Seventh Ray: Revealer of the New Age* and the Lucis Press was promoting the two volumes of *Discipleship in the New Age* at a special price in 1997. But although Melton (1986: 115) reports that the Great Invocation 'is frequently heard' at 'New Age gatherings' and Perry (1992: 29) claims it has even been used at inter-faith events, Bailey's influence upon the idiomatic 'New Age' culture of human potential, healing, and mind, body and spirit pursuits is practically nil. Her books continue to exert a muted impact upon more ascetic spiritual groups, and certainly Steyn (1994: 101) found that nearly two-thirds of her interview sample of white South Africans had been 'markedly influenced' by Bailey in the 1970s and 1980s. But as I argued in

Chapter 2, the distinctiveness of Alice Bailey for a genealogy of the field lies in creating and disseminating a discourse on 'New Age' that early on acquired a life of its own beyond the control of the Lucis Trust.

We can trace the impact of this discourse in the biographies of 'New Age' activists from the 1940s to the 1970s. According to Walker (1994: 287), possession 'of at least one' Bailey book was *de rigueur* at Findhorn in the 1970s and early 1980s and a 'working knowledge' of her system was 'a prerequisite for any serious candidate for high office'. Luminaries of the early 'New Age' networks such as Anthony Brooke (1976: 93) and George Trevelyan (1977: 162) knew and used Bailey's Great Invocation, and later activists such as David Spangler (1984: 30) and William Bloom (1991: 2) acknowledge their debt to Bailey's 'New Age' discourse. Riddell (1991: 285) notes that the Great Invocation was displayed in the original Findhorn sanctuary as recently as the early 1990s, and it is significant that, following the attack on the World Trade Centre in New York in September 2001, a new daily programme of 'Network of Light meditations for peace' began in this sanctuary, based around utterance of the Great Invocation.[17] Walker's (1994: 287) observation that Bailey's influence on Findhorn 'should not be underestimated' is indeed a shrewd one.

All this is by way of showing that, out of all proportion to its small numbers and almost invisible public footprint, the Unit of Service is located in, and derives ideological sustenance from, closely interconnected spiritual circles. These are based partly in specific Lucis Trust projects and partly in a wider field of alternative spiritual practice, which in turn has been watered by Bailey's distinctive 'New Age' discourse.

Persevering

What you've got with the Unit of Service is meditation. It's not a massage group, it's not for self-enlightenment, it's not for holding crystals, it's not for self-development, it's for world service: *that's* its purpose.

(Alison, Unit of Service)[18]

Early in January 1995 I received through the post a photocopied newsletter giving notice of the next full-moon meditation. The date, time and place were given, along with the enigmatic 'keynote' of the month's zodiac sign, Capricorn: 'Lost am I in light supernal, yet on that light I turn my back'. There were also a few quotations from Bailey and a postscript appealing for donations towards the cost of hiring a stall at the next holistic health fair. During my time with the Unit it was invariably Alison who put these newsletters together: sometimes they reproduced one of her engravings, but otherwise the format was much the same each month.

Numbers at this month's meditation were the same, although Iain and Gill were replaced by two individuals new to me: Gordon, an energetic self-employed 'green' businessman who had lived at Findhorn in the 1970s, and Mark, a younger man in his thirties who had trained at art college and now practised 'psychic art' for a small living; he showed me his portraits of the Christ and two other 'Masters', Morya and Koot Humi. Pam, Deirdre, Patrick and Alison were the familiar faces. As I entered the room, Gill telephoned, and Alison relayed her message to the group – 'she can't come, but she's linking up' – meaning that Gill would synchronise with the group meditation in her own home. Patrick had already begun the evening's preliminary talk, in which he correlated 'Capricorn energies' with historical events such as the fall of the Berlin Wall and the collapse of apartheid in South Africa. Several of the group nodded thoughtfully.

At 8.25 p.m., the precise time of the full moon, we began the meditation. I worked hard tonight to bring alive the meditation outline – to put imaginative flesh on its bones – and I noted later that 'by the time of the invocation, I was subtly aware of the group breathing in together, and speaking in the outbreath'.[19] Afterwards Gordon said: 'That was beautiful!' 'Wasn't it?' said Alison, filling the kettle. Over cups of herb tea and a few biscuits, there was more discussion of astrology, and we compared our 'sun', 'moon' and 'rising' signs. It turned out that the group had a preponderance of fire and air signs, which triggered some amused interpretations of the group's fiery energy and extravagant ideas, but a lack of 'grounding' from earth and water signs. Patrick and Alison were quick to point out that in any case these standard interpretations were actually the 'astrology of personality': *esoteric* astrology, on the other hand, which the group should prefer, worked deeper, 'at the Soul level'. Gordon then proposed organising an Edinburgh meditation festival jointly with other interested parties – he suggested Transcendental Meditation and the Brahma Kumaris – but conversation on this idea petered out. I steered talk round to Findhorn, where Deirdre and Mark had done 'Experience Week', and to 'New Age' in general. Alison said she didn't like the term, and there was general agreement. Mark said 'New Age' was 'a media thing', and that many of the groups concerned were actually 'Old Age' in their attitudes, anyway. Alison thought that small groups and meditation were the essence.

At the following month's meeting there were only six of us. Pam was absent – I never saw her again – and Iain had not reappeared. But Gill was back, and this time it was Gordon who telephoned to say he was 'linking up'. As usual, the gathering began with a talk, again by Alison, on astrology. The February full moon was in Aquarius, the keynote being 'Water of Life am I, poured forth for thirsty men', and there was animated discussion of 'Aquarian energy', which, the group felt, showed itself in the increasing numbers of small spiritual groups in the culture at large. After a short pause, we composed ourselves and Alison announced quietly, 'Meditation: letting in the light'. My field notes, written afterwards on the train home, describe the night's meditation as 'a deep and powerful experience':

I was aware tonight of a strong suspension of disbelief on my part. I worked hard at the various visualisations, and intoned the 'responses' with intention and weight. Consequently I felt much more of a participant than previously, and felt my role as a 'researcher' blurring, so that I spontaneously said to Alison on leaving, 'I found the meditation really *worked*' – as though I was an 'apprentice'.[20]

Group profile

The main activity of the Unit of Service is *group meditation*.
(Flyer: *Full Moon Meditation Meetings*)

The true meeting place of the group is the plane of mind.
(*The Science of Meditation*: booklet, p. 12)

By now I had encountered most of the characteristic features of the full-moon meditation meetings over a period of some two years' semi-regular participation. The rhythm of events was predictable: some two weeks before the full moon a newsletter would arrive confirming the date (the gathering being held either on, or at the nearest possible weekday evening to, the full moon) and location (invariably at Alison's flat). Although faces would come and go, there were typically some half a dozen individuals present, including a core of three or four regulars. The meeting lasted about one hour and a half, and consisted in some twenty minutes' introductory talk or reading, twenty minutes to half an hour devoted to the meditation, and another half an hour talking quietly over tea and biscuits. During the latter period, practical matters might be raised such as the details of hiring tables at fairs. The slender finances of the group were covered by a tin for donations, which Alison usually put out during tea, although expenses were never more than marginal (the table, for example, was obtained at a special charity rate from the fair organisers).

The group existed primarily, indeed almost exclusively, for the purposes of meditation: it was understood that we were not gathered for therapy, discussion or chat, but to meditate at an auspicious moment in the occult calendar by way of rendering 'world service'. What exchanges of views there were chiefly revolved around the task in hand and the strengthening or deepening of technique through the application of insights from the publications of the Lucis Trust in general and Alice Bailey in particular. Particular episodes during the time of my involvement with the group reinforced the hegemony of Bailey's scheme in the wider field of alternative spirituality. For example, early on I suggested holding a separate reading group to cater for more discursive interests. The new moon was identified as a good time for this kind of approach, and Patrick, Deirdre and I duly met at the next new moon in my home in Stirling to read and discuss sections from Bailey's *A Treatise on White Magic* (1934). This was a subdued meeting that on Patrick's suggestion began and ended with Lucis Trust meditations and involved some rather guarded discussion, Deirdre and Patrick largely looking to me to raise questions. My tentative comparisons of Bailey's scheme to other spiritual systems were received with indifference, and it was apparent that Deirdre and Patrick largely saw the reading group as an opportunity for the Unit to read more intensively in the Bailey corpus. This new-moon initiative flagged but was revived the following year by Gordon, the most eclectic Unit member, who indicated that he would like a more inclusive forum. Yet the first of the revived series again inclined strongly towards an orthodox curriculum, with Gordon himself suggesting we study a collection of Bailey's astrological writings, *The Labours of Hercules*, and Alison proposing we work with a Lucis Trust study series entitled 'Problems of Humanity'. Even in ostensibly more relaxed and eclectic settings, then, the discourse inclined inexorably towards the Bailey books and their interpretive machinery.

The atmosphere of the Unit in general was one of quiet reflection, concentration and mental work. Conversation was muted and episodic, and bodily contact was at a minimum. There was relatively little discussion of the families, careers and everyday lives of group participants and a period of absence on the part of a semi-regular participant like myself occasioned no comment beyond a welcoming 'good to see you again'. The lack of concern with the private lives of individuals contrasted with a lively interest in politics and current affairs, however, although this tended to be articulated in generalised, impressionistic terms. Furthermore, although the working vocabulary included words such as 'occult' and 'esoteric' – the meditation ritual at one meeting was explicitly explained as '*esoteric* work' – the regular members were keen to stress the group's accessible, non-religious, non-doctrinal nature. Thus Alison spontaneously announced at this same meeting: 'This is not a *cult*, it's very simple and straightforward work'.[21]

In fact the work – performing and correctly interpreting a ritualised full-moon meditation – was anything but simple. Some knowledge of astrology and post-Theosophical cosmology in general, in addition to a keen interest in the Bailey books, was effectively a prerequisite for viable participation. Group conversation and practice was otherwise abstruse and there was only limited opportunity for clarification or analysis of terminology during the evening. Skill in working with visualisation techniques was also required of participants, for a high degree of concentration was required to bring the meditation 'to life'. The heightened subjectivity required and in turn fostered by the internalised ritual also discouraged seeking 'outside' help from the group, and in any case the impressionistic subtleties of the process tended to dissolve once I attempted to formulate them in words. According to the group, the formalised stages were actually 'incredibly open' and 'dynamic' in practice, since each meditator visualised in a manner appropriate to themselves, reflecting their own position on 'the spiritual path': there were no set images or semantic associations. However, for several months in lieu of an opening talk we studied a Lucis Trust booklet called *Meditation at the Full Moon* and it became clear that, through group socialisation over time, one would gradually learn, absorb and recapitulate the characteristic features of Bailey's worldview. Meditation practice as a whole was deeply shaped by Bailey's understanding of 'the Soul' as the realm of ultimate, causative reality with which one strove to 'align' oneself both in meditation and daily life. In other words, the 'mental planes' were seen to be portals to the 'real world' of the soul to which one gained ritual access through correct performance of the sequence of visualisations. It followed that our individual subjectivities were ultimately windows on an objective, causative but occult reality, and the 'group sentiency' generated in the course of meditative work was its manifestation.[22]

Nevertheless, learning to meditate competently was a subtle process involving trial and error practice in a group context. Halting conversations on technique emphasised subjective acts such as refining one's intuition and developing an openness to sensory hints and fragments. So the nature of occult meditation was said to be variously 'active', 'mental', 'imaginative', 'creative', and 'highly visual'.[23] Meditation worked like a 'funnel' to 'channel down energies,' Alison said. Mark explained the technique as 'impressionistic, like a painting. Or maybe you smell things.' Sinclair (1984: 46) refers to 'the art of spiritual impression', an impression being 'like a hint' that can be 'accepted or rejected at will'. But 'it's not an intellectual exercise,' cautioned Deirdre, 'you have to experience it in practice.' 'And you have to keep your consciousness high,' warned Patrick.[24]

Patrick's remark was also a veiled warning against dangerous illusions – 'glamour', in Bailey's terms – which pandered to the pride and ambition of the ego while obscuring the reality of the Soul. Glamour could contaminate any level of enquiry or practice. At one holistic health fair, Mark told me he thought the Transmission Meditation sessions on offer were 'dubious' or, as he put it, 'glamoured'. Transmission meditation was a group ritual devised by a former Alice Bailey student, Benjamin Creme, and Mark was particularly unhappy with the photograph promoted by Creme's group, which showed a tall turbaned man, whom Creme claimed was the Christ, addressing a crowd in Nairobi. If the Christ *had* returned, Mark said passionately, he would be working away quietly and selflessly, not parading for the world's cameras in exotic locations. On another occasion when I asked about the identity of 'the Masters', Patrick warned me that such enquiry was intrinsically 'glamoured'. And when I asked Deirdre which Bailey books she had personally found most informative, she told me gently that 'we've all got our own glamours to deal with and we walk the path alone', implying that what had been illuminating reading for *her* might actively mislead *me*, and that my question had been 'glamoured' in the first place.[25]

In sum, the uniformity of material in Unit newsletters and group practice underscored the fact that, like any other occult system, one needed to invest substantial time and energy in the study of Bailey's cosmology to be able to 'do' the meditations successfully and, indeed, to persist in the group at all. It was not a casual option. The commitment required is reflected in the small attendance at the full-moon meditation meetings. In my span of involvement with the group – part-time over nearly two and a half years – I met seventeen different individuals in all,[26] and although Alison told me she had a list of about fifty people interested in the work of the Unit, she only sent out about fifteen newsletters each month. Both facts point to a very small active constituency, despite the busy 'alternative' milieu in which the Unit was located and in which it advertised itself through hiring tables at health fairs.

However, I was told that achieving a certain quality of practice rather than attracting x numbers of practitioners was the Unit's chief concern. The sustained practice of a core group of meditators could have a spiritual impact on the 'mental planes' almost in inverse proportion to its paltry public footprint. As Alison explains it:

> To maintain the integrity – the inner life – of the group there has to be a spiritual tension at its centre, which is why you need two or three very committed people right at the centre of this group work.

It is also telling that the core group in this Unit (and surely in others) were Arcane School students involved in Triangles work. It is precisely this trio – Alison, Patrick and Deirdre – who generated the 'spiritual tension' in the Unit to keep it vibrant. Alison was a trained painter and engraver who not only hosted the meditation meeting but had founded the group; she had been involved with the Arcane School for twenty-five years as student and 'secretary'. Patrick had been a student for around eight years, and had recently worked as an adult education lecturer; brought up as a Catholic, he had read widely in Hinduism, Taoist yoga and Subud before settling down to the Bailey work. Deirdre had been episodically enrolled in the Arcane School and had recently rejoined; she worked as a nursing auxiliary and had formerly been involved with a different meditation network, Fountain International, associated with the eccentric but charismatic theorist of conspiracies, David Icke. She and Patrick travelled some forty miles to the meetings, often sharing a car. This core group were all single, although Alison and Deirdre had grown-up children. All three were present at the Arcane School conference in London I attended. Patrick's commitment to the Bailey work became deeper still: towards the end of my involvement with the group, he moved to London to work full-time for World Goodwill.

In addition to this core group of 'regulars', there were some half-a-dozen occasional attendees. Some might also be Arcane School students, as was Mark. 'Occasional' actually meant 'semi-regular', since although these individuals, like myself, participated in substantially fewer meetings, they continued to attend over time. For example, Gill, who lived near Alison, was present at about half of the meetings I came to, but when absent she often telephoned to say she was 'linking up', and she regularly helped out on the Unit's table at the health fairs. Gordon attended slightly more regularly, and would also contact Alison if he couldn't come. He lived with his family in a market town some fifteen miles away. Gordon had wide experience of 'New Age' activities: he was a former trustee of the Salisbury Centre and had lived at Findhorn during its period of expansion in the 1970s, where he had known Peter and Eileen Caddy and other luminaries. Gordon was the participant most likely to discuss non-Bailey groups and activities. At various meetings I attended he publicised a 'peace concert' by Indian guru Sri Chimnoy, circulated a newsletter from Anthony Brooke (whom we met in Chapter 4), mentioned his participation in the Lamplighter movement (also Chapter 4) and spoke enthusiastically about alternative politics: he had stood as a Green Party candidate in European elections but now favoured the Natural Law Party, the political wing of Transcendental Meditation. This range of experience made Gordon the unspoken deputy to Alison, even though he did not attend as regularly as Patrick, his nearest contender in this regard. I also met Austin, a young man who was hoping to get into primary-school teacher training. He had been an Arcane School student and had previously come to the meditations for six months or so, but had found it too far to travel. He, too, had attended the Fountain International meditation group a few years ago, where he'd met Deirdre.

Still others attended on a handful of occasions or were one-off visitors. In my time with the group there were some half a dozen 'casual' attenders. At the briefest end of the scale, Andrew, an older man involved in the National Federation of Spiritual Healers, came only once. More persistently, Shaun, a young Australian, attended three consecutive meetings before dropping out; he then rejoined after I left. Pam, a quiet woman in her early thirties whom I never saw again after my early visits, was probably a 'casual' attender although it is possible she was an 'occasional' who had finally moved on. As I've shown, Unit of Service participation requires ideological commitment and adroit ritual technique, as well as social skills to balance the intimate domestic setting of Alison's flat with the restrained formality of group practice. Hence the preponderance of 'regulars' and 'occasionals' over 'casuals' should not surprise.

In summary, a typical full-moon meditation gathering for this Unit of Service numbered about six; a slightly higher representation of men overall was offset by a two to one ratio of women to men in the 'core group'; age tended to be over thirty; single people were to the fore; and access was through personal contact (word of mouth, a friend of a friend, or through contact at a health fair).[27] The group as a whole had an ascetic and somewhat gnostic character. Thus Alison introduced the meditation on one occasion by explaining that we were actually spiritual beings, or 'angelic lords', who had undertaken to incarnate on earth but had forgotten our true identities. An emphasis on selfless 'service' is pervasive: Patrick told me that 'the Path' was by nature lonely, and that the Arcane School discouraged students who were really seeking a social or therapeutic group.[28] Finally, the act of meditation is consistently referred to as a perfectible procedure or technology. Thus a booklet called *The Science of Meditation* describes it as 'a scientific technique which can be relied upon to produce results if followed through with care and precision'. And Bailey herself says in another booklet, *Meditation at the Full Moon*: 'The inevitability of Christ's return is established, scientifically and under law; this constitutes a call which He may not deny and one which He must obey'.

History of the Unit of Service and links with other groups

> We are not working alone for there are many other similar groups all around the world. In this way we are in a very real sense part of a worldwide subjective network. A unit or cell of service is not an organisation so much as an organism.[29]

The genesis of the group is intimately linked with its founder's search for 'some kind of discipline' in her spiritual quest. Alison says she was 'intensely religious, reading, reading, reading, thinking, thinking, thinking since I was very young'. She read mystical and devotional Christian literature, books on Buddhism, and others – 'you name it'. She also absorbed the work of artists like William Blake, Samuel Palmer and Cecil Collins. She became involved in the Bailey work in her late twenties while living in the North-West Highlands with a young baby and her then husband, a native Gaelic speaker. 'There was nobody I could talk to', she recalls, 'you can't get a hold of the minister by the lapels and say, "look, come on, *tell* me!"' A friend advised her to try an 'esoteric school', and so Alison obtained a specialist book catalogue. Out of some 200 titles she chose *Discipleship in the New Age*. 'The minute I read it', she said, 'I'd come home!' She enrolled in the Arcane School. In the late 1970s she was looking for a way to offer 'service' and decided to advertise meditation meetings in her house. She had the Great Invocation printed in the local newspaper, *The West Highland Free Press*, and put up posters in the neighbourhood. 'It was laughed at', she recalls, although she says her father-in-law, a Free Church lay preacher, admired the Great Invocation. For about a year, Alison says, no one came: 'I just meditated on my own'. Once she was visited by an angelic presence during the meditation: 'there was a sudden whoosh!, a beating of wings, then it was gone'. She persisted for four years with a handful of occasional participants. When she moved to the city in the mid-1980s, the Lucis Trust put her in contact with six or seven individuals looking for a group, and a new Unit of Service was born. Since then Alison estimates that 'fifty to a hundred' people have passed through the group:

> People come and go. There's always been a core, an inner core, of dedicated regular people. And then there's the people on the periphery, who come in now and again. But everyone's needed, it's like a little ashram in that sense.

146

While the format of the meetings has become fairly standardised, with the meditation at its heart culminating in group recitation of the Great Invocation, the Unit cautiously incorporates fresh openings when they enhance the dominant Bailey base. During my period of involvement, contact was made at the Arcane School conference with members of two groups in the Irish Republic, and our meetings subsequently incorporated a short mental 'link-up' with a Unit of Service in Cork and a 'Goodwill Group' in Dublin. And as we have seen, spurred initially by my own enquiries into the Bailey cosmology, a 'New Moon' meeting was set up in 1996 to concentrate upon discussion and study of wider Lucis Trust material.

The Unit practises three general kinds of 'networking'. First, through Alison there was an informal connection with the local Quaker meeting house. She occasionally attended meetings for worship there and delivered a paper called 'What is Spirituality?' at a Quaker-sponsored forum in 1997. The Unit had also organised three public events at the meeting house in recent years, on the themes 'Building Wholeness' (1989), 'One Humanity' (1992), and 'Building Right Relations' (1997). These were day-long gatherings featuring speakers and discussion, and attracting audiences of fifty or so: Alison told me she modelled them on the Arcane School conference. Perhaps the most heterogeneous networked connection was a workshop called 'Dancing the Sevenfold Energies of Life', which the Unit effectively sponsored at the Meeting House in June 1996. This was an ambitious programme mixing Alice Bailey's esoteric philosophy of seven rays of creation with 'sacred' or folk dances from Europe and the Middle East.[30] The event was strongly dependent upon Unit of Service input, since Alison herself had suggested the venue to the couple leading the workshop, and in the event five of the eight participants, including myself, were Unit members. However, the workshop involved a degree of physical movement and touch that was rare in our group culture, and not all were comfortable with this – Alison herself made her excuses and left after lunch. We danced in a circle, holding hands, around a simple centrepiece consisting of a sky-blue scarf loosely spread out, with a small brass plate holding a light-blue candle in the middle. This burnt continuously and formed a natural focal point as we concentrated on the dance steps. In between dances we discussed in detail the creative and destructive characteristics of the seven rays according to Bailey's philosophy, and attempted to correlate the ritual movements of specific dances with psychological and spiritual 'inner' states.

In addition to this informal but persistent connection with the Quaker venue, the Unit maintained a more formal public presence at alternative health fairs – which is where I, for one, first met them. The hired tables at these events were deemed a success insofar as a good deal of literature (supplied by Lucis Trust HQ in London) was picked up by browsers, a few pounds accrued in donations, and a newcomer came along to the full-moon meditation now and again. Occasionally, as at the Livingston event mentioned earlier, the group also presented a talk and public meditation: on one occasion in Glasgow this attracted an audience of fifty.[31] Our table was supervised by whoever came along, with the core group predominating as usual. I helped out on several occasions, most prominently in October 1995 in Glasgow when I looked after the display alone for two hours while Deirdre attended a talk on spiritual healing. During this time I self-consciously fielded a variety of enquiries. One man asked about the Unit's relationship with Theosophy, a woman inquired into the 'Triangles' work, a young man involved in the Gnostic School of Anthropology asked me if, like them, we did *kundalini* meditation; a former acquaintance of mine from a writer's group shared his newfound interest in David Icke; and a young woman told me her father had been in the Arcane School and that they still had all the Bailey books in the house.[32] The group was pragmatic about these fairs: Deirdre said they reminded her of 'the hippie thing' and that you had to pick and choose very carefully; Gordon thought that the Unit's stall was 'a great service'; but Alison disliked the fairs and was glad when the Unit stopped participating around 1999.[33]

A third type of outreach was the result of individuals' particular lives and careers. I have noted some of Gordon's networks: he rejoined the Salisbury Centre as a Trustee during my time with the group and once or twice the Unit met there when Alison was away. Like Gordon, Deirdre was familiar with Findhorn, had done 'Experience Week' there, and at one point planned to do its three-month resident programme. Mark made a small living as a psychic artist, and for a time worked for an alternative health promoter: he, too, had visited Findhorn, and like Deirdre had participated in workshops on transpersonal psychology, a therapeutic movement sympathetic to the Bailey work. For her part, Alison occasionally spoke in public about Alice Bailey and the Lucis Trust and she also sometimes exhibited her drawings and paintings in which Bailey's symbology was usually to the fore: for example, at a private gallery during the 1996 Edinburgh festival her display included impressive line and watercolour illustrations to Shakespeare's *King Lear* alongside small woodcuts illustrating passages from the Bailey books.

Five years after my first contact with the Unit there was a significant shift. Alison's new husband assumed leadership of the group and plans were mooted to move the meditation meetings permanently to a public venue such as the Salisbury Centre or the Quaker Meeting House. Alison was relieved: she told me that running the Unit had 'always been a line of great resistance for me', the implication being that the task had been part of her 'soul' training and 'service' and not something her ego would willingly have chosen.[34]

Coda

In his survey of heterodox spiritual groups in the US, Ellwood (1973: 105) considered that the full-moon meditation groups had 'peaked in the early postwar years'. Certainly the eschatological 'New Age' promoted by the Lucis Trust contrasts markedly with the post-1970s turn towards human potential and self-realisation. The stance of the Unit of Service – indeed its very name – recalls many features of early 'New Age' instincts and attitudes, surveyed in Chapters 3 and 4. These include the emphasis on the group as an impersonal organism synthesising individual personalities, or egos, at a 'higher level'; the focus on technique and procedure as 'scientific' methods for achieving occult goals; the acceptance of 'hierarchy' and hence of the principle of organisation, role-differentiation and (implicitly) group statuses; the prominence of mental work in the form of concentration, visualisation, meditation, and correct thinking; a somewhat austere aesthetic emphasising mental and physical hygiene; and the grand idealism of 'world service' and selfless work for a universalised 'humanity'. Not least in this list is the Unit's quiet millennialism, encoded in the key petition 'may Christ return to earth' with which the Great Invocation closes. Indeed, the Lucis Trust confidently expects a conference of the Masters to take place in 2025, at which a decision will be made regarding the reappearance of the Christ. As Patrick quietly pointed out, because this 'great spiritual event' is 'fairly imminent', many of us can expect to see 'significant things happening'.

Finally, the small numbers and slight footprint of the Unit need not, in the emic view, mitigate its potency: indeed, by homeopathic analogy, empirical dilution might occultly *strengthen* its effect in the specific operation of hastening the return of the Christ.[35] And like Sheena Govan's group or the early Findhorn community, the Unit of Service has no commercial dimension: indeed, this was the sole site in my fieldwork in which a money transaction was *not* a prerequisite of entrance.

After the 'Leo' meditation meeting of August 1995 I scribbled this on the train home:

> To use a much-loved Bailey word, it is very *un*-glamorous: nearly half the group travel from out of town; there is only a little social intercourse, and an acknowledgment that the group is there to work – or to *serve* – rather than exist as a 'discussion group'; there is no such thing as a 'recruitment drive' – and the vastness of the Bailey cosmology suggests that – as Alison pointed out tonight – while cause and effect are inextricable (the law of karma), there's no knowing the *timescale* on which it operates. Thus, the 'light' generated tonight during the meditation might take a hundred years to have its particular effect.[36]

For her part Alison simply said:

> It doesn't sound much, does it, what we're doing, just meditating? But I think it's very important, it's fundamental. It's a real commitment.

7

A COLONY OF SEEKERS
Findhorn

> While we have no formal doctrine or creed, we believe that humanity is involved in an evolutionary expansion of consciousness which is creating new patterns of civilization and a planetary culture infused with spiritual values.
>
> (Findhorn Programme,
> April–October 1996, p. 2)

> We provide a training ground for spiritual seekers wishing to understand and express their own unique spirituality.
>
> (Walker 1994: 17)

Findhorn today

> Some people come here seeking to change the world; they may not be aware that the modern method of doing this is by changing themselves.
>
> (Riddell 1991: 133)

Findhorn[1] has grown into a substantial settlement that since 1962 has hosted three generations of spiritual seekers exploring alternative spiritualities, therapies, expressive arts and crafts, and gardening. In the 1960s and early 1970s, as we have seen, Findhorn was known as a 'New Age centre' or a 'centre of light'. More recently 'spiritual community', 'eco-village' and 'mystery school' (Walker 1994) are terms that have peppered its discourse and it now also describes itself as a 'NGO [non-governmental organisation] associated with the Department of Public Information of the United Nations'.[2]

This kaleidoscope of self-representations makes it difficult to pinpoint Findhorn's primary purpose or function. The shifting nomenclature is bound up with fluid organisational structures and a relatively high turnover of personnel: in the early 1990s Metcalf (1993: 10) pointed out that more than half the colony had been there 'less than five years'. The basic organisation consists in a 'core' group, which guards and tends Findhorn's overall vision; a management group, which handles practical decisions; and several work departments with their own budgets. Each department has a 'focaliser' (see below); there is also one focaliser for each of the two main settlements, and a focaliser for the Findhorn Foundation as a whole. Nevertheless, institutional adjustment is endemic to Findhorn: during the winter of 1996–7, for example, a radical overhaul saw the *en masse* resignation of the management committee and a lengthy process of internal consultation on long-term structure and aims. Simultaneously a new body, the Findhorn Bay Community Association, sprang up to speak for the interests of alternative practitioners and small businesses in the area in general, since the colony has attracted wider settlement in the locality by ex-residents and affiliates.[3] A further index of flux at Findhorn is the number of official 'vision statements' floated in recent years, ranging from the succinct – Judy Buhler-McAllister's (1995: 35) simple statement 'we are here to serve the transformation of consciousness' – to the verbose:

> The purpose of the Findhorn Foundation is to create a centre of service and living education for the integration of spiritual principles into everyday life: specifically to create new models for individuals and communities that seek to embody inspired forms of ecology, economy, culture and spirituality.[4]

So Findhorn at the beginning of the twenty-first century continues to be in the near-constant state of reflexive monitoring and organisational experiment that has characterised it from the beginning. The colony now occupies a number of buildings and grounds in and around the market town of Forres and the peninsulate village of Findhorn, twenty-five miles to the north-east of Inverness on the Moray Firth. It has grown and diversified over four decades, and now comprises two main geographical sites. The original settlement is called 'The Park', an abbreviation of 'Findhorn Bay Caravan Park', where the pioneers set up home in their caravan in November 1962; it was finally purchased in 1983. In 1972 the Findhorn Foundation was constituted as an educational trust and in 1975 it bought Cluny Hill Hotel ('God's Hotel' of Chapter 3), now known simply as 'Cluny'. These sites – some seven miles apart – and other Foundation properties, including the home of the Moray Steiner school and Newbold House, an affiliated community household – are linked by a daily minibus shuttle service.[5]

The Park is a small section of land bordered on the west by the main road into Findhorn village and, beyond it, the water of Findhorn Bay, and to the other sides by scrub and afforested land adjoining RAF Kinloss, a busy airbase. The latter is a persistent presence in the area: the main thoroughfare in The Park is a stretch of former aircraft runway. The Park gives the general impression of a well-tended holiday park: a profusion of caravans, chalets and wooden houses provide the bulk of resident accommodation, some community-owned, others now private. A Community Centre caters for the communal life of the settlement; the Universal Hall, a large stone building designed and erected by the community, seats three hundred and is the focus for conferences and meetings as well as touring theatre and music; the Apothecary sells homeopathic and herbal medicines; a Victorian villa accommodates an eclectic library of esoteric literature; and the Phoenix Shop is a sizeable foodstore and bookshop.[6] Communal meditation takes place in The Sanctuary, a large wooden chalet dating from the late 1960s, and also in a small, semi-underground chamber, the Nature Sanctuary, constructed in 1986. A 'green' agenda can be seen in some turf-roofed buildings, an ecological sewage treatment plant, a wind-powered turbine, and 'Trees for Life', a charitable project regenerating native forest in Highland glens. There is a scattering of cars, and some bicycles, but people largely walk around the site.

The 'Cluny' site consists in the massive Victorian hotel building with its sloping garden grounds, including a wooded knoll said to be a 'power point', up and around which a worn spiral path has been trodden over the years. The building itself contains several floors and around two hundred rooms, including large kitchens, a dining room, a ballroom, several large lounges, and a small bookshop. A high-ceilinged room at the rear of the building accommodates Cluny's Sanctuary. It is a busy building, like a large but comfortable youth hostel, and hosts the majority of Findhorn's visitors.

In 1991 the Foundation had about one hundred and seventy 'members', including children and dependents.[7] The community in total – ex-members and associates in addition to the resident core – numbered between four and five hundred. A 1989 count showed that almost two-thirds of the adult residents were women, nearly three-quarters were aged between thirty and fifty, all were white, and a sizeable majority came from the UK, the US and West Germany (Riddell 1991: 132). Participation in Findhorn by Scottish nationals has been, and remains, minimal, with the exception of early figures such as Lena Lamont, one of the 'Nameless Ones' discussed in Chapter 3, and an Edinburgh Theosophist, R. Ogilvie Crombie, who visited regularly in the 1960s. Of two separate fieldwork visits I made in 1995, the 'Experience Week' group contained only one participant resident in Scotland (myself), and less than ten per cent of participants in a sizeable conference on the 'Western Mysteries' lived in Scotland. A simple questionnaire that I circulated within the community supports and clarifies this profile. The self-selected sample of respondents rarely claimed 'New Age' identities, although most could offer sophisticated definitions of the term. They preferred 'spirituality' to 'religion', the latter being understood as 'dogmatic' and 'political'. Alternative medicine and healing were widely advocated, practised, and interwoven with this 'spirituality'. Respondents were overwhelmingly early to late middle-aged: that is, a quarter were aged 30–39, two-thirds 40+. A high level of education was in evidence: almost two-thirds of the sample had attended a university.[8] Another survey, conducted internally in 1997, mapped the kinds of spiritual practice followed at Findhorn: from a sample of one hundred, forty-nine meditated in some way, seventeen prayed, sixteen 'walked in nature', and seventeen studied spiritual texts.[9]

Findhorn ethos and economy

It is a sort of spiritual supermarket, where you can pick and mix and try to find something which suits you.

(Male Findhorn resident)[10]

Life at Findhorn, according to Riddell (1991: 62), is essentially an 'ongoing workshop'.[11] The metaphor appropriately suggests a culture of discussion and experiment, risk and change. In the mid-1990s the Findhorn Foundation had a turnover of around one million pounds a year, most of which stemmed from its year-round programme of residential courses, conferences and workshops. These feature experimental spiritualities, healing practices and ecological concerns and are advertised in brochures distributed via an international mailing list of some twenty thousand individuals, groups and organisations (at the peak of outreach in the mid-1990s). For example, over the winter of 1994–5 there were conferences on 'Process-Oriented Psychology' and 'The Western Mysteries', and a three-month gardening course. Week-long courses included 'Towards Inner Peace and Planetary Wholeness', 'Enlightened Leadership', 'Inner Listening', 'Celtic Creation' and 'Iona – A Landscape Temple'. Multi-week 'spiritual journeys' led by Foundation staff have also been available: for example, 'Sacred Nepal' and 'African Wilderness and the Human Spirit: a Spiritual Journey to Zimbabwe'. More recent workshops have explored 'The Gay Man's Inner Journey', 'Relationships as a Path of Spiritual Growth', and 'Shamanic Consciousness'.[12] The brochures also include details of residential training in the Foundation lifestyle, ranging from the mandatory 'Experience Week' to an apprenticeship of a year or more, after which one might become an employee of the Foundation, settle in the locality, or simply move on.

As one might expect, the demographic profile of visitors closely matches the resident population: Riddell (1991: 112) notes that the majority are white, middle-class professionals, aged 30–45, interested in the environment and self-development; she also notes 'more than average' single and divorced people for the age cohort. But the general profile of Findhorn is changing as more Japanese, Brazilian and East European nationals visit. Such shifts reflect wider trends in the global economy. In the early 1990s, for example, Metcalf (1993: 11) discerned a 'dramatic shift' since the 1970s from an American to a European core of visitors, and from the 'alternative' to the 'mainstream' sector: he claims that two-thirds of contemporary guests increasingly pursue careers in 'mainstream' society, and half again are 'business people'. This, of course, fits Riddell's demography and indicates the acculturation of a general idiom of spirituality, healing and personal growth in the culture at large. Metcalf also perceived a trend in the 1980s 'of privatisation and devolution' in the colony that eroded the oft-perceived 'communality' of Findhorn. But consider a remark of a recent chief focaliser of the community: 'The Findhorn Foundation Community is often talked about as an intentional community. It wasn't, it was an *accidental community*' (Buhler-McAllister 1995: 35; emphasis added). This is further support for using 'colony' or 'settlement' as the most apt descriptors of Findhorn, since these terms accommodate the characteristic to-ing and fro-ing of seekers and the constantly shifting institutional structures, characteristics that are homogenised and reified by the term 'community'.[13] I return to this point at the end of the chapter. In the meantime, as the following ethnography of 'Experience Week' suggests, 'community' is less an agent than a by-product of Findhornian praxis: the main focus of the colony is the reflexivity and regeneration of the individual seeker.

Experience Week: Findhorn in a nutshell

> It is a week spent saying hallo to spirit in very practical ways.
> (Riddell 1991: 117)

Findhorn's mandatory vehicle of socialisation is 'Experience Week', a week-long introduction to the colony's co-operative lifestyle. Riddell (1991: 117) describes it as 'an experience of our life in microcosm'. In contrast to the fluctuating structures and personnel mentioned earlier, Experience Week has demonstrated consistency of form and content over time since its trial run in the mid-1970s and hence serves as a reliable guide to certain norms and values operative at Findhorn (and, by extension, elsewhere in alternative spirituality).[14] The following ethnography is based on my fieldwork notes and observations from one such week in February 1995.[15]

My first contact with Findhorn was an envelope franked with the slogan 'Expect a Miracle'. Inside I read that 'Experience Week' was a 'group experience' designed to enable individuals 'to find personal expression in a group context':

> Work is an integral part of our life here through which many of our spiritual lessons are learnt. The rest of the time is devoted to group activities, which aim to deepen your understanding of the Foundation, to encourage you to give and receive support in the ongoing process of spiritual growth, to bring forth your inner riches of love and truth as unique contributions to the world, and to honour the Divine in all life.[16]

It was clearly a serious undertaking. A 'willingness to meet others with love and respect, to share yourself openly and to participate fully' was stipulated and prospective participants had to submit a personal letter detailing their 'spiritual background, if any' and explaining why they wished to come. I outlined my research interests and also mentioned my personal career as a seeker in the 1980s. I concluded earnestly that

> if pressed, I would probably describe myself as a 'religious humanist': that is, I don't believe in 'God', but I do believe that all relationships, all things, must somehow be experienced 'religiously' if we are to begin to fathom the depths and mystery of our worlds.[17]

What the personnel at Findhorn made of this cerebral play I am not sure, but the process of composing a lengthy personal letter to an unknown institution, and then waiting for a reply, made me both expectant and a little anxious. Had I written the 'right kind' of letter? Would my research be tolerated? In short, would I pass muster? In fact a prompt and friendly reply confirmed my place, but contained otherwise troubling information for a researcher on 'New Age': 'Yes, people seem to associate our Community with the "New Age"', wrote the Foundation employee, 'although the general feeling here is that the "New Age" is over'.

As Brierley and Walker (1995: 33) acknowledge, Findhorn is 'by and large dependent upon people travelling hundreds of miles to visit it'. In fact my own journey from Stirling, in central Scotland, was significantly simpler in cost and mileage than those of the other members of my Experience Week group. Increasingly expensive and time-consuming journeys had to be made by Vicky from Manchester, Nick from the Bristol area, Walter from Torquay on the Devon coast, Conor, an Irishman, from Kent, and Sonja, a Serbian student, from London. Others came from further afield: Anna from the Netherlands; Jutta from Munich; Veronique, a Swiss national, from Berlin; Kathy from Oregon; Martine from Brazil; and Corinne, an American, from Switzerland. Many were thus dependent upon air travel, which increased the financial outlay of the week considerably.[18] Two others – Kirsten from Germany and Ingrid from Sweden – were resident Findhorn staff who were participating as part of an internal training programme in group facilitation, and so were already on site. We were fourteen in all, then: ten women and four men, all white Euro–Americans, and three-quarters aged in our thirties and forties, although the overall age range was wide: the youngest, Martine from Brazil, was twenty-one; the oldest, Walter from Torquay, was seventy-eight. Our group profile thus broadly conformed to typical Findhorn demography.

The week ran from Saturday afternoon to the following Friday evening. Apart from two free evenings and one free afternoon, the days were fully programmed. Concentration and stamina were required, and the atmosphere could be emotionally intense. Built into the week was a variety of activities that exemplified Findhorn's environment and lifestyle: guided tours, group sessions, work placements, and informal talks and 'sharings' from residents.

Saturday

Saturday morning, Experience Week
I'm so nervous I can hardly speak
Arrive at Cluny Hill, half past ten
Almost turned and went home again.[19]

I arrived in Forres just after eleven o'clock on a sunny but cold February morning, prepared for a brisk walk from the station to Cluny in time for registration by noon. However, a handful of individuals had boarded a plain white minibus in the car-park, and on enquiry I learnt that this was the Findhorn Foundation bus and it was going to Cluny. Inside two men in their thirties – Conor and Nick, I later found out – gazed pensively out of opposite windows. An American woman of a similar age – Kathy – asked the driver some questions about Findhorn as we got going. He said non-committally, 'Wait and see, you'll find out for yourself'. We drove through busy shopping traffic. Just outside the town, we headed up a short drive – unsignposted except for 'Private' – and emerged in front of Cluny's imposing bulk. The reception area was busy as our group arrived and another group left: people came and went, parting with smiles and hugs, moving luggage here and there. In the adjoining lounge others read newspapers or talked quietly.

We were directed up a wide staircase to the 'Beech Tree room', a spacious apartment with a bay window. Here it was darker and quieter. A tape of popular songs from the 1940s played and the atmosphere was demure and relaxed. A bursar took outstanding monies and introduced Dagmar and Paul, respectively German and English, both also in their late thirties, who were to be our 'focalisers' for the week ahead. Riddell (1991: 97–8) explains that focalisers are responsible for 'holding the energy' of a group, which means 'connecting with, and making sure others connect with, an inner, spiritual significance of situations, so that things can happen "from the inside out"'. Dagmar gave us a timetable for the week and then led us on a brisk tour of Cluny's facilities: laundry rooms, small shop (books, postcards and candles), dining room, kitchens, Sanctuary, and finally our bedrooms. My notebook records: 'Everything neat, precise, aesthetically quite luscious'. I shared a room with Conor, the Irishman from Kent. On our beds, tucked into folded towels, were 'blessings' cards – small commercially-produced mottoes – left by the housework team. On mine was printed, mysteriously, 'Sisterhood'. I mulled this over. Conor and I chatted. When I explained why I'd come to Findhorn, he said disapprovingly: 'So you're not a heartfelt New Ager, then?'

I wandered outside to admire the view: Cluny sits on a rise overlooking a manicured golf course with small hills beyond. Vicky was sitting on a bench in the sun, apologetically smoking a cigarette. We chatted briefly: like Conor, she'd travelled the previous day and taken a local bed and breakfast for the night. She put out her cigarette – smoking is rare at Findhorn – and we went to join the noon meditation in the Sanctuary.

There are now three Sanctuaries in all, two at the Park and one at Cluny. The main Park Sanctuary is a purpose-built wooden chalet with a low ceiling, net curtains, a circle of plain upholstered armless chairs, and an abstract weaving of a sunrise on the main wall. There is also a more intimate Nature Sanctuary, which I describe later. The Cluny Sanctuary, where we now headed, is a large airy room with high bay windows at one end where several potted shrubs and plants grew. A stained glass panel on the opposite wall pictured the roots and branches of a flourishing tree. Outside the room we followed the etiquette of removing footwear, leaving our shoes alongside other neat pairs. Atmosphere and deportment in preparation for Sanctuary practice was markedly sober, even grave: I noticed that people now avoided body and eye contact where elsewhere they actively sought it.

Inside the Sanctuary about eighty chairs and a dozen cushions were arranged in a circle around a low table holding a large candle in an elaborate artificial flower arrangement. That Saturday there were perhaps only two dozen people present. I took a seat; a few more came in, in ones and twos. Most people chose the comfortable armless chairs, although some used bulky meditation cushions clustered around the centrepiece. A rota volunteer switched on a prominent red bulb outside the room to warn latecomers that the meditation session had begun: no one should now enter or leave (without good reason) in order to avoid disturbing the 'energy' generated by the group meditation. This volunteer read out a few words from Eileen Caddy's book of guidance, *Opening Doors Within* (a copy of which was left in each sanctuary) and then struck a metal bowl. This emitted a low, reverberating note. The meditation had begun, and continued in silence for some twenty minutes. Most meditators had closed eyes – one man wore a sleeping mask – and sat with feet on the floor; some sat cross-legged on the chairs; many rested cupped hands lightly on their laps, palms uppermost, thumbs lightly touching. Twenty minutes later the bowl was struck again to conclude the session. Most left quietly then, although one or two lingered in solitary meditation. Someone picked up the Caddy text and pondered it. As we walked quietly down to the dining room for lunch, Conor asked me 'How was the meditation for you?' His had been 'powerful', he said.

Meditation at Findhorn revolved around two sanctuary sessions daily, in the morning and at noon. Abstract themes supplied a general focus for each session, such as 'love', 'wisdom', 'compassion', and 'healing'. Special meditations also took place: during my stay, for AIDS sufferers. There were also regular singing sessions using songs and chants from the French Christian community, Taizé. Individual use of the Sanctuaries also proceeds more or less around the clock, and it was not unusual to see one or two pairs of shoes or slippers outside the door at most times of the day or evening.

Food at Findhorn is vegetarian with some vegan options, although fish is served on Fridays when alcohol is also available.[20] After a tasty buffet lunch, we gathered in the Beech Tree room for our first group session. We sat on comfortable straight-back chairs in a large circle, in the middle of which was placed, on the floor, a lit candle in an arrangement of dried leaves and pine cones. We discussed the week's schedule and were given a thumbnail sketch of the community by our focalisers. Paul said that Findhorn's focus was getting in touch with divine reality: 'what we call Spirit', he said, 'or the God within'. Dagmar and Paul now introduced us to a ritual practice called 'attunement'.[21] To 'attune', we remained in a circle, facing in, joined hands and closed our eyes. The ritual requires a special way of connecting hands: the right hand is offered palm-up, the left palm-down (we fumbled self-consciously with this at first, some of us giggling). Dagmar spoke a few words – 'let us bless the week ahead and be open to all that it brings' – which we considered quietly for a few moments. Then she lightly squeezed her neighbours' hands and let go: this signal was passed round the circle and we gradually opened our eyes. Our first attunement was over. For a few moments, the group remained quiet and thoughtful, some smiling, others making gentle eye contact. Looking around me, I thought I saw stiller bodies and calmer faces.

We were now ready to be instructed in 'sharing'. In this practice, individuals take it in turns to speak about whatever they wish so long as they express themselves 'from the heart', as a popular expression in the colony has it. Dagmar said: 'We share according to what I call the popcorn principle: when you feel something bubbling inside, it's your turn, you're ready to go!' But Paul carefully explained that sharing is no emotional free-for-all. He introduced some ground rules. First, we were to speak from our own experience, from what we had 'gone through' ourselves, rather than according to opinions we had formed or ideas we had acquired 'second-hand', as it were. Second, we were to speak in the first person only, a speech act known as making an 'I' statement or 'owning' one's communication: speculation and abstraction were out. Third, we should seek eye contact with whomever we were addressing, rather than looking away as we spoke. Fourth, listeners were not to interrupt when someone was sharing – whether to agree, dispute or offer advice – although a challenge could be made to a contribution deemed overly discursive and hence lacking the crucial ingredients of spontaneity and reflexivity. Such a challenge was soon forthcoming from Dagmar to my room-mate Conor, when he began to talk rather abstractly of finding 'things' difficult and depressing. 'Conor, is that an "I" statement you're making?', she prompted, 'are you talking about yourself?' Similarly, when Sonja, the Serbian student, suddenly became self-conscious in the middle of a sentence and dropped her eyes, Paul said: 'Sonja, look up, look around you, look at the group!' Former Findhorn resident Akhurst (1992: 116) has written: 'There is something tender about such a gaze that touches a deep level, a place near the heart that lets the other in, attaching no judgment or expectation'. Perhaps so, but it could be disconcerting to the novice, particularly among a group of people who had only just met. But 'stranger' was a concept that would soon be challenged under the accelerated conditions of Experience Week.

The purpose of this first session quickly became apparent. We were to apply our understanding of the new ritual practices we had been taught – focalising, attuning and sharing – to our personal 'introductions' to the rest of the group: that is, our biographical stories of how and why we had come to Findhorn. Taking it in turns around the circle, we passed two hours in this fashion. The careful choice of words by each speaker, close reciprocal attention from the group, and a general heightening of emotional intensity all round were the noticeable effects of our clumsy but game experimentation with these new interpersonal rituals. Nick, a self-employed computer programmer and Quaker attendee, told us he'd known of Findhorn 'for years' – 'I always knew I'd come' – but had prevaricated 'because I was afraid I'd never leave once I got here!' Vicky, a mother and 'closet' Pagan, was keen to explore the Community's understanding of 'nature', but commitments to her children had prevented her from visiting sooner. Corinne, also a mother, used images of pregnancy and childbirth to celebrate her female creativity; born in America, living now in Switzerland, she described herself as a 'world citizen'. Kathy, another software programmer, had come as part of an extended European holiday she had organised to take stock of her foundering marriage; she claimed to know relatively little about Findhorn and to have come on impulse. Veronique, a Swiss-born midwife from Berlin, had just ended a long-term partnership; like Kathy, she remained preoccupied throughout the week and was particularly unforthcoming in this first session, partly through language difficulties. One exchange in particular underlined the new ethos of expressivity and bodily contact. In the middle of telling us how he had left a secure job in computers to travel on his savings, Conor became tongue-tied and agitated, whereupon Walter, a long-term Theosophist who had previously visited Findhorn in the 1970s, crossed the room and said, 'come on, old son, stand up: you need a hug!' Thus two men who had only just met – one in his late seventies, the other in his mid-thirties – embraced briefly and awkwardly in front of the group: the first of many such hugs.

And so it went on until all had spoken, whereupon we held hands again to 'tune out'.[22] A pattern of interaction and a conceptual framework were deftly set out by Dagmar and Paul during this first session. Whatever else we did in the week ahead, we would meet as a group every day, attuning, sharing and generally taking our cue from the hints and nudges of our focalisers. The willed intensity of this attitudinal transformation on the part of a group of strangers from all over the world was summed up in Corinne's remark to me after dinner: 'We're a family now'. That same morning we had not even met.

In the evening there was a mixed gender sauna, but such self-disclosure was more than anyone in our group was yet ready for. Before bed I spent twenty-five minutes in the Sanctuary, alone, digesting the events of the day. My notes read: 'I decide to go *deep within* and *listen*, rather than look to a lead from others in the group'. Findhorn was already casting its spell.

Sunday

> We do not attempt to come to simple, rational decisions, based on the perceived interests of the parties involved. We seek to find 'what wants to happen', by inner attunement.
>
> (Riddell 1991: 93)

> Something inside me said, *Yeah – that's it*. It wasn't a voice, more a feeling, but I knew it was true. My mind said no, while my heart said yes.
>
> (Tattersall 1996: 22)

'Nothing real can be threatened. Nothing unreal exists. Herein lies the peace of God'. These opening words from *A Course in Miracles*, a massive channelled text first published in America in 1975, were quietly intoned by an Irish woman in her forties to begin morning Sanctuary meditation. I recognised some of our group among the twenty or so present. Yesterday we had been encouraged to join in the community meditation schedule, but although many of our group, including myself, participated most days, on no occasion was the Sanctuary more than about half-full at most. Akhurst (1992: 113) noticed a similar pattern when he lived at Findhorn in the mid-1980s: 'Guests told me they could see all the Experience Week [participants] in the Sanctuary morning and evening, but where were the members? Did they meditate at different times?'[23] I return to this point later.

This morning a visualisation exercise followed the lesson from *A Course in Miracles*. We were invited to imagine ourselves moving towards an intense source of light that was obscured by clouds, and yet to understand that these clouds had no real substance; we were invited to feel them soft and wet against our eyes and forehead as we floated into them and through them . . . and then we were left to the morning silence. A thrush called outside; someone coughed; the candle in the middle flickered and recovered. Walter and Veronique breached Sanctuary etiquette by stumbling in when the red light was on and whispering noisily in the vestibule. Later I overheard the rota volunteer telling Dagmar to make sure our group understood correct procedure.

After Sanctuary we gathered in the ballroom to do 'Sacred Dance': folk dances from Greece, Yugoslavia, Israel and Russia. Introduced into the community by a German musicologist in the 1970s, Sacred Dance – elsewhere called 'circle dance' or 'international community dance' – is now an established feature of Findhorn life.[24] Music was provided by a well-worn tape-recording of the Findhorn Sacred Dance Band. These dances required close physical contact, from holding hands to clasping each others' waists. Once again we were encouraged not to flinch from eye contact nor to 'block the energy' in needless chatter between dances. In my notebook I wrote: 'They're fun, simple steps and neat movements, and a good way to relate without words'.

At brunch in the palatial dining room I sought out Dagmar, who was sitting alone by the large bay window. I tentatively voiced my scepticism about some ingredients in the Findhorn mix – UFOs, 'Spirit', 'power points'. To my surprise, Dagmar laughed: 'Yeah, I don't feel anything when I go up there, either', she said, referring to the 'power point' behind Cluny.

In the afternoon we drove by minibus to Findhorn village. It was cold and wintry; the village was quiet, the large caravan park shut up for the winter. We came to the beach, a long, bare expanse of sand and pebbles. We milled around for a while, skimming stones, scanning the cold sea for dolphins, or simply gazing out on the dark hills across the Moray Firth. Paul chose a special pebble he told us we would need for our group work later in the week. Then we drove the mile or so back to the Park, where an Australian resident took us on a walking tour of the original caravan settlement. Although now considerably expanded and landscaped, the Park retains a 'frontier' atmosphere: despite increasing numbers of new houses, much accommodation is still chalets, caravans, and even whisky-barrels (a cluster of converted distillery casks, known as 'Bag End' after Bilbo's home in *The Hobbit*). The overall impression is simultaneously parochial and countercultural, a cross between a seaside chalet park and an 'alternative' village. Buildings nestle among trees, shrubs and a network of paths. We visited the shabby but welcoming Community Centre, the Universal Hall (an imposing edifice with a large performance hall, basement recording rooms, and cafe), and the Nature Sanctuary, all built by the community. Our tour ended at the latter, a small oval chamber whose site had been chosen, according to our guide, following advice from 'one of the little people': a fairy or nature spirit. Heating kept the room warm, comfortable and curiously womb-like. We sat on cushions around the walls; a candle on the cleft stone centrepiece was lit; and Paul and Dagmar introduced a new exercise. First, as usual, we attuned; then we each silently meditated upon a particular 'quality' we wished to receive from the week. Finally we drew an 'angel card' from a small pile. This represented the reality of the 'quality' or issue we had to 'work with', like it or not. Like the 'blessings' card slipped into our towels at Cluny, the angel card showed an abstract word, but this time illustrated by a rather schmaltzy cartoon of angels.[25] In my meditation I had requested 'Confidence', but actually drew 'Faith'. The picture showed two angels in mid-air flight between trapeze swings. Not unlike the epistemic acrobatics required by the fieldworker, I thought. On the other hand, perhaps the angels were nudging me to rethink my scepticism? Others were not so fortunate: Kathy, for example, struggling with feelings of depression over her failing marriage, drew 'Joy', and bitterly displayed her selection to the group. A card was also drawn to symbolise the group's overall essence: it was 'Release'. 'Mmm', nodded Dagmar. Paul raised his eyebrows and smiled.

Back at Cluny, we gathered after dinner. Paul added the pebble from the beach and the group's 'Release' angel card to the candle arrangement in the centre of the circle. Now we were to attune to find appropriate work placements for each of us in the week ahead. Several of the group – Anna and Vicky in particular – wanted to work in the famous Findhorn gardens. Paul read out a list of the departments currently needing help, and we were asked to meditate to discover which one we felt 'drawn to', the idea being that 'we would feel something inside ourselves' for the right job (Tattersall 1996: 22). The list was then read out again, and by a pragmatic combination of meditation and reflection, the various requirements were resolved. Following half an hour of sharing, the evening concluded with a session entitled 'Inner Life'. 'Frank is coming to share with you on spiritual practice', said Dagmar. Frank was an American in his late forties or early fifties. He enthusiastically described Findhorn to us as 'living Zen'. 'It's about being *here*, *now*', he said, 'rather than *there*, *then*'. He supported this message with readings from Benjamin Hoff's *The Tao of Pooh* and T. S. Eliot's poem *Little Gidding*. Frank spoke charismatically about his own 'spiritual path', which began with Psychosynthesis, took him to Findhorn in the 1970s and then on to Bhagwan Shree Rajneesh in Poona, India, before recently returning to Findhorn. To end the session he led a visualisation exercise in which we were to imagine ourselves sitting in a darkened film theatre ready to watch the 'movie of your own life'. But the film was playing in reverse, running backwards through our recent past, into early adulthood and teenage years, back into our childhoods, and finishing with us as discarnate spirits about to enter our mothers' wombs. We then quickly re-wound the film to the present and visualised ourselves leaving our 'home movies' with fresh understanding of our life purpose. Frank's mellifluous drone wove an atmosphere of drama and empowerment around this simple exercise in the recuperation of popular culture for spiritual practice.

Monday

Work is love in action.

(Findhorn saying)

Today we began our work placements. Jutta, the young German woman from Munich, and I had attuned to posts in the Community Centre at the Park, so we took the morning minibus from Cluny, arriving just in time for meditation in the Park Sanctuary. This is the original Findhorn Sanctuary: as we saw in Chapter 2, it occupies a site said to be a 'power point'. It is a quiet chalet sheltered by trees and shrubs. This morning about forty meditators were present, and the session began with a Taize chant.

The Park Sanctuary is a stone's throw from the Community Centre (known as the 'CC'), where work began just after nine o'clock. We were six in the work group: the CC focaliser, Stella, one of the few Scots residents I met, a

Glaswegian with infectious spontaneity; Jane, a studious American who was enrolled as a Foundation student; a Swiss student, Heidi, who had decided that Findhorn wasn't for her and was in her final week there; Rudi, an Austrian psychotherapist now experimenting with spiritual healing; and the Experience Week neophytes, Jutta and myself. The group gave us a warm welcome, and we sat on benches round one of the dining tables to attune and share. Stella, the focaliser, went first. 'I'm feeling just great!' she announced, throwing out her arms and laughing, 'It's just great to *be* here'. 'Mmm,' said Rudi, smiling and nodding slowly as he looked at each of us in turn, 'I'm feeling *good*.' 'Yeah, I'm feeling pretty good this morning, but tired after a busy weekend' said Jane. Only Heidi was muted: 'I think it's time for me to move on,' she said, and shrugged. The others nodded soberly. But the general enthusiasm was contagious. I said I was glad to be at the Park and among the wider community: indeed, I was beginning to find our group sessions at Cluny claustrophobic and reminiscent of group therapy.

We set to work. Our remit was to clean the entrance hallway, toilets, dining and lounge areas of the CC while the Kitchen staff – including Martine from our group – laboured behind the hatch preparing the lunch. We were to clean the furniture, maintain condiments and candles on the table tops, and vacuum and mop the floors. As it happens, I was working in a celebrated role: no less a figure than Peter Caddy (1996: 328) – presumably with his own catering apprenticeship in mind – thought that cleaning the CC was

> a wonderful training ground for future leaders, for it was necessary to be very aware: to make sure that the tables were lined up, the salt and pepper pots were full, the window sills dusted, and that the tables were laid in time for each meal. It involved real discipline and attention to detail, and was where the founding principles of Findhorn could be put into practice – to love where you are, to love whom you're with, and to love what you're doing.

If the tasks nevertheless seemed menial, the atmosphere was pleasant – Rudi put some orchestral music on – and the pace was leisurely. 'Those toilets look great!', called Jane to me as she wandered past with the vacuum cleaner. We had an extended tea-break, and were comfortably finished in time for noon Sanctuary. We ended the session by tuning out: Stella blessed the morning's work and enjoined us to release our feelings and 'move on' into the rest of the day. After Sanctuary, the CC filled up for lunch with about sixty people, most of them residents and employees. Many lit candles at their tables. The atmosphere was busy and convivial.

Back at Cluny a session of 'trust' games was scheduled under the heading 'Group Discovery'. Two Foundation staff, a young Italian man, Dario, and an older German woman, Helge, were our focalisers. 'You're gonna enjoy this,' said Dario, in heavily Americanised English, 'I just *love* seeing groups open up to the games'. We began with a mirroring exercise. I paired up with Walter, the elderly Theosophist. Facing each other, we took it in turns to initiate movements – facial gestures, arm or torso movements – which the other copied as closely as possible. The aim was to reach a point where movement and response were so seamlessly integrated that it was difficult for an outsider to differentiate them. Next we played 'cars and drivers': the 'cars' closed their eyes, and were directed by the 'drivers', who stood behind them and 'drove' them with hands on shoulders. Paired with Jutta, I found her enthusiastic 'driving' quite unnerving. Although I kept my eyes shut, I tensed my body. Afterwards Jutta said, half-accusingly, half-jokingly: 'You didn't trust me!'

Two exuberant games followed. The first was a children's tag game where you could only escape being 'it' by hugging somebody. This occasioned waves of adrenalin and gales of laughter. In the second, we stood with closed eyes while our focalisers assigned us one of several animal categories. At the command 'dogs!', 'goats! or in my case 'sheep!' (and was this esoterically significant, I wondered?), we had to locate our fellow creatures across the room by making appropriate animal noises and feeling with our hands. This was generally hilarious, and 'baa-ing' at each other became a running joke through the week between myself and Veronique.

There were two quiet physical exercises. In the first, to the accompaniment of ambient music we took it in turns to assume a contorted shape on the floor to symbolise isolation and retreat from the world. The partner – in my case Paul the focaliser – then carefully 'unfolded' my knotted shape, lifting my limbs and rearranging me in a more relaxed position. In the space for feedback afterwards, I told Paul I found his handling of me a bit brisk. 'Sorry', he said, simply. In the second, we closed eyes again and were paired with an anonymous partner. Taking one of their hands in ours, we were to express, with the activity of our fingers only, various stipulated moods and emotions: for example, 'sadness', 'joy' or 'irritation'. I found this an intimate and touching exercise.

This session dramatically promoted a wide spectrum of physical contact, including the rumbustious, the sensual and the tender. Tears, laughter and hugging spread like a contagion through the group as we got into our new behavioural stride, and the afternoon finished in a riot of hugging, in couples, trios and, finally, as one large group. Such close physical contact was encouraged by the pervasive culture at Findhorn of taking the other's hand or touching her arm when speaking, even in brief everyday encounters, and by generous hugging when greeting, sharing or parting, often for a minute or longer. I overheard one individual hail another at Cluny reception with the exclamation 'Hey, give me one of those famous Findhorn full-frontals!', meaning the colony's characteristically close, lingering hug.

That evening, following a relaxed half-hour of sharing, a staff gardener visited us to talk about 'Nature'. First we did a guided meditation to attune to the 'nature spirits' – in my case, unsuccessfully – and then the gardener told us of her favourite gardening techniques, including meditating with the plants and dowsing for 'earth energies'. Some tentative, even awed, questions followed, particularly from Vicky regarding the nature spirits and the 'Pan energy' associated with Findhorn. There was also some approving discussion of the 'Perelandra' method of esoteric gardening in the US, whereby selected rows of crops are 'offered' to local fauna, such as rabbits, in exchange for their not encroaching on the rest of the crop. In my notebook I wrote impatiently: 'Much talk all day on "energy", which is a word that stands for much and anything'. Talismanic use of the term 'energy' is in fact pervasive in the discourse of alternative spirituality. St John (1977: 39–40) notes how 'an individual may feel a lot of energy or a lack of energy', that 'energy in a group may be high or low, may suddenly surge or droop' and that in general 'energy is something that gets blocked (bad) or flows freely and spontaneously (good)'.

Tuesday

Tuesday morning, with a hoover in my hand
Cleaning out the dining room, beginning to understand
Tuning in, tuning out
Startin' to see what Findhorn is all about.

In the morning I was back in the CC at the Park, one moment polishing table tops, the next talking about spiritual healing with Rudi at teabreak. These work placements gave us insight into the day-to-day life of the wider community, a factor also advantageous to Findhorn since without exception prospective students, even those who wish to take further workshops, must begin their career in an Experience Week. The work placement also suggested that the intense interpersonal contact propagated in our group sessions remained high in the colony at large and was not simply an exaggerated distillate of Experience Week. As one might expect, however, effusive and indiscriminate sharing seemed to be particularly redolent of novices like ourselves, and a degree of behavioural routinisation (less demonstrative, more selective) could be detected in other strata in the colony, especially among veteran residents and families (a distinctly minority grouping). But mixing with residents generally reinforced the new behavioural and cognitive norms we had learned. At the same time Stella genuinely encouraged us to re-evaluate our attitude to mundane work: instead of seeing it as a chore to be done as quickly as possible, we should see it as an end in itself and learn how to *enjoy* it. Thus cheery conversation, jokes and bright music were typical punctuations to a week of undemanding but essentially dreary domestic labour.

The morning passed quickly and we tuned out with Stella's simple blessings on the work. Just before lunch there was a special gathering to mark the restoration of the Caddys' original caravan, just across the path from where Eileen Caddy now lived, in a timber house symbolically named 'Cornerstone'. Part of the original garden beside the caravan was also restored and dedicated to the nature spirits. Forty to fifty residents and friends were gathered, including Caddy herself in fresh lipstick, blue-rinsed hair and wellington boots, and carrying a large framed photograph of her husband, Peter, who had been killed in a car crash the previous year. There was some live music from violin and accordion and then the focaliser of the restoration project spoke. The caravan embodied the spirit of Findhorn, he said; it marked the site where 'spirit first came into matter'. Although some had opposed the restoration project, he continued, Eileen herself, the sole founder still in residence, had wanted the caravan to be saved. Then Caddy herself, in a clipped English accent, pronounced a 'blessing of the Christ' on the caravan.

Back at Cluny we gathered on the grass outside the main entrance at 1.50 p.m. sharp (the week was immaculately choreographed) for a group photograph. Next on the schedule was a 'Nature Outing'. We drove to a popular beauty spot on the Findhorn river, attuned beside the swirling peaty water, and were invited by Dagmar simply to '*be* in nature' for the next couple of hours. 'Feel the energy. See what happens', she said with a smile. Some wandered off in pairs; others, including myself, chose to be alone. Apart from Vicky, whom I saw sitting on a boulder beside the spate, swaying and chanting in impromptu Pagan worship, and Sonja, whom I passed in a sandy cove sadly prodding the water with a stick, I scarcely saw the others. My notebook simply records: 'Many thoughts came and went'.

The evening sharing was long and relaxed: 'much giggling, as well as from-the-heart accounts', reads my notebook. But I also wrote: 'When does Findhorn become "easy", "glib"? How open is it to feelings of conflict, of anger?' I realised that the emic response to my query would be to turn it back on itself: or rather, to turn *me* back on *myself* and hence to see the question as a projection of my own suspicion and scepticism, my own negativity. For the second half of the evening Christina, overall focaliser for the Park, joined us to explain management structures at Findhorn. These, she said, were always fluid: the main tension was between 'core group', guardians of Findhorn's spiritual vision, and management group, who budgeted for the bigger picture.[26] To Corinne's complaint about the apparent lack of provision for children and families at Findhorn, Christina replied that the dynamic flux of the place 'throws the spotlight on *you* to create the space *you* want'. Since 'external events are really reflections of internal processes: that is, the world, and everything in it, is a mirror of the self', then it was simply up to us to identify and effect the changes we desired.[27] The goal was to find space for a variety of lifestyles at Findhorn. Christina said she herself was a single parent and sought a 'more feminine vision of leadership' to defuse polarities and embrace opposites. 'There is no such thing as an enemy', she said passionately, 'only friends and potential friends'. When Sonja spoke up emotionally at this point to describe her guilt and paranoia as a Serb demonised by media coverage of the then-raging Balkan war, Christina embraced her warmly, declaring 'as a German, how I know what this feels like!'

Wednesday

Don't leave even a speck of dust. It must be perfect. God made us perfectly, so only perfection is good enough for God. No sweeping things under the carpet!

(The Caddys' instructions to their housekeeper,
in Caddy 1988: 2)

After morning meditation in the Sanctuary we gathered in Cluny's lounge. Paul and Dagmar introduced Sam, a wiry white New Zealander in her late forties who described herself as a 'modern gypsy'. Sam was to focalise a special group project: spring-cleaning the lounge. We began, as usual, with attunement. Sam spoke of the need to clean the external world with the same thoroughness we would apply to our 'inner work' (a pervasive metaphor in Findhorn genealogy, as we have seen). We then attuned to individual jobs. I found myself with Corinne and Sam carrying chairs along the passage to the old ballroom, where we painstakingly polished them. Sam was brisk and resolute: when I suggested we stack the chairs outside the lounge to save time and energy, she said, simply but sharply, 'No!'

In the afternoon we settled down in our circle to study a pamphlet by David Spangler. Dagmar introduced his work as the 'next step' in Findhorn's evolution, after Eileen Caddy's guidance by 'Spirit' and Dorothy Maclean's co-operation with the 'devas' or nature spirits. *Cooperation with Spirit: Further Conversations with John* is a collection of communications received in the 1970s by Spangler from a homely inner guide he calls 'John' (see Chapter 5). Dagmar explained that we would read the text aloud in a circle, taking a paragraph in turn. We shouldn't believe every word, she advised, but should be open to 'resonances', including the esoteric significance of the particular paragraph it fell to each of us to read.

Progress was slow: many of us struggled with Spangler's abstract language. After a while we stopped to share, and a variety of feelings were aired, some at a tangent to the text. Martine spoke of her sadness at living in Brazil in personal comfort, but alongside poverty and homelessness. She said, 'I know it's their karma that they have chosen this purification, but to see little children starving – it makes me feel so unhappy!' Some murmured agreement. But I said I was sceptical of the existence of karma and 'spiritual worlds': I didn't believe that anyone 'chose' to be born in poverty. The group listened impassively. Dagmar nodded thoughtfully. But no debate followed. Later I wondered how much passion might emerge in the group if uncomfortable feelings were enunciated as clearly as more normative emotions and attitudes. Certainly our group was quite conformist, even placid (was this because of, or despite, the 'release' invoked by our group angel?). Everyone attended all sessions; there was little or no challenge to the authority of our focalisers; and most of us worked diligently to adapt to our new environment. Although criticism and 'negative' feelings

167

were not expressly forbidden, scepticism was voiced privately (if at all).[28] However, I would guess that our group's amenability is broadly typical of Experience Week culture, since the considerable travel and expense involved in combination with mythified expectations of the colony are likely to encourage a behavioural 'honeymoon'.[29] As and if neophytes penetrate deeper into colony life, they will inevitably be faced with real interpersonal conflicts and differing social statuses of a kind already hinted at in this account (Bruce 1998).

Frank returned before supper to share a favourite passage from an Alice Bailey book. 'I've carried this around the globe with me', he said, waving a dog-eared paperback called *Glamour: A World Problem* (1950). The extract he had chosen was from the 'Rules of the Road', an allegory of the spiritual quest first published in *Discipleship in the New Age* in 1944. Rule three gives a flavour of the series:

> Upon that Road one wanders not alone. There is no rush, no hurry. And yet there is no time to lose. Each Pilgrim, knowing this, presses his footsteps forward, and finds himself surrounded by his fellowmen. Some move ahead: he follows after. Some move behind; he sets the pace. He travels *not* alone.
>
> (Bailey 1981: 584)[30]

Frank gave another virtuoso performance, slowly and rhythmically reading out the text and then providing an esoteric gloss. I found this quite cathartic. It also triggered a response in Sonja, who became angry and tearful about her Serbian identity. For the first – and last – time that week, a voice charged with real frustration and rage disturbed the equanimity of the Beech Tree room.

Thursday

> When I was still and listened to my inner self, I learned I would never be led astray. What seemed to be trivial coincidences proved to be quite significant. These incidents all had purpose and importance.
>
> (Tattersall 1996: 30)

My notebook today tersely records: 'Morning: work at Park. Conversation from Rudi around chakras and colour energy. I cleaned the toilets.' The afternoon was free. I browsed in the Phoenix Shop, which stocks an extensive selection of books, magazines, Tarot decks, jewellery, wind-chimes, incense, music, clothes, drums, candles, and a wholefood, organic grocery. Then I followed a path that led beyond the whisky-barrel residences and came down over scrubby dunes to the beach. In the lea of the dunes I came across some spiral patterns marked out with pebbles and driftwood, presumably by Findhornians. I followed the largest spiral carefully into its centre: the passage was just wide enough to accommodate one pair of feet.

Friday

We had naturally become as a family to each other in a mere seven days. However, in our final meeting we could feel our group's energy begin to dissipate. We then understood that the appropriate time to leave Findhorn had come.

(Tattersall 1996: 32)

On the minibus to the Park this morning I chatted with Martine, the youngest member of our group. Experience Week was her last port of call in a year of travel that had also included four months on an Israeli kibbutz. 'It was hard work', she said, 'and fun, but not a spiritual place, not like here'. Today's work session in the CC was the last. Just before lunch we gathered and drew 'blessings' cards – appropriately enough, mine was 'movement' – and then we shared and tuned out for the last time.

Back in the Beech Tree room after lunch were copies of the group photograph taken earlier in the week. Paul announced forthcoming workshops, advertised some Findhorn books and explained ways of 'keeping connected': for example, we could join the 'Stewards of Findhorn' network or we could meditate for twenty minutes each day at local noontime to 'align with' Sanctuary practice and help 'create a network of light around the world'. Then we settled down for our last session: 'Completion'. The stone that Paul had chosen on the beach last Sunday was to be the 'talking stone'. Whoever held it, spoke, and when finished, passed it on to the individual whom she or he sensed the stone 'wants to go to' next. 'Say whatever you need to say to complete the week for you', advised Dagmar.

Most of the group took their time, weighing the pebble thoughtfully in their hands as they sought suitable words. Some – Kirsten, Anna, Sonja – were shy or reserved and spoke little; others – Jutta, Kathy, Veronique – tried to articulate difficult feelings; a few – Vicky, Walter – waxed lyrical. Conor described himself as a bird of passage: 'Findhorn is a rock', he said, 'and I'm perched on it for a while, but that's all'. Nick said 'I just want to say thank you' and quickly passed the stone on. I was last. I had a photograph of my son Owen, then just six months old, lying on his back after a bath. I passed it round the circle to general amusement and cries of delight. 'He's lovely!' said Ingrid. 'He's giving you a dirty look!' exclaimed Walter. Suddenly embarrassed, I looked down and away. 'Steve, look up, look at the group!' said Dagmar, touching my knee to get my attention, 'see the pleasure on their faces!' We finished up passing kisses round our circle and then stood quietly together. 'That's it!' said Paul, stretching. 'It's over' said Dagmar. Someone put on a tape and the afternoon broke up amid free-style dancing.

Postscript: the post-Experience Week experience

Although no one left until the following morning, the week had effectively finished, and it felt like it. Some were staying on – Conor to enter the student programme, Anna, Jutta, and Kathy to do 'Experience Week 2'. Kirsten and Ingrid, and our focalisers Paul and Dagmar, melted back into the community. I returned home with a Findhorn candle and a few books and – still in my fuzzy role – made a few attempts to 'link up' with Sanctuary meditation; for a few months, too, I kept my angel card ('Faith') in my wallet. A few communications came out of the blue. Conor sent a note from Orkney and a postcard from Ireland after packing in the student programme. He wrote: 'I think Findhorn is great but it's not right for me at present'. Vicky sent me a birthday card with the Pagan greeting 'bright blessings'. Veronique sent a postcard of people swarming across the Berlin Wall. She wrote: 'I try to remember my angel and the angel of the group. I am feeling better at work; beside that, there has been no great miracle in my life.' In the summer I received a circular letter from Sonja in London promoting a month of meditation and prayers for Bosnia. In an accompanying note, Sonja said she was about to return to Findhorn following involvement in the 'Alternatives' programme at St James's Church, which she described as 'real spirit of Findhorn in the heart of London'.

Nearly two years later, only Sonja, Walter and Anna replied to my letter asking for reflections on the long-term effects of Experience Week. Sonja sent me a lengthy list of the talks, courses and workshops she had been attending in and around London. Walter reiterated the personal strength he found in Theosophical metaphysics and explained how this chimed with the Findhorn worldview. Neither had kept in touch with any of the group except for a few postcards. Nor had Anna. But she had a copy of Eileen Caddy's book *Opening Doors Within*, which she read from daily. 'What I learned from Findhorn is to be present in the moment', she wrote from the Netherlands. 'Don't look too far ahead, because a lot of things come in another way than I expect [*sic*]'.

Accidental community

At the moment I tend towards Eastern religions but I don't follow anything specific, I like to pick out what is true for me and follow that and use it.

(Kirsten, Findhorn resident
and Experience Week participant)

I first came to Findhorn on the track of answers to the Big Questions such as: Who are we? Where do we come from? Where are we going? Whose turn is it to buy the next round? And, your place or mine?

(Dennis Evenson, ex-resident)[31]

Findhorn is a hall of mirrors, a place to meet yourself round every corner, in every object, in every person you meet.

(Nick Rose, resident)[32]

Despite other indices of institutional flux, Findhorn ideology and practice over the years has consistently revolved around 'inner work'. Such a focus is now ideally suited to contemporary cultural conditions where, with the dilution of traditional sources of corporate authority such as a master narrative, a priest-hood and the discipline of the congregation, religion has become by default a self-sited and personally-negotiated practice of strategically-interacting individuals. To be sure, religion has always been this *in part*; but at Findhorn, as elsewhere in the field since the 1970s hermeneutical shift, it is now *largely* this.

At the same time this radical rhetoric of personal and inter-personal transformation and spiritual freedom should not be allowed to obscure the functionalism of group culture in servicing the needs of seekers over the past half-century. In this sense 'New Age' group culture has certain inbuilt constraints, sharing affinities with the evangelically-derived piety of Sheena Govan's Pimlico circle or the secular confessionalism of encounter groups rather than with, say, the shifting forms of the early twentieth-century anarchist movement, the syndicalist committees of the 1968 student movement or the communal drift of 'New Age travellers'. Findhorn's 'pietist' heritage can be seen in the ubiquitous practice of 'sharing', a technique derived in part from Faith Mission evangelism (Sheena Govan) and the Moral Re-Armament movement (Peter and Eileen Caddy). Similarly the encounter group influence of the 1970s persists in the physical culture of touching and hugging, the emotional expressivity and the recuperation of the sensuous, fleshy body as a devotional site through dance, yoga, sauna and massage. Indeed, the role of this hybrid group praxis in fomenting lay expressions of spirituality explains in part the vituperation heaped upon all things 'New Age' by conservative evangelicals, particularly in the US, who detect in 'New Age' groups a powerful rival in the expanding market of de-clericised religion.

The confessional culture bequeathed by both pietist and encounter currents is encapsulated in the general injunction at Findhorn to speak 'from the heart', the latter symbolised by the heart-shaped logo placed next to signatures on letters and notes. The heart symbolises authenticity and wholeness, in contrast to the head, which is popularly portrayed as the rather cold and alienated source of reason and calculation. 'Too heady' was a frequent complaint made by members of the audience at the 'Western Mysteries' conference. One of the conference organisers justified this reaction by explaining that Findhorn was not an academic community: rational debate, he said, was 'interesting, but polarising'. Findhorn, on the other hand, sought inclusivity and consensus. Findhornians therefore had a 'right' to be 'suspicious of academics'.[33] As a male resident explained to me: 'I am moving away from the purely mental/conceptual ideas of religion and into the heart': the former, he said, was 'cold/hard/limited in scope' whereas the heart was 'warm/soft/flowing and limitless'.[34] The role of affectivity in late 'New Age' is exemplified in the results of a questionnaire I gave out in my Experience Week group: as a descriptor of the most important type of spiritual experience, almost all respondents ticked my category of 'emotional release: overwhelming feelings of devotion, love, peacefulness, happiness, etc.' The fact that such values are now diffused in Anglo–American popular culture demonstrates the extent to which the gap between 'alternative' and 'mainstream' spirituality has been closed since the 1970s: the biography of Diana, Princess of Wales and 'Queen of Hearts' in the popular mourning following her death, is a case in point (Woodhead 1999).

In sum, Experience Week offers visitors competence in managing a particular style of spirituality partly imported from the wider culture and partly fine-tuned at Findhorn itself. The groundrules for Experience Week (making 'I' statements, seeking eye-contact, not interrupting) articulate a practical, accessible and portable interpersonal ethos. And a metaphysical message is built into this simple behavioural script: divinity is no longer 'out there', where traditional models of religion would like to consign it (so the popular discourse goes), but 'in here', within 'us', seeking release. We need to 'get in touch with' the vital 'energy' (St John 1977: 39–40) circulating in this subtle inner world. A range of techniques is available for tapping this 'biological electricity' in the daily round, including meditation, visualisation, touch, confession, and devotional reading. The result is a user-friendly, problem-solving spirituality well-suited to the everyday world of housework and jobs, kin and peer groups. Encouraging mottoes help keep spirits up and minds focused: 'work is love in action' or 'love where you are, whom you're with and what you're doing'. Trial and error sampling under the rule of attunement determines what is appropriate, in spiritual life as in careers and relationships. 'Try it', suggests Eileen Caddy (1992: 11) of the technique of 'guidance' passed on to her by Sheena Govan, 'it really does work'. 'If you had an experience of the sacred ... why aren't you repeating it?', asks William Bloom (1993: 18). Successful navigation between the promptings of 'inner' world, 'emotional intelligence' and fleshy body can equip the whole person to function as a compact, efficient organism. In sum, a focused brain and relaxed body, animated by 'spirit' or 'the god within', can generate a confident sense of self well prepared to handle both the risks and the opportunities of contemporary social, cultural and technological change.

That, at least, is the gist of the ideology now driving the 'New Age' idiom. What actually obtains will be affected by other variables, including the realistic constraints of social life that operate here as anywhere else. Sanctuary attendance offers a useful test case on the balance between organismic self-expression and institutional routinisation. Clearly, attending Sanctuary, like collective worship anywhere, constrains the charisma of spiritual expression. On the other hand, as I've noted, the Sanctuaries were rarely more than half-full, suggesting a reluctance to surrender spiritual spontaneity to the Foundation's timetable. Akhurst (1992:

113) says this trend of declining attendance developed during the 1980s, in sharp contrast to the mid-1970s, when one newspaper article reports 'a hundred people crowded together' in the Park Sanctuary.[35] The implication, of course, is that Findhorn residents have come to regulate, even to resist, participation in the central collective ritual to which they must perforce direct new recruits if the colony is to continue. Note also the chronology of this change from 'crowded' to 'half-empty' sanctuary, which accompanies the shift in 'New Age' hermeneutic from circumscribed emblem to promiscuous idiom in the 1970s and 1980s, demonstrating once again the symbiotic relationship between 'congregational' discipline and public self-representation that has haunted the field.

But, forty years on, the colony has developed considerable skill in managing the inherent tensions between seekers and host institution, drawing extensively on small-group culture as an interface between the two. The women and men at Findhorn come to represent themselves less as 'members' of, or 'converts' to, a demarcated religious organisation than as individuals practising a spirituality liberated from bureaucratic hegemony. As seekers, they are sceptical of the revelations proffered by traditional and new religions alike and are interested less in 'making up the numbers' than in fully engaging with life's experiences. In other words they see themselves as an ensemble of individuals or an orchestra of soloists: in Troeltsch's pungent phrase 'a parallelism of spontaneous religious personalities' (cited in Hill 1973: 56).

The paradox at the heart of Findhorn culture, and of 'New Age' discourse in general, is how to reconcile the conflictual demands of the virtuosic 'seeking' that connects and gathers people with the 'congregational' discipline that must be at least minimally maintained if a collectivity is to survive at all. For creating a communal lifestyle is not and has never been an end in 'New Age' networks.[36] The group is not the goal but a means to another, always deferred, end: just as individuals come and go at Findhorn, so do its various groups ceaselessly form, disband and reconstitute in workshops, conferences, management meetings, and meditation. The net effect is to intensify the present moment and current experience. The ensuing sense of a heightened, even feverish, present-tense is suggested by Corinne's remark to me after our very first group session on day one: 'We're a family now'. What this means is that the authority of the group – and by extension, the colony as a whole – is contingent upon, and hence ultimately secondary to, that of its individual constituents. The group merely serves as a strategic device to gather, affirm, and sooner or later disseminate its participants. And this returns us to the moot question of collective structure and identity at Findhorn with which this chapter began. The evidence suggests that Buhler-McAllister (1995: 35) is correct to consider Findhorn an 'accidental' rather than 'intentional' community, for the real focus of the colony is the reflexivity and regeneration of individual persons. Hence Findhorn is better described as a 'colony' or 'training ground' (op. cit. Walker 1994: 17), terms which better express its aggregative, ceaselessly reconstituting ecology of spiritual seekers.

8

A NETWORK OF SEEKERS
Holistic healing

Many new age seekers are now using a therapy or combination
of therapies as part of the process of inner development and
spiritual growth.

(Wilson 1989: 82)

Healing is any process that enhances our physical, mental,
emotional, and spiritual well-being.

(Waters 1996: 106)

Diseases do not exist in holistic health, only imbalanced
individuals.

(English-Lueck 1990: 50)

Health, well-being and 'New Age':
modes and metaphors

There is plenty of evidence in secondary sources that major concerns of 'New
Age' as both emblem and idiom overlap with those of 'alternative' or 'holistic'
healthcare. As Albanese (1992: 75) points out for North America:

It is no accident that the network of communication that has
promoted the message of the New Age has relied noticeably on
massage therapists and chiropractors, on bulletin boards in natural food
stores and in alternative healing clinics, on ephemeral publications
strongly supported by advertisers who purvey one or another form of
physical, mental, and/or spiritual healing.

In *Health in the New Age*, an ethnographic study of holistic healing networks
in California, English-Lueck (1990: 2) argues that the 'New Age' idiom and
alternative healthcare had converged by the early 1980s. She describes
practitioners of 'alternative health' as 'not simply a group of people favoring
one health care system over the prevailing paradigm' but as 'an ideological

174

community actively pursuing a desired future'. Nor is this a peculiarly American development: in South Africa, Steyn (1994: 288–9) found that a fifth of her interviewees were practising healers. Levin and Coreil (1986) and Danforth (1989: 253) have even proposed a discrete category, 'New Age healing', to include phenomena as diverse as 'astral projection, guided visualisation, iridology, reflexology, chromotherapy, rebirthing, shiatsu, and pyramids and crystals' (Danforth 1989: 253).[1]

There is also an abundance of primary evidence. In Scotland, three-quarters of my small sample of customers at an alternative health fair in Edinburgh considered 'New Age ideas' to be 'positive' or at least 'interesting' (Sutcliffe 1995). A number of autobiographies interweave themes of healing and spirituality, such as actress Shirley MacLaine's international odyssey *Out On a Limb* (1983) or Lori Forsyth's British quest, *Journey Towards Healing* (1993). And entries in surveys and directories associated with 'New Age' typically include substantial space for 'holistic healing' (Osmond and Graham 1984) or 'alternative health' (Considine 1992).

The present chapter adds to this body of primary evidence through profiles of popular hybrids of healing, well-being and spirituality in Scotland in the mid-to-late 1990s. In these circles, people come and go and pick and choose with very few, if any, boundaries to negotiate, unlike the tricky balance required at the Findhorn colony or the more rigorous commitment required by the Unit of Service. Personal involvement in healing, whether receiving treatment as a client or participating in a workshop of some kind, may last no longer than an afternoon. Structurally, this has the effect of dramatically highlighting the individual's agency: the 'solo seeker' is a prominent role-type in this field and the ideology of the group is perhaps at its weakest. Yet at the same time the intricate networks of healing practices and their concrete nodes – fairs, workshops and small centres – draw seekers together in a busy exchange of news, views and practices. In this context, following one's own path or truth may be the rhetoric, but the practice is eminently social, and elements of a common culture can be mapped in the field.

By 'alternative' or 'holistic' health I mean a cluster of aetiologies and treatments that are quite differently formulated in comparison with the kind of medicine regulated by the 1858 Medical Act and since institutionalised in the UK in the National Health Service of 1948 onwards. Saks (1992: 5) correctly argues that this institutionalisation of allopathic medicine legitimated 'a single register of legally recognised practitioners with self-regulatory powers and a monopoly not only over the title of "doctor", but also state medical employment'. Allopathic medicine involves a 'parts-oriented' diagnosis and intervention though drugs and, if necessary, surgery, with 'cure' of the organism the ultimate goal: as Saks (1992: 4) puts it, the body is seen as 'a machine whose individual parts can be repaired when breakdown occurs'. On the other hand, non-allopathic treatment promotes the recovery, under optimal conditions, of a 'whole' person through her or his latent resources. There has been some debate over the most appropriate terminology for non-allopathic approaches. 'Alternative', 'complementary' and 'holistic' are in practice near-cognates and choice of one or the other arguably reflects a particular political agenda towards the medical establishment (respectively to confront, co-operate or synthesise) rather than an essential divergence in methodology.[2] Whatever the term chosen, Saks (ibid.: 4) points out that the approach is likely to be holistic, meaning 'an emphasis on stimulating the life force of the individual in his or her total social environment'. I return shortly to these notions of vitalism and holism. But the gist is that non-allopathic health systems seek

> to recruit the self-healing capacities of the body. They amplify natural recuperative processes and augment the energy upon which the patient's health depends, helping him to adapt harmoniously to his surroundings.
>
> (Fulder 1996: 4)

In addition to undergoing specialist treatment regimes the person will be kept busy at an everyday level, assessing and choosing systems and techniques from a variety of sources including popular magazines and television as well as from accredited practitioners and dedicated outlets. The holistic health world is imbued with a strongly populistic ethos, seen in the teaching and learning of such practices as aromatherapy, massage and yoga through evening classes, magazines and paperback books. Accreditation is widely available: some long-established systems, like homeopathy, offer relatively high-status legitimation after substantial training, while other less complex systems that are essentially single techniques, such as crystal healing or Reiki, offer simpler, faster accreditation.[3] But a 'do-it-yourself' approach predominates, embracing both the simple self-prescription of Bach flower remedies on the one hand and the sophisticated self-monitoring of brainwave activity in Biofeedback training on the other. Even when a trained practitioner or a group of patients are involved in treatment, their role will be – in Saks's words – to 'stimulate the life force' of the subject in question: exterior intervention simply functions as a trigger for internal recuperation. In this sense self-healing is the paradigmatic model of holistic healthcare. As I was told at a Bach flower remedies workshop in Edinburgh in 1996, 'health is listening to our inner voice' and the flower remedies function 'to connect you with your higher self'. Not for nothing was founder Edward Bach's breakthrough publication called *Heal Thyself* (1931).

It is important to note that it is 'healing' and not 'curing' that is the goal here: that is, an open-ended engagement with the illness or disease (often rendered 'dis-ease') is encouraged over attempts to stifle or eradicate its symptoms. Emphasis is upon process rather than goal, on supporting the organism while the illness follows its course. This may or may not lead to quantifiable 'recovery'. While a successful allopathic treatment may have the effect of neutralising an illness relatively painlessly and quickly, proper healing in emic eyes consists rather in re-evaluating one's emotional attitude to illness, which means taking into account the wider context of the disease and subtler interpretations of what it *is*, what it *does* and the *meaning* it has for the sufferer.

There is evidently a strong degree of abstraction involved in making this move from a physiological to an essentially metaphysical model of illness. A popular theodicy is implied: illness is 'no random event' but 'a lesson' (English-Lueck 1990: 19–20), a 'sign that body and mind are not being used properly'. Ill-health has moral significance: it can even be 'a very fruitful teacher, at times the only one to whom we would be willing to listen' (St Aubyn 1990: 87). Bloom (1991: 75) goes so far as to describe his own severe episode of hepatitis-B as 'a blessing'. Such statements challenge allopathic understandings of healing as curing, as a tangible restoration of physical health. For example, the 'philosophy of care' statement displayed in the waiting room in Glasgow's homoeopathic hospital where I attended for consultation in 1996 began: 'We aim to help people self-heal – if possible from their disease, but always from their suffering'. According to St Aubyn (1990: 31), the outcome of a course of healing will 'be the right one for the person's overall soul evolution': that is, 'it may not include an alleviation of physical suffering, but will almost certainly comprise a shift in attitude or perspective'. In a wider metaphysical context in which death has been deferred through widespread acceptance of reincarnation and karma,[4] authentic healing does not necessarily obviate a painful illness: death may even be part of the process. For as St Aubyn (1990: 87) explains 'death itself cannot be regarded as frightening once we accept it as an adventure we have already undertaken many times'. In a similar mode, at a packed workshop I attended in Glasgow in October 1996, the American 'clown doctor' Patch Adams said his so-called 'silly hospitals' were designed to demystify death; one of his first publications, he said, was called 'Fun Death'.

A demonstration of spiritual healing given at a health fair I attended in Glasgow in October 1995 provides a case study of this approach in action. Eighty people, around three-quarters of whom were women aged mid-thirties and above, gathered in a seminar room while harp music played softly on tape. Ian Scott, vice-president of the National Federation of Spiritual Healers (NFSH), explained that the aim of spiritual healing was to achieve balance or harmony between body, mind and spirit – the 'inner being' or soul, as he put it. It was said to be particularly effective for stress-related conditions. A central premise was the availability to the healer of a 'central energy source – you can call it god', he said. The healer acts as a channel for this energy, which may then 'kick-start' the client's own energy resources.

Two volunteers from the audience, both women in their thirties, came up for healing from Scott and a colleague. Scott gave a running commentary on his own healing ritual. He began by 'balancing' himself, with eyes closed, and then asked permission from the 'central energy source' to be a conduit for healing. Next he laid his hands on the client's shoulders to allow the 'inner being' of healer and client to make contact. Then he removed his hands and, keeping them several inches away with palms facing inwards, moved them over the body, working down from the crown of the head, 'scanning' and 'balancing' the energy points or 'chakras' within the body. He would not, he said, touch the body again during the healing process unless he intuitively felt it would help to 'cool' the client's pain. He also worked briefly on the client's 'aura' which, he said, emanated from the chest area and enveloped the person in a subtle 'cloak' of energy. To finish, he 'closed down' the chakras – which he had 'opened up' by passing his hands over the body – and gave thanks for the healing. The actual healing ritual lasted about fifteen minutes. Afterwards, the volunteers reported feeling 'really relaxed' and 'growing stronger in balance'. Scott said 'we merely help what is supposed to be the situation': his most profound act of healing, he added, had been a case in which he 'helped' a young woman with cancer 'to die' – that is, to accept her death with serenity and grace.

The concept of self-healing helps to substantiate the interrelationship between holistic health and 'New Age' spirituality. The elevation of the organic unity and agency of the person over and above the invasive, scientific 'doctoring' of allopathic medicine recalls preferences in 'New Age' circles for the 'inner' agency of the soul (Alice Bailey) and for 'speaking from the heart' rather than the 'head' (Findhorn). In short, self-healing and self-realisation go hand-in-hand in post-Seventies 'New Age' discourse. Both require modification of the actor's conventional vector of engagement with the world in favour of self-referentiality and reflexivity.

Moreover, the kind of worldview associated with 'New Age' provides an ideal backdrop to specific healing practices and models of well-being since the alternative cosmology it provides can supply a higher-level, metaphysical legitimation for the esoteric aetiologies and anatomies of holistic healthcare. For example, the chakras, aura and 'energy source' invoked by the NFSH vice-president, and the references to reincarnation and karma by St Aubyn, are widely disseminated as causal agents in the discourse of alternative spirituality. In her study of healing practices in suburban America, McGuire (1998: 5) went so far as to conclude that particular healing practices were used by exponents predominantly as a means of locating themselves within an overarching cosmology. That is,

> only a tiny minority of adherents initially came to their alternative healing group or healer out of a need to heal a prior condition. Most adherents were initially attracted by the larger system of beliefs, of which health–illness related beliefs and practices are only one part.

In other words, seekers may approach holistic therapies as accessible, concrete portals into an attractive yet otherwise abstract framework of popular beliefs and values. At the very least, particular spiritual practices and alternative treatments go hand-in-hand, as when I was told that the Bach remedies were 'a good adjunct to meditation' since they could 'fine tune' the user's emotional state. Additional support for a cross-fertilisation hypothesis comes from English-Lueck (1990: 111) who found that a significant percentage of her holistic health informants were also 'religious defectors' or 'apostates' from American mainstream religion.

But despite more recent calls for a genuinely 'complementary' medicine (meaning a partnership between allopathic and holistic treatment) and the increasing availability in the UK of assorted holistic treatments from NHS-funded surgeries, there remains considerable tension, even incompatibility, between 'scientific' and 'holistic' aetiologies of health and healing. The British Holistic Medical Association's agenda for desirable healthcare, for example, includes such abstract, esoteric affirmations as 'matter and energy are interchangeable' and 'there is an interconnectedness between all things, microscopic–macroscopic, living–non-living' (BHMA 1992: 239). The difference in approach extends to training and accreditation: 'even the simplest' of holistic treatments 'involves a view of the body unrecognisable to anyone trained in medical school', claims Fulder (1996: 4). No doubt he has in mind the recondite anatomies of 'astral/etheric bodies', 'zones', 'meridians', 'auras' and 'chakras' typical of alternative–holistic discourse. A simple index of difference here is that while one can learn how to use these terms competently in discourse and interpretation, they cannot be falsified according to Popperian methodology, as can aetiologies of bacteria and cell subdivision, for example. In practical terms this often means that the instructions explicitly given for the self-prescription of Bach flower remedies apply across the board: 'if you need a remedy, it'll work; if not, it'll do you no harm'.

As I mentioned earlier, there are two major premises through which holistic health finds a larger grounding in 'New Age' cosmology: vitalism and holism. Briefly, vitalism claims that the body is animated by a 'life force' (Saks 1992: 4) or, simply, 'energy' (Fulder 1996: 4). In this, the body is the microcosm of a wider cosmic order: both are ultimately animated by the same divine energy source (recall St John's 'biological electricity', cited in the previous chapter). At the Bach Flower Remedies workshop, for example, we were told that distilled water should never be used in the preparation of flower essences since, unlike spring or boiled water, 'it doesn't carry the life force'.

The second premise, holism, is a talismanic word in contemporary religious discourse. The term itself was coined from the Greek ολοζ, 'whole', by the South African statesman and amateur philosopher Jan Smuts (1870–1950) in his book *Holism and Evolution*, and refers to 'the making or creation of wholes in the universe' (Smuts 1927: 98). Smuts thought that 'wholes' were 'self-acting and self-moving' units exemplifying a 'principle of movement or action not external to itself but internal' (ibid.: 101). Wholes could be found as ordered, synthesised units at all levels of creation, from the 'organic biological world' to the 'highest expressions' on 'mental and spiritual planes of existence' (ibid.: 99).[5]

Smuts's term, if not his particular exposition, has acquired wide currency in popular discourse, perhaps on account of its combination of etymological parsimony and referential abstraction that gives it an emblematic lustre similar to 'New Age'. Olsen's (1989: 4) definition of a 'whole' as a system that is 'something *more than* the sum of its parts' conveys the flavour of popular understanding. In California, English-Lueck (1990: 16) found that the term 'holistic health' could function as 'a keyword trigger' for a popular discourse on spirituality. She also notes the logical conclusion entailed by applying holism to health aetiologies: 'diseases do not exist' but 'imbalanced individuals' do. Consequently 'medical histories become life histories' (ibid.: 50), a logical slippage that helps to explain the functional pairing of 'healing' and 'seeking' in personal biographies.

Where holistic health works out these premises in the tangible context of afflicted organisms, 'New Age' discourse plays them out in an abstract populist metaphysic. Through the pervasive privileging of belief over practice in modern constructions of religion, this discourse has come to rationalise and legitimate alternative healing practices, providing a popular intellectual framework for often bewilderingly diverse treatments and practices. The discussion has indicated some central ideas and behaviours in holistic healing networks and their seamless connection with the 'New Age' idiom. In the emic view the individual, traditionally the passive object of hierarchical medical and ecclesiastical establishments alike, can metamorphose into a fully active subject: a spiritually empowered, hale organism, 'self-acting and self-moving' (Smuts 1927: 101), for whom self-realisation and self-healing are two sides of the same coin. Or in Olsen's (1989: 31) terms, the 'healing journey' becomes a 'spiral revolving around an essential core of who we are'.

The snapshot ethnographies that follow map some particular locales in this broad terrain of holistic training. I begin with a profile of an alternative health fair in Scotland which exemplifies contemporary cultural trends in the UK and north-western Europe (York 2000). I sketch a demonstration of Reiki healing at the fair, before moving on to discuss the function of small healing centres. Finally, I describe a workshop in firewalking, a popular model of healing and personal growth developed in the US from indigenous rituals. The chief interest of holistic healing for me here is its function as a significant domain of popular cultural practice, legitimated by the alternative cosmology of 'New Age', and reflexively constructed by participants seeking what Smuts (1927: 222) stirringly calls 'the great overplus of the whole'.[6]

Browsing at an alternative health fair

Those who attended the festival were seeking something: . . . Almost every path on view began in the same place, inside the seeker.

(Bernard Levin, *The Times*,
on the 1978 'Festival for Mind and Body' in London)[7]

Of the nineteenth century's major sources of heterodox healing – herbalism, hydropathy, homeopathy and mesmerism – Cooter (1988: xiv) remarks:

> It was not uncommon for the exponents of these systems to commit themselves to several in tandem and sometimes to orthodox medicine at the same time. . . . The engagements could be multiple and the splicings, conjoinings and abandonments frequent.

A similar situation holds good at the turn of the twenty-first century. Interested parties may pick and choose not only between treatments, but how and where they are delivered. In contemporary Scotland as elsewhere, alternative health provision is a pervasive 'cottage' industry conducted in a variety of settings: in the home, in hired public rooms, or in a small co-operative practice. Locale is no obstacle: while alternative treatments find their largest social base in towns and cities, a thriving rural culture also exists. Forsyth's (1995) directory of holistic health care in the Highlands and Islands of Scotland is a case in point, collecting over forty individual practitioners and a handful of group practices scattered across a vast and superficially inhospitable rural terrain. Holistic and alternative healthcare is also available through adult education classes, public fairs and – increasingly – mainstream medical outlets, including the National Health Service, where it is promoted under its 'complementary' tag.

A good cross-section of what is available at any one time in the industry is provided by the display of goods, services and practitioners in alternative or holistic health fairs. In contemporary Scotland, day or week-end events can be found in large conurbations, smaller towns and rural villages alike. These fairs are neither new nor discrete phenomena. They incorporate elements of spiritual and political – usually 'green' or libertarian – countercultures as well as perennial 'health' concerns. As D. and L. Jorgensen (1982: 375) summarise the function of a similar event in late-1970s America, such gatherings allow a sometimes scattered community to 'make new friends, exchange ideas and services, reaffirm established relationships, develop business arrangements, present positive images to the public, make converts, and recruit members'. The Jorgensens are in fact describing a 'psychic fair', but there is considerable cross-over in content and function with 'health and healing' fairs. For example, the 'Mind Body Spirit' Twentieth Anniversary festival in London in 1996 incorporated a 'psychics and mystics' section to cater for demand in Tarot, palmistry and clairvoyance, while to muddle categories further, the Edinburgh Body and Soul bookshop currently organises separate 'health' and 'psychic and healing' fairs. Broadly speaking, 'psychic' events serve a more plebeian constituency and are rooted in divination and prophecy on supernaturalistic models, while a naturalistic expansivity of self dominates 'health' events and attracts more middle-class seekers. Fuller (1989: 103) generalises the contrast like this:

While holistic healing groups are trying to broaden conventional medical theory to include a role for spiritual factors, psychic healing groups are primarily concerned with establishing the lawful activity of an extrasensory reality.

In practice, the two inclinations push and tug in a popular dialogue that undermines tidy compartmentalisations of culture. Alternative health fairs anchor this discourse in a material form, providing a 'foundation for a common culture' (D. and L. Jorgensen 1982: 375), seen in the gentle ritualising of ordinary acts, exchanges and spaces of everyday life, and cheerful, pragmatic boundary transgressions.

In October 1994 I visited the 'Scottish Alternative Health Exhibition' in central Glasgow. Organised by the editors of a small Scottish alternative health magazine called *Connections*, these weekend gatherings have run more-or-less regularly since the early 1980s and conform to a general format successfully established in Britain in the late 1970s by the 'Mind Body Spirit' festival in London (Hamilton 2000). The fair was held in the City Halls, a large municipal building with a central hall and ancillary rooms. I spent Sunday afternoon at the event, taking the role of a casual customer, browsing from stall to stall, chatting here and there, and picking up leaflets. This pattern of behaviour was typical of the general public, of whom some three thousand visited over the week-end. It was at this event, and in this role, that I first ran into the Unit of Service (see Chapter 6), which demonstrates the lively reticulation of contemporary fields of spirituality and healing. Women constituted well over half the numbers present, both as stallholders and customers.[8] The vast majority were white; I heard Scottish accents, both east and west coast, but also English and North American intonation. Participants looked to be predominantly middle-aged: that is, between early thirties and late fifties.[9]

Around seventy different groups were represented. Available techniques and practices included the Bates Method of eyesight improvement, the Alexander Technique and a locally-devised system, the Circle Method, in addition to more generic approaches such as massage, herbalism, aromatherapy, and homoeopathy. 'Eastern' treatments and techniques included acupuncture, shiatsu, Chinese herbal medicine, T'ai Chi, and Qigong. Variations upon spiritual healing were offered by the Order of the Ascending Spirit and the NFSH, as well as Reiki – which I profile shortly – and SHEN therapy, a new 'hands-on energy field intervention' from America. All offered dedicated training programmes to capitalise on the teach-yourself impulse fuelling the field, for as English-Lueck (1990: 146) comments, 'learning to become a practitioner is an extension of the role of the client'.

A handful of new religious movements were also in attendance, including the Brahma Kumaris and the Friends of the Western Buddhist Order. A post-Theosophical current was represented by the Unit of Service and the local

Rudolf Steiner School, which provided a creche. Material provisions available at the fair included incense, toiletries, candles, crystals and books, and technological aids such as treatment couches and meditation stools could be purchased. Two bookshops had large stands, testifying once more to a vigorous reading culture. Organic vegetables and groceries were available from the well-established Grassroots wholefood shop, and the cafe served vegetarian food.

Around thirty free talks and demonstrations were offered over the weekend by participating stallholders. This was evidently a draw for the crowd: most of these forty-minute sessions were full. Experiential learning was characteristic of the event as a whole, and various 'taster' sessions – in massage, shiatsu, spiritual healing, magnet therapy, aura photography, and Tarot readings – were available beside stalls. Browsers – like myself – would stand and watch a treatment for a few minutes before signing up or wandering on. Massage and spiritual healing were particularly popular: the latter had spread onto the large stage area where clients, sitting upright with closed eyes and hands in laps, were treated by several busy NFSH practitioners.

A market atmosphere predominated: goods both tangible or intangible were for sale and the flow of money from customer to stallholder was close to the surface. Yet despite a busy turnover of customers, the prevailing mood was relaxed, comfortable, slightly sensuous. Incense burned at several stalls and clothing was loose and colourful. I browsed, watching people receive neck and shoulder massages, shiatsu and Tarot readings. Ambient music played on tape with indigenous sounds of didjeridoos and gongs, and samples of birdsong and whale calls. At one table I picked up the 'New World Music' catalogue, retailing music 'to calm you, to relax you, to inspire, balance and heal you'. It listed around one hundred recordings with titles like 'Spirit of Tibet', 'Illumination: A Celtic Blessing', 'Return of the Angels' and 'Mystic Heart'. 'Music for Healing' was said to provide 'waves of soft melodic music' to 'spiral around the listener, bathing the senses in delightful ripples of serene relaxation'. At 'Avalon', a Pagan-oriented 'healing crafts' shop from Edinburgh, I bought some hand-mixed herbal incense to burn on small charcoal tablets. At 'Grassroots' I bought organic apples and fairly-traded peanut butter. At the table occupied by the 'Order of the Ascending Spirit', I talked briefly with its charismatic foundress, an American woman in her late forties presently based in a country village an hour's drive from the city. In her literature she described herself as 'a healer and spiritual teacher' offering counselling, psychic skills and landscape tours. The Order provided a variety of classes at 'Steppingstone', an alternative centre in Glasgow, including a weekly 'healing circle' and courses such as 'Rites of Passage' and the 'Nearly Everything Class': this was described as 'an ongoing psychic and spiritual development course in which we'll do a little of almost everything – meditation, healing, imagery, Tarot, biscuit reading, and more'.

With the exception of one broadsheet I picked up, entitled 'Reflections on the New Age' (cited in the introduction to the present book), the emblem 'New

Age' was scarcely in evidence, although ideas and images associated with the post-seventies hermeneutic turn suffused the event as a whole. In fact the mixture of psychotherapeutic, dietary and spiritual idioms was such as to baffle an easy distinction between a 'health treatment', a 'therapy' and a 'religious tradition'. The ensuing collage of ideas and practices is precisely what has become popularly identified with – indeed, taken to *be* – 'New Age'.

A Reiki demonstration

It is one thing for me to describe how an apple tastes; it is quite another thing for you to have your own 'bite'. . . . It is the same with Reiki.

(Hall 1999: 4)

Just for today do not worry/Just for today do not anger/Honour your parents, teachers and elders/Earn your living honestly/Show gratitude to everything.

('Five Spiritual Principles of Reiki', in McKenzie 1998: 52–3)

After lunch in the busy cafeteria, I joined the queue for a Reiki demonstration in one of the large ancillary rooms. A leaflet I had picked up described Reiki as 'a powerful tool for both physical healing and for expanding our conscious understanding of life and the nature of reality'.[10] A relatively new treatment in Britain – Stanway (1982), an otherwise comprehensive guide, does not mention it – Reiki is now 'flavour of the month' among healers, according to Lee (1997: 36).[11] The Reiki demonstration today was given to a full house by 'Reiki Master' Kim Hastie and a female student. Hastie, a dynamic woman in early middle-age, operates from 'The Silverdale Centre' in Cheshire. She began by outlining the history and philosophy of Reiki. The transliteration from the Japanese means 'universal' (*rei*) 'life force energy' (*ki*), and the system was devised in Japan in the early twentieth century by Mikao Usui.[12] In due course, Usui is said to have 'cured' the 'serious tumour' of a Hawaiian woman who duly became a 'Master' under his tutelage, and who in the 1970s trained some twenty successors (Lee 1997: 37, 56). From these small beginnings the practice has proliferated, and there are now both 'orthodox' teachers (known as 'Usui Reiki') as well as mavericks, some trained in Usui Reiki but founding their own line, others self-appointed and self-accredited.[13]

The claim that Usui *cured* a cancerous growth vouches for the founder's charismatic touch, and McKenzie (1998: 48) reports no less than four miracles worked by Usui on the same day the secret symbols of Reiki were revealed to him, according to tradition, on Mount Kuri Yama in Japan. But 'curing' is by no means ubiquitous in Reiki, and claims to *heal* and claims to *cure* dynamically co-exist in comparative spiritual healing. Consider for example the case of Mari Hall, who describes herself as the UK's first Reiki Master, founding the

International Association of Reiki in Scotland in 1990 before moving to the Czech Republic. In vivid contrast to Ian Scott's statement that his most profound act of healing had been to help a client face death, Hall includes testimonies of five 'miracles' she has witnessed in the course of her practice as a Reiki healer, including her own recovery from partial paralysis (Hall 1999: 33–40). At the same time Hall undercuts her own agency in these strong examples of healing-as-curing by stating that 'many miracles come through Reiki but I am not doing them' (Hall 1999: 6, 33). In other words, the healer is a channel for transcendent, god-like powers.

In her talk, Kim Hastie stressed the universality of Reiki, claiming that Mikao Usui had had to find a 'spiritual path' beyond both Christianity and Buddhism in order to receive (or devise) his system. The technique was thus open to all, irrespective of creed or personal perspective. Like Hall, Hastie understood the 'opening of the healing channels' in a Reiki treatment to be an impersonal process giving direct, unmediated access to the divine. She was at pains to stress that we all instinctively 'knew' what she meant by the words 'divine' and 'God'. If necessary we should translate her words into our own terms – 'cosmic energy' or 'the source', for example.

Hastie concluded her lucid introduction by inviting the audience to 'come up for healing', as Scott had done in the NFSH demonstration discussed earlier. A steady supply of clients, mostly women, took the opportunity to sit, relaxed but upright, for ten-minute sessions with the Reiki master and her student. Treatment was simple and consisted in the healer placing one hand on the top of the client's head and the other on the upper back. The hands stayed in motionless contact while Hastie continued to talk.[14] She used illustrations from popular science to explain that Reiki viewed the world as a vibrant 'energy field', rather than as a collection of static 'things'. Recalling Smuts, she claimed that all entities were 'wholes' with different levels of atomic vibration. Reiki healing was a matter of 'restoring the appropriate vibrationary level' to the body in question, be it person, animal or plant. The healer draws the 'energy' from a universal source, using her own body as a channel. In popular discourse, 'you realise you are acting only as a conduit or transformer for "something" much greater than you' (Heavens 1992). Self-healing and other-healing become inextricable:

> The channel is never drained when giving healing, because they [*sic*] too are treated in the process of giving another a treatment. This also means that the more we use the energy, the more we assist our own healing process.
>
> (Silverdale Centre leaflet)

Reiki is effectively a modern oral tradition, depending upon an initiatic transmission (for a fee) from Reiki master to student. Hastie emphasised that training required hands-on tuition from 'a living Master'. It wasn't possible, she insisted, to learn the technique from books. McKenzie (1998: 46) agrees and infuses the ambivalence and mystery that accompany the oral history and practice of Reiki into the total package transmitted from master to student:

> as with all storytelling, some versions are more satisfying than others, but when we choose a Master we also choose the story we will hear. Afterwards we can create our own story based on our own experience of Reiki.

There were various levels of initiation, involving 'fine tuning the physical and etheric bodies to a higher vibratory level and opening a purified channel for the energy to pass through'. In particular, second-level students are taught the Reiki symbols, a series of signs drawn in the air. Hastie also offered 'energy exchanges', in which 'advanced' and 'master' practitioners could gather to transmit energy among themselves. Her dynamic exposition made it plain that Reiki was more than a specific healing technique: it was esoteric, initiatic and gently utopian. In her leaflet *Reiki Training: A Powerful Tool for Personal Transformation*, she writes:

> As Reiki begins to move in and heal our whole system, it begins to move us into the next step in our evolution. It starts to work on and break through our limiting beliefs and attitudes thus increasing our ability to take responsibility for our lives and well being.

Not just a therapeutic technique but a pragmatic theology and accessible cosmology – a self-contained spiritual system, in fact – Reiki packages central concerns of holistic health.

Centres

> Outside the Christian Church in this country we are witnessing a rise of centres of spiritual power and transformation. I do not refer to drop-out communes or fringe Christian groups.
>
> (Peter Spink, letter to *The Times*, in Spink 1980: 3)

An additional node in holistic healing networks is the 'centre', which provides a concrete base where participants can interact. An example on the grand scale is Findhorn, discussed in the previous chapter. The kind of centres Spink has in mind are private or co-operative houses scattered throughout Britain, Western Europe, the US and Australasia.[15] Healing may be the sole focus of the centre or it may co-exist with a variety of spiritual practices. Indeed, the same individuals and groups often reappear in local fairs and centres. Spink (1980: 4) catches the flavour of these centres:

Each is independent and autonomous. . . . They exist both in town and country, occupying large old country houses or tenement buildings in the suburbs. . . . Some are constituted as educational charitable trusts, others function in private houses. . . . They range in size from the now world-famous Findhorn Community in the North of Scotland . . . to the recently formed Portland Centre at Brighton in Sussex which centres around a small book shop and which organises festivals on the south coast.

Three representative examples in Scotland are the Salisbury Centre in Edinburgh, Steppingstone in Glasgow, and the Westbank Centre in rural Fife. These are all projects of at least a generation's standing, two of them dating from the 1970s and the latter from 1959 (we first came across Westbank in Chapter 4). Let me begin with the Salisbury Centre, a large Georgian house in an affluent Edinburgh suburb complete with library, meeting rooms and an organic garden. It was set up in 1973 through the joint efforts of a Sufi group and a Jungian psychotherapist, Winifred Rushforth (1984: 136–43) and is maintained by a resident core of mostly young adults guided by a smaller group of trustees. It describes itself as a 'holistic education centre' promoting 'spiritual, emotional and physical wellbeing'.[16] The Salisbury Centre belongs to a loose network served in the UK in the 1990s by a newsletter called 'Open Centres', which linked 'Centres, Groups, Private Houses and Friends' involved in 'the awakening of the individual to a deeper spiritual consciousness'.[17]

In contrast, 'Steppingstone' is a private Victorian flat in the west end of Glasgow. It was set up by the owner in 1978 to pursue her interests in Anthroposophy and the White Eagle Lodge, but has since become more eclectic. The owner is a Londoner in her mid-fifties who lives in an equally spacious apartment next door. During my visit in January 1995 she told me that contemporary Christianity had been 'pruned' and that her interests as a 'heretic' lay rather in what she called the 'secret teachings of Jesus', the legends of the Holy Grail, and the Culdee tradition that she claimed had inherited 'the Druidic spirit'. Steppingstone is now vigorously inclusivist: the Order of the Ascending Spirit, whose representatives I met at the alternative health fair, ran classes there, and I later attended an Aetherius Society meeting there entitled 'UFOs: Their Mission to Earth'. The centre consists in several large rooms hired out to groups and individuals, a long hall with posters and leaflets, and one room, a 'universal sanctuary', set aside for silent meditation and 'developing peaceful energies', with Islamic calligraphy on the fireplace tiles, a small electric water fountain and a driftwood sculpture embedded with crystals.

My final example is the Westbank Natural Health Centre in the village of Strathmiglo, Fife. Established in 1959 by a retired army major and spiritual healer, the late Bruce MacManaway, and his wife Patricia, Westbank claims to be 'Scotland's longest running healing centre' and has as its motto 'helping people to better health'.[18] In contrast to the Salisbury Centre's oligarchy and

Steppingstone's individual direction, Westbank is a family-based concern: the Macmanaway's sons practice geomancy and healing at the Centre, including work with animals, particularly horses (Holland 1998). Westbank claims to teach 'upward of 500 students each year' in subjects such as meditation, stress control, healing, ESP and yoga. The family also owns a house on the island of Iona. As we saw in Chapter 4, Westbank was a significant node in the 1960s 'New Age' network: Peter Caddy, then a regular visitor, considered Bruce MacManaway 'one of the finest healers in Britain' (Caddy 1996: 243). Given this lineage, it is appropriate that Westbank should be the venue for the final ethnography of this chapter and of the book as a whole.

A firewalking workshop

The firewalk was the perfect metaphor to encompass all aspects of life, the full spectrum: from anguish to bliss.

(Tolly Burkan, founder of American firewalking,
in Danforth 1989: 261–2)

To walk unharmed over incandescent coals is to take a step into a different and somehow magical world where all things become possible, where we begin to see clearly that all limits are self-imposed and ultimately illusory.

(Shango 1996: 12)

Alternative metaphors of health and well-being are dramatised in the ritual of the firewalk. Firewalking enjoyed considerable popularity in Anglo–American culture in the 1980s and 1990s. In its contemporary popular form – that is, largely isolated from indigenous context and packaged in a workshop format – it substantiates Waters' (1996: 105) remark that, in holistic health and the 'New Age' idiom alike, 'healing and personal development are very nearly synonymous'. The ritual of firewalking encapsulates the self-expressive dynamic of contemporary healing, in which a nebulous sense of well-being and a discourse of spiritual self-empowerment blend.

My account actually begins some time after the event. On a Wednesday morning in March 1997 I received a letter addressed in a familiar hand: mine. I had written it just over a year ago at the end of a firewalking workshop, on the instructions of the leader, and in a flush of excitement and relief. The workshop's host – the Westbank Centre – had agreed to post on our letters in one year's time, as the final reflexive fruit of the event. I read it now self-consciously:

Dear Steve
Remember this night? You've just walked over burning charcoal, from the fire we built earlier this afternoon at the raised garden here at

Westbank. Now we've just had coffee and cake, preparing to go home on the slow road to Stirling.

Your PhD will be just about finished – or at least, getting that way. I hope you feel pleased with it, and feel that this night helped get something together. Remember the word you chose tonight: CLARITY.

And by the way, the other word that you toyed with, but didn't quite use, was WRITE. You can do this. You will do this. After all, you can walk on fire.[19]

I had discovered Westbank through a combination of serendipity and 'networking'[20] typical of the field. I first read about the centre in a book, then heard of it by word of mouth (from the proprietor of the new shop Healthworks, in fact, mentioned in Chapter 5). Next I found a historical reference in Peter Caddy's (1996) memoirs, and finally an address in the alternative health magazine *Connections*. Moreover, Westbank was less than an hour's drive from where I lived. In short, the contact was ideal for 'seeker' and researcher alike and invited exploration. I got on the Centre's mailing list and early in 1996 received a poster headed 'Firewalking: A Sacred Ritual of Personal Empowerment':

> Firewalking is an ancient practice intended to empower and heal. Walking barefoot over hot coals burning at over 1200 degrees Fahrenheit seems impossible, yet over half a million Americans and many in the UK have done it. How many other things in your life seem impossible?[21]

On a cold day in February I telephoned Westbank for further information. 'Let me put you on to the firewalker herself', said the secretary. 'Hi, Hazel here', said a relaxed American voice. 'I'm interested in doing the firewalk', I say. 'How long does the workshop last?' 'Well, once we're into sacred time it's difficult to say exactly', says Hazel. I ask about the risk of 'getting burned'. 'That's a *big* question', she replies. 'Three-quarters of a million Americans have done this, and thousands elsewhere. There are only a few cases of burns – but what interests me is, why *those* people, compared to all those who make it through?' In any case, Hazel tells me, she is a doctor 'if necessary' (of Chiropractic, it turns out). 'Wait until you're standing in front of the coals before you decide whether or not to walk', she says, 'but I promise you, it'll impact on the whole of your life'. I check on the price reduction offered for early registration. 'It's an added bonus', she confirms, 'the workshop actually begins the moment you're committed to it'.[22]

Snow was lying on the fields as I drove to Strathmiglo in the prime farming country of central Fife on a grey February Sunday. The Westbank Centre is behind the village, a cluster of buildings with a slightly worn and rambling appearance. Parked tightly in the cramped courtyard space were a dozen middle-range cars. We gathered in a large rectangular room, with french windows leading out to a small garden. Chairs stood in rows facing a flip-chart and about thirty people had gathered, including members of the MacManaway family. Some were chatting, evidently on familiar terms. Apart from two boys, all looked over thirty, with a scattering of older people. Women were slightly in the majority, and with two exceptions, all were white. I sat beside Annie from Edinburgh, who described herself as a 'regular' at Westbank and also at the MacManaway's house on Iona. We chatted briefly about my research, and her own explorations in alternative healing. She had an 'evangelical' son, she told me, who thought that 'this sort of thing' – firewalking – was 'devil-worship'.

Hazel Price, the firewalker, appeared. Aged around late thirties, she had long, straight hair and wore a full skirt with bands of primary colours, a turquoise blouse and a 'devil's eye' pendant. 'Okay', she said, 'I think we're ready to go'. She flipped over the top page on her chart. It read:

1   Whoever shows up are exactly the right people
2   Whenever it begins is always the right time
3   Whatever we co-create here together is the only thing that can possibly happen
4   When it's over it's over.

Hazel launched into an explanation of these statements, strolling backwards and forwards in front of us as if on a small stage. Firewalking, she said, was about breaking down limiting 'cages' of belief, our self-imposed structures of thinking and expectation. These cages are not fixed: they can expand. We can make them. It followed that anything we might not currently understand in our lives – including what was happening right here, right now at this workshop – must be referring to something beyond our present 'cage' of beliefs. But we would 'get it' eventually – if we really wanted to. So certain things might or might not make sense during the evening: it all depended on how flexible our individual cages were at this moment in time. 'But that's OK', she laughed, 'don't worry, that's how it is!' Some of us nodded uncertainly.

'Let's break the ice a bit', she said, sizing us up. 'Do you know this one?' She began to sing 'If you're happy and you know it, clap your hands'. 'Come on!' she called out. People began to join in, and soon we were all singing, clapping and stamping feet. 'OK', Hazel said, 'that's good, we're getting some energy moving'. Now she spoke of Tolly Burkan, the 'father of the firewalking movement',[23] who had personally instructed her. Burkan stressed the significance of intentionality: that *how* we do what we do, and not necessarily *what* we do, is the real basis of healing and growth. Heather gave the example of eating ice cream: we could choose to eat it 'with guilt' (the typical adult mode, she said) or 'with glee' (the child's proper attitude). In either case our intent would have greater effect than calories. By analogy, she claimed, 'fire burns *or* fire heals', the difference being intent or faith. 'Flesh cannot firewalk, but Spirit can, moving *through* the flesh', she concluded earnestly.

Hazel showed us slides of her visits to native firewalkers in Hawaii and Sri Lanka. Originally the preserve of 'mystics and shamans', she said, firewalking was now opening up to everyone – 'with the shift in human consciousness I think we're all aware of'. But first we needed to get to grips with fear and its potentially crippling effect on our lives. She said that opinion polls had discovered that peoples' greatest fear was public speaking. 'So let's do it!', she announced, rubbing her hands, 'I want each of you to stand up and tell us all why you're here tonight!' Dutifully we stood up around the room to introduce ourselves. Brief aspirations or confessions quickly became the norm: 'I've *always* wanted to walk on fire', said one; 'I want to walk on fire because I'm scared of being myself', said another. 'I've walked three times already, but I'm trembling here at the thought of walking again'; 'I got lost coming here tonight, and I think that says something about my life'. After each introduction, we applauded vigorously.

In this first session, which lasted around an hour and a half, Hazel spoke rapidly and with great energy, sometimes acting out figures of speech or walking in a direct, determined line to mimic the act of the firewalk, sometimes cracking a joke, sometimes delivering an insight or aphorism with fiery conviction. Pre-written charts structured her monologues. This was very much a performance: we were the audience, responding to her leads, mimicking the behaviour and internalising the rationale of the successful firewalker. Now it was time to build the fire. As part of our mental preparation, we were asked to write down a word expressing our personal 'intention' for the evening and to be ready to place this piece of paper on the fire at the right moment in the ritual. Also, Hazel distributed a form waiving our right to hold her, Westbank or anyone else apart from ourselves responsible for the results of our stepping onto the coals. This was portrayed less as accident cover for the organisers as an opportunity for us to claim responsibility for our intent and actions at the event and therefore to 'own' our decision to firewalk. In other words, if I 'got burned', it was down to nothing or no one but myself and my own bad faith (compounded of guilt and fear, according to Hazel). Even then, evidence of 'failure' is recuperated by firewalking ideology: Danforth (1989: 279) points out that firewalkers emphasise that 'getting burned is simply another opportunity to learn and grow', which means that 'even burning becomes a healing experience'.

The mood became reflective and sombre. Silently we filed out to the small garden. Here turf had been removed to a depth of about six inches to form a shallow rectangular trench five feet by ten. Half-melted snow muffled the earth. Hazel began to shake a rattle to consecrate the space, making slow, swooping gestures as she moved around the trench. We collected one log at a time from a helper beside a large pile, and under Hazel's direction placed it in the middle of the trench to build a square stack. Hazel urged us to carry each log tenderly, 'like a baby', to honour its contribution to the ritual. We solemnly added the slips of paper with our written intentions and formed a circle round the trench, holding hands in the twilight, some of us skipping up and down against the cold. The helper doused the stack with vegetable oil, and Hazel lit it. Then she moved gracefully around our circle, blessing each person's 'aura' and giving us herbs – a twist of sweet grass as a symbol of 'sweetness' and a pinch of sage for 'purification'. Flames took hold of the stack, and smoke billowed out and up. Finally Hazel blessed the fire and thanked the earthworms and other small creatures for giving up their lives for our sakes.

We went back inside. The mood was now restrained. Hazel turned again to her flipchart and unveiled this acronym:

F alse
E vidence
A ppearing
R eal

'Fear', said Hazel, 'is nothing but this'. Our belief cages programme us into interpreting situations misleadingly, she explained: hence the tale of the man who, primed with fearful warnings against poisonous snakes, mistook a coil of rope for a cobra poised to strike. So, if we *think* the fire will burn us, it will, but its heat is actually 'false evidence' that cannot fool an 'awakened spirit'. Here Hazel invoked popular accounts of neurobiology and physics, the gist of which was, simply, the power of mind over matter.[24] 'I'll give you an example', she said, producing a small plank of yellow pine and placing it across two chairs. She concentrated for a few moments, breathing deeply, and then with a fierce 'Hah!' karate-chopped it in half. A buzz went round the audience. 'Come try it', Hazel grinned, 'some folk actually find this bit more difficult than the firewalk'. We gathered round the chairs, Hazel whooping and others applauding as individuals successively smashed their pieces, with just one failure, and one abstention (me, feeling distinctly heretical). In the former case, an older woman tried several times: after her final attempt there was a moment of embarrassed silence before someone called out 'Well *done*!', and people remembered to clap.

We returned to our seats and Hazel delivered a moral fable about life's purpose. Three men are hitting rocks with a sledgehammer (she acted this out with relish). The first man is in a chain-gang: he cries 'I'm breakin' rocks in the hot sun!' The second is a breadwinner: he cries 'I'm workin' to feed my family!' But the third says quietly: 'Me, I'm breaking stone to build a cathedral to the glory of God'. Beside me, Annie caught my eye and nodded approvingly.

So how will we know it's *right* to walk the fire, Hazel asked? We're not to walk from egotism, after all, nor from asceticism or masochism, nor from fear of being left out (the karate exercise demonstrated an instinctive group conformity but at the fireside, in the dark, I suspect that not everyone firewalked – including Hazel herself, as she told us afterwards). The secret was this: our 'Higher Self' would know if and when it was right to walk. We needed to get 'in touch' with this inner source by listening quietly and trusting our guidance. But there was a catch, said Hazel: our Higher Self or inner voice lives *in the present moment only* and is infallible *only then*, not for past or future tenses. Hence, a second too early or too late (the rational mode) will not work. Conditions will have changed and the inner voice will no longer ring true. It has to be accessed and heeded *right now*.

As we digested this, Hazel called us to our feet. 'It's time to dance!', she said, pulling back chairs, 'find a partner!' We formed a circle again, and Hazel taught us a folk dance similar to the sacred dances at Findhorn. We were to sing a song as we danced, and while we danced and sang we were to look each other directly but softly in the eye, recalling the groundrules on eye contact during Experience Week. The words were:

Maybe this is the healing, that we share this feeling
and find a compassionate love,
flowing from my heart to yours,
flowing from my heart to yours.

As we sang the first line, we faced our partner and spread our arms up, out and down to bless each others' auras. To the second line, we crossed hands on our chests, still facing each other. To the third, we placed one hand on each other's chest, just over the 'heart centre' or 'chakra', and as we repeated this line we moved round the circle, taking a new partner. It was tricky to co-ordinate singing, dancing and hand movements, and I found it a little unnerving to look progressively into twenty–nine strangers' eyes. When we finished, Hazel asked us to stand quietly for a few minutes in order to feel 'the energy' around the room. Some of us were breathing heavily. Suddenly her helper entered the room. 'The fire is ready!', he announced. We shuffled nervously. 'OK!' said Hazel, and she swept across the room, mimicking yet another successful firewalk. 'Go for it! *Bliss* is on the other side of that fire!'

Outside there was no moon, but village street lights glowed down the short rise. The stack of logs had burnt into a crumpled heap of glowing charcoal. We stood in a circle, barefoot on the cold grass, holding hands while Hazel raked out the coals to form an even covering over the bed of the trench. Then a few logs were scattered down one side: these flared up. Suddenly Hazel shouted: 'The fire is now open!' and began a chant, with no explanation of the words. We took it up, clapping hands and stamping feet. After a short hiatus, the first person – Hazel's helper – came to the top of the trench, paused, then briskly crossed the coals to a great cry of excitement. The way had been opened. A trickle of followers began, soon becoming a busy procession as people came to the head of the jostling circle and crossed the trench to whoops, applause, continual chanting and clapping. Some walked quickly or half-ran, and were lightly caught by helping hands on the other side; others kept to a regular walking pace; a few danced and skipped across, or stepped slowly and deliberately as if testing the coals.[25] Sparks sometimes jumped up from heels, and a hose of water was kept handy on the far side where hugs and congratulations were exchanged among the neophytes. I went across twice, in four or five longish steps. The bed of charcoal felt crunchy underfoot, like warm cornflakes. My feet were already cold from the ground, so it was difficult to gauge the heat, but as I didn't want to reap the fruits of bad faith, I didn't linger. Eager hands met mine at the far end; someone patted me on the back, someone else said 'Nice one!' In the dark it was hard to tell who was who.

Finally Hazel cried 'One minute' and, shortly after, 'Last call!' One or two cameras flashed, freezing phantom figures on the coals. Then Hazel motioned us to stop chanting. She said solemnly: 'I invite anyone who chooses to walk the fire in silence. Say your intention before walking, and the group will say it back to you.' A few did so, calling out words like 'love', 'healing', and 'transformation'. We stood in silence, watching the coals glow. An hour had passed: it was becoming very cold. 'Let's go inside,' said Hazel quietly.

We talked and joked a little now as we walked down the gravel path. Some said the pain of the cold, or the gravel underfoot, was worse than the fire. There was a sense of comradeship and achievement. At the door we washed each other's feet in bowls of warm water. Inside, people sat chatting with cups of tea. The workshop had lasted nearly six hours. I felt exhausted. Before we dispersed, Hazel – also looking drained – handed out some photocopied sheets. These included a reflexology chart for treating any 'hot spots' on the soles of our feet, and a list of 'The Five Points of Power'. These were 'Pay attention', 'Speak the truth', 'Ask for what you want', 'Take responsibility for your experience' and 'Keep your agreements'. We were also to write down an inspiring message to ourselves, which Westbank would post on to us in one year's time to rekindle memories of the experience. 'Write what you like,' said Hazel, 'but remind yourselves of what you did here tonight. Feel your own power!'

9

THE END OF 'NEW AGE'

The church dissatisfies me. I know all the things they teach. I want more, you know?

(Alison, Unit of Service, 1997)

We are trained to listen to experts in our culture and not to ourselves. The premise of the New Age is the other way around.

(Spangler 1996: 184)

The whole point is our journey, not our destination.

(Edwards 1993: 63)

Recapitulation

In this book I have reconstructed the genealogy of a multivalent emblem, 'New Age', within interconnected networks of 'alternative' spirituality from the 1930s to the 1990s. In the first part, called 'Emblem', I examined Peter Caddy's career in the Rosicrucian Order, the activities of Sheena Govan's group and the early years of the Findhorn settlement. I found evidence of other networks active in England, New Zealand and the US in the late 1950s and early 1960s – George Trevelyan, the Heralds of the New Age, the North American 'subculture' delineated by David Spangler – for whom 'New Age' was an apocalyptic emblem within a cocktail of occult, psychic and spiritualistic ideas and practices. In this early period the expression had objective historical status among communicants: a 'New Age' was imminent, its apocalyptic harbingers were on the horizon and groups had to prepare themselves spiritually in response.

In the second part, 'Idiom', I traced the diffusion and disintegration of this emblem in the 1970s and beyond under the influence of a youthful counter culture and a concomitant decline in the authority of grand narratives (Lyotard 1979) in the culture at large. 'New Age' became, as it were, adjectival, a loose 'quality' of a person, act or social process rather than a negotiated emblem. As a sign of this shift it became self-consciously problematised by both participants and observers – one informant in Lowe and Shaw (1993: 227) said vehemently 'I hate that cliche "New Age"'. It was increasingly rendered in inverted commas ("New Age") or lower case (new age) and it came to qualify everything from an adumbrated religiosity to entire – sometimes mutually contradictory – lifestyles:'alternative','yuppie', holistic,'traveller'.[1] Significantly, the ethnography of the last three chapters is notably thin in use of the emblem although rich in genealogical association and folk memory. The international 'New Age' showcase, Findhorn, is now increasingly reluctant to deploy the term, preferring to describe itself as a 'spiritual community' with 'no formal doctrine or religious creed'. 'New Age' surfaces only serendipitously in holistic health circles, and if it underpins Alice Bailey's writings, it is veiled in Lucis Trust discourse as we enter the twenty-first century.

But I have also uncovered considerable empirical evidence of social networks sporadically associated with 'New Age'. The reconstruction of these has been one task of the present book, rescuing real emic histories from the false etics of a 'New Age movement'. These networks are manifestations of an 'alternative' spirituality that is self-consciously dissenting with regard to established religious institutions and post-Enlightenment rationality alike. Created by self-taught practitioners, amateur thinkers and 'do-it-yourself' seekers, this kind of spirituality has been moulded by populist values and popular culture. It is radically elective – supremely a 'religion of choice' – although constrained by social variables of class, gender and ethnicity. Thus we have a series of interest groups associated with 'New Age' that yet lack sufficient complexity of organisation or public programme to constitute a social movement in any meaningful taxonomy. In fact, far from amounting to a 'movement', the defining properties of 'New Age' at any one time are largely the sum of the activities of x number of mustered seekers: a 'buzzing hive of virtuosic individualists' (Sutcliffe 2000a: 32).

In this final chapter I consolidate my critique of the concept of a 'New Age movement'. Simultaneously I reconstruct the organisational processes that shape the constituencies of actors elided by this concept. This requires further discussion of the role of 'seeker', the act of 'seeking' and the nature of the preferred ideology, 'spirituality'. Finally I argue that the immediate future for seekers – the metaphorical 'children of the new age' – is qualitatively rich but quantitatively limited. By this I mean that inbuilt constraints in the institution of spiritual seekership restrict its political impact compared to the scale and complexity required to achieve the kinds of radical social change invoked in the popular rhetoric. At the same time key features of spiritual seeking and the ideology of spirituality redirect our attention to so-called 'softer' cultural spheres of feelings and relationships – and subjectivities in general – that may play a more significant role in the reconfiguration of contemporary religion in the longer term. The legacy of 'New Age' remains for the time being an ameliorative, domesticated and localised Anglo–American discourse on spirituality, despite its often extravagant claims of universal consciousness and global transformation.

The 'New Age movement': laying the ghost

In Chapter 1 we saw that most commentators understand 'New Age' to be a movement of some kind. I questioned this position then and probed it further in Chapter 5. The historical and ethnographical evidence of the remaining chapters has added considerable cumulative weight to my argument. Let me consolidate it now.

First, emic affiliation with 'New Age' is optional, episodic and declining overall. A good index is the titles of representative source texts. Hanegraaff's (1996: 525ff.) formidable selection of one hundred and eleven primary sources yields only six titles actually featuring the expression 'New Age', and none mentioning a 'New Age Movement'. In Bloom (1991: ix–xii), only two out of fifty-one titles employ the term; in Satin (1978: 221–33), only one out of two hundred. This pattern of marginal usage was confirmed in my fieldwork. In a simple questionnaire I circulated during Experience Week at Findhorn, only two out of ten respondents identified themselves as 'New Age' and even then it was with qualifications: Martine from Brazil used the by-now familiar inverted commas while Patrick, the Irishman, described his identity as 'New Age and still searching'. Nor are the founders of the Findhorn colony keen to invoke the emblem. Dorothy Maclean told me: 'We did not use the term "New Age" much in the early days', and Eileen Caddy likewise wrote: 'No, Peter, Dorothy and I did not think of ourselves as part of a New Age Movement'.[2] In sum, historical, ethnographical and autobiographical evidence strongly suggests that a 'New Age' identity is and has been restricted to the predilections of discrete groups and individuals, instead of defining the agenda of a substantial collectivity, let alone an operative movement.

Certain bodies, of course, have persisted with the expression. The Arcane School continues to offer the 'training in new age discipleship' it began in the 1920s. But such idiosyncratic projects only prove a general rule. Similarly, individuals sometimes invoke the emblem while on other occasions they wear a different hat. Button and Bloom (1992: 17) exemplify this *laissez-faire* approach when they write: 'During the last ten years, "holistic thinking", "the green movement", "new paradigm thinking", the "new age" – *whatever we choose to call it* – has become a significant force' (emphasis added; also note the indeterminacy conveyed by all those inverted commas). Despite Button and Bloom's implicit disavowal, taxonomies matter: they inscribe (or deny) power and legitimacy in social collectivities. The ambiguities and qualifications in their formulation directly reflect political uncertainty. More forthright is David Spangler's confession: 'I have personal doubts that there really is something called the "New Age movement". The New Age *idea*, yes, but a *movement*, no –

at least not in any ideological, organised sense' (in Spangler and Thompson 1991: 64). But how could there be a 'movement' without ideology and organisation? Elsewhere Spangler spills the beans:

> There is no dogma, no orthodoxy, and essentially, no agreement on where the boundaries of the movement are and who is or is not part of it. In this sense, it is not so much a movement as a sprawl.
>
> (Spangler 1996: 34)

The notion of a 'New Age movement' is also problematic in etic terms in that the phenomena lack the requisite sociostructural features to differentiate a distinctive 'New Age' project from looser, slacker types of collective behaviour such as the models of 'crowd', 'fad', 'craze', and 'public' proposed in Turner and Killian's *Collective Behaviour* (1972). Certainly several types of 'movement' have been advanced historically, particularly new religious movements (NRMs) and new social movements (NSMs).[3] Part of the problem in this important but strangely neglected definitional endeavour is that scholars on 'New Age' have generally avoided specifying their usage – York (1995) is an honourable exception – or else, like Melton (1988), have proposed such an eccentric model that 'New Age' is *ipso facto* rendered unique. But the 'New Age' field as a whole is actually deficient in the typical features of NRMs and NSMs. It lacks a distinctive corporate body, a legislative mechanism, historical consciousness, organisational infrastructure, boundaries, and other indices of membership and belonging, and, crucially, unambiguous self-identity and concrete goals. The absence of these features sharply distinguishes 'New Age' from the mass of post-1960s movements and associated fields of study, to which the 'New Age Movement' taxon confines it through a basic category mistake. This point becomes clearer if we contrast 'New Age' with prominent NRMs such as the Church of Scientology, the International Society for Krishna Consciousness or the Unification Church. It is obvious that 'New Age' lacks a founder like L. Ron Hubbard or Sun Myung Moon, has no corporate body to seek tax exemption or 'religious' status (or which could qualify as a 'church' or 'society'), has no equivalent conversion identity to the 'Moonie', no dress code like the Krishna devotee's, and no unique argot like Scientology's terminology of 'clears', 'thetans' and 'orgs'. The comparison fares little better when we turn to examples of social movements. Byrne (1997), for example, bases his analysis on the 'green', peace and women's movements in the UK. These certainly share with 'New Age' characteristics of cultural diffusion and polycentric organisation but they do have in each case a consistent signifier and referent as well as an explicit political platform of self-identity, theory, method, and goal. 'New Age' – taken as a collective behavioural field – has none. Certainly a few organisations tagged 'New Age' might individually meet these criteria, such as Findhorn or the Lucis Trust, but that is an argument for qualification as a

NRM or NSM, not for extrapolating from these very distinctive cases to a generic 'movement'.

I conclude my argument on this score by addressing the most persuasive organisational model so far advanced for 'New Age': the 'SPIN' or 'segmented polycephalous integrated network' advanced in Gerlach and Hine (1968, 1970) and adopted by York (1995). Gerlach and Hine offer a loose yet nuanced definition that appears at first sight promising for 'New Age' studies. For them, a 'movement' is

> a group of people who are organised for, ideologically motivated by, and committed to a purpose which implements some form of personal or social change; who are actively engaged in the recruitment of others; and whose influence is spreading in opposition to the established order within which it originated.
>
> (Gerlach and Hine 1970: xvi)

Despite an unhelpful terminological vagueness, there are resonances if we apply this definition to 'New Age' in the 1950s and 1960s at least: the emphasis on the 'group' as the organisational unit, the ideological motivation provided by an imminent, concrete 'New Age', the active networking with sympathetic others; and the subcultural stance. But the evidence suggests that 'New Age' in its early, emblematic period was only ever 'in opposition to the established order' in its abstract rhetoric of a planetary 'apocalypse': it actually attracted most support from a relatively privileged, occasionally aristocratic, social base and participants clearly expected to be among the elect salvaged from the predicted planetary destruction. Conversely, the later, idiomatic period shows just how easily a countercultural discourse of 'work on oneself' could be recuperated by popular and middle-class cultures increasingly shaped by postmodernising forces (Harvey 1989; Lyon 2000) in which the adjective 'alternative' is as likely to refer to consumer choice in the spiritual marketplace (Roof 1999) as it is to signify political opposition. The fate of the SPIN model is settled once we know that the empirical examples chosen by Gerlach and Hine were Pentecostalism and Black Power, two clearly-demarcated social movements organised according to sustained materialist programmes of recruitment and advancement. As such they are anathema to 'New Age' instincts.

Indeed, one might say that the politics of change pursued by Byrne's examples in the UK and Gerlach and Hine's in the US have been almost completely absent in 'New Age', where a preoccupation with subjectivity, interpersonal relationships and the general quality of experience has sidelined questions of political mobilisation. This methodological individualism has the effect of severely downplaying the historical potency of institutions both to maintain and to resist the social order. Rather it has promulgated – with uncertain results – a popular model of the percolating power of individuals, networks and groups as a kind of 'spiritual yeast' in the social order.

Seekers and Seeking: the popularisation
of an identity and a strategy

Writers [to Alice Bailey in the early 1920s] asked for guidance in their
search for truth without being subjected to the usual limitations of
dogmatic creeds.

(*The Arcane School: Entrance Papers*, Lucis Trust, London, n.d, p. 2)

I began to question many of the things that had been taught by
conventional religions, and started my own search for the truth
through many 'ologies' and 'isms'.

(Peter Caddy *c.* 1933, remembered in Caddy 1996: 25)

For the world, the only hope is for individuals to explore their own
journeys.

(Healer Jill Rakusen, in Coniam and Gibson 1996: 35)

The typical actor in 'New Age' is a religious individualist, mixing and matching
cultural resources in an animated spiritual quest. Standing in sharp contrast to
traditional participatory roles in Anglo–American religion such as 'member',
'communicant', 'congregant' or 'convert', we can call this actor a 'seeker' and the
sum of her or his cultural ploys, 'seeking'. The attendant social institution of
'seekership' raises issues of agency, identity, common culture, and impact.

There are both advantages and disadvantages in employing the term 'seeker'.
In its favour, 'seeker' is a term widely known and used among practitioners
themselves and has its own rich stock of theory and lore. So it carries emic
authority. But it can also function as a comparative anthropological category
connoting subjectivity and reflexivity. The impact of various social variables on
seekership can be mapped and analysed. These include class and ethnicity but
not gender: seekership in theory and practice carries weak gender ascription,
in contrast to the emergent popular discourse on spirituality (which I
discuss below). Seekership also crosses age cohorts and infuses autobiographical
narratives in suggestive but largely unexplored ways. And finally, not least,
the term is parsimonious. Negatively, 'seeker' has overly pious or 'earnest'
connotations and may suggest a theological judgment or a neo-colonialist
interpretation (derived from orientalist fantasies of the 'mystic East'; cf. King
1999) of what the proper approach to 'religion' should be. We must beware of
naturalising a normative role of the 'seeker' as a particularly holy or morally
righteous individual. Nor should we cast the seeker as a role-playing obsessive
or as a systematic theologian in disguise, since in practice the role may be lightly
carried or the person may not construct of her or his behaviour in these terms,
and values and practices are likely to be derived from popularised and syncretic
forms. In any case the boundaries between seeking and other roles and practices
adopted in the life course – in education, relationships, health care, work and

leisure – are often quite fuzzy, as we have seen. In this book, then, 'seeker' functions as an anthropological role, not as a soteriological prescription.

Seekership has its own history; strategies change over time. The act of seeking formerly demonstrated strong affinities with unusual biographies and elite social class, as the examples of Annie Besant (Bevir 1999) and Ronald Nixon/Sri Krishna Prem (Haberman 1993), or Alice Bailey and Sir George Trevelyan in 'New Age' genealogy, amply demonstrate. But globalising cultural flows have democratised and popularised what were previously largely leisured, elite forms of identity and self-expression. The loosening of traditional kinship and community ties during and after the Second World War, particularly in urban and metropolitan centres, compounded already high levels of social and geographical mobility among the general population, and these were stimulated in turn by wartime refugee crises. We can posit that a measure of reflexive seekership in individuals' self-representations emerged across the cultural spectrum – bolstered by middle-class traditions that esteemed the value of qualitative experience and the character-building work of self-reflection – as a strategy for managing the population displacements and exponential 'pluralisation of life-worlds' (Berger *et al.* 1974) characteristic of the post-war world. Early 'New Age' seekers' culture, for example, was in no way pure or *sui generis*. It was a mongrel spiritual culture that, as we saw in Chapters 2 to 4, incorporated occult ideas such as the existence of secret 'Masters' and Indian teachings on karma and reincarnation alongside popular psychological techniques and neo-Christian piety. These and contiguous ingredients can easily be found in other spiritual microcultures of the period, as can the social functions of group interaction, popular reading and the experience and wisdom derived from the 'university of life', displayed as a lay antidote to scientific rationality and the hegemony of 'the experts'. The only really distinctive element in seekership culture, as I have shown, was the 'New Age' emblem itself.

The emergence of the 'seeker' as an etic model of reflexive identity is largely a post-war development. In Canada in the early 1950s, for example, Mann (1962: 39–41) identified a small segment of the population he called 'metaphysical tramps'. These were 'intellectual critics of the churches' who were 'eager to discover some new slant on religion'. From Mann's data they appear to have been single, unattached and mobile; he disapprovingly considered them 'incorrigible drifters'. During the same period, Festinger *et al.* (1964) mapped Mrs Keech and 'The Seekers' in the US and Buckner (1968) later identified a type he called 'the occult seeker' among UFO groups. Lofland and Stark (1965: 868ff.) derived a loose social institution of 'seekership' from their analysis of spiritual consumers in California based on a cognitive model of 'problem solving': that is, the search for 'some satisfactory system of religious meaning' to 'interpret and resolve discontent'. Lofland (1977) subsequently developed a simple typology of 'veteran' and 'freshmen' seekers: the former were typically aged over forty and hence, like the 'New Age' pioneers in Chapters 3 and 4, born in the interwar period or earlier; the latter were implicitly part of the post-war baby-boom generation discussed in Chapter 5. Importantly, Lofland noticed the 'multi-directional, tentative seeking' of the 'freshmen' seekers, which might just as easily lead to deeper commitment as to fresh conversions or even to another kind of cultural 'deviancy' altogether (ibid.: 170). In other words, the trajectories of this new generation of seekers had unstable arcs and unpredictable impact, and were already transgressing boundaries between 'sacred' and 'profane' domains. By now the seeker signalled an emergent type of reflexive cultural identity with diffuse, institutionally destabilising effects.

Further analyses followed in the 1970s. In a seminal paper on the post-Sixties 'cultic milieu', Campbell (1972: 127) found its major institution to be the loose, fluid 'society of seekers'. Straus (1976) sought to rescue seekers' agency and creativity from the reductive, even pathologising, accounts of the 1960s; he also contextualised the phenomenon, like Lofland, within broader processes of cultural change in which 'the quest to change one's life' (ibid.: 269) was now paramount. In a similar vein, Balch and Taylor (1977) explained the 'metaphysical seeker' as a socially-oriented problem-solver, rather than the fantasist or sick individual portrayed in Buckner's dismissive account of UFO seekers. Rehabilitation of the term as an etic construct was completed in the 1990s when Roof (1993) labelled the entire cohort of baby-boomers a 'generation of seekers' and Sutcliffe (2000a) pointed to the entrenched function of seekers and seeking as the biographical motor of 'alternative' and contemporary spiritualities.

As we have seen in this book, seekers' quests are simultaneously projected onto the social world through travel, pilgrimage and social interaction, and introjected within the self to create an expanding field of subjective, qualitative experiences. Exploration of both realms is deemed vital: as Alison from the Unit of Service says, 'the search without will prove little without the inward search'.[4] For example, before setting up 'Gandalf's Garden' in London, Muz Murray (1989: x) spent seven years travelling widely, 'sifting the sands of many spiritual cultures for guidance'. Hollywood actress Shirley MacLaine (1983: 90) demonstrates the diffusion of the model into popular culture when she writes, 'I've always thought I was looking for myself whenever I travelled. Like a journey anywhere was really a journey through myself.' Seeking can cover a wide geography, from regularly visiting a nearby fair or centre to making journeys of, say, several hundred miles to visit an international colony like Findhorn. Judith Boice (1990) narrates a five-year pilgrimage through several international settlements including Findhorn, Auroville in India and the Bear Tribe in North America. Similarly, *Journey: An Adventure of Love and Healing* (Tattersall 1996) chronicles an intense episode in the author's life: an American living in Italy, he visits Findhorn for Experience Week and then travels to Norway with a German man and a Norwegian woman to resolve a series of emotional and spiritual crises. These and other journeys replay Anthony Brooke's international travels or the wanderings of the Findhorn founders, but in a more somatic and affective idiom where bodily contact and emotional expressivity are affirmed as touchstones of spiritual authenticity.

When mapped out reflexively as 'inner work' (Caddy 1988: 84), seeking transforms the self into a portable institution: a rich storehouse of subjectivities with which to interpret the passing world. The books of Alice Bailey are instructive in this regard, since they chart a satisfyingly complex 'inner' world of subtle bodies, angelic forces and unfolding hierarchies of relationship. Similarly, the field of holistic health is replete with esoteric anatomies and aetiologies: meridians, astral and etheric bodies, chakras and zones, the circulation of *chi*, *prana* and *kundalini*. And human potential discourse encourages the seeker to harness the energies of his 'inner team' (Waters 1996: 115) through reflexive processes of 'self-audit', 'self-awareness', 'self help', and 'self-talk', to cite a few entries in a dictionary of 'personal development' (ibid.: 178ff.).

Of course, the notion of intense searching and questioning to resolve specific dissatisfactions, or perhaps a more general anomie, has a long pedigree in theology, literature and folk tradition alike. I am thinking here of Augustine's seminal Christian *Confessions*, the apocryphal wanderings of Siddharta Gautama, or the virtuosity of Hindu yogis, as well as the great variety of reflexive 'journals' and 'confessions' in the modern period. And an implicit search may, consciously or not, propel quite secular biographies in the 'pursuit of worldly success, health or consolation' (Campbell 1972: 124). But the significance of the social institution of seekership in contemporary spirituality lies in its popularisation and diffusion of a previously elite, specialist role, which has specific consequences for Anglo–American corporate religion. So Walker (1994: 27) characterises 'New Age' by its insistence that 'spiritual insight is not just given to a few theologians, adepts, priests or shamans, but is available to all' and in Bloom's (1991: xv–xvi) rhetoric, 'New Age' is merely 'the visible tip of the iceberg of a mass movement in which humanity is reasserting its right to explore spirituality in total freedom'. In 'New Age' discourse and increasingly in popular and middle-class cultures, the 'spiritual quest' is no longer the prerogative of a social elite – superiorly educated monks, clerics and philosophers with commanding cultural capital, or even the aristocratic pioneers of 'New Age' – but a populist norm. This development suggests that the intellectualist model of seeking as a rarefied 'problem-solving' perspective, a strategy to reduce cognitive dissonance among the spiritually sensitive and restless, needs to be contextualised within a wider culture of popular practice in which the 'seeker' is now a familiar and accessible role model. Indeed, evidence from other studies of popular religion (Schneider and Dornbusch 1958, Roof 1999) indicates that a pragmatic heterodoxy and customisation of practice and belief among the 'people in the pew' is more widespread in Anglo–American Christian cultures than ecclesiastical history has allowed. This in turn suggests that a modified seekership culture may be less alien to institutional religion than might at first be assumed.

Two basic dynamic expressions of seeking can be distinguished: 'serial' and 'multiple'.[5] A 'serial' seeker has changed religious or spiritual allegiance, typically more than once. Adhesion to each 'spiritual path' may last months, years or decades, and any number of sequential affiliations may be pursued over the course of a lifetime. This mode of seeking is well illustrated in the biographies of the pioneers of Chapters 3 and 4. At a minimum count, Peter Caddy passed through the Rosicrucian Order, Sheena Govan's neo-Christian piety and UFO prophecy. So orderly was his progression that he himself noted that 'each major change in direction is accompanied by a change in partner' (Caddy 1996: 368). Dorothy Maclean was initiated into Western Sufism, then explored a variety of 'spiritual groups' in the 1950s (Maclean 1980: 13) before establishing contact with the nature spirits at Findhorn. George Trevelyan studied Alexander Technique and Anthroposophy before promoting his eclectic esoteric syllabus at Attingham Park. Liebie Pugh, we are told, had 'travelled along or knew of most spiritual paths' (Caddy 1996: 234). A steady progression of sources of guidance appears in the Heralds of the New Age bulletins from the 1950s to the 1980s. And each of these figures or groups appropriated in some fashion, and for varying periods of time, the 'New Age' emblem.

Seriality remains a feature of 'New Age'. The trajectory of David Icke's 'spiritual journey' in the UK recapitulates early 'New Age' patterns in his sense of 'being guided' (Icke 1991: 13ff.). Olsen (1991: xv) introduces her compendium of alternative health treatments in suitably reflexive mode: 'This book represents just the early phases of my personal health odyssey. I expect to continue exploring health care options for as long as I live'. And McGuire (1998: 116) reports that a 'not atypical' member of one American alternative healing group 'tried (and was generally pleased with) rebirthing, crystal healing, colonics, meditation journals, shiatsu, and dance therapy'. Serial seeking dramatically reflects the impact on autobiography of an expanding cultural menu. Nevertheless, in this mode of seeking one is not so much interested in the thrill of the chase as resolving the quest: reaching closure of some kind. As Gill Edwards (1993: viii) puts it:

> For fifteen years, I had followed personal and spiritual paths – from dreamwork to TM, from Gestalt therapy to yoga, from Buddhism to the Quakers. But while each had enriched my life, none had led to the transformation that I was seeking. I began, day after day, to call out to Spirit, saying that I was 'ready'.

A hankering for certainty instils a teleological undercurrent in the serial search: not just to seek, but to *find*. In contrast, multiple seeking proceeds multi-directionally and synchronically: an array of spiritual resources are exploited more or less simultaneously. Ideas, methods and techniques are decontextualised and reconstituted in new settings and adventurous juxtapositions. The practice of multiple seeking has a particular affinity with late 'New Age', when, according to Bloom (1993a: 82) 'all the spiritual traditions and cosmologies are now available to us'. Data in Rose (1998: 15) support this hypothesis: of some nine hundred *Kindred Spirit* subscribers, he found that fully two-thirds 'follow more than one teaching at any one time'. Of course, serial and multiple tacks on spirituality are not mutually exclusive stances: many seekers alternate between episodes of each. But the multiple strategy seems particularly well-suited to the task implied in the discourse of assembling a customised spiritual 'kit' of ideas, values and practices. Hence Bloom (1993b: 21) advises the tyro: 'Spiritual practice is something that you and you alone can put together for yourself'. *Journey Towards Healing*, the 'personal search' of alternative therapist, counsellor and channeller Lori Forsyth (1993: 7), epitomises this attitude. By her mid-thirties Forsyth had already tried out yoga, alternative medicine, spiritual healing, psychic prediction, spirit guides, and Findhorn, to name just a few resources, and she had also changed her name by deed poll the better to express her personal sense of autonomy and originality. Similarly, McGuire (1998: 95) reports that participants in one healing group 'wove together complex, eclectic, and continually changing strands from several approaches for their personal beliefs and practices'. One respondent vividly illustrates this customised approach to daily practice:

> Her meals were selected for particular nutritional benefits; she used mini-meditations during her hectic moments at the office, applied acupressure and visualization to counter a headache [and] employed breathing techniques and visualization at each stoplight to handle the stress of a difficult commute home. At home she used a mantra, crystal and visualization to 'centre' herself during and after an argument. . . . Most days she spent one hour on exercise followed by stress-reducing visualizations in the sauna . . . Later she had a cup of herbal tea and meditated for half an hour.
>
> (McGuire 1998: 184–5)

Here an inventive mix of spiritual, dietary and exercise practices has permeated everyday life. Closure is spurned: practice remains open and mutable. This is clearly useful in times of rapid cultural 'turnover', allowing new ideas and practices to be slipped into the mix as and when they become available. As Shirley MacLaine has remarked, 'every time I think I've got the answers I think it's different a week later'.[6] Likewise William Bloom (1991: xviii) describes his 'spiritual enquiry' as 'an exploration' whose end 'I cannot now even begin to sense'. Hence the multiple seeker refines a customised lifestyle through pick and mix and trial and error in the 'spiritual marketplace' (Roof 1999). In contrast to the earnest, ascetic lifestyle of the 'New Age' pioneers, multiple seeking can be light, laid-back, even fun. 'Be playful', suggests Spangler (1996: 181); Bloom advertises his talks as 'enjoyable' and 'fun'.[7] Not so much pilgrim's *progress* as pilgrim's *process*, seeking itself has become the end. Gill Edwards (1993: 63) acknowledges this: 'The whole point is our journey, not our destination'.

We can say, then, that a sense of history and alterity marks off the serial approach from the hyperactivity of multiple seeking, which tends to scramble boundaries of time and place. Although a spontaneous eclecticism implicit in the earliest networks undermines a strict dichotomy between serial and multiple dynamics, for analytical purposes we can usefully differentiate the two. This ploy allows us to see a rough fit between early 'New Age' and serial seeking, and late 'New Age' and multiple seeking. The careers of Mary Swainson and Lori Forsyth respectively exemplify this rough template. Swainson, born in the Edwardian era, progressed carefully and selectively through life: she was thirty years old before she joined an esoteric group and almost fifty before she began her 'New Age' work (Swainson 1977: 204, 208). By contrast, Forsyth was born in the late 1950s and her career ranges hungrily in both time and space. Her packed narrative comes to rest when she is still only in her mid-thirties, at which point she has already covered more ground than most serial seekers attempt in a lifetime, nonchalantly concluding: 'My whole life has been an experiment, hasn't it?' (Forsyth 1993: 255).

In practice, both serial and multiple seekers must manage a trade-off between choice and constraint, depending on factors such as whom one meets and where, what one reads, which event one happens to attend, and how 'available' one is to exploit a given opportunity. Here is the route Mary Swainson (1977: 204) took to contact one particular group:

> One day when I was about thirty, I was browsing in a public library. Somehow my hand seemed led to touch an unknown book (many seekers have had this experience). It turned out to be the first publication of an esoteric group which, at long last, 'felt right' for me, at that time.

Notice how Swainson locates this carefully-nuanced act in a social anthropology of readership. 'Many seekers', she casually remarks, 'have had this experience'. Here the outcome is positive: according to her own account, Swainson is proactive and available, and jumps at the chance. But the rationale of seeking can also accommodate negative experiences. A participant in a workshop at Findhorn told us that he had been a long-term member of one esoteric group whose leader was 'exposed' in a scandal. Far from becoming embittered for having followed a corrupted practice, he reported that the leader's exposure had been a profound learning experience on the need for him to repudiate powerful *gurus* on his 'spiritual path'.[8]

These examples also show that seeking is neither naive nor antinomian behaviour, but eminently social, legitimated by a wider cultural institution of 'seekership'. Indices of this diffuse cultural institution in action range from interpersonal networks and small groups to the popular readership tapped by lifestyle directories such as *The Many Ways of Being* (Annett 1976) and *The Seeker's Guide: a New Age Resource Book* (Button and Bloom 1992). Certain reflexive linguistic tropes also operate, such as 'path', 'quest', 'seeking', 'higher self', 'energy', being 'centred', and 'getting in touch', establishing a semantic range nuanced towards American vernacular speech. At Findhorn, one resident speaks of 'a quest, a search for myself'.[9] Across the Atlantic, Mark Satin (1978: 13) confesses to his own 'inner search'. Back in the UK, David Icke (1993: 85) writes: 'It is the *seeking* which expands the mind'. Simmons (1990: 81–2) neatly summarises the gist of this popular discourse:

> Each of us has his or her own path. At any given time we must choose the sources of knowledge and experience that seem intuitively right, moving on to other books, disciplines, and scenarios when the time comes.

These normative claims beg the question of the strength of seekers' agency and its historical impact. There are several possible angles on this. On the one hand, the act of seeking implies some basic level of discontent with religion: a 'lack' or 'loss' of some kind. As Alison from the Unit of Service put it bluntly: 'I know all the things they teach. I want more, you know?' Whether or not they come from socially and financially advantaged backgrounds (and many do), seekers may still feel a lack of more tenuous cultural goods such as security, satisfaction and belonging. In this sense the thesis of relative deprivation holds good enough: that is, seekers feel themselves disadvantaged in access to scarce cultural goods. Another possibility is that seekers have become caught up in the thrill of the chase, with submission to a satisfying process overtaking achievement of a particular goal (cf. Campbell 1972: 127). The mystification imputed to seekership in earlier accounts stems from this interpretation, pathologising the culture by portraying its actors as people 'floundering about among religions' (Lofland and Stark 1965: 869). It is certainly possible to find evidence for this theory in some actors' lives, although we need to proceed from specific instances. Roof (1993: 88), for example, steers his assessment of Mollie Stone (whom we met in Chapter 5) in this direction when he concludes that 'life for her remains a quandary, her quest unfulfilled'. But a more positive interpretation must take seriously (although not unreservedly) seekers' testimony to real empowerment in the social world. This view sees seekers reclaiming a hitherto marginal or avant-garde role whose personal reflexivity and social flexibility actually equips them nicely for the 'pluralisation of life-worlds' inherent in postmodernity. Hence Straus (1976: 252–3) models the seeker as a person 'acting creatively in order to construct a satisfying life', an agent who develops 'tactics' for exploiting 'happenstance situations and encounters'. Likewise Balch and Taylor (1977: 851) propose replacing the tired model of the 'personally disoriented searcher' with that of a role 'socially oriented to the quest for personal growth'. Here seekers are not so much 'at sea' in religion as attempting to refashion the self as an appropriate vessel – organismic, reflexive, relational – for navigating the rapids of contemporary culture.

I do not wish to settle this issue one way or the other – indeed, this would be to draw as false a dichotomy between models of mystification and empowerment as that between serial and multiple seeking – but rather to call for nuanced, reflexive accounts of particular instances such as I have attempted to provide in the present book. In any case, whether as agents or subjects, actors or dupes, seekers and their strategies are relational and contextual. This carries implications for the collective structure and function of seekership, a consideration that returns us to a central morphological issue. If certain collectivities, like those associated with 'New Age', depend entirely on the associative and disassociative impulses of x number of individuals, they function as purely strategic assemblies to gather, affirm and disseminate an aggregate of the same. The collectivity itself has no intrinsic identity, no essential purpose or goal: the ceaseless seeking undermines any overarching agenda beyond the mutual exaltation of spiritual paths. It follows that testimony of belonging to a dynamic, purposeful collectivity will be ambiguous, temporary, and necessarily contingent upon passing moods, needs and instincts. And this is exactly what we find when we look for evidence of clear self-identification as 'New Age' or for signs of a *bona fide* movement. The collectivities associated with 'New Age' resemble simple aggregates of self-reflexive individuals. Indeed, a movement of seekers must be an operative contradiction, since one's subjective freedom – indeed, *imperative* – to 'seek' inevitably relativises congregational commitments and boundaries.

Seekers at large: the structural dynamics of 'New Age'

> The right ordering of the New Society can be seen as a pattern of group relationships, from the small cell of a few closely-linked individuals to the world society of nations.
>
> ('The Significance of the Group in the New Age', October 1965, Attingham Park Prospectus)

Since I argue that there is and has been no 'New Age Movement' it may seem perverse to have given over a good deal of this book to a genealogy of historical collectivities connected with the emblem. But a distinction between collectivity and movement is vital, and the sociology of collective behaviour can help here. As Turner and Killian (1972: 5) explain:

> Although a collectivity has members, it lacks defined procedures for selecting and identifying [them]. Although it has leaders, it lacks defined procedures for selecting and identifying them. The members are those who happen to be participating, and the leaders are those who are being followed.

Contingency has replaced necessity in this account of collective interaction: no one is irreplaceable and agenda and outcomes are left substantially to chance. Such a collectivity may be 'compact' or 'diffuse' (ibid.: 111). The 'compact' collectivity, or crowd, gathers only at particular places for the duration of a specified event, whereas the 'diffuse' crowd is scattered across time and space, articulated partly through genealogies of relationships and partly through popular media. Both types interact in 'New Age' culture, whether we think of the compact collectivities of groups, workshops and conference gatherings or the dispersed networks of seekers. Common characteristics of compact and diffuse crowds, according to Turner and Killian (ibid.: 114), are uncertainty, urgency, the communication of moods and images, constraint, suggestibility, and permissiveness. As with the early analysis of seekership, it is not necessary to swallow the implicit disapproval inscribed in the language of these traits, which with just a little (emic) imagination could be re-described as the recovery of the subjectivities of choice, passion, emotional expressivity, self-control, openness, and tolerance. What actually obtains in a particular case will doubtless mix and muddy the purity of these polarities. But enough has been said to show that Turner and Killian's model allows for a realistic play between agency and constraint in the socialisation of the seeker. Hence

> the individual encounters expressions of the same sentiments, witnesses the same behavioural models, and quickly acquires the sense that he is part of a collectivity, sharing uniform sentiments and encompassing a large number of people.
>
> (ibid.: 114)

In the specific terms of a genealogy of 'New Age', I am arguing that this emblem enjoyed an episodic career as a 'fad' (ibid.: 129) within a diffuse collectivity of seekers in the 1950s and 1960s but dissolved into a loose idiom after the 1970s. Again, we need to read 'fad' not derogatively but anthropologically, for the exposition makes clear its application in explaining the crucial hermeneutic shift from emblem to idiom discussed in Chapter 5:

> A fad does not consist of simple, unimaginative imitation. It has *collective enthusiasm for a wide range of individual innovation around a common theme*, in behaviour that is performed in association with others.
>
> (Turner and Killian 1972: 130; emphasis added)

In other words, thinking of 'New Age' in terms of a social 'fad' or 'craze' allows for substantial latitude of belief and practice while maintaining a minimum common reference point, supplied here by the emblem itself. In short, 'New Age' has been a discursive emblem used *within* certain networks of alternative spirituality rather than constituting an entity in itself, which also means that diffuse collectivities of seekers have predated, and will outlive, 'New Age'.

We must now identify the mechanisms through which this collectivity or diffuse crowd of 'New Age' seekers is articulated. Chapters 6 to 8 show the ubiquitous forms of social organisation associated with 'New Age': the group, the colony and the network. These structures function as secondary institutions to regulate the collectivity, occupying an ambiguous zone somewhere between traditional primary institutions and the virtuosic but unstable displays of innumerable 'wandering stars' (Sutcliffe 2000a). I do not propose to say anything more about 'New Age' colonies here. Although frequently upheld as the premier international 'New Age' settlement, Findhorn is better designated as one of very few colonies, perhaps the *only* colony, for which a sound case can be made for classification as 'New Age'. In other words, the colony is an unusual form in 'New Age', and Findhorn features in the genealogy of 'New Age' *not* because the colony is representative of a wider type but because it is the particular historical outcome of a seminal 'New Age' group. Indeed, as Chapter 7 demonstrated, small interactive groups are effectively the building blocks of Findhorn's organisational structure. So I will concentrate here on developing remarks I made in earlier chapters on the function of networks and groups in socialising the seeker.

First developed in anthropology and in the sociology of the family (Barnes 1954, Bott 1957), the term 'network' has been deployed enthusiastically in 'New Age' studies, Melton *et al.* (1991: 416) describing it as 'the single most important New Age organisational form'. The most sustained treatment is York (1995), who understands 'New Age' to be on the cutting edge of a vast 'emerging network' of postmodern religion. A more modest approach can be made following Mitchell (1969: 12), who makes a simple but useful distinction between 'interactional' and 'morphological' characteristics of a network. Interactional characteristics concern the internal dynamics of networks: the differentials of power among individuals and groups whereby authority is wielded and political agendas are set. By contrast, morphology treats the shape and structure of networks in relation to other patterns of organisation. I brought out the interactional dynamics of the early networks in my discussion of the acceptance and then repudiation of Sheena Govan's authority by the proto-Findhorn group in the late 1950s, in the construction of a common apocalyptic discourse on 'New Age' in the 1960s and in the hermeneutical shift in 'New Age' in the 1970s. The morphology of the networks emerges in the ethnographies of the Unit of Service and holistic health in Chapters 6 and 8, where I showed through my own entry into the field how insertion into a local network can quickly lead to a series of interactions and exchanges.

My own experiences are broadly confirmed by other accounts of social networking in action. In London, Barker (1994: 330–2) briefly plots her passage through what she calls the 'extraordinary "intercommunication" of the New Age scene'. And Luhrmann (1994: 36) has delved into magical networks in the English capital. Her impression of the dynamics of networking is particularly apposite:

I became part of a complex, dense network which kept doubling back upon itself: I would meet someone independently, who turned out to have been initiated by someone I knew and whose name was known to other people I also knew. I was familiar with groups at the centre of this network and at its edge. . . . No matter what my point of entry had been . . . I would have ended up in contact with many of the people I know now.

Networks also function at a regional level. In England, 'North East Network' bulletin, subtitled 'Link up with New Age activities in the North East' and targeted at the 'consciously expanding group of individuals' practising 'personal development and natural/holistic therapies', has been published since 1994 in Sunderland. Since 1993 the more populous and socially-advantaged Bristol–Bath–Glastonbury triangle has had *The Spark*, a forty-page free newspaper of co-operative, ecological and entrepreneurial listings focused very broadly on 'creative solutions for a changing world'.[10] On a larger scale, a similar kind of 'intercommunication' characterises holistic health in California (English-Lueck 1990: 25) and 'New Age' in South Africa (Steyn 1994: 308).

This consensus suggests that a network model of alternative spirituality could function as a predictive tool in plotting the trajectories of selected seekers through an identified network, charting the effect of the network's social and ideological constraints on the development of seekers' careers. As the individual enters the network, a series of options becomes available: at a talk by a teacher at a holistic health fair she buys a pamphlet with an address on the back; she visits this centre to attend a workshop; a study group emerges from this workshop and one evening it is led by a facilitator from a long-term group, which she joins and where she makes a new friend who duly invites her on a spiritual retreat at another centre. In the course of time, to paraphrase Luhrmann, she begins to 'bump into' people, to recognise 'familiar faces', to hear news through the 'grapevine' and in turn to be socialised into the network's norms and values. She may also extend the network by introducing friends and family. In the most attenuated version of networking, intercommunication itself becomes the ritual act. Hence during his talk at an alternative health fair in Glasgow in 1996, Patch Adams said, almost as an aside (and recalling Anthony Brooke's international efforts), 'I correspond regularly with about 1600 people around the world'.

But care is needed with the network model. If 'New Age' is not a movement, neither is it – by the same evidence and logic – a network, for the latter is a dynamic web or process of communication and interaction rather than a material entity. Hence 'New Age' is a term *within* a network, or networks, and should not be confused with the properties of the network itself, which are in any case hardly the preserve of alternative spirituality but a ubiquitous feature of modern culture – 'the institution of our age, an unprecedented source of power for individuals', as Ferguson (1982: 43) puts it. Fields where networking has been formative are as diverse as business marketing, the world wide web, clandestine operations and the so-called 'old boy network' in British public life (Heald 1983). The boundary-crossing and variable-blurring properties of the network can create the impression of the diffusion of a discourse, and a diaspora of exponents, far in excess of what actually obtains. This helps explain the attraction of network imagery in 'New Age' discourse. Melton *et al.* (1991: 416) sketch this exaggerated effect well:

> The very existence of the networks creates an image within the New Age community of a growing movement, permeating mainstream society, and of a public, far beyond the boundaries of the movement itself, which is participating in the creation of a New Age without knowing it.

It is ironic that this exposure of 'New Age' rhetoric problematises the authors' own analysis of a 'New Age movement'. For 'New Age' networks are dynamic, unstable processes of discursive intercommunication and exchange, a mechanism whereby a sense of collective belonging can be generated among otherwise fissiparous individuals and groups. In this way

> the diffuse collectivity creates a sense of permissiveness and of constraint, which aids the individual in resolving the uncertainty that deters him from acting solely on the basis of his own judgment.
>
> (Turner and Killian 1972: 117)

Parameters of behavioural and ideological tolerance and restriction are primarily established face-to-face in couples and small groups, but norms and values are also disseminated via newsletters, mailing lists and telephone trees, and more recently via e-mail, discussion lists and web pages. A scattered matrix of small buildings, rented premises and private houses functions as the set of material nodes in the network, offering seekers places to gather, interact and express their solidarity.

When participants get together, social interaction invariably takes the form of small groups. A few remarks on 'New Age' group culture follow to close this section on the structural dynamics of the field. First, the group is pervasive: it structures all sectors of the spiritual culture associated with 'New Age' now and in the past, whether we look in holistic healing, Findhorn and meditation practice today, inspect the bulletins, meetings and gatherings of the 1950s and 1960s, or unpack Alice Bailey's oligarchic ideology of the 1930s. Groups may be one-off gatherings, formed for a day, week-end or (exceptionally) week-long 'workshop': that is, an experiential, participative learning forum. Examples include the firewalking event at Westbank, the 'New Age' group leaders gathering at Attingham and 'Experience Week' at Findhorn, respectively. Groups may also meet regularly, either for a limited series, such as the various teaching groups run at the Salisbury Centre, or indefinitely and with considerable commitment, like the Unit of Service meditation meetings, or the Rosicrucian Order's week-end gatherings in the late 1930s. Second, the groups tend to be small, meaning for present purposes 'a group all of whose members are known, at least by sight, to everyone of them' (Phillips 1965: 14). There were fourteen in Experience Week, six on average at full moon meditations, eight at the Alice Bailey Sacred Dance day, and five in Sheena Govan's Pimlico group. Low numbers encourage intimacy and interaction among varied, sometimes antagonistic personalities ('chalk and cheese' is how Eileen Caddy described herself and Dorothy Maclean in Sheena Govan's group). As Lucis Trust spokeswoman Jan Nation put it in a workshop at Findhorn: 'groupwork entails the coming together of individuals with completely different points of view, each fulfilling a different function'.[11] The facilitator at the Sacred Dance workshop considered that the optimum group size was between ten and twenty: any less meant insufficient 'energy' was generated, any more and the group might break up or sub-groups hive off. Larger groups in which I participated included twenty-one people at a Bach Flower Remedies day, thirty at the firewalking event at Westbank, and thirty-six at the 'Inner Ashrams' workshop mentioned above. These were more anonymous events, incorporating structured teaching, formal exercises, and firm leadership by a designated 'expert'. But even here participation was encouraged and small group interaction was used to break down a potentially intimidating mass. As firewalker Hazel Price explained, 'no one will be able to stand back – it will affect the energy'. Jan Nation put this more forcefully: 'someone who is critical can be a poison in a group'. In any case size was, in theory at least, no barrier to intercommunion: Nation also claimed that 'if the group in this room had meditated together for ten years we wouldn't need to discuss anything'. Third, a diversity of group leadership and decision-making models can be found, from the relatively modest directives given us by our Experience Week focalisers, and the gentle shepherding by Alison in the Unit of Service, to the rousing poetics of George Trevelyan, the presidential style of Liebie Pugh and Peter Caddy, and the increasingly authoritarian decrees of Sheena Govan. Internal group dynamics varied accordingly: sometimes consensus prevailed, at other times 'spiritual rivalry' might break loose and leaders get toppled or groups disband. In the most sophisticated contexts a transparent obsolescence is built into groups, for example at Findhorn.

The discourse of 'New Age' spirituality

I have never met anyone engaged in any kind of New Age activity who has thought of herself or himself as having joined a new religion.
(Spangler 1993: 79).

As Spangler says, the emic position actively repudiates 'religion' and 'religiousness'. 'I'm not talking of religion',[12] writes Alison of the Unit of Service. MacLaine (1983: 8) says: 'The religions of the world didn't seem to explain or satisfy our spiritual needs'. Trevelyan's (1977: 2) book *A Vision of the Aquarian Age* is emphatically not about 'a religious movement, but a spiritual awakening'. Religion may not only be shunned but positively attacked. William Thompson calls it 'one of the greatest forces for evil at work in the world today' (in Spangler and Thompson 1991: 176). 'I had little respect for the religious institutions and priestly hierarchies', writes Bloom (1990: 2), describing his school vicar as 'an extraordinarily boring man!' (Bloom 1993b: 18).

'Organised religion', then, is constructed in the 'New Age' idiom as unimaginative and socially constricting at best, pathological at worst. It is contrasted unfavourably with a vivid, vital 'spirituality'. In *The New Age in a Nutshell*, Lorna St Aubyn (1990: 84–5) defines religion largely in terms of 'mundane rules', 'Church control' and 'excessive dogma'. Spirituality, on the other hand, is 'not just for Sunday mornings' but 'for all day every day'. Children raised in particular faith traditions, she thinks, have been 'vaccinated by religion' and are thereby 'immune to spirituality'. According to Liz Hodgkinson (1993: 108) in *The Personal Growth Book*: 'You can be genuinely spiritual without ever going near a church or place of worship and, conversely, go to church, synagogue or mosque several times a week without ever understanding what spirituality is all about'. David Icke (1993: 12) encapsulates this impatient discourse when he writes: 'Religion has hijacked spirituality'.

Sometimes the enemy is merely damned by faint praise. Patrick in the Unit of Service told me: 'Without spirituality, there would be no religion, but not vice versa'. Walker (1994: 27) explains that Findhorn is not 'a religion' but 'a context within which all aspects of life, including religious observance, are taking place'. Alternatively, 'spirituality' simply prevails by default. Thus Simmons (1990: 11) portrays a 'new spiritual awakening':

> Traces of this movement are everywhere if one wants to look. Every week now, I hear about another group or activity or institute involved in things spiritual, and they are scattered throughout the entire Western hemisphere.
>
> (ibid.: 204)

This kind of discourse proliferated in the 1980s and 1990s and can now be found widely in newspapers, magazines and popular conversation. If we look back at the ethnographies in this book, we see that an ideology of 'spirituality' underpins the general discourse. In Chapter 6, Patrick privileges spirituality over religion in the work of the Unit of Service while Sinclair (1984: 46) characterises the Bailey work in general as 'the art of spiritual impression'. In Chapter 7 we saw how Findhorn now typically calls itself a 'spiritual' rather than a 'New Age' community, and in the questionnaire I conducted there, 'spirituality' was overwhelmingly preferred by respondents to 'religion'. The latter was associated with ideas like 'the system', 'dogma', 'organised belief', and 'narrow' outlooks, whereas spirituality was linked to 'living experience' and to 'open', 'inner', 'inclusive', and 'natural' discourse.[13] In Chapter 8, nearly three-quarters of respondents to the same questionnaire at an alternative health fair juggled these terms and categories in very similar fashion (Sutcliffe 1995) and the chapter showed that in networks of healing and well-being as much as anywhere else in the general field, talk of 'spirit' and the 'spiritual' was plentiful, of 'god' and 'religion' scant. Firewalker Stephen Mulhearn, for example, made no references at all to the latter pairing; his most explicit theological claim was 'we're not human beings being spiritual but spiritual beings being human'.

Nor is the 'spiritual' merely a contemporary fad. In Chapters 3 and 4 we read how Dorothy Maclean (1980: 12–13) explored avowedly 'spiritual' groups in the late 1940s and early 1950s. Eileen Caddy (1988: 19) recalls of husband-to-be Peter that ' "religious" was not the way to describe him. I knew he didn't go to church, but I sensed a commitment to something spiritual.' In the interwar years, too, we find substantial traces of this discourse. In his very successful book *God is My Adventure*, Landau (1935: vii, 148) addressed himself to 'contemporary spiritual life' and 'modern spiritual pursuits'. And talk of 'spirituality' permeates the *Occult Review*. In 1932 an editorial proposed setting up a 'Spiritual League' to 'weld together' the many 'scattered spiritual units' among its readership while in 1935 the editor remarked approvingly that 'the type of literature which deals with the spiritual quest is becoming increasingly popular'.[14] An article by a Mrs Featherstonehaugh in 1932 concluded that 'the real problem' of the world was 'a spiritual one' and was not adequately represented in the plight of religion, for 'only to the superficial do the empty churches represent the spirituality of the age'.[15] Alice Bailey, too, used this kind of language. In 1925 she wrote that 'behind all subjective phenomena' is a 'latent spiritual cause' which is the proper focus of 'the spiritual man' (Bailey 1991b: 392). And in 1936 she described the vanguards of the 'New Age' as

> not necessarily people who could be termed 'religious' in the ordinary sense of that word, but they will be men of goodwill, of high mental calibre . . . free from personal ambition and selfishness, animated by love of humanity.

> (ibid.: 393)

In sum, since at least the First World War 'spirituality' has developed as a discourse set over and against 'institutional religion'. In contemporary culture 'spirituality' has emerged as a hybrid discourse constructed from 'alternative' and 'popular' sources. Indeed, practising 'spirituality' is no longer confined to denizens of aristocratic, avant-garde or subcultural enclaves: it is increasingly done in the culture at large. An informant in Ferguson (1982: 401) could claim by the end of the 1970s that 'a person is no longer an oddball because he is known to be on a spiritual quest'. By the 1990s, significant percentages in one American survey were describing their identities as explicitly spiritual *and* non-religious (Zinnbauer *et al.* 1997). These individuals were reported to be 'less likely to evaluate religiousness positively' and 'less likely to engage in traditional forms of worship such as church attendance and prayer'. In contrast they were

> more likely to be independent from others . . . to engage in group experiences related to spiritual growth . . . to characterise religiousness and spirituality as different and nonoverlapping concepts . . . to hold nontraditional 'new age' beliefs [and] to have had mystical experiences.
>
> (Zinnbauer *et al.* 1997: 561)

Roof (1999: 177) concurs with these findings, emphasising the reflexive and popular qualities of Anglo–American discourse in which the word 'spiritual' is 'invoked positively as a basis of self-identity' by a heterogeneous constituency who simultaneously use the word 'religious' as a 'counter-identity for clarifying who they are not'.

This emergent 'spiritual' discourse demonstrates significant biographical continuities across the decades, from the interwar seekers targeted by Alice Bailey, through Sheena Govan's post-war Pimlico group and to the new seekers of the late-Sixties counterculture and beyond. It has three broad qualities or instincts: it is dissident, lay and functional. First, it remains a dissident discourse, although increasingly in latent rather than manifest function. The agenda is consistently one of finding or constructing an alternative to institutional religion: something *other*, something *more*, something *better*. 'I decided to give up organised religion', says an informant in Tomory (1996: 86). 'It suited me perfectly that I could have a spiritual understanding and basis that was nothing to do with religion', writes Lori Forsyth (1993: 76). 'The church dissatisfies me', says Alison from the Unit of Service, 'I want more, you know?' Other institutions are similarly scolded for their repression of populist freedoms. 'People here have a *right* to be suspicious of academics', an American told me at Findhorn. A related strategy is to prospect further afield for a replacement for the enemy 'organised religion', particularly in 'Eastern', 'esoteric' and indigenous sources. Hence in the interwar period Alice Bailey located her *guru* in Tibet (following Blavatsky), Paul Brunton prospected 'secret Egypt' and 'secret India', and the White Eagle Lodge sought legitimation in a native American spirit guide. More recently, Bowman (1993b) has charted the creative reconstruction of 'Celtic' spirituality while UFO groups have looked to extraterrestrial realms – perhaps the ultimate 'alternative' source (Melton 1995).

Anti-authoritarian rhetoric seasons the mix. Icke (1991: 127) writes:

> The new spirituality involves a one-to-one relationship with the
> Godhead and the higher intelligences. We will no longer believe
> that all our sins can be forgiven by a priest appointed by the Church
> hierarchy. Why do we need a human to arbitrate between ourselves and
> God when we have our own personal link?

Similarly, Bloom (1990: 8) says: 'I advise people not to be cowardly about their
own spiritual authority'. But even these statements reproduce an established
message in the genealogy of alternative spirituality. Krishnamurti, for example,
told the *Occult Review* as early as 1932 that 'authority is the antithesis of
spirituality', Landau (1935: vii) acknowledged 'something sacriligious' behind
the intent of *God is My Adventure* and in the late Victorian period Helena
Blavatsky is reputed to have said, 'I wouldn't be a slave to God Himself, let alone
man'.[16]

Second, the instinct is lay and populist, seen clearly in the theatre of
operation, which is largely everyday lives and interactions in Anglo–Amercian
culture. This ethnodomain has traditionally (and unaccountably) received little
scrutiny from academics but here it takes centre stage. Among holistic health
practitioners in California, for example, English-Lueck (1990: 138–9) noticed
that 'conversations flip casually between discussions of hairdressers, spouses, and
massage oil to reincarnations, sensing auras, and chatting with one's spirit
guides'. Gill Edwards (1993: 178) speaks of 'the spirit of everyday life', William
Bloom (1993a: 59) of 'housework and daily yoga'. The chapters of the Crotona
Fellowship gathered in members' suburban houses; Sheena Govan's group met
in her Pimlico flat; groups associated with Liebie Pugh and the Findhorn
founders met in hotels; Trevelyan's 'New Age group leaders' met at an adult
education college; and the Findhorn colony began in a caravan park.
Contemporary projects typically continue this pattern of domestic operation,
such as the Westbank Centre, a family home, and the Unit of Service, which
invariably met in Alison's flat. And Findhorn now owns the hotel and
caravan site.

The domestic setting undermines traditional boundaries between public and
private space: everyone prepared to cross that threshold and muck in, is
welcome. In Marilyn Ferguson's 'Aquarian conspiracy' – which she sees simply
as a vast networking of like-minded spiritual activists – the key point is that 'a
conspirator can be anyone' (Ferguson 1982: 21). Now, this is a direct populist
appeal, and Worsley (1969: 242–4) has identified two cardinal features of this
syndrome: 'the supremacy of the will of the people' and the desire for a 'direct
relationship between people and leadership, unmediated by institutions'.
Translating these from politics to culture – more specifically, to contemporary
spirituality – is a self-explanatory move: the former feature neatly captures the
collective institution of seekership and the latter addresses the demand for

immediate access to the source of spiritual vitality. Populism's inclusivity is particularly salient here: Worsley explains that it can embrace a variety of small-scale, entrepreneurial, marginal and even disgruntled identities that otherwise repudiate or evade primary institutions. To these and other mobile identities, populism offers 'a new communal transectional identity' (ibid.).

This brief account of the mechanics of cultural populism helps to explain the popular appeal of 'New Age' spirituality. Consider various prominent notions uncovered in this book: that self-identities or 'labels' fundamentally mislead; that anyone can join; that 'doing it' rather than 'talking about it' is what 'New Age' is about; that spirituality is innate and 'instinctive' (Bloom 1991: 221) and that our passions, enthusiasms and feelings − our manifold subjectivities − are clues to its genius; that unmediated experiences of gnosis and charisma are within reach of everyone; that 'spirituality' can function as a unifying factor (a 'universal link') across the world; and that institutions − particularly religion and education − only thwart it. Hence David Spangler (1996: 220) thinks that 'anyone can become a birthforce for a new world', that 'we may all become champions'; and Gill Edwards (1993: 192) declares dramatically: 'It is time for *everyone* to become a shaman, a metaphysician, a dream-weaver, a walker-between-worlds'. Following on the heels of Alice Bailey's prototype 'true Aquarian' of the 1930s (Bailey 1991a: 416), the ultimate 'transectional identity' has been proposed in some 'New Age' quarters: the 'planetary citizen' who cultivates a 'planetary consciousness' for a 'planetary culture'.[17]

Disciplinary control of knowledge and traditional educational credentials are eschewed in these and other expressions of the emergent spirituality, a stance that feeds a self-taught ethos. As Ross (1992: 539) remarks, the discourse urges 'everyone'

> to become the engineer/architect/designer of his or her own environment. Reskilling oneself . . . can be seen as a way of reappropriating, from the experts, folk skills that were once everyday knowledge.

The authority to interpret is reclaimed by practitioners themselves, who are typically not specialists trained by traditional institutions, but lay 'doers' and 'thinkers': 'amateurs' in the literal sense of 'lovers' or 'enthusiasts'. In this manner specialist discourses on psychology, physics and religion are retrieved from university libraries and laboratories and factored into popular teachings on the healing power of positive thinking, the importance of matching IQ with 'EQ' or 'emotional intelligence', the scientific basis of holism and the perennial teachings at the heart of all religions.

Popular culture may also directly trigger amateurist spiritual reflection. For example, an initially sceptical Peter Caddy (1996: 370) describes his visit to Florida's Disney World in the company of George Trevelyan:

I saw Disney World through his eyes, as if through the eyes of a child, and so entered into the spirit of the place. I felt that I'd learnt an important lesson: 'Except ye be as a little child, ye can no wise enter the Kingdom of Heaven'.

David Spangler (1984: 131) cites Richard Adams's epic fantasy novel about a rabbit colony, *Watership Down* (1972), as a favourite book. And in the mid-1990s he kept three miniature models on his desk for inspiration: Mickey Mouse as the sorceror's apprentice in Walt Disney's *Fantasia* (1939), Yoda the wizard in *Star Wars* (1977), and Merlin the magician from Arthurian folklore.[18]

As well as the shamanic and the spectacular, more ordinary daily tasks and transactions are brought to attention. Roof (1993: 64) found Mollie Stone understood 'spiritual' to be 'something very worldly, having to do with relating to the earth and sky and animals and people; and something very bodily, having to do with health, happiness, and feeling good about herself'. In the Findhorn magazine *One Earth*, William Bloom (1993b: 18) lists various everyday activities as opportunities for 'practical spiritual practice' such as 'listening to music, making love, having a baby, painting, fasting or weeding the garden'. Notice how his list casually, even innocently, reclaims intimate and profane acts of everyday life as the stuff of spirituality. In her paperback manual *Stepping into the Magic* Gill Edwards (1993: 179ff.) pursues a similar line, listing some simple everyday tasks through which practitioners can 'connect with Spirit': taking a bath or shower is 'an opportunity to "cleanse" yourself of the past'; mealtimes are a chance 'to remember that the Earth has given this gift of food'; glancing in the mirror is a moment for speaking an affirmation like 'Today, I am open to miracles'; and even such simple acts as climbing stairs can be used to 'affirm that you are reaching for a higher perspective on your life'. Domestic space itself receives special attention, and at the time of writing there is a boom in *feng shui*, a traditional Chinese practice repackaged for Anglo–American culture that deals in the harmonious management of interior environments. The popularisation and diffusion of *feng shui* can be seen in a glut of publishing: one feature in *Here's Health*, a British popular health magazine, is called '20 Ways to Heal your Home' and proposes approaches such as 'light some candles', 'make a small shrine', 'harness crystal power', 'get the "vibes" right', and, simply, 'love your space'.[19]

The tedious side of human domesticity also receives attention. Bloom (1993a: 60) says that 'one woman I know always washes the dishes with divine awareness' and 'another woman taught me how to wash and clean the lavatory with love'. This sacralisation of housework is a persistent strain in Findhorn spirituality: the central aphorism in the colony in the mid-1990s was 'work is love in action'. But despite (or perhaps because of) this celebration of what has traditionally been regarded as 'women's work', an equivocal gender ascription is at work here that exemplifies some wider political ambiguities inherent in 'New Age' spirituality. A full analysis of different stages in the gendering of power in

'New Age' spirituality requires further detailed research, but by exhuming and at least sexing a largely buried field, I hope to have made some empirical inroads. Work traditionally ascribed to women – housework, childcare, emotional labour – has certainly been revalued in 'New Age', even brought to the centre of attention in the case of the incorporation of emotional work into the 'expressive ethic' of the late-1970s onwards (Heelas 2000), seen particularly in Experience Week. Findhorn's domesticated habitat partly explains its persistent popularity for women, and this holds true for 'New Age' circles in general: in crude terms, this is where women's expertise has been confined by a dominant gendered discourse based on the segregation of women to the 'private' domain and men to the 'public' sphere. But determining the actual power wielded by women in 'New Age' circles is complicated by several factors. On the one hand, women are prominent in the sex profile of 'New Age', typically in a two-to-one ratio, and this is confirmed by my own findings: the 'core group' in the Unit of Service, Experience Week participants at Findhorn and my questionnaire sample at an alternative health fair in Edinburgh repeated this two-to-one ratio, and at a Bach Flower Remedies workshop and a talk by firewalker Stephen Mulhearn, it increased to three to one. Rose (2001: 330) also found in his *Kindred Spirit* questionnaire that nearly four out of five alternative therapists were women. On the other hand – and here's the rub – he also found in the same survey that female teachers were 'outnumbered two to one' by men as role models and authoritative sources (ibid.). Now, this is just one study, but its implication is that women may predominate as participants and 'coalface' practitioners (Reiki healers, Findhorn group focalisers, firewalk instructors) without attaining parity in higher-profile leadership.

This pattern is substantiated in my genealogy. On the one hand Alice Bailey can justly lay claim to being the modern ideologue of 'New Age'. But playing the role of 'secretary' to her Tibetan 'Master' effectively inscribed a familiar, hierarchically-gendered relationship at the heart of 'New Age' epistemology. In a different vein, Sheena Govan and Liebie Pugh each became a messianic figure in the 1950s and 1960s – a female Parousia, in effect – but who now remembers them? Sheena Govan's historical memory is almost entirely mediated by Peter Caddy's autobiography (1996) and Paul Hawken's hagiography (1990), and it was Caddy who finally usurped her authority as public face of the group, as we saw in Chapter 3. As for Pugh, she leaves almost no historical footprint. And who remembers women networkers such as Sheila Walker of the Scottish UFO Society, who first put Peter Caddy in touch with George Trevelyan, or indefatigable international correspondents such as May Harvey of the Heralds of the New Age? Likewise, Myrtle Glines was David Spangler's associate when he arrived at Findhorn, and her practical experience in counselling and groupwork evidently grounded the crucial shift in 'New Age' discourse from apocalypse to self-realisation, but her part has been soundly eclipsed by Spangler's role. Likewise Findhorn was settled by more women than men (three to one, if we include Lena Lamont with Eileen Caddy and Dorothy

Maclean) and yet it was the man, Peter Caddy, who was the colony's face to the outside world up to 1979. And while George Trevelyan has been called the 'father of the New Age', I know of no claims for a 'mother'. More recently, Marilyn Ferguson (1982) found in *The Aquarian Conspiracy* that only two out of thirty-seven inspirational figures in a small Californian survey were women, while the Findhorn Foundation continued to be represented by men as overall directors into the late 1980s. The ambiguity of gender roles in 'New Age' is encapsulated in the transgendered economy at 'God's Hotel' in Forres in the late 1950s, where Peter Caddy managed the operation (using his intuition and hunches) and Eileen Caddy changed nappies and cooked (while obtaining hierophantic guidance).

So far I have discussed two qualities or instincts of the field: the dissident and the lay. Third and finally, I wish to point out the functional dynamic of 'New Age' spirituality. That is, the 'New Age' seeker is largely preoccupied with the rational–functional application of spiritual skills. She wants a spiritual practice that will *do* things, that will make things *work*, whether on the intimate scale of biographies and relationships or on the global scale of co-operation and social unity. Hence a problem-solving, 'working' approach to life characterises the 'New Age' ethos, emphasising short- and medium-term achievement of goals and the active creation of meaning in everyday life. Here is Bloom (1993a: 84) again on the ideal method:

> If we commit ourselves to career retraining or returning to formal education, we do so with great care and thought. We research the areas in which we are interested. We taste what they are like before we make long-term plans. We should have the same approach to spiritual education.

In other words, individuals should assess risk and opportunity and make appropriate plans and adjustments in spirituality as much as in anything else. Implementing spiritual strategies is a matter of empirical trial and error, conducted on oneself as the experimental 'site' but duly worked out in relationship with others. Claims have even been made that such an 'empiricised' spirituality upholds scientific method. Bloom implies as much in a typically populist statement on the convergence between spiritual experience and science, which supposedly is

> coming to a more fluid understanding of nature and the cosmos, in which there is a continuum between consciousness and matter, and an understanding that everything is made up of energy in different forms.
>
> (Bloom 1996: 18)

This actually sounds more like a metaphysical than a scientific statement.[20] From Alice Bailey's texts to contemporary takes on holism and energy, imagery lifted from the popular science of the day has invoked the authority of scientific data and method, whether in terms of light waves, electricity, atomic power, nuclear radiation, or extraterrestrial life forms. At the same time, it is not clear that sufficient expertise (or even interest) exists among seekers to evaluate such a statement properly. Yet science connotes modernity, and the effect is to establish 'New Age' as a cutting-edge discourse.

But at the end of the day, personal experience – construed as pure and irreducible – is the touchstone: as Bloom (1996: 18) also says, 'if you have not experienced it, why should you believe it?' Such functionality calls forth an intense pragmatism among seekers. 'Anything can work', says Ferguson (1982: 91). 'Do some sampling of ideas and images', suggests Spangler (1996: 181). 'Do something, anything, to deepen your relationship with the sacred', urges Bloom (1993b: 18). This approach can veer towards a prosperity teaching. 'If you embark on this path you will never actually want for money, friends, or good relationships', says Hodgkinson (1993: 26). Lori Forsyth (1993: 130ff.) lists a new job, a new car and a new home as cumulative examples of 'the way life flows when one works with Spirit'. But material success may also be an intrinsic goal of spiritual practice, as in the Findhorn practice of 'manifestation'. Eileen Caddy recalls that

> sometimes it took a while after the thought was put out to achieve the physical reality, but often it would happen quite quickly. . . . When I received guidance about something, I knew it would come, and often just the right object or amount of money would be given to us.
>
> (In Walker 1994: 191)[21]

Learning and perfecting spiritual practice can be a highly technical matter. Bloom himself (1993b: 19) speaks of 'spiritual technology'[22] while Ferguson (1982: 91) introduced the term 'psychotechnologies', meaning techniques and systems designed to trigger 'a deliberate change in consciousness'. In *A Guide to the New Age*, Stuart Wilson (1989: 51ff.) offers nearly eighty different spiritual techniques and strategies, including Peter Caddy's advice to eliminate 'if' and 'can't' from one's vocabulary, adopt a vegetarian diet, take up meditation and regularly use affirmations. In a clear summary of the lay functionalism informing practice, he concludes: 'We should feel free to *use* any combination of techniques for change that seems *right to us* and gives us good *results*' (ibid.: 66; emphasis added). Finally, several self-styled resource books and catalogues substantiate the 'do-it-yourself' ethos of alternative spiritual practice. Compendiums like *The Whole Person Catalogue* (Considine 1992) and *The Seeker's Guide* (Button and Bloom 1992) list groups, ideas, teachers, techniques, products, courses, and treatments across the spectrum of meditation, healing and personal growth circles. 'Take time to look around', advises Spangler (1996: 181). 'Give yourself plenty of time to dip and to discriminate', suggests Bloom (1993a: 83).

The end of 'New Age'

What was once a mystery is now understandable.

(Wiseman 1979: 113)

I'm a spiritual person. I'm fascinated by all sorts of religions and I pick from them what I want.

(Evelyn Glennie, musician)[23]

Local variation *is all there is!*

(Martin 2000: 282)

The title of this last chapter has deliberately carried a double meaning. We have reached the 'end' in the sense that 'New Age' as a collective moment of utopian change is over – as indeed Findhorn kindly informed me when I began this work. But we have also reached an end in the sense of arriving at the kind of popular, functional, everyday spirituality which is, in significant part, the legacy of 'New Age': a product of its genealogy.

In this book I tested the consensus that New Age is a 'movement' and found instead a diffuse collectivity of questing individuals. These seekers have certainly used the expression 'New Age', and between the mid-1950s and mid-1960s they briefly organised themselves around it, treating it as the emblem of an imminent apocalypse. Apart from this, affiliation has been sporadic and ambiguous. At the same time I have exhumed, described and analysed a series of small groups and networks of seekers from the 1930s to the early twenty-first century. I have also discussed the popular discourse generated in the field. This has in part addressed the timing of an apocalyptic 'New Age', but has increasingly dwelt since the 1970s on the promise of a pragmatic, world-affirming 'spirituality'. As we examine the archive material informing Chapters 3 and 4, the popular literature of Chapters 2, 5 and 9, and the ethnographies of Chapters 6–8, we see that this discourse of 'spirituality' increasingly displaces 'New Age' and inherits the controlling instincts of dissidence, populism and functionality outlined in this final chapter. By the early twenty-first century this diffuse and popularised discourse of spirituality has become fairly comfortably established across the cultural spectrum as a symbolic repudiation of 'organised religion'. It has an almost entirely white, middle-class demography largely made up of professional, managerial, arts, and entrepreneurial occupations.[24] It is also well-represented by women by dint of its reclamation of skills and attributes traditionally consigned to domestic realms and predominantly gendered as 'feminine', such as emotional empathy, bodily awareness and interpersonal skills. However, notwithstanding superiority in numbers (and also in spiritual gifts, according to some emic accounts), the relative social power and status of 'New Age' women remains an unresolved issue.

The demography underscores very real constraints around this spirituality. Despite its rhetoric of inclusivity, it is clear that certain sectors of the population are more likely to get involved than others. Nevertheless, the norm – and in a globalised age, the appeal – is of a universalised lay spirituality, open to all, yet with no stigmatising label or fussy membership criteria. The apparent paradox of how such an amorphous discourse can be learned and transmitted is explained by the role of the seeker, located in a diffuse collectivity of peers and mentors. No other social role has the requisite combination of reflexivity and interdependence to generate the modicum of institutionalisation required while simultaneously sabotaging levels of organisational complexity beyond the most simple. We have seen how 'New Age' seekers resourcefully sift and splice their sources. Consequently the presenting profile of individual (and group) is constantly changing in line with the migration of ideas and techniques (and individuals) in and out of the biography (or collectivity) in question. Should stronger collective identity or mobilisation be sought – when an aspiring leader emerges – there is inbuilt resistance at the heart of the phenomenon, for the logic of seeking encourages movement laterally (to 'share' and 'network' with peers and colleagues) rather than vertically (scaling a hierarchy). Clearly such lateral diffusion does not translate easily into sustainable policy, as we saw in the case of 'New Age' in the 1960s, and as still haunts Findhorn's attempts to come up with a consistent self-identity. Indeed, the history of 'New Age' is littered with temporary groups and mutated identities, which is both a source of the restless, passionate creativity of its actors as well as a factor in its elision from cultural history. As institutions crumble and regroup (an apt term), seekers stand revealed by default, if not by choice. And currently there are rich pickings for seekers: the cultural panorama of the early twenty-first century provides a variegated spiritual landscape for those with sufficient cultural capital, perhaps unique in the history of religions in its sheer range of groups, quests, paths, and trips. In this sense we can see that the instinctual drive of 'New Age' spirituality towards a simple, direct and useful practice (Maldonado 1986) not tied to any particular host institution, is the pre-eminent expression of popular religion in contemporary culture.

But such a spirituality must be inherently unstable. Indeed, the career of 'New Age' exemplifies the fickle public impact of this new spirituality. The restlessness and mobility of its key agents militates against the level of institutionalisation required by a viable NSM or NRM, as I have repeatedly argued, and the fiercely subjective values and experiences of seekers are in any case hostile to institutional recuperation. The revealing advice of Bloom (1990: 8) 'not to be cowardly' about one's 'spiritual authority' returns us to the sociostructural indeterminacy haunting 'New Age', for which the following observation, derived from the work of Max Weber, remains highly pertinent:

> Given the absolutistic moral fervor, the revolutionary disdain of formal procedures, and the inherent instability of the lack of provision for

succession, charismatic activities and orientations because of their close relation to the very sources of social and cultural creativity, contain strong tendencies toward the destruction and decomposition of institutions.

(Eisenstadt 1968: xix)

'Charismatic activities and orientations' perfectly encapsulates the spiritual seekership, groupwork and networking at the heart of 'New Age', and this immediacy and spontaneity must be a major source of the biographical attraction and resilience of 'alternative' forms of spirituality. But in structural terms, this instinct is also the gravest obstacle to the lasting inroads on the primary institutions of the modern world that this spirituality would dearly like to make. For its reflexive biographies, its loose collectivities and its one potentially explosive emblem – 'New Age' – lack a viable level of collective focus and mobilisation effectively to deliver its challenge.

NOTES

INTRODUCTION: ON THE GENEALOGY OF 'NEW AGE'

1 Hebdige (1979: 27) points out that the 'stock imagery' of punk was 'crisis and sudden change'. For example, in 1976 the Clash wore overalls painted with the slogans 'Hate and War' and 'White Riot', while the refrain of the Sex Pistols' 1977 single 'God Save the Queen' was 'No future' (Savage 1991: 236, 348). And punk's successor in popular culture, the ecstasy/acid house scene of the late 1980s and 1990s (Collin and Godfrey 1997), inherited this apocalyptic strain. In her collection of 'end-of-the-millennium' fiction from club culture, Champion (1998: xiv, xii) speaks of 'the whole apocalypse vibe that characterised the eighties and nineties' including 'the classic motifs − hedonism, insanity, religious mania, suicide cults, future technology, chemical excess and media conspiracies − each of them escalating as we near the mythological date'.

2 See Wolf (1992) and Davies (1999) on the pitfalls of unbridled reflexivity.

3 As, I subsequently discovered, does Christoph Bochinger in his *'New Age' und moderne Religion: Religionswissenschaftliche Untersuchungen* (Gutersloh: Chr. Kaiser 1994). From Hanegraaff's (1996: 377−80) brief but valuable exposition of his work, Bochinger would seem to describe 'New Age' as a 'label' and a 'syndrome' rather than a *'Weltanschauung'* or 'social movement', an approach that approximates my use of 'emblem' and 'idiom'. However, I believe that the genealogical, rather than 'history of ideas', analysis that I attempt here resolves the inconsistency, even fallacy − imputed to Bochinger by Hanegraaff (1996: 379) − of denying any substance to 'New Age' while simultaneously reconstructing its intellectual history.

1 THE LIFE AND TIMES OF 'NEW AGE'

1 On emic/etic, see discussion below.

2 The reference here is to the American cataloguer of strange phenomena, Charles Fort (1874−1932), who compiled four books in the 1920s and 1930s on anomalous, marginal and occult phenomena. Fort's practice was ataxonomic: he simply accumulated evidence by *listing* − an unfortunate tendency in 'New Age' studies.

3 See the exhaustive discussion of conservative Christian attacks in Saliba (1999: 39−88).

4 Further on the hegemony of Anglo−American culture, York (1995: 42) sees 'New Age' as 'especially an American−Canadian−British−Dutch−West German− Australian−New Zealand phenomenon'; see also the territory covered in Lewis and Melton (1992). In a search I conducted on the worldwide web on 17 August

2001, Yahoo! found 228 entries by region for 'New Age: faiths and practices'. Eight countries were represented: US, Canada, UK, Australia, New Zealand, Denmark, Sweden and – curiously – Turkey. The vast majority (171) were in the US (California alone amounting to one-third of this total) followed by Australia (20) and the UK (14).

5 In addition to works cited in this section I have also benefited from the discussions in Wiseman (1979), Kleinman (1991), Wagner (1997) and Davies (1999).

6 See also Helfer (1968) and Drijvers (1973). I augment primary sources with a selection of secondary sources in Chapters 2 to 6.

7 'Modus Operandi', *Heralds of the New Age* no. 27, (1964), p. 40.

8 'A Facet of Greatness', *Heralds of the New Age* no. 26, (1963), pp. 34–7.

9 *Heralds of the New Age* no. 94, (1986), inside back cover.

10 Useful if decontextualised discussions of popular textual/theological themes can be found in Bednarowski (1991), Greer (1995), Hanegraaff (1996, 2000), and Partridge (1999).

11 See also Melton (1986: 107–21) and Melton *et al.* (1990, 1991).

12 See the more detailed discussion of NRMs and NSMs in Chapter 9.

13 See respectively Alexander (1992), Diem and Lewis (1992) and Ellwood (1992); Melton (1992), Kelly (1992) and Poggi (1992); Rupert (1992); Albanese (1992) and Riordan (1992).

14 Compare Spangler's (1993: 80) experienced emic view: 'One does not become a "New Ager" in the same sense that one becomes a Christian, a Muslim or a Buddhist'.

15 But see also the popular oral histories in Akhtar and Humphries (1999).

16 Compare McCutcheon's (1997) argument on the confusion generated by *sui generis* religion: that is, 'religion' as a unique, self-existent cultural formation, immune to explanation and critique.

17 Advertisement in *Occult Review* LXXIII/4 (October 1946), p. 221.

18 Another 1967 text is *The Christ Experience in the New Age* by David Spangler, cited in Caddy (1996: 307) but which I have not seen.

19 Peter Caddy, *The Findhorn Story* (Findhorn Trust, 1969), cited in Rigby and Turner (1972: 75).

20 'The difference between Pagan and "new age" is one decimal point . . . a two-day workshop in meditation by a "new age" practitioner might cost $300, while the same course given by a Pagan might cost $30' (Margot Adler, cited in York 1995: 161).

21 See for example the caricatures of 'New Age' in Harvey (1997: 219–21) and Pearson (1998).

2 'OLIGARCHY OF ELECT SOULS': ALICE BAILEY'S NEW AGE IN CONTEXT

1 Compare Ferguson's (1982) notion of an 'Aquarian conspiracy' seeking a 'turnabout in consciousness of a critical number of individuals, enough to bring about a renewal of society'. These formulations of an 'oligarchy' and a 'conspiracy' by Bailey and Ferguson respectively fuelled a rash of inaccurate and tendentious portrayals of New Age as a 'satanic' plot among conservative evangelical Christians in the 1980s (Saliba 1999: 53–6).

2 On these and other developments in the history of the Theosophical movement, see Anonymous (1951), Judah (1967, Chapter 3), Campbell (1980: 147–73), Melton (1986: 45–52), Washington (1993) and Tingay (2000).

3 Hazelgrove (2000: 23, 33) similarly finds in the interwar period 'a variety of fugitive and fragmented supernaturalisms' and 'a culture steeped in supernatural signs'.

4 Advertisement in *The Search Quarterly*, Vol. 1, 1931.

5 *The Shrine of Wisdom*, Vol. 2, No. 1, Autumn 1920.

6 Cf. the thriving culture of small 'esoteric' and 'metaphysical' groups and societies in the US in the 1920s and 1930s, from future UFO contactee George Adamski's 'Royal Order of Tibet' to the 'Brotherhood of the White Temple' (Stupple 1984: 134).

7 'Linking Up', *Occult Review* LVI/1 (July 1932), pp. 2ff.

8 Compare the audience targeted by the large post-1970s publishing fields, now re-described as 'inner development' (Popenoe 1979) and 'New Age' (Hanegraaff 1996).

9 This holds true seventy years later. Although the sociology of the market has changed radically (high street bookstores now stock 'Mind Body Spirit' titles and there is widespread Internet purchasing), the stock in Atlantis and Watkins remains similar to interwar holdings (some titles are even identical) and their function remains the same.

10 Heselton's (2000: 52–125) invaluable, pioneering excavation of the ROCF is from the perspective of a historical reconstruction of Wicca, as are the very brief mentions in Hutton (2001: 205, 211–13). In contrast the present work treats the ROCF in a distinctive 'New Age' genealogy.

11 NLS Acc. 9934/8: correspondence, F. Keen to P. Caddy, 27 October 1971; Caddy to Keen, 11 November 1971 and 23 December 1971 (see Chapter 3, n. 2 for an explanation of this source). Caddy's gravestone is set with Rosicrucian symbology (Caddy 1996: f.p. 321) and Caddy (1996) uses Sullivan's aphorisms as chapter headings, further demonstrating the enduring influence of the ROCF in his biography.

12 Heselton (2000: 78ff.) provides a full account of the circumstances surrounding the building of this theatre, including local newspaper coverage and pictures of the theatre and 'ashrama'.

13 *Pro* was Annie Besant's daughter, Mabel Besant-Scott, then leader of Co-Masonry in Britain (Heselton 2000: 91ff.). *Contra* is the early Wiccan activist, Doreen Valiente (1986: 153), who refers to Sullivan's 'flamboyant personality' and 'highly coloured claims'.

14 The extent to which the ROCF's quasi-Masonic hierarchy of grades – outlined in a rulebook published in 1926 and modified in 1936 – was operative is unclear, although Slocombe (1995: 2) tells us that Caddy soon attained 'the second Point, second degree'.

15 The most public twentieth-century 'Rosicrucian' organisation is AMORC (Ancient and Mystical Order Rosae Crucis), which began in the US in 1915 (and advertised heavily in the *Occult Review* in the 1930s), but Caddy (1996: 31) firmly (and correctly) dissociates the ROCF from this. There are also explicitly Masonic Rosicrucian orders, such as the Societas Rosicruciana in Anglia, formed in the 1860s. The ROCF is best located within the hybrid, quasi-Masonic currents of late nineteenth-/early twentieth-century 'vernacular' Rosicrucianism: see the overview in McIntosh (1987: 129–44) and the popular texts reproduced in Melton (1990).

16 *ROCF Outer Court Manual No. 2. The Rosicrucian Fraternity* (Bohemian Press: Somerford, Christchurch, n.d.). I am grateful to Kevin Tingay for supplying rare ROCF pamphlets. Other ROCF material cited here is from the British Library deposit. The Order's surviving occult library of around 160 items – including some antiquarian works – plus nearly 400 pamphlets by Sullivan was gifted to the University of Southampton's Hartley Library, special collections, in 1977.

17 Heselton (2000: 72) tells us that although Sullivan had a wife and child in Liverpool, he lived in later years with the ROCF's secretary, Ivy Keen (known as 'Francesca').

18 From 'First Point Lecture No. 13: The Chapter' by 'Aureolis', n.d. (early 1920s).

19 See the accessions register for the ROCF collection in the Hartley Library, op. cit.

20 See the 1953 picture of an ROCF member in ritual robes (Heselton 2000: 109).

21 'First Point Lecture No. 13', op. cit.

22 Cp. Schneider and Dornbusch (1958), Judah (1967: 12–19) and Hanegraaff (1996: 229ff.) on positive thinking in popular Christianity, 'metaphysical' religion and 'New Age' respectively.

23 NLS Acc. 9934/8: correspondence between P. Caddy and F. Keen.

24 As noted, the ROCF also circumscribes a key period in the genealogy of Wicca.

25 *Occult Review* LV/2, p. 125, from a five-page letter entitled 'Fear: A World Problem'.

26 *Occult Review* LXXI/2, pp. 117–18.

27 Their substantial house is photographed in Sinclair (1984: 56). This sketch of Bailey's life is based on Bailey (1973), Judah (1967: 119–122), Sinclair (1984) and Balyoz (1986: 191–217).

28 By way of indicating the immense labour involved, the quantity of text published under the name of the Tibetan alone (officially 'through' Alice Bailey) comes to over 9,000 pages; and Bailey also wrote some half a dozen texts under her own name.

29 Leaflet: *Lucis Trust* (London, n.d.). The Lucis Trust prints and distributes an immense range of leaflets, cards, booklets, and fliers advertising and explaining aspects of Bailey's work. Although often undated, their phraseological and typographical conservatism suggests standardisation of content and format over time (for example, some carry previous addresses of the Trust, now scored out). Unattributed quotations in this chapter come from my collection of these primary sources.

30 Lucis Press leaflet: *Twenty-four Books of Esoteric Philosophy by Alice Bailey* (London, n.d.). Bailey (1991a: 603) defines 'esoteric' as 'the power to live and to function subjectively, to possess a constant inner contact with the soul'.

31 *The Arcane School: Entrance Papers* (London, n.d), p. 2.

32 The Lucis Trust's success over the years in targeting high-profile political causes is shown by Ellwood (1973: 104), who notes an audio recording of Eleanor Roosevelt (1884–1962) reciting Alice Bailey's 'Great Invocation', and the recent manifesto by former Lucis Trust workers McLaughlin and Davidson (1994), which carries an introduction by the present Dalai Lama.

33 In fact the Great Invocation is the last of three such 'Invocations' composed in the mid-1930s (Bailey 1981: xvi).

34 For example, three column inches in *The Times* on 13 June 1995 reproduce the text and announce 'Today is World Invocation Day. People of goodwill around the world will be linking in meditation and prayer and using this invocation. *Will you join them?*'

35 As well, it should be noted, as triggering familiar associations in occult culture regarding the special 'spirituality' and 'wisdom' of Tibet: cf. W. Y. Evans-Wentz's *Tibetan Book of the Dead* (1927) and James Hilton's bestselling novel *Lost Horizon* (1933) about the Tibetan lamasery of 'Shangri-La'. Further on occult representations of Tibet, see Lopez (1998).

36 For example, in the pamphlet *My Work, by the Tibetan* (Lucis Trust: London, 1943, p. 10) Blavatsky is explicitly referred to as Bailey's 'predecessor'.

37 See *The Arcane School: Entrance Papers* (booklet, London, n.d., p. 2). Bailey's concern to establish an authentic 'school' must be set in context. Most of the gurus discussed by Landau in *God is My Adventure* were exploring similar projects to consolidate and transmit their teachings, from Gurdjieff's 'Institute for the Harmonious Development of Man' and Count Keyserling's 'School of Wisdom' to Rudolf Steiner's Waldorf school and the more informal, mobile units of Frank Buchman's 'Oxford Groups'.

38 However, the official relationship between the Theosophical Society and Alice Bailey has remained frosty since the rift in 1920. Miller (1988: 190), for example, defends Bailey against long-standing 'defamation' from Theosophists: 'Of the three outstanding members of the Theosophical Society who felt obliged to leave, Krishnamurti was never completely ostracised, Rudolf Steiner is tacitly ignored, but Alice Bailey has earned the greatest odium'.

39 Most of this was first published in the 1930s and 1940s, further volumes appearing posthumously (Bailey died in 1949).

40 An event which continued a tradition of countercultural spirituality in the locality (Green 1986) and anticipated the Eranos conferences (Webb 1976: 396–7).

41 *Occult Review* (LV/2, February 1932, pp. 120–5), *Occult Review* LXI/2 (February 1935, pp. 117–19).

42 The books are *From Intellect to Intuition* (1932), *A Treatise on White Magic* (1934), *Esoteric Psychology I* (1936) and *Esoteric Psychology II* (1942).

43 *The Spiritual Hierarchy*, pamphlet, n.d., pp. 4, 8.

44 Correspondence: 8 September 1997.

3 THE 'NAMELESS ONES': SMALL GROUPS IN THE NUCLEAR AGE

1 Dorothy Maclean, 1950s seeker and Findhorn co-founder: personal correspondence, 20 May 1997. Other unattributed remarks by Maclean in this chapter are from this source.

2 I refer here and in following chapters to Findhorn's archives in the National Library of Scotland (hereafter 'NLS'), Edinburgh, to which I was kindly granted access by the Findhorn Foundation. Deposits carry the following accession numbers (and dates): 9934 (1989), 10381 (1991), 10560 (1992). Small additions are ongoing. The material is extensive but uncatalogued. It includes original diaries, correspondence, minutes of meetings, audiotapes, financial accounts, and ephemera.

3 The Principal of the Faith Mission Bible College in Edinburgh described her as 'a mystery person' whose experimental spirituality was 'totally out of context in the Govan household' and a 'source of embarrassment and disgrace' (Rev. Dr C. N. Peckham, personal correspondence, 4 December 1996).

4 'My Childhood Days' and 'The Anguish of a Mother': *Sunday Mail* (Glasgow), 5 May 1957, 12 May 1957.

5 Conversation with David Govan, Edinburgh, 5 September 1996. Rev. Dr Peckham also commented: 'The Govans had plenty of "spark" and leadership qualities, so I suppose she had this quality in abundance' (see n. 3).

6 From telephone conversations with Daphne Davies (8 December 1996) and Rosemary Main (16 December 1996).

7 *Scottish Daily Express*, 18 January 1957, front page.

8 Daphne Davies, see n. 6. ENSA = Entertainments National Service Association.

9 Davies, n. 6, who recalled that Govan's income came from music lessons and sibling support.

10 She married Peter Caddy in Glasgow in 1957 (his third marriage). For convenience I refer to her throughout as Eileen Caddy.

11 Eileen Caddy: letter, 13 August 1997. Other unattributed remarks by Caddy are from this source.

12 The essay was published in the *Royal Airforce Quarterly* in April 1952 and is reproduced in Caddy (1996: 449ff.).

13 So-called in Caddy (1988: 64)

14 Maclean sometimes transcribed these and remembers, as an example of Govan's subjects, the life of Jesus as a model for human development (see n. 1).

15 Further on Glastonbury in 'New Age' genealogy, see Chapters 4 and 5.

16 Govan's niece Daphne Davies, a regular visitor to the Pimlico flat in the early 1950s, has confirmed this impression: see n. 6. For details of Govan's earlier sexual relationship in 1947 with Peter Caddy's former mentor, and now chief, in the ROCF, Walter Bullock – during a period when she and Caddy were living together – see Caddy (1996: 77–80): this sexual relationship was (unsuccessfully) designed to conceive 'the next Messiah' (Caddy 1996: 79).

17 Headline, subtitled 'This is what Sheena calls her disciples': *Sunday Mail* (Glasgow), 5 May 1957, pp. 12–13.

18 Cited in 'An Artist Quits the Fleshpots to follow Sheena', *Sunday Mail*, 26 May 1957, p. 13.

19 By 1957 a reporter for the *Scottish Daily Express* (17 January 1957, p. 2) could write 'The urgency of their belief is their conviction that the "second coming" is imminent'.

20 David Govan (n. 5) and Daphne Davies (n. 6) both remembered that Govan thought she was 'Jesus Christ returned' and that the group reciprocated. In 'The amazing story of Peter Caddy's life' in the *Sunday Mail* (5 May 1957, p. 13), Peter Caddy calls Sheena the 'World Teacher' and in 'Eileen gets her first message from God' (*Sunday Mail*, 12 May 1957, p. 11), he says: 'God, in his infinite love and mercy for mankind, has, at the eleventh hour, sent Sheena to save the world ... a Redeemer in the form of a woman'.

21 *Sunday Mail*, 12 May 1957, pp. 10–11.

22 Newspaper stories began on 14 January 1957 in the *Daily Record* (Glasgow), p. 9, and *Scottish Daily Express*, p. 5, referring to 'the Sect' or 'the Nameless Sect'. In the former, the group is described as 'a group of people of all denominations ... who have given up everything for God'. The *Scottish Daily Express* of 17 January 1957 carried a large front page photograph of Sheena. Both newspapers focused upon the 'scandal' of a young English family divided by Govan's claims. The coverage is an interesting early example of the kind of 'cult controversy' (Beckford 1985) which later became commonplace with the burgeoning of NRMs in post-war culture.

23 *Scottish Daily Express*, 17 January 1957, p. 2.

24 *Sunday Mail*, 5 May 1957, front page and pp. 12–13. The seven are Peter and Eileen Caddy, Dorothy Maclean and Jimmy Flangon from the original Pimlico group; Lena and Hugh Lamont, whom the Caddys and Maclean lodged with in Glasgow; and Fred Astell, an engineer from Bradford, England, whose split from his family to follow Govan triggered the media bonanza.

25 *Sunday Mail*, 12 May 1957, pp. 10–11; 19 May 1957, pp. 14–15; 26 May 1957, pp. 12–13. An editorial on 12 May 1957 sketched events under the title 'Good – or Evil?'; another on 19 May 1957 stated that 'hundreds of letters' on the group had been received – 'mostly highly critical'.

26 Compare other groups and societies explored by Peter Caddy and Dorothy Maclean in the period. Other useful profiles of alternative spirituality in the 1940s and 1950s are included in Mann (1962) on Canada, Davies (1954) and Leech (1976) on Britain, and Ellwood (1997) on the US.

27 NLS Acc. 9934/8 holds sporadic correspondence between Sheena Govan (living in Croy) and Peter Caddy at this time.

28 NLS Acc. 9934/8: P. Caddy to W. Bullock, 10 February 1965.

29 Caddy's (1996: 169) name for the group's new abode.

30 Cf. the widespread practice in alternative spirituality of assuming spiritual alter egos to designate one's sensitive inner nature or 'soul': 'Aureolis' (Sullivan); 'Elixir' (Eileen Caddy), 'Divina' (Dorothy Maclean).

31 NLS Acc. 9934/101, 'Network of Light – Connection Points' and 'Network of Light – Contacts 1964'. Following Naomi's lead, Findhorn has consistently presented itself as a 'Centre of Light'. For example, at the close of Experience Week (see Chapter 7), participants were encouraged to 'tune in' to the daily noon meditation at Findhorn to help maintain a 'network of light' around the planet; and a new daily programme called 'Network of Light Meditations for Peace' began at Findhorn in response to the attack on the World Trade Centre in New York in September 2001.

32 Ibid.: see typescript 'Directions to 7VXC . . .' in 'Network of Light – Contacts 1964'.

33 NLS Acc. 9934/Item 138: 'Dorothy 1957–1962'. This bulky typescript includes other brooding forecasts of 'great disasters' (17 February 1962) and 'the end' (7 November 1961).

34 This is not morally to decry practice but to raise questions of mystification in the discourse. In this connection we might just bear in mind Harris's (1990: 55) blunt warning against 'the human capacity to . . . obfuscate, forget, and disguise our inner lives; to say one thing and do another; and to produce in the aggregate effects that were not intended by any individual'.

35 NLS Acc. 9934/50: letter to J. Gemmell, 23 August 1969.

36 Heelas and Woodhead (2001: 62ff.) in particular have recently drawn attention to the role of small groups as 'secondary spiritual institutions' in contemporary culture.

37 Maclean alludes to an extensive but differentiated domain of alternative spirituality when, in response to my enquiries on specific contacts, she replied: 'I had no direct contact with J. G. Bennett, Maurice Nicoll or Ouspensky, though I did read their books. . . . Nor do I remember coming across Gerald Gardner, but I do have a horribly bad memory for both names and faces' (letter, 8 September 1997).

38 'Contactees' meet space beings, 'channels' receive communications from them. The roles are largely gendered according to an active/passive code – the former tend to be men, the latter women. For a bibliography of early UFO publishing exemplifying the American cultural base, see Melton and Eberhart (1995; some items are cited in Chapter 4).

39 The book's fieldwork methodology has since been discredited but this does not affect the descriptive evidence deployed here.

40 Information from 'The Heralds of the New Age: An Explanation of its Nature and Objectives': double-sided typewritten foolscap sheet, n.d. (early 1960s) and 'Modus Operandi', *Heralds of the New Age*, no. 27, n.d. (1964), pp. 39–40.

41 Typically 40–50 pages of messages, guidance and network news.

42 *Heralds of the New Age*, no. 10, 'Further telepathic Communications from Venus and the satellites of Jupiter' (n.d. [1959?] 21 pp.).

43 *Heralds of the New Age*, no. 14 (n.d. [1960?]), back cover.

44 *Heralds of the New Age*, 1962 Revelations. Letter Lesson No. 9.

45 Although bulletin no. 94 (July 1986, p. 31) lists 40 countries in which the Heralds' bulletins had been distributed since the mid-1950s.

46 'Modus Operandi': see n. 40.

4 'THE END IS NIGH': DOOMSDAY PREMONITIONS

1 Excerpt from a letter in *Heralds of the New Age*, no. 26, 1963, p. 44.

2 NLS 9934/101, 'Network of Light contacts 1964, loose typewritten sheets.

3 NLS Acc. 9934/21, correspondence.

4 Quoted in 'Life in the "Sanctuary": where the world is left behind', *Scottish Daily Express*, 17 November 1970, p. 12.
5 Cf. a recent Findhorn resident cited in *Scotland on Sunday*, 29 December 1996: 'I feel rooted here, yet at the same time I don't know how long I'm going to stay'.
6 Her extensive diaries of 'transmissions' from this period are in NLS Acc. 10381/21–43.
7 NLS Acc. 9934/6, P. Caddy to N. Hurst, 9 February 1965.
8 Biographical material comes largely from four obituaries: 'Craftsman at work on the New Age', Fiona MacCarthy, *Guardian*, 16 February 1996; Anne MacEwen, *Independent*, 26 February 1996; Anonymous, *The Times*, 17 February 1996; 'Sir George Trevelyan's "Release into Light"', Ruth Nesfield-Cookson, *One Earth* 21 (Spring 1996), p. 29. I am grateful to Ruth Nesfield-Cookson – Trevelyan's secretary throughout the 1960s – for additional information and for comments on an earlier draft of this section.
9 Dedicated adult education was taken particularly seriously: 'by 1948 there were already more than a dozen [new establishments], by 1950 more than a score. All over England stately country houses were being bought up and brought into use' (Kelly 1992: 393).
10 Telephone conversation with Ruth Nesfield-Cookson, 13 July 1997, who also kindly supplied other records, quotations and general information on Attingham's alternative curriculum cited in this section.
11 Such as ornithology, amateur drama, historic houses: see 'Open Residential Courses: The Shropshire Adult College at Attingham Park', Summer 1965 programme (Shropshire County Council Records and Research Centre, Shrewsbury, England).
12 Attingham Park, Autumn 1965 programme: see n. 11.
13 Leaflet for a Centre for Spiritual and Religious Studies weekend in Brighton in November 1965 entitled 'Man – Known and Unknown'.
14 *Heralds of the New Age*, no. 34, n.d. [1966], p. 22.
15 All following quotes from correspondence between Best and Caddy in 1967 and transcriptions of Best's mediumship at Findhorn: NLS Acc. 9934/6.
16 NLS Acc. 9934/6: correspondence.
17 NLS Acc. 9934/21: correspondence, P. Caddy to M. Parish, 1 July 1967.
18 Date of birth inferred from Brooke (1976: 51) who gives Pugh's age at death as seventy-eight.
19 NLS Acc. 9934/67: 'correspondence with key individuals, 1966–88, n.d.', P. Caddy to P. Shaw, 25 April 1966.
20 Dorothy Maclean, letter: 8 September 1997: see the frontispiece photograph of Pugh in Brooke (1967). Maclean's reference to Tibet is in a long line of popular Western invocations of Tibet as guarantor of spiritual profundity, as we saw in Chapter 2.
21 M. Barbanell, '*De mortuis nil nisi bonum*', *Psychic News*, 31 December 1966.
22 Anthony Brooke, personal correspondence: 25 April 1997.
23 NLS Acc. 9934/128, R.Nesfield-Cookson to Peter Caddy, 5 April 1966.
24 NLS Acc. 9934/21: correspondence, M. Parish to P. Caddy, 25 June 1966.
25 Craig Gibsone: 'Obituary – Joan Hartnell-Beavis (1910–1996)', *Findhorn Foundation Stewards Network News*, No. 9, October 1996, p. 4.
26 Personal correspondence, 25 April 1997.
27 NLS Acc. 9934/191: 'Library'. Anthony Brooke, card pamphlet, n.d. [1966?], p. 3.
28 Universal Foundation letter heading, e.g., NLS Acc. 9934/21.
29 NLS Acc. 9934/21: Universal Foundation, January 1968. NLS Acc. 9934/7, 'correspondence: Anthony Brooke', contains a profusion of letters and postcards sent by Brooke to Findhorn from international locations.

30 Newsletter: *Operation Peace Through Unity*, Vol. 57 (n.d., prob. 1996, New Zealand). I acquired my copy at a Unit of Service meditation meeting, described in Chapter 6, which demonstrates the fertile synchronous and diachronous further intercommunication of 'New Age' culture.

31 Pole's biography can be reconstructed in part from Gaythorpe (1979) and Benham (1993).

32 In the 1990s the 'silent minute' was revived 'at this important and critical period of our evolution': see website at www.thesilentminute.org.uk.

33 From 'The Lamplighter Movement', A5 flyer obtained in 1996 (private address).

34 NLS Acc. 9934/128: Peter Caddy to George Trevelyan, 19 December 1965.

35 Letter: 20 May 1997. Further on 'alternative' and 'New Age' Glastonbury, see Hexham (1983), Benham (1993), Bowman (1993a, 2000) and Prince and Riches (2001).

36 NLS Acc. 9934/128: letter, Peter Caddy to Wellesley Tudor Pole, 15 February 1968. Strathmiglo in Fife is home to the Westbank Centre: see Chapters 5 and 8.

37 'Harmonic Convergence', *Kindred Spirit*, No. 1, Winter 1987, p. 9.

38 In the early 1970s the 'Michael' group moved to England and changed its name to 'World Movement for United Prayer': see NLS Acc. 9934/6.

39 *Heralds of the New Age* Bulletin, no. 29, n.d. [1964], p. 40.

40 NLS Acc. 9934/21: correspondence, P. Caddy to M. Parish, 19 February 1969.

41 Letter: 8 September 1997.

42 Ruth Nesfield-Cookson: telephone conversation, 16 July 1997.

43 From her work with George Trevelyan, Ruth Nesfield-Cookson estimates between two and three thousand (telephone conversation, 13 July 1997).

44 To take just one example: Tod (1989) chronicles an autobiographical quest from the 1950s to the early 1970s to find the best site at which to conduct a twelve-year cycle of 'light ceremonies' using Alice Bailey's *Great Invocation* (ibid.: 127). According to the account, a location in the Brendon Hills, Somerset, was finally chosen and quarterly ceremonies held here from 1971 to 1982 involving twenty-seven regular participants (ibid.: 187). But although the story was finally published by Findhorn Press – and with an introduction by Peter Caddy – I can find no significant cross-references in the text to people, groups and networks discussed in the present book.

45 NLS Acc. 9934/189: Press Cuttings File No. 1: 'Visionaries of New Age Keeping an Eye on Earth', *Milwaukee Journal*, 26 June 1977.

46 NLS Acc. 9934/8: correspondence, P. Caddy to W. Bullock, 5 June 1965.

47 NLS Acc. 9934/21: correspondence, P. Caddy and M. Parish, n.d. and 27 October 1965.

48 NLS Acc. 9934/30: P. Caddy to S. Walker, 30 January 1968.

49 NLS Acc. 9934/6: correspondence, P. Caddy to L. Brandt, 17 July 1970. Other unattributed quotes in this section also come from letters in this file written in September 1970 and June 1973.

5 HEAVEN ON EARTH: FROM APOCALYPSE TO SELF-REALISATION

1 Subheading glossing the *Zeitgeist* of the late 1960s in Neville (1971: 52).

2 Melton (1988: 36): 'The New Age Movement can best be dated from around 1971. . . . Baba Ram Dass, a transformed refugee from the psychedelic age, emerged as its first national prophet'; York (1995: 37–8): ' "New Age" is becoming recognised as a "generic term" for the exploding re-interest in 1960s counterculture concerns'; Hanegraaff (1996: 10): 'The New Age movement is commonly, and rightly, regarded

as rooted in the so-called counterculture of the 1960s'; Heelas (1996: 1) pictures 'the Movement' as having 'expand[ed] with the counter-culture of the later 1960s and earlier 1970s'.

3 *Oxford English Dictionary* (1989): 'A hipster; a person, usually exotically dressed, who is, or is taken to be, given to the use of hallucinogenic drugs; a beatnik'. 'Freak' and 'head' were emic correlates which, according to Tomory (1996: 236), came to be preferred to 'hippie' as this term acquired pejorative connotations.

4 The classic portrayal of the 'underground' in England is Nuttall (1970).

5 The *Oxford English Dictionary*'s first citation of 'alternative' in the sense of an 'oppositional' or 'dissident' culture dates from 1970. See also Nicholas Saunders's 1971 handbook *Alternative London*, the informal model for a series including his *Alternative England and Wales* (1975) and *Alternative Scotland* (Wright and Worsley 1975).

6 On which, see Strachan (1970), Campbell (1972) and Webb (1976: 417ff.) and the extensive bibliographies in Galbreath (1972) and Truzzi (1972).

7 *Gandalf's Garden*, No. 3, 1968, p. 4: cited in Leech (1976: 75).

8 Compare also the lack of significant reference to 'New Age' in the US in Ellwood (1973).

9 William Bloom in conversation at Alternatives, St James's Church, Piccadilly, London, 3 June 1996. In his text *First Steps: an Introduction to Spiritual Practice*, Bloom (1993a: 65) notes in passing: 'At the very least you should know about [psychedelic drugs], for they are – albeit secretly – a portal of change and illumination for many people'.

10 D. Sheff, *Rolling Stone*, 5 May 1988, cited in Roof (1993: 33).

11 Masters (1985: 17–18) notes: 'The old (that is, people over thirty) were contemptibly dismissed as unworthy guardians of ridiculous values'.

12 Willy Wegner, 'The Orthon Cult: Doomsday in Denmark 1967': web publication at www.skeptica.dk/arkiv_us/pa_us004.htm, visited 2 January 2002.

13 'Liebie Speaks', *Heralds of the New Age*, No. 38 (1967), p. 16.

14 NLS Acc. 9934/21, letter from M. Parish to Findhorn (14 November 1967).

15 NLS Acc. 9934/21: circular letter, January 1968. Other unattributed quotes in this section of the discussion are from this source.

16 NLS Acc. 9934/30: letter, P. Caddy to S. Walker, 28 May 1967.

17 NLS Acc. 9934/17, letter, P. Caddy to Lucis Trust, 29 June 1972.

18 D. Black: 'The Findhorn Trust', *Scottish International Review* 5/1 (January 1972), p. 14.

19 NLS Acc. 9934/21: letter, P. Caddy to M. Parish, 12 December 1969.

20 Although the counterculture's 'sex revolution' (Leech 1976: 17ff.) was certainly anticipated by the cohabitations in Sheena Govan's circle: see Chapter 3.

21 On the human potential movement, see Stone (1976), Wallis (1985), and Drury (1989).

22 Nick Rose: oral contribution to a symposium entitled 'Findhorn and the Western Mystery Tradition', 20 March 1995, during the conference 'The Western Mysteries: Which Way Today?'

23 See the list of Spangler's various sources of guidance in Walker (1994: 406–12) and compare the similarly demotic character of American channelled sources in the 1980s and 1990s in Riordan (1992) and Brown (1997). A booklet of Spangler's conversations with 'John' (Spangler, ed., n.d.) was used as a discussion text during the Experience Week I attended: see Chapter 7.

24 Field notes: 'The Magician's Wound', Bloom's talk during 'The Western Mysteries: Which Way Today?' conference, Findhorn, 20 April 1995.

25 Conversation, 3 June 1996: 'Alternatives', St James's Church, Piccadilly, London.

26 *Newsweek*, 25 January 1993: cited in McLaughlin and Davidson (1994: 57).

27 Steven Kull 1992: *Burying Lenin* (Westview Press: Boulder, Colorado), p. 26: cited in McLaughlin and Davidson (1994: 26).

28 Personal letter: 25 April 1997.

29 William Bloom: 'Conscious Energy Work, Sword and Chalice Talks' (1996 brochure).

30 *Alternatives* Autumn and Spring/Summer Programmes 1996, St James's Church, Piccadilly, London.

31 Details from *Skyros: World Leader in Alternative Holidays*, 1998 brochure.

32 See the introduction and individual chapters in Sutcliffe and Bowman (2000) for further exploration of this lateral move in post-New Age studies.

33 Compare the Californian informant in Drane (1991: 18): 'It was OK in the '70s to say "New Age" . . . but now people think "rip-off" '. See also Lewis and Melton (1992: x): 'participants have distanced themselves from this label because of the mass media's focus on the more superficial and outlandish aspects of the New Age'.

34 On British television, Channel Four's series *The New Age* (1991) and *Desperately Seeking Something* (1995, 1996) led the field, although this does not take into account the airing of 'New Age' themes on chat shows and in magazines. In two separate searches of the worldwide web four years apart (17 April 1997, 17 August 2001) using the popular Yahoo! search engine, I found on each occasion some 120 main category matches under 'New Age' alone.

35 John Hancox, 'Clan of the Outsiders', *Guardian*, 8 July 1992 ('Society', p. 23).

36 Pat Kane: 'In Thrall to New Age Thrills', *Guardian*, 4 January 1995.

37 Elspeth Thompson: 'Room of Our Own', *Observer*, 1 May 1994, 'Life' section, pp. 44–5; Li Min Lim: 'Pick and Mix at the New Age bazaar', *Scotland on Sunday*, 26 May 1996.

38 Jonathan Petre: 'The Church on its Knees', *Sunday Telegraph*, 9 February 1997, p. 22.

39 David Morgan: 'New Age devotees unshaken in quirky beliefs', *Scotland on Sunday*, 30 March 1997, p. 21; Tony Allen-Mills: 'Caught in the Net', *Sunday Times*, 30 March 1997, News Review, p. 1.

40 Lindsay Baker: 'Natural Remedy', *Observer*, 19 November 1995, 'Life' section, p. 72.

41 Catherine Pepinster: 'Nineties woman has a new worry – typecasting', *Independent on Sunday*, 2 March 1997, p. 7.

6 A GROUP OF SEEKERS: THE UNIT OF SERVICE

1 Henceforth all unattributed quotes are from Lucis Trust leaflets and flyers, usually with no date or place of publication (London).

2 From the typescript of a talk given by Alison at a public forum organised by the Unit of Service in October 1992.

3 Ibid. All names, and some personal details, have been changed to ensure anonymity.

4 According to the Lucis Press in 1998.

5 Lecture typescript, 3 December 1994. Hanegraaff (1996: 384) dates modern usage of the term 'esoteric' to the mid- and late nineteenth century. Historically, Faivre (1994: 20) tells us that ' "Esotericism" is sometimes called "interiorism": a knowledge that passes through a gnosis to reach a form of individual illumination and salvation'. According to C. Bochinger, in 'New Age' parlance 'esoteric' primarily refers to an *'individualkultur* according to the motto: "You have it all inside yourself, check it out!" ' (C. Bochinger, *'New Age' und moderne Religion*, 1994, p. 376, cited in Hanegraaff [1996: 385]). Compare Bailey's definition in her 1934 script *A Treatise on White Magic* (1991a: 603): 'the power to live and to function subjectively . . . an interiorly held attitude of mind which can orient itself at will in any direction'.

6 Unit of Service newsletter, August 1995.
7 Lucis Trust advertisement in the alternative newspaper *Planetary Connections* (No. 11, Autumn 1996), 'Networking Resource' Section, p. 13.
8 *Units of Service Forum*, No. 10, January–December 1993/4, p. 1.
9 Alice Bailey's *Esoteric Psychology II* (1942: 681–2) discusses the characteristics of 'Units of Service'.
10 *The Arcane School: Entrance Papers* (London, n.d), p. 2.
11 Information from conversation with trustee Steve Nation, London, 3 June 1996. Alison told me it took her twenty-five years to complete the whole course, and also that '*lots* of students don't finish – which is fine' (letter, 12 April 1999).
12 Telephone conversation, 20 April 1997.
13 Unless in the context of a group meeting (when they come from my field notes), all unattributed quotes in this chapter are from an interview with Patrick, 22 January 1997. Further on the Arcane School, see Sinclair (1984: 58–61), who claims that 'formerly' the School was structured in a series of degrees analogous to Freemasonry. The mention of 'Rosicrucians' as a significant minority among School participants encourages comparison of its early structure with the contemporary ceremonial of the Rosicrucian Order, Crotona Fellowship.
14 Letter from Alison, 12 April 1999.
15 In the mid-1990s the Lucis Trust in Britain and the Commonwealth had an annual income of around £250,000 (Lucis Trust financial summaries, 1994–6).
16 Booklet: *The Spiritual Hierarchy* (n.d.).
17 www.findhorn.org/about_us/comnews, accessed 30 December 2001.
18 Interview, 22 April 1997. All other unattributed quotes by Alison in this chapter apart from dialogue in group settings (which is from my field notes) are from this source.
19 Field notes: 16 January 1995.
20 Field notes: 14 February 1995. By 'apprentice' I had in mind Forrest's (1986) discussion of 'apprentice-participation' in psychic/mediumistic groups.
21 Field notes: 26 September 1996.
22 Cf. the opening address in *Discipleship in the New Age* (Bailey 1981: 3): 'the Kingdom of God . . . is precipitating on earth and will be composed of those who are becoming group-conscious and who can work in group formation. . . . [T]hese people . . . will be identified with certain group expansions of consciousness'.
23 Field notes: 16 March 1995.
24 Field notes: 10 August 1995.
25 Field notes: Holistic Health Exhibition, Glasgow, 21 October 1995.
26 I attended fourteen full-moon meditations between December 1994 and April 1997 – around half of the total number convened during the period. My comments about 'regulars' and 'occasionals' must therefore be understood in the light of my semi-regular presence.
27 In half of the meetings I attended there were seven in the group; in the smallest, four, in the largest, nine. In only four meetings did women equal or outnumber men. On the basis both of structural constraints and group ideology I would predict broadly similar profiles in other Units of Service.
28 Field notes: 8 September 1995.
29 See n. 2.
30 A similar kind of 'sacred dance' is incorporated into Experience Week at Findhorn: see Chapter 7.
31 Field notes: 'Connections' Alternative Health Exhibition, Glasgow, 20 October 1996.
32 Field notes: 'Connections' Alternative Health Exhibition, Glasgow, 21 October 1995.

33 Personal letter, 12 April 1999.

34 Letter, 12 April 1999.

35 'Of course the Unit of Service meditation at the full moon is very esoteric (as was always understood) and would not and will not appeal to many' (Alison: correspondence, 24 July 1997).

36 Field notes: 10 August 1995. Compare Bailey (1981: 45): 'Inner work which does not work out into objective activity upon the physical plane is wrongly oriented and inspired'.

7 A COLONY OF SEEKERS: FINDHORN

1 Officially the 'Findhorn Foundation and Community', a title differentiating the legal functions of a charitable body, the Findhorn Foundation (created in May 1972), and the wider colony of residents and affiliates (Walker 1994: 59, 71–8). But as Riddell (1991: 5) notes, 'for spiritual seekers, the Findhorn Foundation or the Findhorn Community is just "Findhorn"'. I follow popular usage, although readers should be aware that this effectively conflates 'alternative' colony and rural village, and has caused tensions between the two over the years.

2 As, for example, in the Guest Programme, October 1998 to April 1999, p. 3.

3 *Stewards of the Findhorn Foundation Network News*, No. 10, January 1997, p. 14. There are also some dissident voices in the vicinity: see York (1997) on a recent 'expose' of Findhorn by ex-residents.

4 *Network News*, op. cit., p. 6. Walker (1994: 21–2) lists four other variations of mission statements in use in the early 1990s.

5 The Foundation also owns a small crofthouse on the island of Iona, where retreat weeks are regularly held; and the neighbouring island of Erraid hosts an affiliated community.

6 Following a down-turn in the Foundation's finances in 2001, the shop was sold to staff and supporters and is now an independent concern.

7 The catch-all category 'member' has been discredited. In the mid-1990s Buhler-McAllister (1995: 33) distinguished between four categories of participation: guest, employee, student, volunteer. Data in the following paragraphs draw on aforementioned texts plus Brierley and Walker (1995). For other emic perspectives on Findhorn's history see Findhorn Community (1978) and Hawken (1990).

8 'Spirituality, Experience and the "New Age"': 185 copies of this questionnaire were distributed among Findhorn residents in the autumn of 1995 and 37 replies were forthcoming, i.e. a 20% response rate. Compare these data with Rose's (1998: 11) findings from a survey of subscribers to the British magazine *Kindred Spirit*: 'Almost without exception, participants are middle-class. . . . Almost three-quarters . . . are women. . . . Over half are middle-aged'. Findhorn demography is thus broadly consistent with this (and other) indices of 'New Age' and 'Mind Body Spirit' spirituality.

9 *Stewards of the Findhorn Foundation Network News*, No. 11, April 1997, p. 5. These practices were also central to early 'New Age', although its cult of landscape has broadened into a more diffuse nature veneration under the cultural impact of post-sixties environmentalism.

10 Quoted in 'Clan of the Outsiders', John Hancox, *The Guardian* (8 July 1992), 'Society' section, p. 23.

11 Defined in the *Oxford English Dictionary* (second edition, 1989) as 'a meeting for discussion, study, experiment, etc.'

12 See Guest Programmes, October 1994–April 1995, October 1996–April 1997 and October 1998–April 1999. Conferences can be large events: 'The Western

Mysteries: Which Way Today?' and 'Eco-Villages and Sustainable Communities: Models for 21st Century Living', both in 1995, attracted 120 and 400+ participants respectively. At the end of 2001 the Foundation was reviewing its plans following a drop in numbers of visitors.

13 'Colony' also taps comparative history, illuminating Findhorn's resemblance to earlier European settlements like Germany's Schloss Mainburg, opened in 1903 as a 'centre for organic life' (Webb 1976: 55ff.), or the Monte Verita settlement – the 'mountain of truth' – at Ascona, Switzerland (Green 1986).

14 Compare the accounts in Boice (1990: 60–77), Riddell (1991: 115–18) and Tattersall (1996: 11–32).

15 Some of what follows first appeared in Sutcliffe (2000b). All names, and some personal details, have been changed. My thanks to Findhorn and to my fellow participants for agreeing to my presence in the group as a participant–observer.

16 This and the following citations from Findhorn Programme, October 1994–April 1995, p. 5.

17 From my application letter, November 1994. Incidentally – and in keeping with contemporary 'quest culture' (Roof 1999: 46ff.) – I would no longer endorse this statement.

18 In 1995 it cost between £225 and £335 according to means; in 2001, a flat rate of £295. Bursaries are also advertised.

19 From the song 'Experience Week', written during an Experience Week in 1992 by Mike Scott of British pop/folk group, The Waterboys; lyrics were reproduced in the Findhorn magazine One Earth, No. 17, Spring 1995, p. 24. I use other verses as day headings below.

20 See Twigg (1979) and Hamilton et al. (1995) on connections between dietary and religious alternativism.

21 Walker (1994: 136) claims that this practice was introduced to Findhorn in the 1960s by Anthony Brooke and Monica Parish (see Chapter 4). According to R. Ogilvie Crombie 'the fundamental purpose of attunement is to link together so that the group works well'; David Spangler describes it as 'the New Age method of prayer, of communication with vaster and freer levels of Life' (ibid.: 167, 174).

22 'At the end of the period of work, it is helpful if there is a completion or "detuning" – a holding of hands, a "thank you", or whatever is appropriate': William Bloom, cited in Walker (1994: 170).

23 Compare the altogether stricter regime in the 1970s when one of Peter Caddy's maxims was: 'People who pray together stay together'. Akhurst (1992: 35) adds: 'More often freely translated as "You come to Sanctuary – or else you're out"'.

24 Later the same year I attended a workshop in Edinburgh that partnered these dances with Alice Bailey's teachings: see Chapter 6.

25 Angel cards originated in the 'Transformation game' in the late 1970s (see Chapter 5) but have since acquired an independent retail career as contemplative aids.

26 In terms of Weberian sociology, the 'core' and 'management' groups embody the struggle between charisma and routinisation in social life: see Metcalf (1993).

27 My gloss (in field notes) of Christina's exposition, but a common theme in 'New Age' discourse – see Hanegraaff (1996: 229–45).

28 And generally not in my presence, in any case, due to my liminal status in the group as a participant–observer. Recall Conor's question to me, 'So you're not a heartfelt New Ager, then?' Jutta asked me early on if I were 'a minister or something', and Vicky enquired later why, exactly, I was at Findhorn, since I appeared to her to be 'too together' (the unspoken ending being: '. . . for this place'). This last remark was striking and highlighted the latent therapeutic function of Findhorn ritual practice.

29 One resident at Findhorn told me he found 'most visitors so desperate to believe in the myth of Findhorn that they "overlook" any evidence that might conflict with it' (e-mail communication, 21 September 1996).

30 Frank's use of Bailey material provides further evidence of its continuing influence at Findhorn: see Chapters 2 and 6.

31 From 'The Easter Mysteries – an Esoteric Perspective', typescript circulated at 'The Western Mysteries: Which Way Today?' conference, March 1995, Findhorn.

32 Oral contribution to the symposium 'Findhorn and the Western Mystery Tradition', 20 April 1995, during the 'Western Mysteries' conference, op. cit.

33 Opinions on this subject are in fact diverse: on the one hand the delivery of some academic modules, mostly validated by American universities, has been viewed with uncertainty within the colony; on the other hand I personally received a helpful response to my own – definitely 'heady' – questionnaire.

34 Personal letter, 4 September 1995.

35 *The Scotsman* (Edinburgh), 9 September 1975.

36 In sharp contrast to some post-Sixties countercultures: see for example Rigby (1974), Pepper (1991), Hetherington (2000).

8 A NETWORK OF SEEKERS: HOLISTIC HEALING

1 Compare the expanding range of alternative/holistic treatments that can be mapped from Stanway (1982) through Olsen (1991) to Fulder (1996). As early as 1973 there were 135 therapies on the agenda of the first 'World Congress on Alternative Medicine' in Rome (Stanway 1982: 9). On the acculturation of the field in the UK in the 1980s and 1990s, compare the consumer reports in *Which?* 1986 ('Magic or Medicine?') and *Which?* 1995 ('Healthy Choice'). A *New Scientist* report ('Hype, Hope and Healing', 26 May 2001) assesses recent scientific findings.

2 A contributor to Adams (1982: 4) writes: '[It] used to be called Fringe Medicine . . . during the 1970s was termed Alternative Medicine and . . . is now becoming established as Complementary Medicine'. CAM (Complementary and Alternative Medicine) is now an acronym increasingly used (see for example *New Scientist*, 26 May 2001).

3 See the review of English healing courses and accreditation in Bowman (1999).

4 See Hanegraaff (1996: 262–75) for a discussion.

5 For a brief comment on Smuts' ideas in historical–cultural context, see Steyn (2001).

6 Other specialist debates can be traced in McGuire (1998), English-Lueck (1990) and Ross (1992) in the US, and Sharma (1992), Bowman (1999), Hamilton (2000) and Hedges and Beckford (2000) in England.

7 Cited in Ferguson (1982: 42).

8 Sutcliffe (1995) records a two to one female to male ratio from a sample of seventy-three at a *Connections'* fair in Edinburgh in March 1995. A survey by the organisers returned about the same percentage for an earlier fair (70%, *Connections* 18, 1992, p. 21). Women as majority participants and practitioners is a constant across the field, from just over 50% to 75% and more. For example, 75% were women at the Bach Flower Remedies workshop I attended at the Salisbury Centre in Edinburgh in March 1996, as were 75%+ of practitioners in the Highlands and Islands (Forsyth 1995), around 66% of the audience at a talk by firewalker Stephen Mulhearn in Stirling in January 2000, and a slight majority at the firewalking workshop in Fife in 1996, described below.

9 Three-quarters of the sample for Sutcliffe (1995) were in this age bracket. Compare the similar demographies of Findhorn (Chapter 7) and *Kindred Spirit* subscribers (Rose 1998, 2001).

10 This and other unattributed quotes are from field notes and flyers in my fieldwork collection.
11 Lee's article, published in the English alternative/holistic health magazine *Caduceus*, was flanked by advertisements from some twenty different British Reiki 'Masters' offering courses and accreditation. Globally, Lee (1997: 36) reckons that there are now 'over 4,000 Usui Masters [descended from the founder] plus countless "New Age" [i.e. self-accredited] Reiki masters'. Interest has grown further as Reiki (like yoga previously) has entered popular publishing and community education.
12 In Heavens' (1992) popular account, Usui created Reiki by combining information from '2500 year old Sanskrit sutras' with wisdom derived from his own 'spiritual searching'. According to McKenzie (1998: 46), Usui was a practitioner of Shinto, Japanese Buddhism and Christianity who also studied comparative religion in the US. See also Mellon (2001).
13 Reiki practitioners exemplify fissiparous propensities within alternative healing and spirituality in general: Fulder (1992: 177) notices 'a continuous splintering process' as therapists found their own small institutions and teaching lineages.
14 Compare the detailed schemes of hand positions in McKenzie (1998), Hall (1999) and other popular manuals.
15 For a cross-section of international 'centres' at the end of the 1970s, see the listings in Khalsa (1981) and Adams (1982).
16 Salisbury Centre Autumn Programme, 2001 (booklet).
17 *Open Centres* newsletter, Winter 1994/95, pp. 3, 29. The newsletter was established in 1977 and is issued bi-annually.
18 This and the following unattributed quotations from Westbank leaflets, 1995–7.
19 Letter to myself written 11 February 1996, received 12 March 1997.
20 'Network: to make use of one's membership of a network, one's contacts, etc.; to acquire information or some professional advantage, often while appearing to be engaged only in social activity' (Tulloch 1991: 211).
21 Poster dated 11 February 1996.
22 This and the following account is from my field notes of 1 February 1996 and 11 February 1996. My thanks to Hazel (a pseudonym) for agreeing to my participation in the event.
23 See Danforth (1989) for a detailed account of the emergence of American fire-walking.
24 Cf. the folk science of firewalk enthusiast John Sangster: 'when a person whose mind has been prepared to hold a suitable thought walks upon the burning embers of a fire-track, he does so *with feet atomically changed*'. ('Firewalking – the Facts', *The Seeker*, Vol. 4 no. 1 [Sussex, England], pp. 30–4, n.d, *c.* 1967.)
25 During a talk at a Body and Soul health fair in Stirling in January 2000, firewalker Stephen Mulhearn mentioned examples of 'miraculous' behaviour he'd witnessed on the coals, including one person praying on their knees and another doing a handstand.

9 THE END OF 'NEW AGE'

1 On 'yuppie' see Tulloch (1991: 318), who dates the acronym from the 1980s: 'young upwardly mobile professional people . . . college-educated, getting on and even getting up in the world, but with a bit of the hippie-dippie counterculture clinging to them still'.
2 Letters, 20 May 1997 and 13 August 1997.
3 From an enormous literature see Barker (1982), Beckford (1985), Clarke (1987) and Wilson and Cresswell (1999) on NRMs, and Eder (1985), Beckford (1989), Byrne (1997) and Bloch (1998) on NSMs.

4 'What is Spirituality?': unpublished typescript by Alison (1997), p. 9.
5 Some of the following first appeared in Sutcliffe (1997).
6 Interview in *Scotland on Sunday* (Edinburgh), 9 March 1997.
7 'Conscious Energy Work: Sword and Chalice Talks', W. Bloom, A4 pamphlet, London 1996.
8 During the workshop 'From Darkness to Light: True and False Initiations' during the Findhorn conference 'The Western Mysteries: Which Way Today?', April 1995.
9 Radio Scotland: 'Cover Stories', 28 August 1995.
10 *North East Network*, no. 21 (winter 2000); *The Spark*, no. 9, Winter/Spring 1996/7.
11 'Cooperation with the Inner Ashrams': a workshop during the 'Western Mysteries' conference, Findhorn: 20 April 1995.
12 See n. 4.
13 See Chapter 7 for further details of this questionnaire.
14 Respectively, 'Linking Up' (editorial), *Occult Review*, LVI/1 (July 1932), pp. 2–7; *The London Forum*, (temporary title), LXII/4 (October 1935), p. 219.
15 'Can Occultism Help?', *Occult Review*, LV/5, May 1932, p. 330.
16 J. Krishnamurti, 'Through Many Lives to Contentment', *Occult Review*, LV/5 (May 1932), p. 327; M. Neff 1937, *Personal Memoirs of H. P. Blavatsky*, New York: Dutton, p. 37, cited in Campbell (1980: 4).
17 On 'Planetary Citizens', a pressure group begun in 1972 and affiliated to the United Nations, see the excerpt by its co-founder, Donald Keyes, in Bloom (1991: 208ff.). Peter Russell's concept of 'the emerging unified consciousness of humanity', or 'global brain', is cited in Hanegraaff (1996: 156). Introductory statements in Findhorn brochures in the mid-1990s advocate 'a planetary culture infused with spiritual values'.
18 'The Once and Future Mysteries', Spangler's opening talk for 'The Western Mysteries: Which Way Today?', Findhorn, 15 April 1995.
19 *Here's Health* (London), November 1996, pp. 22–3.
20 See the extensive discussion of 'New Age science' in Hanegraaff (1996: 62ff.).
21 In the early Findhorn colony successful manifestations included money for car repair bills, caravans and bungalows: see the brief discussion in Chapter 4.
22 A phrase also used by Schneider and Dornbusch (1958: 60) on popular religion in the US to indicate 'an instrumental attitude toward religion, an accordant emphasis upon technique or "science", and a magicalisation of spiritual notions or principles'.
23 'Good Vibrations', *Face to Face* (Bank of Scotland consumer magazine), Summer 1997, p. 12.
24 Largely social grades B and C1: see Sutcliffe (1995) and Rose (1998, 2001), and n. 4, Chapter 1, on the underlying Anglo–American cultural geography. Earlier demographic generalisations in Danforth (1989: 254), English-Lueck (1990: 26), Lewis (1992: 11), Steyn (1994: 27–8), Heelas (1996: 125) and McGuire (1998: 11–13) provide additional evidence.

BIBLIOGRAPHY

Primary sources

Archive and manuscript sources

British Library, London: Rosicrucian Order, Crotona Fellowship, miscellaneous leaflets and pamphlets, Liverpool and Christchurch, 1923–39, shelfmark 4786.h.21.

National Library of Scotland, Edinburgh: Findhorn Foundation papers, Acc. no. 9934, 10381, 10560.

Shropshire County Council Records and Research Centre, Shrewsbury, England: 'Open Residential Courses: The Shropshire Adult College at Attingham Park', Summer and Autumn 1965 programmes.

Magazines and periodicals

Caduceus, 1996–7
Connections: Alternative Health in Scotland, 1992, 1995, 1998
Gandalf's Garden, 1968
Heralds of the New Age, 1959–67, 1986
Here's Health, 1996
Kindred Spirit, 1987
Network News (Stewards of the Findhorn Foundation bulletin), 1996–7
Occult Review, 1931–5, 1946
One Earth (Findhorn), 1988–96
Pagan Dawn, 1995
Planetary Connections, 1994–6
The Quest, 1909–30
Psychic News, 1966
Scottish International Review, 1972
The Search, 1931–4
The Seeker: A Magazine in Search of Truth, 1967
The Shrine of Wisdom, 1920
The Spark, 1995, 1996–7
Which? 1986, 1995.

Newspapers

Daily Record, 1957
Scottish Daily Express, 1957, 1970
Sunday Mail, 1957.

Fieldwork collection: bulletins, pamphlets and leaflets

Alternative health fairs: assorted workshop and stall flyers, 1994–2000
'Alternatives' at St James's Church, Piccadilly: programmes, 1996–9
Findhorn Foundation Programmes and Workshops, 1994–2001
Lucis Trust (including Arcane School, Triangles, World Goodwill) leaflets, cards, pamphlets, n.d.
'Mind Body Spirit' festival programmes, 1995–6, 2001
'North East Network' (England) bulletins, 1995–2000
'Open Centres' newsletter, 1994–5
'Operation Peace Through Unity' newsletter, n.d. (1996)
Salisbury Centre programmes, 1995–2001
Scottish Alternative Health Exhibition programmes (*Connections*), 1994–2000
Skyros: World Leader in Alternative Holidays, programmes, 1995–8
Westbank Natural Health Centre, programmes, 1995–7.

Primary published sources

Adams, R. (ed.) 1982, *The New Times Network: Groups and Centres for Personal Growth*, London: Routledge and Kegan Paul.
Akhurst, R. 1992, *My Life and the Findhorn Community*, Falmouth, Cornwall: Honey Press.
Alder, V. S. 1938, *The Finding of the Third Eye*, London: Rider.
Annett, S. (ed.) 1976, *The Many Ways of Being: A Guide to Spiritual Groups and Growth Centres in Britain*, London: Abacus/Turnstone.
Anon 1985 [1975], *A Course in Miracles*, Arkana.
Argyris, C. and Ward, E. 1991, 'Of Angels and the Earth: an Interview with Dorothy Maclean', *One Earth* 3: 8–10.
Bach, E. 1931, *Heal Thyself*, London: C. W. Daniel.
Bailey, A. 1922, *Initiation, Human and Solar*, New York: Lucis Publishing Company.
—— 1925, *A Treatise on Cosmic Fire*, New York: Lucis Publishing Company.
—— 1936, *Esoteric Psychlogy I*, New York: Lucis Publishing Company.
—— 1948, *The Reappearance of the Christ*, New York: Lucis Publishing Company.
—— 1950a, *Glamour: A World Problem*, New York: Lucis Publishing Company.
—— 1950b, *Telepathy and the Etheric Vehicle*, New York: Lucis Publishing Company.
—— 1951, *Esoteric Astrology*, New York: Lucis Publishing Company.
—— 1954, *Education in the New Age*, New York: Lucis Publishing Company.
—— 1955, *Discipleship in the New Age II*, New York: Lucis Publishing Company.
—— 1957, *The Externalisation of the Hierarchy*, New York: Lucis Publishing Company.
—— 1960 [1942], *Esoteric Psychology II*, New York: Lucis Publishing Company.
—— 1973, *The Unfinished Autobiography*, New York: Lucis Publishing Company.
—— 1981 [1944], *Discipleship in the New Age I*, New York: Lucis Publishing Company.
—— 1987 [1932], *From Intellect to Intuition*, New York: Lucis Publishing Company.

—— 1991a [1934], *A Treatise on White Magic*, New York: Lucis Publishing Company.

—— 1991b [1971], *Ponder On This*, New York: Lucis Publishing Company.

Baker-Beall, E. 1932, 'Occultism as a Guide to Life', *Occult Review* 56/5: 299–306.

Balyoz, H. 1986, *Three Remarkable Women*, Flagstaff, Arizona: Altai Publishers.

Bennet, J. 1925, *The Riddle of the Aquarian Age*, London: London Astrological Research Society.

Bennett, J. 1962, *Witness: The Story of a Search*, London: Hodder and Stoughton.

Blavatsky, H. P. 1974 [1888], *The Secret Doctrine: The Synthesis of Science, Religion and Philosophy*, Pasadena, CA: Theosophical University Press.

Bloom, W. 1971 [1970], *Softly, Children, I'm Coming*, London: Pan Books.

—— 1990, *Sacred Times: A New Approach to Festivals*, Forres: Findhorn Press.

—— (ed.) 1991, *The New Age*, London: Channel 4/Rider: London.

—— 1992, *The Sacred Magician: A Ceremonial Diary*, Glastonbury: Gothic Image.

—— 1993a, *First Steps: an Introduction to Spiritual Practice*, Forres: Findhorn Press.

—— 1993b, 'Practical Spiritual Practice', *One Earth* 12: 18–21.

—— 1995, *The Christ Sparks: The Inner Dynamics of Group Consciousness*, Forres: Findhorn Press.

—— 1996, *Psychic Protection: Creating Positive Energies for People and Places*, London: Piatkus.

Boice, J. 1990, *At One With All Life: A Personal Journey in Gaian Communities*, Forres: Findhorn Press.

Brierley, J. and Walker, A. 1995, 'Financing a Sustainable Dream', *One Earth* 18: 32–4.

British Holistic Medicine Association 1992, 'Response to the British Medical Association Report', in Saks, M. (ed.) 1992, *Alternative Medicine in Britain*, pp. 232–40.

Brooke, A. 1967, *Revelation for the New Age*, London: Regency Press.

—— 1976, *Towards Human Unity*, London: Mitre Press.

Brunton, P. 1934, *A Search in Secret India*, London: Rider.

—— 1935, *The Secret Path*, London: Rider.

Buhler-McAllister, J. 1995, 'The State of the Foundation', *One Earth* 19: 32–6.

Button, J. 1990 [1988], *New Green Pages: A Directory of Natural Products, Services, Resources and Ideas*, London: Macdonald.

Button, J. and Bloom, W (eds) 1992, *The Seeker's Guide: A New Age Resource Book*, London: Aquarian Press.

Caddy, E. 1987, *Opening Doors Within*, Forres: Findhorn Press.

—— 1988, *Flight into Freedom*, Shaftesbury, Dorset: Element.

—— 1992 [1971], *God Spoke to Me*, Forres: Findhorn Press.

Caddy, P. 1996, *In Perfect Timing: Memoirs of a Man for the New Millennium*, Forres: Findhorn Press.

Champion, S. (ed.) 1998, *Disco 2000: Nineteen New Stories from the Last Hours of 1999*, London: Sceptre.

Considine, M. (ed.) 1992, *The Whole Person Catalogue*, London: Brainwave.

Crowley, A. 1989 [1969], *The Confessions of Aleister Crowley: An Autohagiography*, ed. J. Symonds and K. Grant, London: Arkana.

Curtiss, H. and Frank, H. 1921, *The Message of Aquaria: The Significance and Mission of the Aquarian Age*, San Francisco: Curtiss Philosophic Book Co.

Daily Express 1935, *The Book of Fortune-Telling: How to Tell Character and the Future by Palmistry, Cards, Numbers, Phrenology, Handwriting, Dreams, Astrology, Etc*, London: Daily Express Publications.

Davies, H. 1954, *Christian Deviations*, London: SPCK.

Edwards, G. 1993, *Stepping into the Magic: A New Approach to Everyday Life*, London: Piatkus.

Evans-Wentz, W. Y. 1927, *Tibetan Book of the Dead*, Oxford: Oxford University Press.

Ferguson, M. 1982 [1980], *The Aquarian Conspiracy: Personal and Social Transformation in the 1980s*, St Albans, Herts: Paladin/Granada.

Findhorn Community 1978 [1975], *The Findhorn Garden*, London: Turnstone/ Wildwood House.

Forsyth, L. 1993, *Journey Towards Healing*, Nairn: Balnain Books.

—— 1995, *Directory of Holistic Health Care in the Highlands and Islands of Scotland 1995–1996*, Achnasheen, Invernesshire: Watershed Publications.

Fortune, D. 1931, 'Power Centres of Britain', *Occult Review* 52/2: 106–10.

Gardner, G. 1954, *Witchcraft Today*, London: Rider.

Gaythorpe, E. (ed.) 1979, *My Dear Alexias: Letters from Wellesley Tudor Pole to Rosamond Lehmann*, Jersey: Neville Spearman.

Goddard, V. 1975, *Flight Towards Reality*, London: Turnstone.

Govan I. 1978 [1938], *Spirit of Revival: The Story of J. G. Govan and the Faith Mission*, Edinburgh: Faith Mission.

Hall, M. 1999, *Reiki for Common Ailments: A Practical Guide to Healing*, London: Piatkus.

Hawken, P. 1990 [1975], *The Magic of Findhorn*, London: Fontana.

Heavens, J. 1992, 'Reiki', *Connections: Alternative Health in Scotland* 18, p. 19.

Hilton, J. 1933, *Lost Horizon*, London: Macmillan.

Hodgkinson, L. 1993, *The Personal Growth Book: Dozens of Ways to Develop Your Inner Self*, London: Piatkus.

Hoff, B. 1989 [1982], *The Tao of Pooh*, London: Mandarin.

Huxley, A. 1932, *Brave New World*, London: Chatto and Windus.

Icke, D. 1991, *The Truth Vibrations*, London: Aquarian Press.

—— 1993, *Heal the World*, Bath: Gateway.

Inglis, M. 1992, 'The Game of Transformation at Findhorn', in Fleming, B. and Loose, G. (eds) 1992, *The Holistic Handbook for Scotland*, Glasgow: Green Crane Press, pp. viii–ix.

Khalsa, P. S. (ed.) 1981, *A Pilgrim's Guide to Planet Earth: A Traveller's Handbook and Spiritual Directory*, San Rafael, CA: Spiritual Community Publications/London: Wildwood House.

Landau, R. 1935, *God is My Adventure: A Book on Modern Mystics, Masters and Teachers*, London: Ivor Nicholson and Watson.

—— 1945, *God is My Adventure*, revised edition, eleventh impression, London: Faber and Faber.

Lee, B. 1997, 'Reiki, "the Healing Power of the Universe" – at a Turning Point?', *Caduceus* 35: 36–7, 56–8.

Leslie, D. and Adamski, G. 1953, *Flying Saucers Have Landed*, London: Werner Laurie.

McKenzie, E. 1998, *Healing Reiki*, London: Hamlyn.

MacLaine, S. 1983, *Out on a Limb*, London: Hamish Hamilton.

McLaughlin, C. and Davidson, G. 1994, *Spiritual Politics: Changing the World from the Inside Out*, Forres: Findhorn Press.

Maclean, D. 1980, *To Hear the Angels Sing*, Forres: Findhorn Press.

Murray, M. 1989, *Sharing the Quest*, Shaftesbury, Dorset: Element.

Nation, S. 1989, 'World Goodwill: the Evolution of a Movement', unpublished paper delivered at the 1989 Theosophical History conference, London.

Neville, R. 1971 [1970], *Playpower*, St Albans, Herts: Paladin/Granada.

Nuttall, J. 1970 [1968], *Bomb Culture*, London: Paladin/Granada.

Olsen, K. 1991 [1989], *The Encyclopedia of Alternative Health Care*, London: Piatkus.

Osmond, J. and Graham, A. 1984, *Alternatives: New Approaches to Health, Education, Energy, the Family and the Aquarian Age*, Wellingborough, Northants: Thorsons.

Pole, W. T. 1917, *Private Dowding*, London: John Watkins..

Popenoe, C. 1979, *Inner Development: The Yes! Bookshop Guide*, Harmondsworth: Penguin.

Pugh, L. 1957, *Nothing Else Matters: News from the White House*, London: Regency Press.

Redfield, J. 1994, *The Celestine Prophecy*, London: Bantam.

Roddick, A. 1991, *Body and Soul*, London: Ebury Press.

Rushforth, W. 1984, *Ten Decades of Happenings: The Autobiography of Winifred Rushforth*, London: Gateway.

St Aubyn, L. 1990, *The New Age in a Nutshell: A Guide to Living in New Times*, Bath: Gateway.

St John, J. 1977, *Travels in Inner Space: One Man's Exploration of Encounter Groups, Meditation and Altered States of Consciousness*, London: Victor Gollancz.

Satin, M. 1978, *New Age Politics: Healing Self and Society*, West Vancouver, BC: Whitecap Books.

Saunders, N. 1971, *Alternative London*, London: The Author.

—— 1975a, *Alternative England and Wales*, London: The Author.

—— 1975b, *Self Exploration: A Guide to Groups Involved*, London: The Author.

Scott, C. 1920, *The Initiate*, London: Routledge.

—— 1927, *The Initiate in the New World*, London: Routledge.

—— 1932, *The Initiate in the Dark Cycle*, London: Routledge.

—— 1935, *An Outline of Modern Occultism*, London: Routledge.

Shango, J. 1996, 'The Firewalk: a Tool for Healing and Growth', *Caduceus* 33: 11–12.

Simmons, J. 1990, *The Emerging New Age*, Santa Fé, NM: Bear and Co.

Sinclair, J. 1984, *The Alice Bailey Inheritance*, Wellingborough, Northants: Turnstone.

Slocombe, J. 1995, 'Peter Caddy, the Rosicrucians and the Foundations of the Findhorn Community', unpublished paper circulated at 'The Western Mysteries: Which Way Today?' conference, Findhorn, 1995.

Smuts, J. C. 1927, *Holism and Evolution*, London: Macmillan.

Snelling, J. *et al.* 1988 [1987], *The Early Writings of Alan Watts*, London: Century/Rider.

Spangler, D. (ed.) n.d., *Cooperation with Spirit: Further Conversations with John*.

—— 1977 [1971], *Revelation: The Birth of a New Age*, Forres: Findhorn Foundation.

—— 1984, *Emergence: The Rebirth of the Sacred*, New York: Dell.

—— 1993, 'The New Age: The Movement towards the Divine', in Ferguson D. (ed.) 1993, *New Age Spirituality: an Assessment*, Louisville, KY: Westminster/John Knox Press, pp. 79–105.

—— 1996, *Pilgrim in Aquarius*, Forres: Findhorn Press.

Spangler, D. and Thompson, W. 1991, *Reimagination of the World: A Critique of the New Age, Science and Popular Culture*, Santa Fé, NM: Bear and Co.

Spink, P. 1980, *Spiritual Man in a New Age*, London: Dartman, Longman and Todd.

Stewart, B. 1942, *The Aquarian Age: What it Connotes and the Phenomena that Will Usher it In*, The Author: Worthing, Sussex.

Stewart, Basil (n.d. 1952?), *Spiritual Truth: The Pure and Universal Religion of the New Era of the Aquarian Age*, The Author: Bridgwater, Somerset.

Strachan, F. (ed.) 1970, *The Aquarian Guide to Occult, Mystical, Religious, Magical London and Around*, London: Aquarian Press.

Swainson, M. 1977, *The Spirit of Counsel: the Story of a Pioneer in Student Counselling*, Sudbury, Suffolk: Neville Spearman.

Tattersall, T. 1996, *Journey: An Adventure of Love and Healing*, Forres: Findhorn Press: Forres.

Thomas, J. 1957, *Psychic Surgeon*, London: Arthur Barker.

Thompson, W. I. 1975 [1973], *Passages about Earth: An Exploration of the New Planetary Culture*, London: Rider.

Tod, H. 1989, *The Maze and the Arc of Light: A Journey with a Purpose*, Forres: Findhorn Press.

Trevelyan, G. 1977, *A Vision of the Aquarian Age*, London: Coventure.

—— 1981, *Operation Redemption: A Vision of Hope in an Age of Turmoil*, Wellingborough, Northants: Turnstone.

—— 1986, *Summons to a High Crusade*, Forres: Findhorn Press.

Valiente, D. 1986 [1973], *An ABC of Witchcraft Past and Present*, London: Robert Hale.

Vaughan, D. 1967, *A Faith for the New Age*, London: Regency Press.

Walker, A. (ed.) 1994, *The Kingdom Within: A Guide to the Spiritual Work of the Findhorn Community*, Forres: Findhorn Press.

Waters, M. 1996, *The Element Dictionary of Personal Development: An A–Z of the Most Widely-Used Terms, Theories and Concepts*, Shaftesbury, Dorset: Element.

Watkins, A. 1925, *The Old Straight Track*, London: Methuen.

Watts, A. 1973, *In My Own Way: An Autobiography 1915–1965*, London: Jonathan Cape.

Wells, H. G. 1923, *Men Like Gods*, London: Cassell.

—— 1932, *The Work, Wealth and Happiness of Mankind*, Garden City, NY: Doubleday Doran and Co.

—— 1974 [1933], *The Shape of Things to Come*, London: Corgi.

White R. and Swainson, M. 1971, *Gildas Communicates: The Story and the Scripts*, London: Neville Spearman.

Wilson, C. 1956, *The Outsider*, London: Gollancz.

—— 1978 [1971], *The Occult*, London: Hodder and Stoughton.

Wilson, S. 1989, *A Guide to the New Age*, Newton Abbot, Devon: Wayseeker Books.

Wise, C. 1995, 'The Legendary Atlantis Bookshop', *Pagan Dawn*, no. 116, p. 14.

Wright, B. and Worsley, C. (eds) 1975, *Alternative Scotland*, Edinburgh: Edinburgh University Students' Publishing Board.

Secondary sources

Adler, M. 1981 [1979], *Drawing Down the Moon: Witches, Druids, Goddess-Worshippers, and Other Pagans in America Today*, Boston: Beacon Press.

Akhtar, M. and Humphries, S. (1999), *Far Out: the Dawning of New Age Britain*, Bristol: Sansom and Co/Channel 4.

Albanese, C. 1992, 'The Magical Staff: Quantum Healing in the New Age' in Lewis, J. and Melton, J. G. (eds) 1992, *Perspectives on the New Age*, pp. 68–84.

Alexander, K. 1992, 'Roots of the New Age', in Lewis, J. and Melton, J. G. (eds) 1992, *Perspectives on the New Age*, pp. 30–47.

Anonymous 1951, *The Theosophical Movement 1875–1950*, Los Angeles: The Cunningham Press.

Asad, T. 1993, *Genealogies of Religion: Discipline and Reasons of Power in Christianity and Islam*, London: Johns Hopkins University Press.

Baird, R. 1971, *Category Formation and the History of Religions*, The Hague: Mouton.

Balch, R. and Taylor, D. 1977, 'Seekers and Saucers: The Role of the Cultic Milieu in Joining a UFO Cult', *American Behavioural Scientist* 20/6: 839–60.

Barker, E. (ed.) 1982, *New Religious Movements: a Perspective for Understanding Society*, New York: Edwin Mellen.

Barker, E. 1994, 'The New Age in Britain', in Martin, J.-B. and Laplantine, F. (eds) 1994, *Le Defi Magique Vol. 1: Esoterisme, Occultisme, Spiritisme*, Lyon: Presses Universitaires de Lyon, pp. 327–37.

Barnes, J. 1954, 'Class and Committees in a Norwegian Island Parish', *Human Relations* 7/1: 39–58.

Basil, R. (ed.) 1988, *Not Necessarily the New Age*, Buffalo, NY: Prometheus Books.

Beckford, J. 1985, *Cult Controversies: The Societal Response to New Religious Movements*, London: Tavistock.

—— 1989, *Religion and Advanced Industrial Society*, London: Unwin Hyman.

Bednarowski, M. 1991, 'Literature of the New Age: A Review of Representative Sources', *Religious Studies Review* 17/3: 209–16.

—— 1992, 'The New Age Movement and Feminist Spirituality: Overlapping Conversations at the End of the Century', in Lewis, J. and Melton, J. G. (eds) 1992, *Perspectives on the New Age*, pp. 167–78.

Benham, P. 1993, *The Avalonians*, Glastonbury: Gothic Image.

Berger, P. *et al.* 1974 [1973], *The Homeless Mind: Modernization and Consciousness*, Harmondsworth: Penguin.

Bevir, M. 1999, 'Annie Besant's Quest for Truth: Christianity, Secularism and New Age Thought', *Journal of Ecclesiastical History* 50/1: 62–93.

Bloch, J. 1998, *New Spirituality, Self and Belonging: How New Agers and Neo-Pagans Talk about Themselves*, Westport, CT: Praeger.

Bott, E. 1957, *Family and Social Networks*, London: Tavistock.

Bowman, M. 1993a, 'Drawn to Glastonbury', in Reader, I. and Walter, T. (eds) 1993, *Pilgrimage in Contemporary Culture*, London: Macmillan, pp. 29–62.

—— 1993b, 'Reinventing the Celts', *Religion* 23: 147–56.

—— 1999, 'Healing in the Spiritual Marketplace: Consumers, Courses and Credentialism', *Social Compass* 46/2, pp. 181–9.

—— 2000, 'More of the Same? Christianity, Vernacular Religion and Alternative Spirituality in Glastonbury', in Sutcliffe, S. and Bowman, M. (eds) 2000, *Beyond New Age*, Edinburgh: Edinburgh University Press, pp. 83–104.

Brown, M. 1997, *The Channeling Zone: American Spirituality in an Anxious Age*, London: Harvard University Press.

Bruce, S. 1998, 'Good Intentions and Bad Sociology: New Age Authenticity and Social Roles', *Journal of Contemporary Religion* 13/1: 22–33.

Buckner, H. 1968, 'The Flying Saucerians: An Open Door Cult', in Truzzi, M. (ed.) 1968, *Sociology and Everyday Life*, Englewood Cliffs, NJ: Prentice-Hall, pp. 223–30.

Byrne, P. 1997, *Social Movements in Britain*, London: Routledge.

Campbell, B. 1980, *Ancient Wisdom Revived: A History of the Theosophical Movement*, London: University of California Press.

Campbell, C. 1972, 'The Cult, the Cultic Milieu and Secularization', in Hill, M. (ed.) 1972, *A Sociological Yearbook of Religion in Britain* 5, pp. 119–36.

Church of Scotland 1993, Board of Social Responsibility Study Group, section 7.5, 'Young People and the Media: The New Age', Edinburgh: Church of Scotland.

Clark, J. 1990, 'UFOs in the New Age', in Melton, J. G. *et al.* (eds) 1990, *New Age Encyclopedia*, pp. 476–80.

Clark, S. 1992, 'Myth, Metaphor and Manifestation: The Negotiation of Belief in a New Age Community', in Lewis, J. and Melton, J. G. (eds) 1992, *Perspectives on the New Age*, pp. 97–104.

Clarke, P. (ed.) 1987, *The New Evangelists*, London: Ethnographica.

Clarke, P. 1996, *Hope and Glory: Britain 1900–1990*, London: Penguin.

Collin, M. and Godfrey, J. 1997, *Altered State: The Story of Ecstasy Culture and Acid House*, London: Serpent's Tail.

Coniam, S. and Gibson, L. 1996, 'Interview: Giving Voice with Jill Rakusen', *Journal of Contemporary Health* 4: 34–5.

Cooter, R. 1988, 'Introduction: the Alternations of Past and Present' in Cooter R. (ed.) 1988, *Studies in the History of Alternative Medicine*, London: Macmillan, pp. x–xx.

Cumbey, C. 1983, *The Hidden Dangers of the Rainbow: The New Age Movement and the Coming of Barbarism*, Shreveporto, LA: Huntington House.

Danforth, L. 1989, *Firewalking and Religious Healing: The Anastenaria of Greece and the American Firewalking Movement*, Princeton, NJ: Princeton University Press.

Davies, C. 1999, *Reflexive Ethnography: A Guide to Researching Selves and Others*, London: Routledge.

Davies, J. 1993, 'Lapidary Texts: A Liturgy Fit for Heroes?', in Davies, J. and Wollaston, I. (eds) 1993, *The Sociology of Sacred Texts*, Sheffield: Sheffield Academic Press, pp. 26–36.

Deleuze, G. and Guattari, F. 1988, *A Thousand Plateaus: Capitalism and Schizophrenia*, London: Athlone.

Denzin, N. 1970, *The Research Act: A Theoretical Introduction to Sociological Methods*, Chicago: Aldine.

Dickson, L. 1976 [1973], *Wilderness Man: The Strange Story of Grey Owl*, London: Abacus.

Diem, A. and Lewis, J. 1992, 'Imagining India: the Influence of Hinduism on the New Age Movement', in Lewis, J. and Melton, J. G. (eds) 1992, *Perspectives on the New Age*, pp. 48–58.

Drane, J. 1991, *What is the New Age Saying to the Church?*, London: Marshall Pickering.

—— 1993, 'Coming to Terms with the New Age Movement', in Church of Scotland 1993, Appendix C, pp. 54–7.

Drijvers, H. 1973, 'Theory Formation in Science of Religion and the Study of the History of Religions', in van Baaren, T. and Drijvers, H. (eds) 1973, *Religion, Culture and Methodology*, The Hague: Mouton, pp. 57–77.

Drury, N. 1989, *The Elements of Human Potential*, Shaftesbury, Dorset: Element.

Eder, K. 1985, 'The New Social Movements', *Social Research* 52: 869–90.

Eisenstadt, S. 1968, 'Charisma and Institution Building: Max Weber and Modern Sociology', in Eisenstadt, S. (ed.) 1968, *Max Weber On Charisma and Institution Building*, Chicago: University of Chicago Press, pp. ix–lvi.

Ellwood, R. 1973, *Religious and Spiritual Groups in Modern America*, Englewood Cliffs, NJ: Prentice-Hall.

—— 1992, 'How New is the New Age?', in Lewis, J. and Melton, J. G. (eds) 1992, *Perspectives on the New Age*, pp. 59–67.

—— 1995, 'Theosophy', in Miller, T. (ed.) 1995, *America's Alternative Religions*, Albany, NY: SUNY Press, pp. 315–24.

—— 1997, *The Fifties' Spiritual Marketplace*, Rutgers University Press.

English-Lueck, J. 1990, *Health in the New Age: A Study in California Holistic Practices*, Albuquerque, NM: University of New Mexico Press.

Faivre, A. 1994, *Access to Western Esotericism*, New York: SUNY Press.

Festinger, L. *et al*. 1964 [1956], *When Prophecy Fails*, New York: Harper and Row.

Fine, G. 1993, 'Ten Lies of Ethnography', *Journal of Contemporary Ethnography* 22/3: 267–94.

Fitzgerald, T. 2000, *The Ideology of Religious Studies*, New York: Oxford University Press.

Forrest, B. 1986, 'Apprentice–Participation: Methodology and the Study of Subjective Reality', *Urban Life* 14/4: 431–53.

Foucault, M 1977, 'Nietzsche, Genealogy, History', in *Michel Foucault: Language, Counter-Memory, Practice. Selected Essays and Interviews* (ed./trans. D. Bouchard) 1977, Oxford: Blackwell, pp. 139–64.

Fulder, S. 1992, 'Alternative Therapists in Britain', in Saks, M. (ed.) 1992, *Alternative Medicine in Britain*, pp. 166–82.

—— 1996/1984: *The Handbook of Alternative and Complementary Medicine* (third edition), New York: Oxford University Press.

Fuller, R. 1989, *Alternative Medicine and American Religious Life*, New York: Oxford University Press.

Galbreath, R. 1972, 'The History of Modern Occultism: A Bibliographical Survey', *Journal of Popular Culture* 5: 726–54.

Gerlach, L. and Hine, V. 1968, 'Five Factors Crucial to the Growth and Spread of a Modern Religious Movement', *Journal for the Scientific Study of Religion* 7/1: 23–40.

—— 1970, *People, Power, Change: Movements of Social Transformation*, Indianapolis: Bobbs-Merrill.

Green, J. 1998, *All Dressed Up: The Sixties and the Counterculture*, London: Jonathan Cape.

Green, M. 1986, *Mountain of Truth. The Counterculture Begins: Ascona 1900–1920*, London: University Press of New England.

Greer, P. 1995, 'The Aquarian Confusion: Conflicting Theologies of the New Age', *Journal of Contemporary Religion* 10/2: 151–66.

Haberman, D. 1993, 'A Cross-Cultural Adventure: The Transformation of Ronald Nixon', *Religion* 23/3: 217–27.

Hamilton, M. *et al*. 1995, 'Eat, Drink and Be Saved: The Spiritual Significance of Alternative Diets', *Social Compass* 42/4: 497–511.

—— 2000, 'An Analysis of the Festival for Mind–Body–Spirit, London', in Sutcliffe, S. and Bowman, M. (eds) 2000, *Beyond New Age*, pp. 188–200.

Hammersley, M. and Atkinson, P. 1992 [1983], *Ethnography: Principles in Practice*, London: Routledge.

Hanegraaff, W. J. 1996: *New Age Religion and Western Culture: Esotericism in the Mirror of Secular Thought*, Leiden: E. J. Brill.

—— 2000: 'New Age and Secularization', *Numen* 47/3: 288–312.

Harris, M. 1969, *The Rise of Anthropological Theory: A History of Theories of Culture*, London: Routledge and Kegan Paul.

—— 1990, 'Emics and Etics Revisited', in Headland, T. *et al*. (eds) 1990, *Emics and Etics: the Insider/Outsider Debate*, Newbury Park, CA: Sage, pp. 48–61.

Harvey, D. 1989, *The Condition of Postmodernity: An Enquiry into the Origins of Cultural Change*, Oxford: Blackwell.

Harvey, G. 1997, *Listening People, Speaking Earth: Contemporary Paganism*, London: Hurst and Co.

Hazelgrove, J. 2000: *Spiritualism and British Society between the Wars*, Manchester: Manchester University Press.

Headland, T. 1990, 'Introduction: a Dialogue between Kenneth Pike and Marvin Harris on Emics and Etics', in Headland, T. *et al.* (eds) 1990, *Emics and Etics: The Insider/Outsider Debate*, Newbury Park, CA: Sage, pp. 13–27.

Heald, T. 1983, *Networks: Who We Know and How We Use Them*, London: Hodder and Stoughton.

Hebdige, D. 1979, *Subculture: The Meaning of Style*, London: Methuen.

Hedges, E. and Beckford, J. 2000, 'Holism, Healing and the New Age', in Sutcliffe, S. and Bowman, M. (eds) 2000, *Beyond New Age*, pp. 169–87.

Heelas, P. 1996, *The New Age Movement*, Oxford: Blackwell.

—— 1999, 'Diana's Self and the Quest Within', in Richards, J. *et al.* (eds) 1999, *Diana: The Making of a Media Saint*, London: I. B. Tauris, pp. 98–118.

—— 2000, 'Expressive Spirituality and Humanistic Expressivism: Sources of Significance Beyond Church and Chapel', in Sutcliffe, S. and Bowman, M. (eds) 2000, *Beyond New Age*, pp. 237–54.

Heelas, P. and Woodhead, L. 2001, 'Homeless Minds Today?' in Woodhead, L. *et al.* (2001), *Peter Berger and the Study of Religion*, London: Routledge, pp. 43–72.

Helfer, J. (ed.) 1968, *On Method in the History of Religions*, Middletown, CT: Wesleyan University Press.

Heselton, P. 2000, *Wiccan Roots: Gerald Gardner and the Modern Witchcraft Revival*, Chievely, Berks: Capall Bann.

Hetherington, K. 2000, *New Age Travellers: Vanloads of Uproarious Humanity*, London: Cassell.

Hexham, I. 1983, 'The "Freaks" of Glastonbury: Conversion and Consolidation in an English Country Town', *Update* 7/1: 3–12.

Highet, J. 1972, 'Great Britain: Scotland', in Mol, H. (ed.) 1972, *Western Religion: a Country by Country Sociological Enquiry*, The Hague: Mouton, pp. 249–69.

Hill, M. 1973, *A Sociology of Religion*, London: Heinemann.

Hobsbawm, E. 1995 [1994], *Age of Extremes: The Short Twentieth Century 1914–1991*, London: Abacus.

Holland, I. 1998, '40 Years of Westbank Health Centre', *Connections* 33 (Autumn/Winter 1998), pp. 4–7.

Hutton, R. 2001 [1999], *The Triumph of the Moon: A History of Modern Pagan Witchcraft*, Oxford: Oxford University Press.

Joad, C. 1944 [1933], *Guide to Modern Thought*, London: Faber and Faber.

Jorgensen, D. and L. 1982, 'Social Meanings of the Occult', *Sociological Quarterly* 23/3: 373–89.

Judah, J. S. 1967, *The History and Philosophy of the Metaphysical Movements in America*, Philadelphia: Westminster Press.

Karolyi, O. 1995, *Introducing Modern Music*, Harmondsworth: Penguin.

Kelly, A. 1990, 'Astrology in the New Age', in Melton *et al.* (eds) 1990, *New Age Encyclopedia*, Detroit: Gale Research, pp. 37–44.

—— 1992, 'An Update on Neopagan Witchcraft in America', in Lewis, J. and Melton, J. G. (eds) 1992, *Perspectives on the New Age*, pp. 136–51.

252

Kelly, T. 1992, *A History of Adult Education in Great Britain*, Liverpool: Liverpool University Press.

King, R. 1999, *Orientalism and Religion: Postcolonial Theory, India and 'The Mystic East'*, London: Routledge.

Kleinman, S. 1991, 'Fieldworkers' Feelings: What We Feel, Who We Are, How We Analyse', in Shaffir, W. and Stebbins, R. (eds) 1991, *Experiencing Fieldwork: an Insider's View of Qualitative Research*, Newbury Park, CA.: Sage, pp. 184–95.

Leech, K. 1976 [1973], *Youthquake: Spirituality and the Growth of a Counter-Culture*, London: Abacus/Sphere.

Lett, J. 1990, 'Emics and Etics: Notes on the Epistemology of Anthropology' in Headland, T. *et al.* (1990), *Emics and Etics: the Insider/Outsider Debate*, Newbury Park, CA: Sage, pp. 127–42.

Levin, J. and Coreil, J. 1986, ' "New Age" Healing in the US', *Social Science and Medicine* 23/9: 889–97.

Lewis, J. 1992, 'Approaches to the Study of the New Age Movement', in Lewis, J. and Melton, J. G. (eds) 1992, *Perspectives on the New Age*, pp. 1–12.

Lewis, J. and Melton, J. G. 1992, 'Introduction', in Lewis, J. and Melton, J. G. (eds) 1992, *Perspectives on the New Age*, pp. ix–xii.

Lewis, J. and Melton, J. G. (eds) 1992, *Perspectives on the New Age*, Albany, NY: SUNY Press.

Lofland, J. 1977 [1966], *Doomsday Cult*, second edition, Irvington, NY: John Wiley.

Lofland, J. and Stark, R. 1965, 'Becoming a World-Saver: A Theory of Conversion to a Deviant Perspective', *American Sociological Review* 30: 862–75.

Lopez, D., Jr 1998, *Prisoners of Shangri-La: Tibetan Buddhism and the West*, Chicago: University of Chicago Press.

Lowe, J. 1970, *Adult Education in England and Wales: A Critical Survey*, London: Michael Joseph.

Lowe, R. and Shaw, W. 1993, *Travellers: Voices of the New Age Nomads*, London: Fourth Estate.

Luhrmann, T. 1994 [1989], *Persuasions of the Witch's Craft: Ritual Magic in Contemporary England*, London: Picador.

Lyon, D. 2000, *Jesus in Disneyland: Religion in Postmodern Times*, Cambridge: Polity Press.

Lyotard, J.-F. 1979, *The Postmodern Condition: A Report on Knowledge*, Manchester: Manchester University Press.

McCutcheon, R. 1997, *Manufacturing Religion: The Discourse on Sui Generis Religion and the Politics of Nostalgia*, New York: Oxford University Press.

McGuire, M. 1998 [1988], *Ritual Healing in Suburban America*, London: Rutgers University Press.

McIntosh, C. 1987, *The Rosicrucians: The History, Mythology and Rituals of an Occult Order*, Wellingborough, Northants: Crucible/Thorsons.

Main, R. (ed.) 1997, *Jung on Synchronicity and the Paranormal*, London: Routledge.

Makower, J. 1989, *Woodstock: The Oral History*, London: Sidgwick and Jackson.

Maldonado, L. 1986, 'Popular Religion: its Dimensions, Levels and Types', *Concilium* [special issue on 'Popular Religion'], Greinacher, N. and Mette, N. (eds) 1986, Edinburgh: T & T Clark, pp. 3–11.

Mann, W. 1962 [1955], *Sect, Cult and Church in Alberta*, Toronto: University of Toronto Press.

Marrs, T. 1987, *Dark Secrets of the New Age*, Westchester, IL: Crossway.

Martin, L. 1990, 'The Study of Religion: a Field for Historical or Social Scientific Enquiry?', in Tyloch, W. (ed.) 1990, *Studies on Religions in the Context of Social Sciences*, Warsaw: Polish Society for the Science of Religions, pp. 111–16.

—— 2000, 'Of Religious Syncretism, Comparative Religion and Spiritual Quests', in Geertz, A. and McCutcheon, R. (eds) 2000, *Perspectives on Method and Theory in the Study of Religion*, Leiden: Brill, pp. 277–86.

Marwick, A. 1982, *British Society Since 1945*, Harmondsworth, Middlesex: Penguin.

—— 1998, *The Sixties: Cultural Revolution in Britain, France, Italy and the United States, c.1958–c.1974*, Oxford: Oxford University Press.

Masters, B. 1985, *The Swinging Sixties*, London: Constable.

Meek, D. 2000, *The Quest for Celtic Christianity*, Boat of Garten: Handsel Press.

Melton J. G. 1986, *Encyclopedic Handbook of Cults in America*, New York: Garland.

—— 1988, 'A History of the New Age Movement', in Basil R. (ed.) 1988, *Not Necessarily the New Age*, Buffalo, NY: Prometheus Books, pp. 35–53.

—— 1992, 'New Thought and the New Age', in Lewis, J. and Melton, J. G. (eds), 1992, pp. 15–29.

—— 1995, 'The Contactees: a Survey', in Lewis, J. (ed.) 1995, *The Gods have Landed: New Religions from Other Worlds*, Albany, NY: SUNY Press, pp. 1–13.

—— 2001, 'Reiki: the International Spread of a New Age Healing Movement', in Rothstein, M. (ed.) 2001, *New Age Religion and Globalization*, Aarhus: Aarhus University Press, pp. 73–93.

Melton, J. G. (ed.) 1990, *Rosicrucianism in America*, New York: Garland.

—— *et al.* (eds) 1990, *New Age Encyclopedia*, Detroit: Gale Research.

—— 1991, *New Age Almanac*, New York: Visible Ink.

Melton, J. G. and Eberhart, G. 1995, 'The Flying Saucer Contactee Movement, 1950–1994: A Bibliography', in Lewis, J. (ed.) 1995, *The Gods Have Landed*, pp. 251–332.

Metcalf, W. 1993, 'Findhorn: the Routinization of Charisma', *Communal Societies* 13: 1–21.

Mews, S. 1994, 'Religious Life between the Wars, 1920–1940', in Gilley, S. and Shields, W. (eds) 1994, *A History of Religion in Britain*, Oxford: Blackwell, pp. 449–66.

Miller, J. 1988, 'In Defence of Alice A. Bailey', *Theosophical History* 2/6: 190–206.

Mills, R. 1973, *Young Outsiders: A Study of Alternative Communities*, London: Routledge and Kegan Paul.

Mitchell, J. C. 1969, 'The Concept and Use of Social Networks', in Mitchell, J. C. (ed.) 1969, *Social Networks in Urban Situations*, Manchester: Manchester University Press, pp. 1–50.

Monteith, W. G. 2000, 'Iona and Healing: A Discourse Analysis', in Sutcliffe, S. and Bowman, M. (eds) 2000, *Beyond New Age: Exploring Alternative Spirituality*, Edinburgh: Edinburgh University Press, pp. 105–17.

Mouledoux, J. 1972, 'Ideological Aspects of a Drug Dealership', in Westhues, K. (ed.) 1972, *Society's Shadow: Studies in the Sociology of Countercultures*, Toronto and Montreal: McGraw-Hill Ryerson, pp. 110–22.

Musgrove, F. 1974, *Ecstasy and Holiness: Counter Culture and the Open Society*, London: Methuen.

Nelson, G. 1969, *Spiritualism and Society*, London: Routledge and Kegan Paul.

Obelkevich, J. 1976, *Religion and Rural Society: South Lindsey 1825–1875*, Oxford: Clarendon Press.

Oosthuizen, G. 1992, 'The "Newness" of the New Age in South Africa and Reactions to it', in Lewis, J. and Melton, J. G. (eds) 1992, *Perspectives on the New Age*, pp. 247–70.

Partridge, C. 1999, 'Truth, Authority and Epistemological Individualism in New Age Thought', *Journal of Contemporary Religion* 14/1, pp. 77–95.

Paterson, L. 1998, *A Diverse Assembly: The Debate on a Scottish Parliament*, Edinburgh: Edinburgh University Press.

Pearson, J. 1998, 'Assumed Affinities: Wicca and the New Age', in Pearson, J. *et al.* (eds) 1998, *Nature Religion Today: Paganism in the Modern World*, Edinburgh: Edinburgh University Press, pp. 45–56.

Pepper, D. 1991, *Communes and the Green Vision: Counterculture, Lifestyle and the New Age*, London: Merlin Press.

Perry, M. 1992, *Gods Within: A Critical Guide to the New Age*, London: SPCK.

Pevsner, N. 1975 [1936], *Pioneers of Modern Design: From William Morris to Walter Gropius* [first published as *Pioneers of the Modern Movement*], Pelican: Harmondsworth.

Phillips, M. 1965, *Small Social Groups in England*, London: Methuen.

Pike, K. 1990, 'On the Emics and Etics of Pike and Harris', in Headland, T. *et al.* (eds) 1990, *Emics and Etics: the Insider/Outsider Debate*, Newbury Park, CA: Sage, pp. 28–47.

Poggi, I. 1992, 'Alternative Spirituality in Italy', in Lewis, J. and Melton, J. G. (eds) 1992, *Perspectives on the New Age*, pp. 271–86.

Prince, R. and Riches, D. 2000, *The New Age in Glastonbury*, Oxford: Bergahn.

Puttick, L. 2000, 'Personal Development: the Spiritualisation and Secularization of the Human Potential Movement', in Sutcliffe, S. and Bowman, M. (eds) 2000, *Beyond New Age: Exploring Alternative Spirituality*, Edinburgh: Edinburgh University Press, pp. 201–19.

Randall, I. 1999, *Evangelical Experiences: A Study in the Spirituality of English Evangelicalism 1918–1939*, Carlisle: Paternoster Press.

Richardson, J. 1991, 'Experiencing Research on New Religions and Cults: Practical and Ethical Considerations', in Shaffir, W. and Stebbins, R. (eds) 1991, *Experiencing Fieldwork: An Insider's View of Qualitative Research*, Newbury Park, CA: Sage, pp. 62–71.

Ricoeur, P. 1970, *Freud and Philosophy: An Essay on Interpretation*, New Haven, CT: Yale University Press.

Riddell, C. 1991, *The Findhorn Community: Creating a Human Identity for the 21st Century*, Forres: Findhorn Press.

Rigby, A. and Turner, B. 1972, 'Findhorn Community, Centre of Light: A Sociological Study of New Forms of Religion', in Hill, M. (ed.) 1972, *A Sociological Yearbook of Religion in Britain 5*, London: SCM, pp. 72–86.

Rigby, A. 1974, *Communes in Britain*, London: Routledge and Kegan Paul.

Riordan, S. 1992, 'Channeling: a New Revelation?', in Lewis, J. and Melton, J. G. (eds) 1992, *Perspectives on the New Age*, pp. 105–26.

Roof, W. 1993, *A Generation of Seekers: The Spiritual Journeys of the Baby Boom Generation*, San Francisco: HarperCollins.

—— 1999, *Spiritual Supermarket: Baby Boomers and the Remaking of American Religion*, Princeton: Princeton University Press.

Rose, S. 1998, 'An Examination of the New Age Movement: Who is Involved and What Constitutes its Spirituality', *Journal of Contemporary Religion* 13/1:5–22.

—— 2001, 'New Age Women: Spearheading the Movement?', *Women's Studies* 30/3: 329–50.

Ross, A. 1992, 'New Age Technoculture' in Grossberg, L. *et al.* (eds) 1992, *Cultural Studies*, London: Routledge, pp. 531–55.

Roszak, T. 1971 [1970], *The Making of a Counter Culture: Reflections on the Technocratic Society and its Youthful Opposition*, London: Faber and Faber.

Rupert, G. 1992, 'Employing the New Age: Training Seminars', in Lewis, J. and Melton, J. G. (eds) 1992, *Perspectives on the New Age*, Albany, NY: SUNY Press, pp. 127–35.

Saks, M. 1992, 'Introduction', in Saks, M. (ed.) 1992, *Alternative Medicine in Britain*, Oxford: Oxford University Press, pp. 1–21.

Saliba, J. 1999, *Christian Responses to the New Age Movement*, London: Chapman/ Cassell.

Savage, J. 1991, *England's Dreaming: Sex Pistols and Punk Rock*, London: Faber and Faber.

Schneider, L. and Dornbusch, S. 1958, *Popular Religion: Inspirational Books in America*, Chicago: University of Chicago Press.

Seaman, L. 1970, *Life in Britain Between the Wars*, London: B. T. Batsford.

Shaffir, W. 1991, 'Managing a Convincing Self-Presentation', in Shaffir, W. and Stebbins, R. (eds) 1991, *Experiencing Fieldwork: an Insider's View of Qualitative Research*, Newbury Park, CA: Sage, pp. 72–81.

Sharma, U. 1992, *Complementary Medicine Today: Practitioners and Patients*, London: Routledge.

—— 1993, 'Contextualizing Alternative Medicine', *Anthropology Today* 9/4: 15–18.

Stanway, A. 1982, *Alternative Medicine: A Guide to Natural Therapies*, Harmondsworth: Penguin.

Stevenson, J. and Cook, C. 1994 [1977], *Britain in the Depression: Society and Politics 1929–1939*, second edition, London: Longman.

Steyn, C. 1994, *Worldviews in Transition: An Investigation into the New Age Movement in South Africa*, Pretoria, University of South Africa Press.

—— 2001, 'South African New Age Prophets: Past and Present', *Religion and Theology* 8/4.

Stone, D. 1976, 'The Human Potential Movement', in Glock, C. and Bellah, R. (eds) 1976, *The New Religious Consciousness*, Berkeley: University of California Press, pp. 93–115.

Storm, R. 1991, *In Search of Heaven on Earth*, London: Bloomsbury.

Straus, R. 1976, 'Changing Oneself: Seekers and the Creative Transformation of Life Experience', in Lofland, J. (ed.) 1976, *Doing Social Life: the Qualitative Study of Human Interaction in Natural Settings*, New York: John Wiley, pp. 252–72.

Stupple, D. 1984, 'Mahatmas and Space Brothers: The Ideologies of Alleged Contact with Extraterrestrials', *Journal of American Culture* 7: 131–9.

Sutcliffe, S. 1995, 'Alternative Health Questionnaire Report', *Connections* 26: 48–9.

—— 1997, 'Seekers, Networks and "New Age"', *Scottish Journal Of Religious Studies* 15/2: 97–114.

—— 2000a, 'Wandering Stars: Seekers and Gurus in the Modern World', in Sutcliffe, S. and Bowman, M. (eds) 2000, *Beyond New Age*, pp. 17–36.

—— 2000b, 'A Colony of Seekers: Findhorn in the 1990s', *Journal of Contemporary Religion* 15/2: 215–31.

—— 2002, 'Unfinished Business: Devolving Scotland/Devolving Religion', in Coleman, S. and Collins, P. (eds) 2002, *Religion, Identity and Change: British Perspectives on Global Transformations*, Aldershot: Ashgate.

Sutcliffe, S. and Bowman, M. (eds) 2000, *Beyond New Age: Exploring Alternative Spirituality*, Edinburgh: Edinburgh University Press.

Thomas, T. 1995, 'Popular Religion', in Hinnells, J. (ed.) 1995, *A New Dictionary of Religions*, London: Allen Lane, pp. 386–8.

Thorpe, A. 1992, *Britain in the 1930s: The Deceptive Decade*, Oxford: Blackwell.

Tingay, K. 2000, 'Madame Blavatsky's Children', in Sutcliffe. S. and Bowman, M. (eds) 2000, *Beyond New Age: Exploring Alternative Spirituality*, Edinburgh: Edinburgh University Press, pp. 37–50.

Tomory, D. 1996, *A Season in Heaven: True Tales from the Road to Kathmandu*, London: Thorsons/HarperCollins.

Tosh, J. 1984, *The Pursuit of History: Aims, Methods and New Directions in the Study of Modern History*, London: Longman.

Truzzi, M. 1972, 'The Occult Revival as Popular Culture: Some Random Observations on the Old and the Nouveau Witch', *Sociological Quarterly* 13: 16–36.

Tulloch, S. (ed.) 1991, *The Oxford Dictionary of New Words*, Oxford: Oxford University Press.

Turner, R. and Killian, L. 1972, *Collective Behavior*, second edition, Englewood Cliffs, NJ: Prentice-Hall.

Twigg J. 1979, 'Food for Thought: Purity and Vegetarianism', *Religion* 9: 13–35.

Wagner, M. 1997, 'The Study of Religion in American Society', in Glazier, S. (ed.) 1997, *Anthropology of Religion: A Handbook*, Westport, CT: Praeger, pp. 85–101.

Wallis, R. 1985, 'Betwixt Therapy and Salvation: the Changing Form of the Human Potential Movement', in Jones, R. (ed.) 1985, *Sickness and Sectarianism: Exploratory Studies in Medical and Religious Sectarianism*, Aldershot: Gower, pp. 23–51.

Walter, T. 1993, 'War Grave Pilgrimage', in Reader, I. and Walter, T., *Pilgrimage in Popular Culture*, Basingstoke: Macmillan, pp. 63–91.

Warburton, T. R. 1969, 'The Faith Mission: A Study in Interdenominationalism', in Martin, D. (ed.) 1969, *A Sociological Yearbook of Religion in Britain 2*, London: SCM, pp. 75–102.

Washington, P. 1993, *Madame Blavatsky's Baboon: Theosophy and the Emergence of the Western Guru*, London: Secker and Warburg.

Webb, J. 1976, *The Occult Establishment*, La Salle, Illinois: Open Court.

Which? The Consumer Magazine 1986, 'Magic or Medicine?', pp. 443–7.

—— 1995, 'Healthy Choice', pp. 8–13.

White, D. 1974, 'Glastonbury Pilgrims', *New Society*, Vol. 29 no. 615, pp. 133–4.

Wilson, B. 1965, 'A Sociologist's Footnote', in Phillips, M. 1965, *Small Social Groups in England*, London: Methuen, pp. 292–306.

Wilson, B. and Cresswell, J. (eds) 1999, *New Religious Movements: Challenge and Response*, London: Routledge.

Winter, J. 1992, 'Spiritualism and the First World War', in Davies, R. and Helmstadter, R. (eds) 1992, *Religion and Irreligion in Victorian Society*, London: Routledge, pp. 185–200.

—— 1995, *Sites of Memory, Sites of Mourning: The Great War in European Cultural History*, Cambridge: Cambridge University Press.

Wiseman, J. 1979, 'The Research Web' in Bynner, J. and Stribley, K. (eds), 1979, *Social Research: Principles and Procedures*, London: Longman/Open University Press, pp. 113–21.

Wojcik, D. 1997, *The End of the World As We Know It: Faith, Fatalism and Apocalypse in America*, New York: New York University Press.

Wolf, M. 1992, *A Thrice-Told Tale: Feminism, Postmodernism, and Ethnographic Responsibility*, Stanford, CA: Stanford University Press.

Woodhead, L. 1999, 'Diana and the Religion of the Heart', in Richards, J. *et al.* (eds) 1999, *Diana: The Making of a Media Saint*, London: I. B. Tauris, pp. 119–39.

Worsley, P. 1969, 'The Concept of Populism', in Ionescu, G. and Gellner, E. (eds) 1969, *Populism: its Meaning and National Characteristics*, London: Weidenfeld and Nicolson, pp. 212–50.

York, M. 1995, *The Emerging Network: A Sociology of the New Age and Neo-Pagan Movements*, Lanham, Maryland: Rowman and Littlefield.

—— 1997, 'Review Article: S. J. Castro. "Hypocrisy and Dissent within the Findhorn Foundation: Towards a Sociology of a New Age Community" ', *Journal of Contemporary Religion* 12(2): 229–38.

—— 2000, 'Alternative Spirituality in Europe: Amsterdam, Aups and Bath', in Sutcliffe, S. and Bowman, M. (eds) 2000, *Beyond New Age*, pp. 118–34.

Zinnbauer, B. *et al.* 1997, 'Religion and Spirituality: Unfuzzying the Fuzzy', *Journal for the Scientific Study of Religion* 36/4: 549–64.

INDEX